DATA-DRIVEN PERSONALISATION IN MARKETS, POLITICS AND LAW

The most fascinating and profitable subject of predictive algorithms is the human actor. Analysing big data through learning algorithms to predict and pre-empt individual decisions gives a powerful tool to corporations, political parties and the state. Algorithmic analysis of digital footprints, as an omnipresent form of surveillance, has already been used in diverse contexts: behavioural advertising, personalised pricing, political micro-targeting, precision medicine, and predictive policing and prison sentencing. This volume brings together experts to offer philosophical, sociological, and legal perspectives on these personalised data practices. It explores common themes such as choice, personal autonomy, equality, privacy, and corporate and governmental efficiency against the normative frameworks of the market, democracy and the rule of law. By offering these insights, this collection on data-driven personalisation seeks to stimulate an interdisciplinary debate on one of the most pervasive, transformative, and insidious socio-technical developments of our time.

Uta Kohl is Professor of Commercial Law at Southampton Law School. Her previous work on IT law issues includes *Jurisdiction and the Internet* (Cambridge University Press, 2007) and *The Net and the Nation State* (Cambridge University Press, 2016). She acted as the Human Rights Trustee on the board of the Internet Watch Foundation (2014–2020) and is currently exploring the legal treatment of memories, funded by a Leverhulme grant on the Privacy of the Dead.

Jacob Eisler is Associate Professor at Southampton Law School where he focuses on democratic theory, election law, and corruption. Prior to joining Southampton Law School, he was the Yates-Glazebrook Fellow in Law at Jesus College, University of Cambridge, and clerked for the Honorable Gerard E. Lynch, Federal Second Circuit Court of Appeals.

T0370957

Data-Driven Personalisation in Markets, Politics and Law

Edited by

UTA KOHL

University of Southampton

JACOB EISLER

University of Southampton

Shaftesbury Road, Cambridge CB2 8EA, United Kingdom

One Liberty Plaza, 20th Floor, New York, NY 10006, USA

477 Williamstown Road, Port Melbourne, VIC 3207, Australia

314–321, 3rd Floor, Plot 3, Splendor Forum, Jasola District Centre, New Delhi – 110025, India

103 Penang Road, #05–06/07, Visioncrest Commercial, Singapore 238467

Cambridge University Press is part of Cambridge University Press & Assessment,
a department of the University of Cambridge.

We share the University's mission to contribute to society through the pursuit of
education, learning and research at the highest international levels of excellence.

www.cambridge.org
Information on this title: www.cambridge.org/9781108813082

DOI: 10.1017/9781108891325

First published 2021
First paperback edition 2024

A catalogue record for this publication is available from the British Library

Library of Congress Cataloging-in-Publication data
NAMES: Kohl, Uta, editor. | Eisler, Jacob, 1982- editor.
TITLE: Data-driven personalisation in markets, politics and law / edited by Uta Kohl, University of Southampton; Jacob
Eisler, University of Southampton.
DESCRIPTION: Cambridge, United Kingdom; New York, NY: Cambridge University Press, 2021. | Includes index.
IDENTIFIERS: LCCN 2021000184 (print) | LCCN 2021000185 (ebook) | ISBN 9781108835695 (hardback) | ISBN
9781108813082 (paperback) | ISBN 9781108891325 (epub)
SUBJECTS: LCSH: Law–Statistical methods. | Big data.
CLASSIFICATION: LCC K212 .D38 2021 (print) | LCC K212 (ebook) | DDC 343.09/99–dc23
LC record available at https://lccn.loc.gov/2021000184
LC ebook record available at https://lccn.loc.gov/2021000185

ISBN   978-1-108-83569-5   Hardback
ISBN   978-1-108-81308-2   Paperback

Contents

Figures

Tables

Contributors

TT Arvind Professor, York Law School, University of York, York, England

Frederik Zuiderveen Borgesius Professor, iHub (Interdisciplinary Hub for Security, Privacy and Data Governance), Radboud University, The Hague, the Netherlands

Andrew Charlesworth Professor of Law, Innovation & Society, School of Law, University of Bristol, Bristol, England

Noelia Collado-Rodriguez Lecturer, Faculty of Law, University of A Coruña, A Coruña, Spain

Jacob Eisler Associate Professor, Southampton Law School, University of Southampton, Southampton, England

Michèle Finck Senior Research Fellow, Max Planck Institute for Innovation and Competition, Munich, Germany

Alun Gibbs Associate Professor, Southampton Law School, University of Southampton, Southampton, England

David Gurnham Professor of Criminal Law and Interdisciplinary Legal Studies, Southampton Law School, University of Southampton, Southampton, England

Konstantinos V Katsikopoulos Associate Professor, Department of Decision Analytics and Risk, University of Southampton, Southampton, England

Uta Kohl Professor, Southampton Law School, University of Southampton, Southampton, England

Daithí Mac Síthigh Professor of Law and Innovation, Queen's University, Belfast, Northern Ireland

Nick O'Donovan Senior Lecturer, Future Economies Research Centre, Manchester Metropolitan University, Manchester, England

Kieron O'Hara Emeritus fellow, Web and Internet Science Group, Electronics and Computer Science, University of Southampton, Southampton, England

Moira Paterson Adjunct Professor, Faculty of Law, Monash University, Melbourne, Australia

Joost Poort Associate Professor Institute for Information Law (IViR), University of Amsterdam, Amsterdam, the Netherlands

Keith Syrett Professor of Public Health Law, Centre for Health, Law, and Society, School of Law, University of Bristol, Bristol, England

Pamela Ugwudike Associate Professor in Criminilogy, Economic, Social and Political Sciences Department University of Southampton, Southampton, England

Marc Welsh Lecturer, Department of Geography and Earth Sciences, Aberystwyth University, Aberystwyth, Wales

Normann Witzleb Associate Professor, Faculty of Law, The Chinese University of Hong Kong, and Monash University, Melbourne, Australia

Preface

It is almost certain that your life is awash in data-driven personalisation, which gathers your personal information and compares it to personal information gathered about others to provide tailored outputs and decisions. It's shifted your life in the past day, probably in the past hour, and – if you're reading this on a screen – perhaps in the past minute. It has tried to influence what you buy, what media you watch, who you vote for, how you spend your time, what you believe, who you want to be. In short, the very things that make you you.

Yet the omnipresence of data-driven personalisation does not mean it is easily perceived or controlled by those it influences. This personalisation is often implemented through machine learning algorithms that are subtly embedded into day-to-day life. The most familiar type may be the humble internet advertisement, which predicts, rather than just echoes, your latest interests and desires. But as this book shows, personalisation ranges far wider than that, shaping interactions with private and public parties, with both a predictable influence in domains of technological innovation (think Facebook and Uber) as well as surprising infiltrations into domains as old as human society itself (think politics, medicine and law enforcement).

This collection of articles examines data-driven personalisation in all its hopeful potentials and insidious dangers. In its critiques, this collection emphasises diversity of perspective – while it is unified by an interest in law and governance, its focus is on the parallels and themes that cut across topics, private and public, personal and systemic, philosophical and practical. Methodologically it emphasises interdisciplinary analysis and draws from disciplines as diverse as philosophy, economics, penology, systems theory, survey methods and medical ethics.

In light of the disruptive potential of personalisation, for good or ill, we hope you are able to gain three benefits from this book. Firstly, we hope it provides a better sense of what personalisation is, how predictive analytics works and how it is profoundly changing society, and often not for the better. Secondly, we hope you have the chance to see how it operates in specific contexts, or has particular ramifications. And finally – leaning on the last word of the title of this volume, *law* – we hope you come to see how you can, both as a person and as a participant in a number of communities, work to discipline and shape personalisation.

This book can be approached in any number of ways. It has been arranged to form a narrative that is coherent yet retains the individual voices of the authors, and reading it straight through will provide a diverse set of perspectives on personalisation, guided by an introduction and conclusion that seek to tie together the topics at hand. To this end, the chapters are grouped into parts. The first part looks at the general principles and themes of personalisation, serving not merely as an introduction but as a critical context. The second looks at different key themes and methodological approaches to personalisation. The third part consists of topic-specific chapters, emphasising applications to particular domains and problems. The fourth part offers critical and reflective perspectives on personalisation, with a focus on critical broad-view consideration. Yet the chapters are also sufficiently independent, offering readers the possibility to go for specific topics of interest. Your reasons for reading this book will change how you approach it. We would only note that it is meant to accommodate being read both as a single volume and as a collection of contributions.

This book had its genesis in a conference held at the University of Southampton in June 2019. The conference was arranged by Professor Uta Kohl, Professor James Davey and Dr Jacob Eisler and was generously supported by the University of Southampton Faculty of Social Sciences and Southampton Law School. For support of both the conference and this edited volume, we would like to thank Professor Brenda Hannigan, Professor David Gurnham, Professor Nina Jorgensen and Clare Old in particular.

We would also like to take this chance to extend our thanks to Matthew Gallaway, our editor at Cambridge University Press, who has proven both his patience and his expertise during the process of writing this volume. We would also like to thank Julie Duran-Gelléri for providing prompt, thoughtful and extraordinarily attentive editing.

PART I

Introduction: Theoretical Perspectives

1

The Pixelated Person: Humanity in the Grip of Algorithmic Personalisation

Uta Kohl

1.1 INTRODUCTION

By far the most fascinating and profitable subject of predictive algorithms is the human actor. The capacity to predict human preferences, responses and behaviours offers endless possibilities for science, commerce, politics and regulation, and promises convenience and efficiency that further private and public interests in equal measure. There is nothing inherently new about the attempt to predict buying choices, political leanings and likely votes of individuals and groups, the probable effectiveness of medical treatments, likely defaults on loans, the chance of fraudulent insurance claims or of reoffending. Yet, the capacity to 'know' the individual and the group, and to predict their constitution and behaviour has witnessed a sudden upturn of unprecedented scale. The rise of network society and smart technology is generating endless trails of personal data, finely pixelated digital footprints, that are aggregated into big data sets – that involve large collections (volume) of real-time (velocity), diverse and relational personal data (variety)[1] – about virtually all aspects of human life from shopping, food and entertainment preferences, friendship networks, romantic attachments, social activities, health concerns, physical movements, driving behaviour or sporting activities, to biometric data, such as voice, face, gait or keystroke, or physiological data on heart rate, blood pressure or sleeping patterns. These data sets, when mined by algorithms, can reveal significant patterns and correlations and, ultimately, produce knowledge about the group (e.g. behavioural trends, economic activity, delinquency, spread of disease, political trends, etc.[2]) *and* about the individual (e.g. educational level, social status, political leaning, sexual orientation, emotional states and psychological vulnerabilities as well as predilections for activities and movements). This knowledge then lies at the disposal of the private sector and government to be used for a wide range of purposes, implemented through 'personalised' services, treatments and regulation – some beneficial, some harmful, but mostly a mixture of both.

For example, only a few Facebook 'likes' are needed to reveal correlations with personal attributes, such as sexual orientation, ethnicity, religious and political views, personality traits, intelligence, happiness, use of addictive substances, parental separation, age and gender.[3] These granular insights into the individual or micro-groups can be, and are, used to select and deselect content and advertisement to match their profile. Such 'personalisation' serves as essential information management (in response to the overwhelming amount of information available), and promotes efficiency (by saving users' time in searching through masses of content, and businesses the expense of serving adverts to uninterested users). For many, personalisation offers the customisation and optimisation previously only available to the elite, e.g. the personal advisor or trainer, whilst the great masses had to be content with mass production. Mass-personalisation or individualised consumption at scale is now possible at least in the service industry.[4] Yet, the very same practices that appear so beneficial show their exploitative dimension when used to extract extra value from the consumer as, for example, when an inferred desperate search for a loan is translated into an offering of credit with a 'personalised' higher interest rate that reflects the urgency of the search. Equally, the manipulative aspects of personalisation shine through in the practice of micro-targeting political adverts to profiled users, and undecided voters, in the lead up to elections or referendums, as revealed in the Cambridge Analytica scandal.[5] Although the scandal centred on the deceptive collection of data and the absence of user consent to such collection and use, consent seems to only marginally address the manipulative inflection of political (and other) micro-targeting. Even where targeting is consensual, the 'opted-in' lack of choice and consequential lack of exposure to alternative narratives still seem problematic. By the same token, if a patient's personal medical history is supplemented by a genetic profile from an ancestry service, like 23andMe, and life-style data from a Fitbit watch in order to decide on the most effective made-to-measure medical treatment,[6] this process seems in the patient's interest (most effective treatment) and in the public interest (efficient allocation of scarce resources). Yet, the same practice becomes more suspect when used to limit otherwise available treatment options or deny treatment altogether, on the basis of unfavourable DNA or life-style profiles. Finally, the possibility of predictive policing through micro-segmentation of populations promises to employ scarce police resources more efficiently by concentrating on likely serious delinquents and thus to pre-empt crime and disorder more effectively. Yet, he who seeks finds: the distorting impacts of such targeted practices have been well documented, and one of their concomitant side effects is that some sections of the population are granted leeway from which others do not benefit, often along historic racial and ethnic lines of division.[7]

Whether beneficial or detrimental, what these scenarios have in common is the data-driven profiling of consumers or citizens to deliver a customised or personalised service, advert or legal response. Personal data in conjunction with big data is interpreted by algorithms to create a picture of who someone *is* based on who they *were* – their past preferences, activities, networks and behaviours – in order to make a future-oriented prediction of what they might like (i.e. which film), what might persuade them (i.e. which ad) and how they might act (i.e. commit a crime or succeed in a job). A key problematic of profiling and customisation practices lies in their very virtue: the pre-selection and pre-emption of individual choices by those with access to big data sets and profiling technology. Thaler and Sunstein have called them 'choice architects' in the context of 'nudging'.[8] The pre-management of individual choices by these architects is rendered at times more benign by the triviality of the personalised service, e.g. a recommended book, film or song; or by the perspective of those upon whom personalisation bestows a benefit based on their 'good' profiles, e.g., the healthy patient, the unlikely delinquent, the creditworthy or price-sensitive consumer.[9] The core of the problem, however, remains the same and lies, first, in taking the human agent out of the loop of participating and directing her individual and collective life through making active choices,[10] in potentially two capacities: one, the algorithm replaces the traditional human decision-maker (e.g. the judge or the editor or the business person) and, two, those decisions then also pre-empt the choices of the profilee (e.g. the defendant or consumer). Choices are made for her, or at least the framework is created within which she can make her choices. The *second* problematic underlying personalisation practices is that big data analytics is generated by autonomous technology whose complex processes, optimised through feedback loops and machine learning capabilities, often place it beyond human comprehension, and thus *prima* facie also outside human oversight and contestation.

This collection of essays engages with these problematics in various social domains and academic fields of inquiry, and brings together scholars from different walks of law (data protection and privacy law, criminal, medical, and contract law as well as constitutional theory) and other social sciences, such as political theory, human geography, criminology, behavioural economics and philosophy, to interrogate this new powerful phenomenon that is sweeping across economic, political, social and legal domains, and dramatically reconfigures our social structures. What is striking about the contributions is that, despite the different contexts and perspectives, persistent themes emerge. On a practice-focused level, data-driven profiling and its myriad uses raise questions about *substance* (e.g. what is the accuracy of the profile and the legitimacy of using probabilistic predictions in favour of, or against, an individual, particularly in light of the possibility of mistakes or discrimination; what are the wider unintended consequences of profiling on private and public or collective interests) and about *process* (e.g. what oversight, if any, is exercised over the autonomous decision-making technology?; can informed consent ensure the empowerment of users in their profile creation and, more generally, to what extent can and should individuals be able to resist and challenge the collection of their data, its aggregation and use?; and how does it impact on avenues for collective resistance?).

On a theoretical level, there are also clusters of ideas that cut across subject-matters and disciplines, and flock around two themes. The first focuses on the foundational premise of predictive technology which is that future actions can (and should) be inferred from past behaviour or from the behaviour of like actors – a premise which is at odds with ideas of moral agency and free will. Yet, agency lies at the heart of our social orders and underpins the *homo economicus*, the self-determining citizen, and the moral actor who can only be held responsible for their actions on the basis of the freedom to act otherwise. Moral agency is also closely related to our conceptions of identity and personhood, and the open-ended evolving nature of human individuality. These conceptions are profoundly challenged by the creation of the *pixelated human* – a digitally constructed, two-dimensional, instrumentalised, commodified representation of individuality – and yet, this entity is frequently treated as the authentic self. Furthermore, under this deterministic view of human behaviour, normative questions are reduced to, or disguised behind, empirical observations about individual and group histories. This essentialist approach has the effect of continuously reasserting the status quo, and thereby consolidating and exacerbating it, including existing inequalities, structural disadvantages or political world views, and concomitantly reducing the room for individual or collective betterment.

The second cluster of ideas places the granularly profiled user from whom value can be extracted (generally in the name of efficiency) within a sharpened capitalist economic order. Shoshana Zuboff argued that the new data practices have given rise to surveillance capitalism: 'surveillance capitalists discovered that the most predictive behavioral data come from intervening in the state of play in order to nudge, coax, tune and herd behavior toward profitable outcomes.'[11] This perspective helps to frame the heightened user-pay model that various personalisation practices (e.g. personalised health care, credit or insurance products) implement as instantiations of liberal ideas of individualist fairness or just desert in opposition to notions of communal solidarity or distributive justice.[12] The free market lens also helps to explain why consent and personal autonomy should so systematically underwrite profiling practices, regardless of the facts that users exercise that autonomy within vastly asymmetrical power relations; that it legitimises value extraction as opposed to offering protection; and that invariably more is at stake than individual private interests. Equally the commodification of personal data is only intelligible against market logic. When consumers can sell their personal data in return for 'free' services, and corporations can buy and ring-fence this vast resource, the potential of these data sets as a (global) public good to be used for the benefit of all becomes much more circumscribed.[13] At the same time, the micro-segmentation of communities through personalisation practices, legitimised by individual consent, fragments political communities and distorts democratic processes, with the compounding effect of weakening a key mechanism for holding corporate and governmental actors to account, and for restraining the very processes that undermine those democratic processes.[14] In short, profiling and personalisation practices are deeply inscribed with capitalist market values – from their initial conception and rationalisation to their implementation within economic, social and political spheres and their continuing legitimation.

If there is one theme that carries through the whole collection, it is that this newly emerging and highly disruptive phenomenon has continuities with previous practices, concepts and ideologies, through which it may be analysed and critiqued. It is also only against these previously established understandings and processes that we may recognise how it presents a paradigmatic shift that really deserves our assiduous attention before it has pervasively and conclusively reshaped our social orders in its own image. This introductory chapter provides reflections on two distinct intellectual hinterlands to the more specific themes and applications of data-driven personalisation practices in this collection. First, it situates these discussions against a general framework of profiling and defends data-driven individual and group profiling against some critiques of stereotyping, on the basis that our cognition of the external environment is necessarily reliant on relevant abstractions or non-universal generalisations. The second set of reflections centres around the philosophical tradition of empiricism as a basis of knowledge or truth production, and uses this tradition to critique data-driven profiling and personalisation practices in its numerous manifestations. The final part of the chapter summarises the chapters in this volume and their individual contribution to the overall narrative.

1.2 INDIVIDUAL AND GROUP PROFILING AND THE VIRTUES OF STEREOTYPING

1.2.1 *The Interdependence of Individual and Group Profiling*

An initial controversy surrounding algorithmic profiling based on large sets of digital footprints is whether the individual or the group is its real target and the potential object of manipulative practices. Whilst the language of personalisation and customisation suggests the individual is the focal point, in some ways 'personalisation' is a misnomer, as individual profiling is always a form of classification whereby the individual is assessed against group attributes (more on that below) and then put in a micro-category for the purpose of delivering the 'personalised' response or service. Thus although the individual is the target of the customised message, service or treatment, the outcome is based on group features and multiplied across the micro-group. Furthermore, the fact that individual profiling is premised on analysing data sets about populations – mined for correlations and leading to the construction of groups in the process – has led some to conclude that *group* profiling is the critical new phenomenon that challenges existing legal modalities:

> The search for group privacy can be explained in part by the fact that with big data analyses, the particular and the individual is no longer central. In these types of

processes, data is no longer gathered about one specific individual or a small group of people, but rather about large and undefined groups. Data is analysed on the basis of patterns and group profiles; the result is often used for general policies and applied on a large scale.[15]

This argument has some validity (given that privacy regimes envisage an individual victim, and harm to the group only derivatively), but the ability to micro-profile individuals is still at least as valuable to corporate and governmental actors as knowledge about the group, as borne out by the widespread emergence of personalisation practices. In any event, the individual-versus-group dichotomy may largely be misconceived because they reflexively interact with each other. Individual data feeds into population data sets and these sets produce, through correlations, knowledge about populations, that is patterns and groups within them (inductive), which in turn are instructive about the individual (deductive).

The close, yet varying, integration of individual and group profiles has been subject to some debate and conceptualised in the distinction between distributive and non-distributive group profiling.[16] For *distributive* profiles (universal generalisations) attributes of the group are 'actually and unconditionally manifested by all the members of that group'[17] and thus group membership also allows for definitive inferences about the attributes of its members.[18] Every member of university staff (the group) has an employment contract with the university and a salary (attributes). In contrast, *non-distributive* profiles (non-universal generalisations or stereotyping) refer to groups where a family resemblance unites members, but not every member shares every attribute.[19] Here 'a group is defined in terms of... *significant deviances from other groups*. They are based on comparisons of members of the group with each other and/ or on comparisons of one particular group with other groups.'[20] The group boundaries in non-distributed profiles are inevitably fuzzy. Those with a high risk of cardiovascular disease (group) share a number of risk factors, for example, lifestyle, genes, age, weight, etc. (attributes),[21] but membership does not allow for definitive inferences about the particular attribute of a particular member. The non-universal generalisation that 'young men drive recklessly' does not allow for a definitive inference about the driving of any particular young man but, as argued below, mistakes on the individual level are often legitimated by the benefits of identifying (empirically sound) tendential truths.

Whilst non-distributive profiling explicitly compares one group *vis-à-vis* other groups, ultimately the distinctiveness of a distributive group profile (university staff) can also only be understood against other groups, that is what it is not (police or hospital staff, or university students). Indeed, the difference between these two types of profiling may in practice (and theory) not be that clear cut (i.e. is the whiteness of swans 'necessarily manifest' or non-essential?) and becomes largely a function of the profiler's knowledge, pre-conceptions and attendant construction of the group. This suggests that the certainty of (empirically based) distributive profiles may be illusory.[22] The two types of profiling may simply reflect different philosophical traditions: distributive profiles adopt a Platonic top-down perspective on a concept or class that assumes and finds a common essence underlying all its manifestations, whilst non-distributive profiling builds on Wittgenstein's bottom-up (and empiricist) notion of family resemblance whereby concepts or words just refer to clusters of similar or related phenomena:

> Consider for example the proceedings that we call 'games'. I mean board-games, card-games, ball-games, Olympic games and so on. What is common to them all? – Don't say: "There *must* be something common, or they would not be called 'games'" – but *look and see* whether there is anything common to all. – ... [W]e see a complicated network of similarities overlapping and criss-crossing: sometimes overall similarities, sometimes similarities of detail..[23]

So arguably distributive and non-distributing group profiling does not refer to different types of groups, but rather to different ways of looking at the same group, or, more precisely, to different ways of *constructing* groups.

As non-distributive profiling can capture a wider range of relevant, albeit non-essential, attributes (as opposed to seeking a group's essence), it yields a much richer picture of groups and individuals, but also has blurry edges and is fallible in respect of making definitive inferences about its members.[24] This is significant for big-data individual profiling, or any form of statistical profiling: when individual profiles are inferred from comparison with the group (indirect profiling), it may be tempting to fill 'gaps' in an imperfect overlap with the missing group attributes. For example, in the policing context, a large aggregated criminal justice database with data on criminal activities mapped onto post codes, on criminal records and recidivism, social media activities and networks, education and employment histories of offenders, and personality traits may – based on strong correlations – predict for a particular offender a high risk of recidivism. The Harm Assessment Risk Tool, or the HART algorithm, used by Durham Constabulary makes such predictions based on 509 'votes' by the system.[25] A digital footprint on social media may, in the absence of explicit evidence, be analysed to 'reveal' the missing attribute of a single person's status, a left-wing political outlook or homosexuality. Based on the strength of the correlation, an unknown attribute may be 'highly likely' and in this respect fall somewhere between the distributive and non-distributive profiles – as neither necessarily manifest nor simply possible. However, the effect of the use of the predictive technology will often be such as to treat highly likely predictions as effectively established, along the lines of Plato's essentialism. Yet, there may be rights-based reasons, such as the presumption of innocence or the right to privacy, why a particular inferred attribute should be treated as non-essential and its absence presumed, as, for example, when sensitive data may be inferred from a range of non-sensitive data points. (Chapter 5)

1.2.2 *The Virtues of Stereotyping*

One persistent objection to individual profiling based on comparisons to group data, including big data profiling, is that the resultant stereotyping (or non-universal generalisations) leads to the 'deindividualisation of the person' which occurs when '[p]ersons are judged and treated more and more as members of a group (i.e. the reference group that makes up the data or information subject) rather than as individuals with their own characteristics and merits.'[26] This critique is directed at *indirect profiling* that draws inferences about the individual from group data (invariably through non-universal generalisations), as opposed to *direct profiling* that is ostensibly based on data only about the particular individual and therefore arguably more accurate.[27] The objection to the 'deindividualisation of the person' or stereotyping based on comparisons with the group is flawed for a number of reasons. First, the argument that direct profiling delivers *prima facie* more legitimate profiles as it is solely focused on the digital footprint of the single individual assumes that someone's past activities and preferences provide a valid yardstick for his future behaviour and preferences, and implicitly assumes that personhood is fixed in time. Such reasoning relies as much on stereotyping of the individual (and on denying agency) as indirect profiling, as it does not allow for the possibility of continual reinvention and development of individuality through repeated assertions of free choice. Indirect profiling has at least the virtue of squarely acknowledging that 'no man is an island' and that individuality is intimately tied up with social forces within which it develops and against which it may be understood. Still, *all* profiling used for predictive purposes is inherently irreconcilable with the notion of free will as underwriting moral and legal responsibility as well as autonomous participation in democratic processes.

Second, direct profiling is also necessarily comparative with the group, much like indirect profiling, and cannot but invoke the social dimension of human existence. Individuality can only be understood against an assumed 'normality' which contextualises individual divergence.[28] An individual's social media digital footprint is entirely meaningless by itself, in a social vacuum. It can only signal depression or creditworthiness or criminogenic tendencies against data sets, drawn from the group, that display the whole spectrums of psychological, financial or criminogenic states.[29] The interdependence of the individual and the group, the particular and the general, uniqueness and commonality, may best be illustrated with reference to DNA profiling as the biological equivalent to behavioural profiling:

> DNA fingerprinting (also called DNA profiling or forensic genetics) is a technique employed by forensic scientists to assist in the identification of individuals or samples by their respective DNA profiles. Although more than 99.1 per cent of the genome is the same throughout the human population, the remaining 0.9 per cent of human DNA shows variations between individuals.[30]

In parallel with the biological profile, where commonality far outweighs uniqueness, and individual genomic variations operate, and are identifiable, against genomic commonality, individual behavioural uniqueness can also *only* be conceptualised against the broad brush of collective humanity. The specific and the general are co-dependent. (See Chapter 5.)

Last, but not the least, even if direct and indirect profiling are, after all, not so fundamentally different from each other by being comparative and engaging in stereotyping, the crux of the problem may lie in stereotyping *per se*. The argument against stereotyping appears to have found legal recognition in antidiscrimination law: 'Stereotyping, or the imposition of assumptions about a group on an individual, has been central to antidiscrimination law because of the prominence of individual autonomy as a juridical value.'[31] This assertion, however, is misleading in its generality, considering that antidiscrimination law only addresses stereotyping based on a very limited range of factors, for example, race, gender or age. It does not outlaw stereotyping *per se*, nor could it. Human judgment and knowledge invariably, and necessarily, involves stereotyping – or non-universal generalisations – and this is neither irrational nor immoral, assuming it has a sound empirical basis *and* excepting certain historically disadvantaged groups, as protected by antidiscrimination law. Frederic Schauer in *Profiles, Probabilities, and Stereotypes* has argued for the ubiquity of stereotyping and its *prima facie* legitimacy:

> We operate actuarially when we choose airlines on the basis of their records for safety, on-time performance or not losing checked luggage. We operate actuarially when we associate personal characteristics such as a shaved head, a tattoo and black clothing with behavioral characteristics, such as racist beliefs and a propensity to violence, that the personal characteristics seem probabilistically but not inexorably to indicate… Still, once we see… that employers stereotype when they assume that certain characteristics (good grades from a prestigious university) will predict successful job performance, that police detectives focus on suspects by aggregating stereotypes, and that most of us stereotype in much of our daily lives, we cannot so easily dismiss the practice of stereotyping – or profiling – as necessarily morally wrong.[32]

In all these cases, stereotyping, or non-universal generalisation, is based on an acceptance of inaccurate results in particular cases (e.g. in a job, a particular student with poor grades might outperform the students with good grades; a plane from an airline with a good record may crash), but is still justifiable on the ground of efficiency. Shortcuts and proxies (e.g. the grade, the tattoo, the airline brand) reduce informational complexity and thereby facilitate decision-making that is faster and, if empirically sound, also tendentially correct, albeit not 100 per cent. In fact, as Schauer shows, such stereotyping often leads overall to fewer mistakes than a case-by-case approach where wide discretion and factual granularity and complexity introduce far more room for errors of judgement and inconsistencies.[33] In other words, from an efficiency perspective, empirically sound stereotyping allows *overall* for faster and better decisions. Having said that, the possibility of mistakes *is* problematic in serious contexts, such as criminal justice, which has traditionally been deeply individualistic and thus preoccupied with avoiding false positives.

Considering that the antithesis of stereotyping is a case-by-case or particularised approach, stereotyping is a form of rule-based decision-making: a proxy provides a simple instrumentalised yardstick against which individuals (or products or situations) are measured, and can be seen to be measured. So counterintuitively, stereotyping has the moral virtue, first, of facilitating – at least in principle – transparency and accountability, as judging by proxy creates simplicity (by removing informational noise) and makes it possible to understand how a judgment was reached. Given this transparency, the stereotyped individual is also often, not always, able to actively participate in his perception by others, for example, by working towards good grades or getting a tattoo. Stereotyping is then a two-way process whereby the individual deliberately sends relevant signals for the judgment of others, or contests the accuracy of the perceived stereotype in her particular case. Second, generalisation or stereotyping is also virtuous because applying a proxy equally to all, in disregard of individual differences, is aligned with the concept of formal equality, which in turn is fundamental to our understanding of fairness and justice. Resorting once more to Schauer, the value of formal equality lies in 'understanding our common situation and our common plight as one in which there are limits to how much difference our own personal individual situations ought to make. It is no accident that Justice wears a blindfold. And she wears a blindfold not because she needs to steel herself against her own biases, prejudices, and mistakes, but because it is central to one conception of justice that equal treatment for its own sake – treating unlikes alike – serves important functions.'[34] Thus stereotyping applies a social framing to individual treatment, stressing commonality over differences, and thereby reinforces community and affinity.

Outside the legal or social context, the systematic use of proxies to make non-universal generalisations about the external environment (e.g. brown bears = danger; koalas ≠ danger) produces knowledge that enables choices about alternative courses of action and is thus fundamental to evolutionary success. Mireille Hildebrandt observed that 'all living organisms, in order to survive, must continuously profile their environment to be able to adapt themselves and/or adapt the environment.'[35] Taking this perspective, profiling and stereotyping is an essential survival mechanism that consists of abstracting (life-critical) information from the environment in order to adapt to it, or vice versa. It is goal oriented and selective by focusing only on relevant features and by making generalisations that are tendentially true but not always – much like present day profiling by autonomous technology.

In short, whilst there may often be valid arguments about the empirical (un)soundness or other (il)legitimacy of a *particular* basis of stereotyping, in general, judging by proxy is not just intrinsic to the cognitive processing of external reality and fellow humanity, but also has solid moral foundations. Therefore, in so far as objections to direct and indirect profiling are centred on the intrinsic wrongfulness of stereotyping, they are based on a misunderstanding about its role in knowledge production and moral discourse. By the same token, big data-driven profiling and personalisation practices may be criticised for *undue* stereotyping, where the profiling is empirically unsound, or draws on proxies for groups that have suffered long-standing structural disadvantages. (Chapter 11) Furthermore, big data profiling does not facilitate stereotyping practices in which everyone engages equally, but is underwritten by power asymmetries which it consolidates and sharpens, to which the discussion will turn now.

1.3 KNOWLEDGE AND TRUTH PRODUCTION THROUGH AI – THE NEW AGE OF EMPIRICISM

1.3.1 *Blind Knowledge of Data-driven Profiling: Correlations, Not Causation*

Big data analytics, of which individual and group profiling is a prominent example, constitutes – in method, if not aim – the quintessential manifestation of the epistemological tradition of empiricism. For empiricists, in contradistinction to rationalists, the only reliable source of knowledge is information gathered through sense experience or observation. Knowledge follows experience rather than precedes it. For the early English philosopher of science and Enlightenment empiricist Francis Bacon, scientific knowledge had to be based on observations of nature and could only be produced through inductive reasoning – yet not without being guided by some form of hypothesis: 'the true method of experience, on the contrary, first lights the candle, and then by means of the candle shows the way'.[36] David Hume, writing more than a century later, was equally persuaded of the need for observation in matters of fact (as opposed to relations of ideas, i.e. mathematics or logic):

> In reality, all arguments from experience are founded on the similarity which we discover among natural objects, and by which we are induced to expect effects similar to those which we have found to follow from such objects. And though none but a fool or madman will ever pretend to dispute the authority of experience, or to reject that great guide of human life, it may surely be allowed a philosopher to have so much curiosity at least as to examine the principle of human nature, which gives this mighty authority to experience.[37]

As a philosopher, Hume was sceptical about inductive reasoning as a source of true knowledge. For him an observed 'constant conjunction' or correlation (i.e. the sun has risen in the past) does not give us an epistemic basis to *know with certainty* that the same will occur in the future (i.e. the sun will rise tomorrow) – even if observers generally jump to such conclusions and thereby imply an underlying scientific law about cause and effect, from which the future can *demonstratively* be known.

Hume's sceptical empiricism is uncannily enacted by big data analytics in general, and individual and group profiling in particular – even if in a distorted fashion. Big data analytics produces 'blind' knowledge, or knowledge of 'constant conjunctions' or correlations, and often stops at that. *Prima facie* it is the correlation, rather than an explanation for the correlation or true knowledge, that matters. Methodologically, big data analytics makes a hypothesis drawing on a theory – as the foundation for trial-and-error scientific method – far less important than it is for traditional scientific discovery. Knowledge discovery in databases occurs by search-ing for relevant correlations or patterns with the help of algorithms, and 'these algorithms can be supervised, that is they can start with a hypothesis that is tested on the data, or they can be unsupervised,... and just check for any patterns... [in line with a particular] mathematical function.'[38] Thus an unsupervised algorithm proceeds – without Bacon's candle – to search itself for structures (or groups) in the input data towards a desired output. Having said that, there is a hybrid methodology whereby initial data results are used to generate the hypothesis for further statistical testing on other (validation) data.[39] Second and overlapping, in *Big Data: A Revolution That Will Transform How We Live, Work, and Think*,[40] Viktor Mayer-Schönberger and Kenneth Cukier commented that the move from a small-data to a big-data world has unleashed the power of correlations. The abundance of data and sophisticated analytical tools allow for faster and cheaper identification of correlations on a much wider range of subjects – with or without *a posteriori* explanations about cause and effect. Indeed, attempts to explain correlations are, according to the authors, often 'caught in a web of competing causal hypotheses... [and] only make them cloudier. Correlations exist; we can show them mathematic-ally. We can't easily do the same for causal links. So we would do well to hold off from trying to explain the reason behind the correlations: the *why* instead of the *what*.'[41] Thus they conclude, in a twisted nod to Hume, that '[c]ausality won't be discarded, but it is being knocked off its pedestal as the primary fountain of meaning.'[42] Similarly, Chris Anderson had previously – in 'The End of Theory: The Data Deluge makes the Scientific Method Obsolete'[43] – argued that the abundance of data displaces every theory of human behaviour, from linguistics to sociology or psychology, given that it no longer matters knowing 'why people do what they do[.] The point is they do it, and we can track and measure it with unprecedented fidelity. With enough data, the numbers speak for themselves.'[44] These commentators effectively dissolve Hume's intractable dilemma about the possibility of true knowledge (which Kant had already done rather effectively in 1781[45]) by asserting that such knowledge is now redundant.

This argument for the virtues of instrumentalised blind 'knowledge' of big data analytics (if it can be called knowledge) presents a full inversion of Enlightenment ideals of rationality and scientific discovery, even if the claim of a paradigmatic shift in science is to some extent exaggerated. Some theory invariably drives and follows the search for correlations.[46] Mireille Hildebrandt has shown how wider theoretical assumptions are necessarily embedded, even within unsupervised learning algo-rithms, in the constructions of a model of reality by translating external reality into data sets, and 'theory' is also implicated in reviewing the validity of found correl-ations.[47] Furthermore, data simply never speaks for itself: 'Making sense of data is always framed – data are examined through a particular lens that influences how they are interpreted.'[48] Still, whilst exaggerated, the core assertion about the new approach to discoveries stands, even if it over-promises results outside retail and marketing. (Chapter 15) Peter Coveney and others have argued – using precision or personalised medicine and human genomics projects as an example – that big data knowledge discoveries often fail beyond the big-yet-finite data sets on which they are trained precisely 'because they are not designed to model the structure characteristics of the underlying system.'[49] In the human behavioural domain, data sets may prove to be 'finite' in terms of being time-specific or valid only for certain sections of the population. From a scientific perspective, there is also the rather more principled objection about discarding the quest for real knowledge in favour of the new instrumentalised 'knowledge': 'In subjects where the level of theoretical understanding [i.e. physics and chemistry] is deep, it is deemed aberrant to ignore it all and resort to collecting data in a blind manner. Yet, this is precisely what is advocated in the less theoretically grounded disciplines of biology and medicine, let alone social sciences and economics.'[50] Notably, these latter disciplines provide the scientific backdrop within which individual and group profiling generally falls.

From an economic perspective, the blind 'knowledge' of big data analytics is wholly legitimated by efficiencies: if data-driven profiling generates revenue or saves scarce public resources, and effectively predicts (or moulds) choices, it matters not what the underlying reasons may be. On a more generic level, Andrew Feenberg has argued that *efficiency* and *control* are the inherent animating forces of 'technology' rather than values that offer an outside perspective on technology: 'To judge an action as more or less efficient is already to have determined it to be technical and therefore an appropriate object of such a judgment. Similarly, the concept of control implied in technique is "technical" and so not a distinguishing criterion.'[51] In other words, the very adoption of predictive algorithms in various social domains signals the entry of 'efficiency and control' as a dominant frame *vis-à-vis* alternative ways of engaging in the activity (e.g. research or understanding voters) and *vis-à-vis* alternative perspectives for evaluating the merit of the activity or outcome (e.g. 'pure' knowledge discovery, moral and political deliberation, human rights, equality, the rule of law or production of happiness). Feenberg's observation also helps to explain why 'efficiency' should loom so large as justification for predictive and profiling technology, whilst 'control' or potential abuses of control feature heavily in its critique.[52]

Given the 'natural' home of efficient technology in an economic conception of reality, it is perhaps not surprising that individual profiling and personalisation practices have been the most 'successful' in retail and marketing, that is, in terms of maximising efficiencies and control from a corporation's perspective (although not necessarily from other perspectives, e.g., democratic deliberation). Famously, Amazon's phenomenal rise was grounded in its recommender system that benefits from constant feedback loops for auto-correction, and can predict highly accurately the buying preferences of their customers and so helped to dramatically increase sales.[53] Such micro-targeting is now ubiquitously used by platforms, retailers and advertisers to order content and push products. Within the commercial realm, it is clear that the correlations themselves are valuable for the profilers, who would hold no further interest in the explanations behind the correlations.[54] If there were a correlation between a behavioural pattern on social media and excessive purchasing behaviour, it would be irrelevant to an online retailer for targeting adverts, that the common cause of the behavioural and purchasing patterns may be varying stages of depression. Being ignorant of the causes behind non-spurious correlations makes the extraction of economic value morally neutral, particularly as algorithmic value extraction generally draws on some weakness or susceptibility of the consumer. Empiricism's apparently neutral focus on facts or corrections, not framed by explanations, provides the toolkit for de-moralising economic activity. Big data analytics realises that ambition more fully and forcefully than any previous metric or actuarial practice, as it has the strongest claim yet about the self-generated emergence of insights from data sets without human intervention.[55]

This new 'empiricism on steroids'[56] or the pursuit of data-driven blind knowledge has been equally attractive to governments that likewise chase efficiencies for their governing economies. Predictive algorithmic tools used for policing or sentencing are designed to use public recourses in a more targeted fashion and thereby deliver 'better' (more efficient) results, as in turn assessed by metrics. In the civil domain, smart city projects are driven by the prospect of efficiency gains by measuring traffic and footfall to enable live-management of traffic, parking, services, utilities, waste, etc. (Chapter 12) The continuous profiling of human activity aimed at facilitating efficient city life also provides ample opportunities for embedding policing activities, for example, speeding on smart motorways or unauthorised smoking,[57] whilst, at the same time, insidiously nudging populations – with a low-level awareness of an ever-present intelligent environment – into self-disciplining (control). (Chapter 3) Much like in the commercial context, the new algorithmic empiricism offers the added bonus of disassociating government from sensitive decisions. For the impersonal bureaucracies of governments – long familiar with cost-benefit analysis, evidence-based practice and impact metrics – big data algorithmic decision-making holds the promise of removing further residues of:

> individual authority [that] is perceived or portrayed as inadequate, inefficient, partial, paternalistic, corrupt, or illegitimate. In these areas, fully formalized, auto-mated decisions have become more and more attractive as effective and supposedly neutral or even democratic procedures, in particular if they implement an empir-ical component that can be presented as 'carrying' the actual decision. Responsibility can then be shifted to the data themselves.[58]

So the combination of 'self-generated' data and insights and automated decisions allows for standard normative evaluations to be shifted from political, legal or economic domains into the technical realm. Whilst the former require reasoning, judgment and communications that are necessarily contestable (Chapter 16), decisions made by technology appear to be incontestable and are, for that reason, as democratically problematic as tempting for bureaucracies. They appear incontestable not just because of the natural opacity of predictive analytics (recalling that unsupervised learning algorithms operate without a formal 'theory' within black boxes and are 'adaptive' to new data), but also because machine-generated decisions seem objective, neutral and rational, and not infested with human prejudice and fallibility. Notably, there is evidence that decisions based on experience and intuition are inferior to decisions based on simple rules implemented in weighted checklists, and the latter rival machine learning algorithms.[59] (Chapter 15) The justification for decisions by technology is thus arguably higher quality, but also, incidentally, it allows for responsibility to be shifted. Yet, 'the choice of a technical rather than a political or moral solution to a social problem is politically and morally significant,'[60] and neither technology itself nor its decisions are apolitical or amoral.[61]

1.3.2 *The 'truth' and 'accuracy' of Big Data Profiling*

A related set of questions that flow from the empiricism of data-driven profiling and predictive practices centre around issues of truth and accuracy in light of the apparent impartiality and objectivity of statistical analysis: facts do not lie, they speak for themselves; numbers can be trusted. Implicit truth or accuracy claims bolster the authoritativeness of predictive algorithms, resulting in their apparently superior fairness. These claims can be unpacked on multiple levels as has already been comprehensively in existing scholarship.[62] For the purposes of framing this collection, three brief reflections will suffice.

First, big data analytics, much like all statistical evaluation, is neither neutral nor objective. It inevitably embeds value judgments, and often perpetuates societal prejudices and biases. Just because unsupervised learning algorithms act ostensibly on their own does not mean their outcomes are free from biases. All algorithms are trained on data sets and replicate, in developing predictive models, the biases implicit in these sets, known *inter alia* as the 'black data' problem.[63] With traditional statistical modelling based on smaller and more structured data, it was possible to make conscious efforts to counteract biases against disadvantaged groups by deselecting obvious proxies of sensitive attributes (e.g. postcodes for race). Such editing is less feasible in respect of large sets of non-traditional, behavioural data, given that much apparently innocent data (e.g. cultural preferences or educational achievement) is correlated to sensitive attributes, as shown in research.[64] This means that big-data profiling based on innocent variables is still liable to be discriminatory in effect. Although the correlations are more easily identifiable, they are more difficult to eliminate as cleansing data of all proxies would leave little or no valuable data to be analysed. (Chapters 7 and 11) It also shows the depth of societal stratification; in Rieder's words: 'The problem, here, is not that data mining can be biased, but that, after centuries of inequality and discrimination, *empirical reality is biased.*'[65] Still, predictive analytics often exacerbates the problem by whitewashing those biases, whilst perpetuating inequalities under the cover of impartiality and objectivity. Of course, additional biases may also be built into the models. Furthermore, predictive algorithms are also not neutral or objective in so far as the goal-oriented perspective of the corporate or governmental profiler drives the choice of data and its interpretative framing. A government concerned with securing a maximum level of public safety is likely to define 'recidivism' or riskiness more expansively than one focused on rehabilitation, and will select and interpret data with that objective in mind. A corporation's algorithmic model for hiring decisions may, at times of heightened competition, emphasise ruthlessness over competence. A predictive model for creditworthiness might prioritise profit over affordability. These perspectives provide 'interested readings of reality', rather than impartial descriptions.[66] They do not aspire to any 'objective truth' but to an instrumentalised vision of the past to make useful judgements for the future.

Second, even if not 'true' in any objective sense, algorithmic predictions may or may not be accurate. If the model increases profits or reduces expenditure, it is valid; it works. The accuracy of data-driven profiling and attendant predictive practices is measured against subsequent individual consumption or behavioural choices. Did the user click on the recommended news story, film or advertisement, did she default on the loan, defraud the insurance company or buy the product with the increased personalised price? Did the accused reoffend; and did the employee become the rain-maker? One objection is that mistakes can be costly especially in grave contexts, such as sentencing of offenders, creditworthiness assessments or employment decisions. This is not unique to predictive algorithms (and present in all predictions about future human actions drawn from non-universal generalisations) but arguably aggravated here as the outcomes are often not contestable (see below). Still, the more accurate the algorithmic prediction, the greater its legitimacy against alternatives. A more profound objection against predictive algorithms and their proliferation across societal domains – justified by their (assumed, for the time being) superior accuracy – relates to the underlying assumption that they do no more than actualise a future that would have occurred in any event. If they turn out to be largely accurate, interference with reality is marginal. Yet, is this really the case? Predictive practices do not simply 'follow' expected futures, but in the course of implementing them intervene, encroach, manipulate and *make* these futures. As early as 1988, Jonathan Simon commented that actuarial practices 'cannot be dismissed as merely forms of knowing, when to be known is to be subject to significant alterations in life opportunities.'[67] By the same token, predictive algorithmic practices are not passive, but active in nudging the profilee towards the profiler's choice of pre-destinies,[68] whilst foreclosing other opportunities. An offender with a predicted high risk of recidivism is deprived of the chance to enact a different future of law-abiding behaviour; a social media user targeted with particular political messages is deprived of alternative perspectives on the subject-matter. The effect of personalisation practices is to 'normalise' populations within sub-groups. Lawrence Lessig's take on data-driven 'normalisation' (a Foucauldian concept associated with disciplinary regimes, e.g. schools or prisons, to institutionalise populations) is this: 'The observing will affect the observed. The system watches what you do; it fits you into a pattern; the pattern is then fed back to you in the form of options set by the pattern; the options reinforce the patterns; the cycle begins again.'[69] Mireille Hildebrandt thus observes that although customisation 'may seem the opposite to normalisation, in fact has a similar effect.'[70] It is not the profiler that adjusts to individual uniqueness, but rather individuals are – after an initial impetus of data – fitted into the profiler's instrumentalised patterns. Uniqueness is supressed; everyone is *like* others in crucial respects. It is not the profile that is 'accurate', but predictive analytics cajoles the individual into becoming 'accurate' to fit the pattern, into becoming compliant. (Chapters 2 and 3)

That having been said, actuarial practices present a subtler and more insidious form of normalisation than that exerted by the disciplinary institutions Foucault had in mind. Simon argued for the strategic distinctiveness of actuarial practices: 'Rather than seeking to change people ("normalize" them...), an actuarial regime seeks to manage them in place... While the disciplinary regime attempts to alter individual behavior and motivation, the actuarial regime alters the physical and social structures within which individuals behave,'[71] and thereby increases the efficiency of power through making populations more docile and manageable.[72] (Chapter 3) Still, predictive practices impact on, and shape, individual identity, including subjectivities about (group) belonging, or the lack of belonging: algorithmic or actuarial groups have 'no experienced meaning for the members, and therefore lack the capacity to realise common goals or purposes.'[73] Whilst stereotyping in the analogue world generally entails reflexive communications between profiler, profilee, the stereotyped group and the community, which generate a sense of belonging and internal solidarity within the group, algorithmic groups are often artificial, seemingly arbitrary, opaque and transient aggregates.[74] (Chapter 2) This 'makes it more difficult for group subjecthood to develop (or reproduce itself)'[75] and undermines the possibility of collective practices of resistance (see below) which in turn also reinforces their apparent accuracy.

Third, accuracy claims legitimising algorithmic profiling also have repercussions for moral agency, free will and normative domains. Predictive practices are in substance, if not in name, enabled by assumptions of character essentialism. (See Front Cover of the Book) Nicola Lacey commented: 'new technologies in fields such as neuroscience and genetics, and computer programs that identify crime "hot spots"... offer, or perhaps threaten, yet more sophisticated mechanisms of responsibility attribution based on notions of character essentialism combined with assessments of character-based risk, just as the emerging sciences of the mind, the brain, and statistics did in the late nineteenth century.'[76] If individual preferences and behaviour can be foretold 'accurately', it is tempting to conclude that the human actor is after all not the autonomous decision-maker the Enlightenment ideals of human rationality and freedom envisaged. The implications of this are stark, albeit not unprecedented. In criminal justice, forms of character essentialism have long grounded predictive practices that draw deterministic inferences from the delinquent's past to her future behaviour, in an uncomfortable tension with moral agency as the foundation of criminal responsibility and punishment. (Chapter 8). Liberal democracy and the market economy are equally dependant on the presence of autonomous citizens and consumers that can make rational choices between competing political parties and manifestos, or competing goods and services. Whilst in natural sciences, an overarching theory facilitates and constitutes the jump from 'is' (sun rose yesterday and today) to 'ought' (sun rise will rise tomorrow), within the legal and other normative domains, the notion of free choice is a moral imperative that prevents precisely such deterministic reasoning. Free choice entails the possibility of future difference, unexpectedness and new-ness. Importantly, the presumptive existence of personal autonomy (and an underlying understanding of human individuality as open-ended) allows for the possibility of normative demands in the first place. As such, moral agency is a necessary political requirement, even a necessary political fiction, not amenable to empirical disproof by algorithms or otherwise, no matter how great their apparent 'accuracy' is. Within a political and moral community, the open-endedness of human individuality is also essential for the possibility of collective betterment, premised on an understanding that the future is not, need not be, a replication of the past. Such betterment tends to lie in 'unknowable and unpredictable outlier-events' which are wholly outside 'accurate' statistical framings of reality.[77]

1.3.3 *Contesting Big Data Profiling within Spaces of Contestation*

The contestability of algorithmic processes and outcomes, and their reflexive impact on existing spaces of contestation, are likely to emerge as an overall touchstone for their differential legitimacies.[78] Contestation takes different forms in different social domains, but goes some way towards enlisting reasoning and explanations of and for the profiling, and could in principle discipline the uses and nature of predictive analytics. The source of the imperative for contestability varies across social spheres. In the *scientific community*, contestability is an integral part of the scientific method, and can be found explicitly in Karl Popper's concept of falsification that provides for the existence of scientific *knowledge or truth*, but always on a provisional basis, as long as it has not been falsified. In fact, according to Popper, the possibility of falsification is the hallmark of science and scientific knowledge as opposed to non-scientific ones, such as psychoanalysis.[79] Against this reading, insights of big data analytics are not, as such, falsifiable (and in that sense not 'scientific'), considering that algorithms deliver probabilities based on past patterns (facts) rather than (dis) proving universal propositions (normative claims). Even where the predicted probabilities are not borne out against new data sets, for example, Google's flu predictions,[80] and thus false, in the absence of a universal and grounded claim there is no theory that could be 'falsified' in the Popperian sense. This does not mean that these insights cannot be informative or useful (including in the development of theories), but rather that their standing as scientific knowledge or truths needs to be treated with caution. This holds significance beyond science in that data-driven 'scientific' knowledge and its methods routinely inform, for example, legal and political reasoning, propped up with the claim of 'scientific authority'.

In the *legal sphere*, the imperative of the contestability of governmental decisions flows from the State's unique power over individual life and liberty (classically expressed as the state's monopoly on the legitimate use of violence) and oversight in administering public life, and is designed to stem abuses of that power. The contestability (or reviewability) of governmental decisions is integral to the rule of law and actualised in a host of constitutional conventions, rights and guarantees that create spaces for individual or collective contestation. The right to judicial review of administrative decisions, the right of defence,[81] as well as data subject access rights are prime examples of individual rights to contest governmental decisions that affect the individual, underwritten by the understanding that such contestation makes for better decisions with greater legitimacy. Public decision-making based on black-box technology is thus, by its very nature, an anomaly. Its problematic is put in sharp relief within criminal justice, where data-driven profiling of delinquents falls uncomfortably between the countervailing forces of the *efficient* pursuit of public safety (economic perspective), on the one hand, and the presumption of innocence and moral agency as a basis for criminal responsibility, on the other hand. (Chapter 8) In the US case of *State of Wisconsin v. Loomis* (2016)[82] (Chapter 11 and 15) the Wisconsin Supreme Court upheld the denial of parole and consequential six-year prison term (for a drive-by shooting) which was based, in parts, on the 'Correctional Offender Management Profiling for Alternative Sanctions' black-box algorithm, otherwise known as COMPAS, that had classified Loomis as high risk to the community and of recidivism. For the court, it was not fatal to the defendant's constitutional due-process right, that neither the sentencing court nor Loomis had any insight into the workings of COMPAS to review the risk assessment for 'accuracy and scientific validity' – in light of the facts that the tool was only used to corroborate the judge's opinion *and* that Loomis had known the personal information that fed into the algorithm (which arguably also gave him some derivative insight about the algorithm's variables.)[83] The court's attempt to trivialise the tool suggests a keen awareness of its poor fit with the demands of a fair trial, which at the very minimum would require a reasoned decision (even 'black-box' jury decisions are foregrounded by testing of opposite narratives in the adversarial trial). Still, it approved the legitimacy of COMPAS, and thus, in the end, efficiency and blind knowledge trumped due process and articulated reasoning. Collective contestation to these algorithmic tools is unlikely by a public that is increasingly habituated to criminal justice as instrumentalist, preventative risk-management administration towards 'law and order' as opposed to the traditional retrospective, individualised model focused on moral accountability and just punishment, enacted through a trial that serves as a communicative process between defendant, state and community.[84]

In the *political domain*, contestability lies at the heart of democracy and democratic accountability, most prominently manifested in representative government, free elections and free speech protection. John Stuart Mill in reflecting on representative government insisted on the 'function of Antagonism' which, if unfulfilled, would condemn a 'government to infallible degeneracy and decay'.[85] Antagonism serves progress: 'No community has ever long continued progressive, but while a conflict was going on between the strongest power in the community and some rival power... When the victory on either side was so complete as to put an end to the strife, and no other conflict took its place, first stagnation followed, and then decay.'[86] Similarly and overlapping, the marketplace of ideas rationale for free speech protection is animated by the notion that the best or most truthful ideas will emerge victoriously in the free and robust competition (or contestation) of ideas and opinions.[87] Although the reverse may well be the case (i.e. the marketplace of ideas produces rather than reveals 'truths'), in approach it resonates with the concept of falsification in the scientific community. And yet again, personalisation or data-driven political micro-targeting provides for an uneasy fit with the public sphere and political deliberation, and at best disrupts and at worst diminishes existing practices of contestation. First and most importantly, unlike in the legal context, political micro-targeting taps into user preferences, and so almost inevitably incapacitates resistance to itself. Individuals have no or little incentive to question the accuracy or appropriateness of the profiling or personalisation practice, that is continuously adjusted in light of feedback loops. Second, although the overall effect of micro-targeting on the public sphere as a shared space for political deliberation remains ambivalent (Chapter 13), the problematisation of filter bubbles and echo chambers arises from a concern that micro-targeting profoundly undermines the practice of testing and contesting individual political standpoints through exposure to alternative narratives – with strong self-reinforcing dynamics.[88] (Chapter 17) The lack of exposure to such alternative narratives due to personalised context arguably generates more insular, polarised and extremist political perspectives, making them even less amenable to challenge. Thus third, increased political homogeneity and polarisation within echo chambers translates, at the collective, heterogeneous level, into a weakened willingness and capacity to communicate across political sub-communities, and thus tends to diminish social cohesion and conflict resolution, both of which traditional mass media fostered as a prerequisite for effective democratic governance.[89] Thus Cass Sunstein has argued that citizens in a well-functioning democracy ought to be exposed to *chance encounters* and to *shared experiences* which act as social glue, stressing affinity over difference, necessary for solving social problems.[90] Both demands are diametrically opposed to targeted personalised experiences, and up against a powerful alliance of commercial, political and individual interests in the practice of personalisation.

In the *commercial sphere*, contestability is implicit in the idea of the market which is, in its very conception, a space of contestation between providers, enacted by consumers through consumption choices freely and autonomously made and who thereby allocate resources to the 'best' providers. So, much like in the scientific, governmental and political arenas, market contestation also performs a type of 'quality control' with consumers as final arbiters. Whilst data-driven profiling and personalisation are apparently wholly in tune with such market contestation, in fact they undermine the market in significant ways – and again with the blessing of users. *First*, as Nick O'Donovan explores in Chapter 4, data-driven personalisation exerts strong secondary network effects that have led to further online concentration with a diminishing choice for consumers, especially amongst non-profiling providers. *Second*, consumers exercise their autonomy in favour of data-driven personalisation in an environment that is deeply hostile to alternative (and contesting) choices and nudges them towards personalisation, often in non-compliance with the General Data Protection Regulation[91] (Chapter 5) but not necessarily so. Against the immediate personal benefits gained (e.g. access to the site or free use of a service), the distant and often collective harms caused by mass algorithmic profiling, for example, filter bubbles, user-pay models, surveillance, manipulation, pale into insignificance. Facebook's 'emotional contagions study' of 2014 involved 689,003 users and showed how easily Facebook could manipulate the emotions of its subscribers.[92] Although this study was 'corporate research' in response to popular narratives,[93] in fact Facebook's core business lies in continually adjusting its algorithm to increase user time spent on the platform ('stickiness') and decrease buying resistance. The research caused outrage at the time, but did not lead to a mass exodus of its subscribers, as the collective and distant harms failed to trump the immediate personal gains. In that sense algorithmic profiling presents a classic tragedy of the commons, or collective action, problem. Even on a personal level, the collection of personal micro-data points drawn from online behaviour that are generally by themselves neither sensitive nor significant, does not easily translate – in the mind of users – into highly sophisticated individual profiles that may be used across a range of purposes from insurance to pricing to credit risks, and become virtual alter-egos which are hard, if not impossible, to escape. For privileged users, these virtual alter egos may give them significant leeway. Once in place, personalisation, which is designed to break down consumer resistance (i.e. create zero buying resistance[94]) as continuously perfected through feedback loops, becomes fully self-perpetuating, and thus pre-empts contestation. (See Chapter 17) The sheer profitability of profiling also makes corporate 'AI ethics' an unlikely candidate for (self)disciplining these practices. (Chapter 14) *Third*, a 'personalised' market is a highly fragmented market and in fact no marketplace at all; it fails as a communication network within which consumers can get (price) signals that would enable rational decision making and collective action that are defining features of a market. (Chapter 6) Typically, personalised pricing (or price discrimination) disempowers consumers as market participants, given the absence of stable reference points (i.e. the standard price offered to all consumers by a provider) against which buying choices may be made.[95] (Chapter 10)

Against these dynamics, any legal attempt to empower consumers and citizens individually, as the General Data Protection Regulation does as a primary strategy, is immediately met by the resistance-breaking features underlying personalisation. In the commercial context, individual contestation of profiles, similar to the challenge in *Loomis*, is likely only in respect of more significant transactions with an obviously negative outcome, for example, a rejected credit, employment or insurance application. In these very limited contexts (considering the overall ubiquity of personalisation), Article 22 of the GDPR might be useful as it gives profiled subjects the right to human oversight over 'significant' automated decisions,[96] including 'meaningful information about the logic involved [in the algorithm], as well as the significance and the envisaged consequences [of the profile] for the data subject.'[97] This entitlement does not extend to an explanation for the actual decision, or normative justification, but would probably entail information about variables governing the predictive algorithms and their relevance to the decision, thus amounting to something *vaguely* approaching causation, or normative justification.

In summary, the use of predictive analytics has, in different social domains, encountered and, more or less successfully, disabled resistance to itself and thereby also chipped away at the broader spaces of contestation, which traditionally have served core *public values*, such as promoting knowledge, accountable government and functioning markets. Yet, the possibility of contestation also enfranchises the individual by allowing her to become an active participant or critical listener in processes and decisions that have an impact on her life. The inscrutability of profiling algorithms in criminal justice is blatantly problematic as its attendant decisions have an immediate and significant impact on individuals. The systematic exposure to mundane algorithmic personalised outcomes shrouded in darkness is perhaps even more challenging precisely because their all-embracing effects are more insidious, diffuse and evasive. Daniel Solove has argued for the inscrutability of personal data usage as a core harm that privacy is, or should be, concerned about. Using Kafka's *The Trial*, he has shown how – beyond the harms caused by a surveillance environment when personal data is continuously collected – the inscrutability of the storage of data, its analysis and use creates a 'suffocating powerlessness and vulnerability' that repositions the individual *vis-à-vis* the state: 'a bureaucracy with inscrutable purposes... uses people's information to make important decisions about them, yet denies the people the ability to participate in how their information is used.'[98] His commentary was addressed to government but arguably extends to private actors whose inscrutable data practices are in their exertion of impersonal domination equally harmful,[99] particularly where those actors control the infrastructure of collective social, economic and political life. (Chapter 4) In the private sphere, the collection of non-traditional non-volunteered data, its aggregation and open-ended secondary uses (e.g. 'All data is credit data' Chapter 7) magnifies inscrutability and, by implication, the power asymmetries between profiler and profilee. It is this profound asymmetry that undermines the legitimacy of stereotyping which, as argued above, is *prima facie* necessary and useful. This asymmetry also means that whilst stereotyped individuals are in the analogue world, at least in some circumstances, able to participate in the creation of their own stereotype or contest it subsequently, the inscrutability of algorithmic decisions largely prevents active participation in, or contestation of, stereotyping. The individual is kept out of the loop in the processes and decisions that affect his life; or, in Rieder's words, kept 'in the conditions of paranoid meritocracy, constantly wondering whether their practices and preferences signal their adherence to "economic morality."'[100] Corporate actors – and derivatively governmental actors, considering the amount of data sharing – know us *intimately* and much more closely than we know them. Such intimate knowledge is neither harmless nor *prima facie* legitimate. It amplifies corporate and governmental power over consumers and citizens in a reversal of existing understandings of effective democracy and markets, which, even absent abuses, reshapes social relationships. The emergent judicial recognition of the non-domination principle, as advocated by academics as a new privacy standard, is a small tentative step towards acknowledging these paradigmatic shifts in power differentials and redressing them.[101] However, much wider systematic thinking about profiling and personalisation practices will be needed to retain and regain the foundations of a humanist digital society, grounded in individual and institutional responsibility, reason and articulated reasoning; individuality, community and solidarity; and communication as a means for expressing conflicts and work towards their resolution.

1.4 CHAPTERS: THE VOICES OF SUBJECT-MATTER EXPERTS

This collection contributes to the live debate of data-driven profiling and personalisation that has already attracted some impressive scholarship.[102] The volume's particular contribution lies in creating room for the voices of subject-matter experts from various disciplines within law as well as from human geography, philosophy, behavioural economics and criminology, who are not first and foremost 'technologists'. This reflects the philosophy and ambition behind the collection to construct this new phenomenon of data-driven profiling and personalisation, not as a technological problematic to be analysed and 'solved' by computer specialists, IT law or policy experts, but rather as a social, economic and political phenomenon that can and must be understood through existing subject-specific discourses within which it falls. It is through these discourses that compelling continuities and discontinuities with past legal approaches, economic constructs, political, sociological and jurisprudential narratives and underlying ideologies may be observed and critiqued. Equally, the volume speaks to the pressing need for the big data phenomenon, that is sweeping across many societal domains, to be integrated within existing disciplinary scholarship *and* across them.

Running these different discourses about different manifestations of the same phenomenon next to each other is insightful, not least because of the divergent terminology used to describe it. What is known in the market under the enticing labels of 'personalisation', 'customisation', 'optimisation' or 'smart' technology, becomes 'micro-targeting' in the political context, a term that gives a sense of the aggressive and exploitative dimension of the practice. In the legal and criminal justice environment, the terminology 'predictive policing', 'algorithmic profiling' or 'actuarial justice' brings out the more overtly controlling aspects of algorithmic profiling as well as its grounding in the 'scientific' method. In the medical context, the language of 'precision' or P4 medicine (referring to 'predictive, preventive, personalised and participatory') arguably emphasises both the technical nature of the approach and the benefits it brings to patients. The diversity of the terminology provides a snapshot of the particular framing and values that corporate or governmental profilers seek to highlight, but also shows traces of the value that can be found in most profiling practices more or less strongly.

The volume is divided into four parts. It starts and finishes with overarching theoretical accounts of algorithmic personalisation practices and offers in the two middle parts, first, general key themes that emerge from specific legal environments, and, second, a range of social spheres and discourses in which these themes are reconstituted and adjusted within particularised contexts. All in all, the emphasis throughout the volume lies in presenting different disciplinary perspectives in antagonism and rapport with each other. A unifying theme running through the chapters in the first part is the profound power unleashed by big data profiling technology, and its impact on long-standing social structures, modalities of governance and market constellations. In *'Personalisation and Digital Modernity: Deconstructing the Myths of the Subjunctive World'* **Kieron O'Hara** situates data-driven personalisation within a sociological narrative of modernity and its Enlightenment values of rationality, progress and individuality, which has given way to *digital modernity*, characterised by 'communication... supercharged by always-on networked linking using digital technology... the migration of many interactions online... exponentially positive network effects... [and] the capture and reuse of data as a resource.' O'Hara's focus is on the individual who has his world moulded around him through personalised recommendations. Personalisation replaces authentic choice that served as a core tenet of modernity –

and necessarily requires privacy. For digital modernity, choice is now 'the preroga-tive of the data infrastructure which constructs the personalised world.' The data infrastructure knows much better what one *should* prefer, and also requires the abandonment of privacy. O'Hara provocatively sets the tone for later discussions that seek refuge from the excesses of profiling in data protection law, by showing quite how systematically privacy has to be and in fact is abandoned to make space for this brave new digital world. The implications of the datafication for new modalities of government – in close proximity to or through the market – are explored by **Marc Welsh** in *'Personalisation, Power and the Datafied Subject'* from a Foucauldian perspective. Here the individual is an important cog in the wheel of the govern-mental project of 'improving populations'. The individual becomes the locus for the construction of the datafied self, through which self-disciplining control can be exerted. Personalisation technology shifts responsibility for 'correct' forms of actions and behaviours to individuals, whose co-option in algorithmic governmentality is not forced at all, but enticed by rewards, like lower insurance premiums for good driving behaviour (driving metrics) or for healthy lifestyle behaviour (health metrics). Consent is the enabler, power asymmetries the starting and end point: 'The data-poor voluntarily proffer their data to be monetized by companies who combine it with the data lives of others to produce population wide correlations and inferences that can be utilised to generate profit or reduce losses through forms of algorithmic government.' In fact, algorithmic personalisation amplifies those asym-metries by weakening markets. **Nick O'Donovan** in his chapter on *'Personal Data and Collective Value: Data-Driven Personalisation as Network Effect'* shows how algorithmic personalisation exerts subtle secondary network effects of a qualitative type that lead to even more intensive concentration in markets already heavily impacted by primary network effects: the more intensive and sophisticated the data practices, the more fine-tuned the personalised recommendations, and the more willing, and less resistant the consumer who in any event has fewer choices. And, as with all network effects, it has strong self-reinforcing dynamics.

Against these deeply critical and dystopian social science accounts of data-driven personalisation, the second part of the volume hears the voices of legal scholars whose disciplinary methods, toolkits and temperaments mean that the tone of the conversation becomes more practice-focused, technical and cautious, even if the verdicts are ultimately not dissimilar. Existing legal regimes and doctrines, whether data protection, contract, antidiscrimination or criminal law, are profoundly chal-lenged by algorithmic prediction and personalisation. Not only do they fail to act as a break against unfair or exploitative predictive practices, but they have their regulatory integrity and objectives undermined by the structural and operative distinctiveness of algorithmic personalisation. An obvious starting point is data protection law, and in particular the GDPR, that has been much celebrated for its regulatory rigour. Yet, **Michèle Finck's** analysis in *'Hidden Personal Insights and Entangled in the Algorithmic Model: The Limits of the GDPR in the Personalisation*

Context' shows why neither a framework based on consent nor other user empowerment effectively disciplines corporate algorithmic personalisation. The chapter also
conveys a strong sense that binary divisions or understandings between sensitive and
non-sensitive data, individual and group data, personal and non-personal data simply
fail to do justice to the workings of big data analytics and belong to a bygone
analogue, small-data world. In a similar vein, **TT Arvind** in *'Personalisation,
Markets, and Contract: The Limits of Legal Incrementalism'* argues that the phenomenon of algorithmic personalisation presents a paradigmatic challenge to both
privacy and contract law. Privacy conceptions had never before so systematically
been underwritten by contractual arrangements and the ability to commodify one's
privacy. Yet, contract law itself is challenged by data-driven personalisation.
A traditional personalised contract (e.g. the tailored suit) assumed a joint project
and a two-way relationship between buyer and service provider, whilst current
personalised contracts are de-relationalised and so no longer moderated by such
two-way dependency. A personalised, de-relationalised contract creates a one-way
dependency or informational asymmetry that profoundly undermines the user's
effective participation in the market. In *"All Data Is Credit Data': Personalised
Consumer Credit Score and Anti-Discrimination Law'* **Noelia Collado-Rogriguez
and Uta Kohl** explore, with reference to big data use for consumer credit scores,
whether anti-discrimination law offers any realistic opportunity to review algorithmic predictions. Whilst the concept of indirect discrimination – focused on the
actual effect or outcome of a practice – offers in principle a viable method for
overcoming the opacity of black-box algorithms, it can do little to overcome the
structural socio-economic disadvantages that sit at the root of much unequal treatment. Disconcertingly, such inequality is potentially aggravated by big data credit
score models that follow the logic of 'all data as credit data' which threatens to apply
an all-encompassing judgement of the individual to all social domains, regardless of
their functional separation. Moving from civil to criminal law, **David Gurnham's**
discussion in *'Sentencing Dangerous Offenders in the Era of Predictive Technologies:
New Skin, Same Old Snake?'* places novel predictive algorithms that assess the
dangerousness of offenders for sentencing purposes within a long-standing practice
of actuarial risk assessment. Although predictive technology is in that sense merely a
sophisticated version of the old, it powerfully underlines its fundamental mismatch
with liberal principles of retrospective, responsibility-based punishment.

The third part of the book situates data-driven personalisation within various
social domains and disciplinary discourses. The richness of the different languages
and conceptual framings illustrates both the textual variety and the common nature
of the problematics. Starting off with *"P4 Medicine' and the Purview of Health Law:
the Patient or the Public?'*, **Keith Syrett** traces precision or personalised medicine
back to the inception of the Human Genome Project in 1985 and a systems
approach to biology that has recently been augmented by the digital revolution.
Significantly, the rise of personalised medicine mirrors a shift from medical

paternalism to patient choice as a central tenet of UK medical jurisprudence – in that sense law (and ethics) act as key facilitators of precision medicine. Syrett then argues that personalised medicine's fundamental focus on the particular patient, as supported by legal and ethical trends, underplays the important collective nature of health and its social stratification and thus must be treated with caution as a wholesale welcome development. Different yet similar, **Joost Poort and Frederik Zuiderveen Borgesius** explore in *'Personalised Pricing: The Demise of the Fixed Price?'* the practice of price discrimination based on predictive algorithms and its underlying basis in economic theory. Although the net welfare impact of personalised pricing is not clear-cut, the more prices are personalised, 'the more welfare will generally shift from consumers to suppliers.' Surprisingly, the authors' empirical studies show that consumers are overall not supportive of price discrimination even when it works in their favour. This suggests either an intuitive commitment to collective fairness or, more likely, a rejection of a highly fragmented market within which making rational buying choices is fundamentally undermined. Although such user rejection is in theory accommodated by the GDPR's requirement of consent, whether price discrimination is, or can be, effectively stopped remains shrouded in the opacity of online pricing practices. Moving from law disciplining data-driven personalisation, to data-driven personalisation employed as a disciplining device, **Pamela Ugwudike** takes a criminological perspective on the rise of predictive algorithms in criminal justice. In *'Data-Driven Algorithms in Criminal Justice: Predictions as Self-fulfilling Prophecies'* she critiques their fairness by arguing that 'profiling algorithms generate labels that counterproductively evoke a self-fulfilling prophecy and foment future criminalisation.' Biases against minorities – already ingrained in the data sets and the algorithmic models and then reinforced through the profiling – are not just problematic from a penal perspective, where accuracy claims must at the very least be supported by evidence of their differential validity. A social justice perspective can also expose the structural unfairness of predictive technology, and its grounding in historic social and economic disadvantage. 'Smart city' developments – discussed by **Daithí Mac Síthigh** in *'From Global Village to Smart City: Reputation, Recognition, Personalisation, and Ubiquity'* – subtly merge the commercial functionality and controlling dimension of big data analytics. In smart city projects, the ubiquitous physical presence of algorithmic technology is promoted and justified as a more efficient way to 'manage the relationship between the responsible authority and individual residents or other users' mediated by privately owned technology. Mac Síthigh's discussion of the Chinese social credit system and various facial recognition technologies, as enabling devices for effective service delivery within city environs, suggests that policing functions are never far behind the creation of corporate digital infrastructure. The smart city simultaneously enacts a utopian and dystopian vision of a technologically infused society where government and corporations 'know' in detail the individual and the group and act upon that knowledge. A different, but equally powerful, merger of private and public interests occurs in the course of political micro-targeting, as discussed by **Normann Witzleb and Moira Paterson** in *'Micro-targeting in Political Campaigns: Political Promise and Democratic Risk.'* The Facebook/Cambridge Analytica scandal of 2018 provides a natural starting point to explore the virtues and vices of targeting individuals with personalised messages during political campaigns. The authors argue that applying data protection law to political micro-targeting (i.e. lifting the current derogations and exemptions) would provide a useful restraint and garner the benefits and minimise the costs of such personalisation. Yet, perhaps their arguments are too optimistic – considering, on the one hand, Finck's exposition (see above) about the problems associated with consent and the structural peculiarities of big data analytics not acknowledged by data protection law and, on the other hand, the powerful alliance between commercial, political and private interests in favour of micro-targeting.

The final part of the collection is confidently entitled 'The Future...' suggesting that we – as data-limited humans – may *know* the future of data-driven personalisation and its impact on society, even without the aid of a predictive algorithm. What the chapters make clear is that whilst we may not be able to predict what the future *will* be, we can have views of what it *ought* to be. This is where we infinitely outperform even the most complex algorithms: in making normative judgements about the good life and the contours of a society that would support it. This part starts off with **Andrew Charlesworth's** discussion on *'Regulating Algorithmic Assemblages: Looking Beyond Corporatist AI Ethics'* about the confidence that we might place in corporate AI ethics as a mechanism for restraining the excesses of data-driven personalisation, given its dominant position in the current discourse on regulating technology. Situating 'AI ethics' within traditions of corporate social responsibility and institutional ethical frameworks shows its systemic shortcomings and inability to be truly Other-regarding. The chapter further argues that making 'ethical' corrections to AI applications rarely, if ever, addresses their wider societal consequences which arise from their deep integration into social structures, as captured by the idea of 'algorithmic assemblage'. If corporate ethics is a weak answer, **Konstantinos Katsikopoulos's** proposal might be more fruitful, at least in regulatory contexts. In *'Scepticism about Big Data's Predictive Power about Human Behaviour: Making a Case for Theory and Simplicity'* he argues that simple algorithms, supported by theory, do not just have the virtues of intelligibility and thus allow for transparency and accountability, but are also often in performance at least as good as their complex black-box equivalents. This argument is important in respect of predictive technology within the legal and regulatory environments, but holds less force within commerce or political advertising where the corporate bottom-line and party political success are the clear and simple arbiter of whether personalisation 'works'. Another 'process' within and against which algorithmic personalisation may be judged is the role of communication and language in society. In *'Building Personalisation: Language and the Law'* **Alun Gibbs** argues that algorithmic personalisation replaces and competes with language; technology delivers choices and results, but not arguments, explanations or justifications. Yet, it is language that underpins and supports personhood, agency and authentic choice which create social meanings and solidarities and are the key building blocks of our wider understanding of constitutionalism as a political way of life. The more widespread the adoption of personalisation technologies in the building of the 'self', the more we endanger and deconstruct those building blocks and, with them, our political way of life. **Jacob Eisler's** *'Conclusion: Balancing Data-Driven Personalisation and Law as Social Systems'* synthesises the chapters of the volume, and offers a new perspective, by using the socio-legal approach of systems theory. He argues that the real force of personalisation is that it becomes an internal component of the self-perpetuating systems it touches: society as a whole, and even more intimately, individual persons themselves. Its deep integration into these systems illuminates two themes of this volume: why data-driven personalisation's impact is so difficult for standard consent-based mechanisms of legal interpretation to manage; and why the power that elite actors have over the mechanisms of algorithmic personalisation is so insidious. Personalisation does not merely affect society; it becomes part of its constitution. It does not merely affect persons, it becomes part of their identity and self-constitution. Law may counterbalance personalisation, but to do so effectively it must ensure that practices and norms of personalisation do not infiltrate it, as they have infiltrated so many other domains of our society.

NOTES

* Many thanks to Nick O'Donovan, Jacob Eisler, Jörn Werner and Carrie Fox for insightful comments and suggestions.

1 For a description of the novelties of big data, see Rob Kitchin, 'Big Data, new epistemologies and paradigm shifts' (April–June 2014) *Big Data & Society* 1; or Doug Laney, '3D Data Management: Controlling Data Volume, Velocity, and Variety' (2001) *META Group. Application Delivery Strategies* https://blogs.gartner.com/doug-laney/files/2012/01/ad9493D-Data-Management-Controlling-Data-Volume-Velocity-and-Variety.pdf

2 Andrew Whitby, *The Sum of the People: How the Census Has Shaped Nations, from the Ancient World to the Modern Age* (Basic Books, 2020). In the UK, the 2021 census will be the last: www.bbc.co.uk/news/uk-51468919.

3 Michal Kosinski, David Stillwell, Thore Graepel, 'Private traits and attributes are predictable from digital records of human behavior' (2013) *PNAS* www.pnas.org/content/pnas/early/2013/03/06/1218772110.full.pdf.

4 Shoshana Zuboff, 'Big Other: surveillance capitalism and the prospect of an informal civilization' (2015) 30 *Journal of information technology* 75; Karen Yeung, 'Five fears about mass predictive personalisation in an age of surveillance capitalism' (2018) *International data privacy law* (forthcoming) https://papers.ssrn.com/sol3/papers.cfm?abstract_id=3266800.

5 Daniel Susser, Beate Roessler, Helen Nissenbaum, 'Technology, autonomy, and manipulation' (2019) 8(2) *Internet Policy Review*.

6 Btihaj Ajana, 'Digital health and the biopolitics of the quantified self' (2017) 3 *Digital Health* 1.

7 Bernard E Harcourt, *Against Prediction* (University of Chicago Press 2007); Ben Bowling, Shruti Iyer, 'Automated policing: the case of body-worn video' (2019) 15 *International Journal of Law in Context* 140, 153ff.

8 Richard H Thaler, Cass R Sunstein, *Nudge: Improving Decisions about Health, Wealth and Happiness* (Penguin Books 2009). This phenomenon is reminiscent of Foucault's notion of necessary, or tolerated, or popular illegality: Michel Foucault, *Discipline and Punish* (Vintage Books 1995) 82f. (Thanks to Nick O'Donovan for pointing it out.)

9 Notably in the context of price discrimination, consumers find the practice unfair regardless of whether they get a benefit or not. (Chapter 10)

10 Mireille Hildebrandt, *Smart Technologies and the End(s) of Law* (Edward Elgar 2016); Roger Brownsword, *Law, Technology and Society* (Routledge 2019).

11 Shoshana Zuboff, *The Age of Surveillance Capitalism* (Profile Books 2019) 8.

12 John Rawls, *A Theory of Justice* (Harvard University Press 1971); Michael Walzer, *Spheres of Justice* (Basic Books 1984).

13 Julia Lawn and others (eds.), *Privacy, Big Data and the Public Good – Frameworks for Engagement* (Cambridge University Press 2014).

14 Cass R Sunstein, *#Republic: Divided Democracy in the Age of Social Media* (Princeton University Press 2017).

15 Linnet Taylor, Luciano Floridi and Bart van der Sloot, 'Introduction: a new perspective on privacy' in Linnet Taylor, Luciano Floridi and Bart van der Sloot (eds.), *Group Privacy* (Springer 2017).

16 Anton Vedder, 'KDD: the challenge to individualism' (1999) 1(4) *Ethics and Information Technology* 275. Mireille Hildebrandt, 'Defining profiling: a new type of knowledge?' in Mireille Hildebrandt and Serge Gutwirth (eds.), *Profiling the European Citizen* (Springer 2008).

17 Vedder (n 16) 277.

18 Schauer refers to these as universal generalisation which may be based on linguistic definition; for example, all bachelors are unmarried, or empirical observation, for example, all humans are less than 9 feet tall, in Frederic Schauer, *Profiles, Probabilities, and Stereotypes* (Belknap Press 2006) 8f.

19 Hildebrandt (n16) 21.

20 Vedder (n17) [emphasis added].

21 V Ferraris and others, 'Working paper: defining profiling' 6f https://papers.ssrn.com/sol3/papers.cfm?abstract_id=2366564.

22 'Bachelors are unmarried' is a linguistically based profile and necessarily true.

23 Ludwig Wittgenstein, *Philosophical Investigations* (G E Anscombe tr, Blackwell 1958) para 66; Hanoch Ben-Yami, 'Vagueness and family resemblance' in Hans-Joann Glock and John Hyman (eds.), *A Companion to Wittgenstein* (Wiley & Sons 2017) 407 https://publications.ceu.edu/sites/default/files/publications/vagueness-and-family-resemblance.pdf.

24 Patrick Allo, 'The Epistemology of Non-distributive Profiles' (2019) *Philosophy & Technology* 1.

25 Matt Burgess, 'UK police are using AI to inform custodial decisions – but it could be discriminating against the poor' (*Wired*, 1 March 2018) www.wired.co.uk/article/

police-ai-uk-durham-hart-checkpoint-algorithm-edit; Marion Oswald and others, 'Algorithmic risk assessment policing models: lessons from the Durham HART Model and "experimental" proportionality' (2018) *International & Communications Technology Law.*

26 Vedder (n17).

27 This would be achieved through, for example, a content-based filtering system that collects data on the interactions of the particular user with the site (e.g., Like buttons, browsing and purchase history, etc.) and makes predictions based on these historic interactions. This is in contrast to a collaborative filtering systems where big data really comes into its own, as it relies on a vast amount of data about *other* users to identify compelling similarities between different users.

28 Schauer (n18) 64ff, using the example of pitbulls to make the same point.

29 Behavioural scientists have analysed 45,000 photos from 166 Instagram users and have been able to identify correlations between depression and preferences for certain photos. Similar results have been achieved in relation to Twitter feeds. Andrew G Reece and others, 'Forecasting the onset and course of mental illness with Twitter data' (2017) 7 *Nature Scientific Reports* www.nature.com/articles/s41598-017-12961-9; Andrew G Reece and Christopher M Danforth, 'Instagram photos reveal predictive markers of depression' (2017) 6 *EPJ Data Science* https://epjdatascience.springeropen.com/articles/10.1140/epjds/ s13688-017-0110-z.

30 E Giardina, 'DNA fingerprinting' in *Brenner's Encyclopaedia of Genetics* (2nd edn., Academic Press 2013) www.sciencedirect.com/topics/biochemistry-genetics-and-molecu lar-biology/dna-profiling.

31 Jonathan Simon, 'The ideological effects of actuarial practices' (1988) 22 *Law & Society Review* 771, 778.

32 Schauer (n18) 6.

33 Ibid. 100, 251ff.

34 Ibid. 261.

35 Hildebrandt (n16) 26.

36 Francis Bacon, *Novum organum* (1620) in RM Hutchins and MJ Adler (eds.), *Great Books of the Western World* (Encyclopædia Britannica 1952) vol 35.

37 David Hume, *An Enquiry concerning Human Understanding, in Enquiries concerning Human Understanding and concerning the Principles of Morals* (first published 1748, reprinted from 1777 ed., Lewis Amherst Selby-Bigge ed., Clarendon Press 1963) 31.

38 Hildebrandt (n 10) 33.

39 Rob Kitchin, 'Big data, new epistemologies and paradigm shifts' (2014) *Big Data & Society* 1, 5.

40 Viktor Mayer-Schönberger and Kenneth Cukier, *Data: A Revolution That Will Transform How We Live, Work, and Think* (Eamon Dolan Books, 2013)

41 Ibid. 67 [emphasis in the original].

42 Ibid. 68.

43 Chris Anderson, 'The end of theory: the data deluge makes the scientific method obsolete' (*Wired*, 23 June 2008) www.wired.com/2008/06/pb-theory/.

44 Ibid.

45 Immanuel Kant, *Critique of Pure Reason* (first published 1781, Penguin Classics 2007).

46 Kitchin (n 39).

47 Hildebrandt (n 10) 36.

48 Kitchin (n 39) 5.

49 Peter V Coveney, ER Dougherty and R Highfield, 'Big data need big theory too' (2016) *Philosophical Transactions of the Royal Society* 374.

50 Sauro Succi, Peter V Coveney, 'Big data: the end of the scientific method?' (2019) *Philosophical Transactions of the Royal Society* 377.

51 Andrew Feenberg, 'Critical theory of technology: an overview' (2005) 1 *Tailoring Biotechnologies* 47, 47.

52 Amy Fleming, 'The case for... making low-tech "dumb" cities instead of "smart" ones'" *The Guardian* (London, 15 January 2020) www.theguardian.com/cities/2020/jan/15/the-case-for-making-low-tech-dumb-cities-instead-of-smart-ones.

53 Mayer-Schönberger and Cukier (n 40) 50f.

54 E Siegel, *Predictive Analytics* (Wiley 2013) 90.

55 Kitchin (n 39) 4.

56 Bernhard Rieder, 'Big Data and the paradox of diversity' (2016) 2(2) *Digital Culture and Society* 39, 40.

57 Elizabeth E Joh, 'Policing the smart city' (2019) 15(2) *International Journal of Law in Context* 177; Jake Maxwell Watts and Newley Purnell, 'Singapore is taking the 'smart city' to a whole new level' *Wall Street Journal* (New York, 24 April 2016) www.wsj.com/articles/singapore-is-taking-the-smart-city-to-a-whole-new-level-1461550026.

58 Rieder (n 56) 43.

59 Jongbin Jung and others, 'Simple rules for complex decisions' (2017) SSRN *Electronic Journal* https://papers.ssrn.com/sol3/papers.cfm?abstract_id=2919024.

60 Feenberg (n 51) 49, approving Herbert Marcuse's argument in *One-Dimensional Man* (Beacon Press 1964).

61 Langdon Winner, '*Do artefacts have politics?*' (Winter 1980) 109 *Daedalus* 121.

62 Gernot Rieder and Judith Simon, 'Big Data: a new empiricism and its epistemic and socio-political consequences' in W Pietsch, J Wernecke and M Ott (eds.), *Berechenbarkeit der Welt? Philosophie und Wissenschaft im Zeitalter von Big Data* (Springer 2017) 85.

63 Bowling and Iyer (n 7) 153ff.

64 Rieder (n 56) 50. See also Kate Crawford, 'The hidden biases of big data,' *Harvard Business Review* (1 April 2013) https://hbr.org/2013/04/the-hidden-biases-in-big-data.

65 Rieder (n 56) 50 [emphasis in the original].

66 Rieder (n 56) 44ff.

67 Simon (n 31) 772.

68 Put slightly differently by Allo (n24): 'Even though profiling is just the grouping of individuals relative to a selection of features, profiling is more than the sheer adoption of a level of abstraction. Generalisations have pragmatic encroachment: via the actions they inform they affect the world rather than just our models of the world.'

69 Lawrence Lessig, *Code: and Other Laws of Cyberspace, Version 2.0* (2nd revised ed., Basic Books 2006) 220.

70 Hildebrandt (n 10) 307. See also Helen Nissenbaum and Kazys Varnelis, *Modulated Cities: Networked Spaces, Reconstituted Subjects* (The Architectural League 2012).

71 Simon (n 31) 773.

72 Ibid.

73 Ibid. 774.

74 Allo (n24).

75 Simon (n 31) 788.

76 Nicola Lacey, *In Search of Criminal Responsibility: Ideas, Interests, and Institutions* (Oxford University Press 2016) 170f.

77 Nassim Nicholas Taleb, *The Black Swan: The Impact of the Highly Improbable* (Allen Lane 2007).

78 Hildebrandt (n 10) 30.

79 Karl Popper, *Conjecture and Refutations: The Growth of Scientific Knowledge* (first published 1963, Routledge 2002) 44ff.

80 D Butler, 'When Google got flu wrong' (2013) 494 *Nature* 155.

81 Also, on the importance of the possibility of violating laws in the first place, as a form of testing and revalidating the law and its appropriateness (or otherwise), see Brownsword (n 10) 68ff; Hildebrandt (n 10) 10.

82 *Loomis v Wisconsin* 881 NW 2d 749 (Wis 2016); see also *Malenchik v State* 928 NE 2d 564 (Ind 2010).

83 *Loomis v Wisconsin* 881 NW 2d 749 (Wis 2016); see also US Solicitor General, *Brief amicus curiae of United States in Eric L Loomis v State of Wisconsin* (23 May 2017). In contrast to *Gardner v Florida* 430 US 349 (1977) where undisclosed information which the defendant had no 'opportunity to refuse, supplement or explain' had been considered in deciding a capital punishment sentence, was held to be a violation of due process.

84 Brownsword (n 10) 207ff.

85 Ibid. 275.

86 John Stuart Mill, 'Considerations on Representative Government' (1891) in John Stuart Mill, *On Liberty, Utilitarianism and Other Essays* (Mark Philp and Frederick Rosen eds., Oxford University Press 2015) 275.

87 See dissenting US Supreme Court judgement by Justice Holmes Jr in *Abrams v United States* 250 US 616 (1919): 'the best test of truth is the power of the thought to get itself accepted in the competition of the market, and that truth is the only ground upon which their wishes safely can be carried out.'

88 The evidence on this is not clear-cut; see for example, Efrat Nechushtai and Seth C Lewis, 'What kind of news gatekeepers do we want machines to be? Filter bubbles, fragmentation, and the normative dimensions of algorithmic recommendations' (2019) 90 *Computers in Human Behavior* 298; Amja Bechmann and Kristoffer L Nielbo, 'Are we exposed to the same "news" in the news feed?' (2018) 6 *Digital Journalism* 990.

89 James Curran, *Media and Power* (Routledge 2002) 239.

90 Sunstein (n 14) 143f.

91 Regulation (EU) 2016/679 of the European Parliament and of the Council of 27 April 2016 on the protection of natural persons with regard to the processing of personal data and on the free movement of such data [2016] *OJ L* 119.

92 J Jouhki and others, 'Facebook's emotional contagion experiment as a challenge to research ethics' (2016) 4 (4) *Media and Communication* 75.

93 Danah Boyd, 'Untangling research and practice: what Facebook's "emotional contagion" study teaches us' (2016) 12 *Research Ethics* 4.

94 'Flurry of Boris Johnson adverts tested on Facebook' BBC (25 July 2019) www.bbc.co.uk/news/technology-49114147.

95 'Ad-targeting should be made transparent, data ethics body says' BBC (5 February 2020) www.bbc.co.uk/news/technology-51384858.

96 Art 22(1) GDPR: The data subject shall have the right not to be subject to a decision based solely on automated processing, including profiling, which produces legal effects concerning him or her or similarly significantly affects him or her.

97 Art 13(2)(f), Art 14(2)(g), Art15(1)(h) and Recital 63 GDPR.

98 Daniel J Solove, '"I've got nothing to hide" and other misunderstandings of privacy' (2007) 44 *San Diego Law Review* 745.

99 On technical actions/technology delivering impersonal domination inherent in capitalism in contrast to the personal domination of earlier social formations, see Feenberg (n 51) 53.

100 Rieder (n 56) 51 [internal emphasis removed].

101 Bart van der Sloot, 'A new approach to the right to privacy, or how the European Court of Human Rights embraced the non-domination principle' (2018) 34 *Computer Law & Security Review* 539, discusses *Zakharov v Russia* App no 471343/06 (ECHR, 4 December 2015).

102 Most notably: Hildebrandt and Gutwirth (n 16); Hildebrandt (n 10); David Beer, *Metric Power* (Palgrave Macmillan 2016,); David Beer, *The Data Gaze – Capitalism, Power and Perception* (Sage 2018); Zuboff (n 11); Brownsword (n 10); Brownsword (ed.), 'Law, liberty and technology: criminal justice in the context of smart machines' (2019) 15 *International Journal of Law in Context* Special Issue 2.

2

Personalisation and Digital Modernity: Deconstructing the Myths of the Subjunctive World

Kieron O'Hara

2.1 INTRODUCTION

In this chapter, I will discuss the role of personalisation in a wider narrative of the development of democratic societies, that of *digital modernity*. Digital modernity is a species of modernity, in which the key values of modernity – rationality, progress and most of all the individual – are preserved, but with the twist provided by ubiquitous digital networks. One can be sceptical of the difference this makes, as much of the technology is unproven and many of its claims hyped,[1] but it is disingenuous to claim that digital modernity has left everything unchanged. It is qualitatively different from analogue modernity, even if many practices and assumptions have carried through from one to the other.

This chapter deals with *narratives* of how modernity plays out and is implemented by institutions and technologies, which are inevitably partial, and selective in what they foreground and ignore. It is misleading to think of global narratives about technology in society as true or false; rather they are convincing or unconvincing, inspiring or uninspiring. In this chapter, I do *not* endorse any of the narratives spelt out, while exploring their internal logic. The main point is that these narratives are found convincing by powerful people and organisations, sometimes because they serve their purposes and sometimes because they really do seem to explain the direction of travel. For that reason, they are politically influential and worth our attention and critique.

I begin by setting out the context of narratives of modernisation and modernity and follow that with a discussion of digital modernity, showing how personalisation is central to it. Section 2.4 will look briefly at the technologies of personalisation, before a final substantive section drills down a little further into the operation of digital modernity.

2.2 NARRATIVES OF MODERNITY

Modernity is a concept that emerged in sociology in the mid-twentieth century, trading on the intuition that a qualitatively different society had emerged from the medieval world following a number of major historical and economic developments, particularly in Western Europe and later North America and some mainly Anglophone colonies.[2] 'Modern' society had many advantages when it came to competition between societies, in terms of economics (and therefore prosperity), and technology and innovation (and therefore warfare). Key to modernisation was the Enlightenment, the period that roughly coincided with the eighteenth century, in which Western thinkers made the welfare of the *individual* a political value, applied *sceptical principles* to previously unchallenged authorities, and demanded *rational justifications* of policy.[3] Differential experience of Enlightenment was and is still expected to explain many of the inequalities and much of the diversity in social conditions across the globe, despite globalisation; witness the oft-regretted 'fact' that Islam never had its Enlightenment: 'For those whose idea of progress was so narrow as to consist only of what they themselves had experienced, and who were disposed to see repose and decay in unfamiliar societies, repose and decay was indeed what they saw.'[4] Certainly the concept remains ubiquitous:[5]

> However reluctant we are to make value judgements about other cultures, we nevertheless continue to apply the standard of modernization as a matter of course, at least in the economic measures of unit-labour costs and competitiveness. Every day we read about the 'backwardness' of the Southern European countries compared to the exporting countries of the North.[6]

Modernisation so understood is a process, and modernity is relative rather than binary; one society is *more* modern than another. Conceived in temporal, evolutionary terms, we can compare societies using the vocabulary of Habermas and Dirlik; one is more *advanced*, another more *backward*. Typically, societies become more advanced through time, but they can revert to a backward state (the growth in populism in the twenty-first century has been seen as such a reversion[7]). Conceived in spatial terms, we can compare *peripheral* societies (the provinces, rural areas, the developing world, edgelands) with the *centre* (cities, centres of excellence, creative hubs).[8] Again, change need not always be positive: economic or cultural shifts can result in somewhere becoming peripheral, as many worry about the United Kingdom following Brexit, which is sometimes described as the revenge of the periphery upon the centre.[9] These narratives, or myths, of modernity are naturally selective. They can be *descriptive*: societies are changing according to these patterns and processes. They can be *teleological*: this is the direction of travel and it is where we are bound to end up (Giddens wrote of modernity as an unstoppable 'juggernaut' in 1990[10]). Or they can be *normative*: these are the processes we *ought* to be fostering. The valorisation of modernisation itself is a vital tool for its own implementation; as policymakers, businesspeople, technologists, journalists and trade unionists subscribe to the myths, they are more likely to become true. And indeed modern societies were and are, by most standards, highly successful. Bourgeois democracies are, generally speaking, humane, secure, tolerant and prosperous, and by and large only academics and *avant garde* artists persist in adolescent rebellion against them.

As the literature of modernity has extended, the basic Weberian narrative of expanding rationality has been amended in various ways. Firstly, modernisation plays out differently in different societies, and it is increasingly accepted that modernity is as diverse as the societies that host it.[11] However, in this chapter, I will bind the context to the wealthy capitalist democracies of Western Europe, North America and elsewhere. Secondly, the proliferation of the literature on modernity means that social commentators have intellectual resources to consider conditions of modernity, thereby introducing the complexities of reflexivity into modernity's trajectory.[12] In particular, from the perspective of the individual, modernity can be seen as a development in which the individual became the ontological unit of social analysis, displacing the pre-modern focus on communities and their health. As the individual emerges in social analysis, we begin to see accounts in which individuals are damaged or alienated by their position in society.[13] Such accounts add to our reflexive responses here. In particular, the clustering of individuals into social groups takes a more 'objective' turn in modernity; as well as the groups with which individuals readily identify (such as kin groups and those centred on religious practice and belief), more objective analyses can focus on the similarities between people based on broad attributes such as gender and class. These analyses postulate similarities and commonalities of interest of which individuals often have to be persuaded, leading to the evolution of the major ideologies characteristic of modernity, such as socialism, Marxism, feminism and nationalism.

Thirdly, technology has also played a part in lightening modernity's touch, for instance with Bauman's concept of liquidity,[14] which contrasts 'heavy', 'solid', hardware-focused modernity and 'light', 'liquid', software-based modernity, nodding to the technological context. Thanks to Lyotard's conception of postmodernism,[15] many have assumed that we have entered a postmodern period. However, it is interesting to note that Lyotard's *The Postmodern Condition* was originally written in 1979 as a report for the *Conseil des Universités du Québec*, about the effects that technology would have on knowledge production in the exact sciences, and so is centred not on the literature and art whose criticism first prompted the use of the term 'postmodern', but rather on exactly the digital technologies under discussion in this chapter. Lyotard, writing at the beginning of the age of digital technology, was admittedly not an expert on the technologies he wrote about, and may have mistaken signs of a transition within modernity for signals of its demise. Nevertheless, much in *The Postmodern Condition* is consistent with the technologically enabled modernity we are beginning to understand now, and although his chosen term 'postmodernism' is a misnomer, we can credit Lyotard with being one of the first to spot a nascent *digital modernity*.[16]

2.2.1 *Digital Modernity*

Digital modernity is that species of modernity that emerges when communication is supercharged by always-on networked linking using digital technology, resulting in the migration of many interactions online, which not only creates exponentially positive network effects, but also allows the capture and reuse of data as a resource. The data itself can then create a rich picture of the world, while simultaneously fuelling increasingly accurate machine learning or artificial intelligence (AI) to reason about it. So dramatically has internet usage increased that at the time of writing around 50 per cent of the world's population can be considered to be 'online' in some sense, and therefore visible to the technology.

Digital modernity is a narrative or myth (once more, descriptive, teleological or normative) about how this data-driven technology affects society and how the future is unfolding in our present. Versions of the myth suggest that humans are becoming informational beings, or 'inforgs',[17] as a result of a fusion of the physical, digital and biological,[18] our human knowledge and skills to be augmented and connected by vastly more efficient artificial systems.[19] Infrastructure will give us access to a vast range of cultural and personal goods;[20] our familiar notions of work, production and value will be reshaped and free markets and private property destroyed.[21] Professions will be transformed.[22] Widespread change, of conflict, of politics and of our own identities, will be driven by increasingly active and global citizenries.[23] Data will provide immeasurable insight into what activities will produce the best results,[24] but not why.[25] On the downside (for not all these narratives are positive), superintelligent AI might turn out to exceed our own by orders of magnitude, and might develop survival drives of its own; perhaps it may even begin to disregard human interests and pursue a different set of goals.[26] To reiterate, this chapter does not endorse these narratives, but their cumulative rhetorical power should not be underestimated.

2.2.2 *Digital Modernity across Time and Space*

How will these play out? It is helpful to contrast digital modernity with what we might call 'analogue' modernity, i.e. the rational, bureaucratic modernity of the twentieth century, and with pre-modernity, non-rational, non-industrialised societies where local and community considerations are paramount.[27] Temporally, in Europe, the sixteenth century is usually marked as the rough point at which the first modern societies emerged.

On the linear scale where modernity implies advance, and pre-modernity backwardness, digital modernity stands for even further advance. In digitally modern societies, innovation happens routinely, almost at will,[28] and existing social processes are disintermediated and rendered more efficient.[29] Disruption is the order of the day in a world of continuous Schumpeterian creative destruction,[30] where the incumbent and the intermediary are always under pressure from entrepreneurs and startups. Once a system has disrupted and displaced another, it is itself ripe for disruption.[31] In this world, to be advanced is to be a disruptor, and therefore *to exist is already to be backward.*

In space, modernisation marginalises the periphery and privileges the centre. As modernity goes digital, acquaintance is no longer rationed in any sense by geography, and the most productive connections can be sought rationally through search, matching digital doubles or avatars, quantified selves rather than flesh and blood people.[32] Smart cities are designed and optimised using data,[33] and smaller environments instrumented and controlled via the Internet of Things.[34] Space collapses into *cyberspace*, in a famous early description: 'A graphic representation of data abstracted from the banks of every computer in the human system.'[35] Policy depends on the state of an individual's or an environment's data, not on the thing itself. The virtual world affords opportunities for order and rationality, and the most that hapless reality can achieve is *to get closer to the perfection of the algorithm and the data.*

In terms of how it treats individuals, I noted above the shift from the social to the individual as we move from the pre-modern to the modern. This shift continues as we enter the digitally modern, to the data about the individual; the individual is treated as an inforg.[36] Furthermore, the social groups in which an individual is understood to be participating become even less intuitive to the individuals concerned – rather than the large interest groups theorised by the great nineteenth-century ideologies, they become temporary and data-relative, depending on which clusters make sense to machine learning algorithms. The group becomes contingent, fluid and determined by the data.

I earlier suggested that Lyotard's discussion of postmodernism was better understood as his spotting the green shoots of digital modernity. We see here at least one of the misleading parallels and characteristic distinctions between postmodernity and digital modernity, which is that, although both treat the individual as a construction, digital modernity is far more specific about the mechanics of and constraints on that process, as well as the roles of technology and knowledge within it. It is therefore, I would suggest, a far more valuable conceptual scheme than postmodernism, although this is a topic well beyond the scope of this chapter.

In the remainder of this section, I will briefly consider some of the central aspects of the digital modernity narrative.

2.2.3 *The Emergence of Personalisation*

Modernity prizes the uniqueness of the individual, and the individual's reason outweighs tradition and practice as the provider of justifications for acting. Kant's essay 'What is Enlightenment?'[37] expresses this exactly, in its opening sentence 'Enlightenment is man's release from his self-incurred tutelage', and in the 'motto of enlightenment' *sapere aude!*, 'Dare to be wise!'. Individuality is expressed in modernity via *choice*: democracy, free markets, freedom of association, freedom of conscience, romantic love (as opposed to arranged or dynastic marriage), choice of career, freedom of speech and freedom from censorship and so on. The world presents itself to us, and we choose the aspects of it that we wish to consume or pursue at that time. No doubt we are constrained by earlier choices and the choices of others, but in principle our preferences at the point of choice are paramount.

Digital modernity preserves individuality as a central value, but expresses it differently. The data accumulated by the digital infrastructure can be used to make recommendations, tailor choices and target marketing, with sensitivity to an individual's past behaviour and tastes, and current location, as well as records of comparable individuals. Hence individuality is now expressed through *personalisation*: rather than being presented, the world is moulded around the individual, so that everyone gets a different experience, adapted to his or her own preferences.

Let us take the example of association, the people with whom a person has significant contact. In pre-modern societies association is often given or imposed. Extended families, kin, tribes, villages and guilds were important social groups. Association was drastically constrained by geography. Under modernity, one had far more choice over those with whom one associated, and many traditional groupings declined in importance.[38] Under digital modernity, on the other hand, recommendation has increasingly come to govern, if not determine, association. Apps are routinely used to suggest people to date, marry, go to bed with, befriend, employ or boost careers.[39]

Personalisation is a central mechanism for the implementation of the values of digital modernity. A critique of the latter, then, will of necessity involve a critique of the former, which will be the business of the following sections of this chapter (and indeed of the other chapters in this volume).

2.3 CRITIQUES OF DIGITAL MODERNITY AND PERSONALISATION AS ITS CORE MECHANISMS

2.3.1 *Abandoning Privacy and Authentic Choice*

Because the chief mechanism for expressing individuality under modernity was choice, it was essential for those choices to be considered, uncoerced, autonomous and authentic – in other words, that they *did* express individuality rather than being manipulated. For this to be the case, some real or metaphorical space into which individuals could withdraw and reflect was needed, insulated from commercial, family, religious, ideological, economic or political pressures. In other words, the need for privacy is baked into the ideals of modernity,[40] and it is no coincidence that the high point of rational, bureaucratic modernity, the long twentieth century, is the period in which principled privacy protection was constructed as a set of rights, regulations and tools for individuals to police their private space, beginning with the detection of a right to be let alone in common law,[41] via statements of rights to privacy at the mid-century, and culminating in the EU's General Data Protection Regulation of 2018.

Digital modernity shifts its stance on privacy radically. Because choice is now the prerogative of the data infrastructure which constructs the personalised world, the rationale for principled privacy protection falls away – the guarantors of authentic choice are no longer necessary. Indeed, the change is more drastic still, because for personalisation to be an effective expression of individuality, the requisite algorithms must have sufficiently specific input about the individual.[42] Privacy is now not only not required, but it will impede the implementation of the ideals of digital modernity. It is unsurprising therefore that privacy has become a major ideological battleground as digital technology flourishes.

2.3.2 *Social Grammar: The Subjunctive World*

The neglect of autonomy can be given further context by understanding the structural aspects of narratives of society and technology that restrict or constrain categories of relevant phenomena, the judgements made about them and the types of narrative that are characteristic of the societies in which they occur, because they support expression of the key normative assumptions. We can call these structural aspects a society's *social grammar*, because they govern ways in which meaningful social actions are understood to be composed from smaller-scale behaviours and cognitive states, analogously to the way that a linguistic grammar governs how sentences and other meaningful units can be constructed from words and clauses. The governing tense or moods of social grammar in the triad of social narratives we are concerned with in this chapter reflect the shrinkage of time and space from pre-modern to modern to digitally modern. As the reference points for moral, social or practical narratives become less expansive, social grammar adapts to accommodate them.

Under pre-modernity, the governing grammatical tense is *eternal*. Traditions and practices are treated as if they had always been in place (although of course they had to appear at a point in time, and evolve, this is not how it appears from the inside), and innovation is neither sought nor welcomed. A reason for doing something is that 'we've always done it this way'. Practices and institutions are understood to be in tune with social, religious and metaphysical conditions, and though they adapt as those conditions change, the conditions themselves are usually understood as being eternal (for example, pre-modern societies have often seen the growth and spread of universal religions), and so the significance of change, evolution and adaptation are played down.

Meanwhile, modernity is a *present tense* narrative; today's choices based on current preferences are what count, with no requirement for consistency, rationality or coherence. Reason is part of the Enlightenment ideal, but it does not determine preferences; the Enlightened individual applies his or her reason to the job of achieving preferences. (As David Hume put it, reason is and ought only to be the slave of the passions.) It may well be the case that one has, for example, second-order preferences about the preferences one has (one may wish to give up smoking, based on rational evaluation of the medical evidence, a second-order preference with which one hopes to override first-order preferences to smoke a cigarette in a particular context), but it is the individual's job to manage his or her first- and second-order preferences.[43] As arch-modernist Henry Ford said, 'history is bunk'; there is no requirement on the individual to refer to past practices or others' behaviour to express his or her preferences; one can buy what one wants now, vote for whomever one supports now, join whatever groups one wishes to associate with now (and act differently tomorrow). Ethicists such as Kant did argue about the conditions which would apply to, say, good or rational behaviour, and some Kantian principles inform some of the social structures and institutions that have grown out of modernity, in order to support ethical or rational behaviour over the unethical or irrational. However, in modern societies, Kantian interventions on the large scale tended to be seen as excessively paternalistic, and the expression of individuality came to be seen as requiring rejection of 'normal' conventional feeling.[44] Rational choice economics, and the notion of revealed preference, evolved to express the present tense world; one prefers to perform action A, and so one As. The evidence for one's preference for A is precisely the performance of A.[45]

However, digital modernity has a different rationale. One is not supposed to choose what one prefers; one instead chooses from a diminished list which nudges one towards *what one would have chosen if only one had known all the relevant facts*. But the data infrastructure has far more of the facts than the individual, with the gap growing all the time. The infrastructure is a better judge of what the individual should prefer, and so the infrastructure quite properly makes the choice.[46] The grammar is therefore in *subjunctive mood*, the grammatical verb form that expresses events that have not (yet) happened – in this case, choices that should be, but have not yet been, made. The subjunctive world that digital modernity creates is the context for the valorisation of personalisation.

2.4 THE TECHNOLOGY OF PERSONALISATION

The implementation of personalisation is naturally less well honed than the narrative suggests. The technology is less effective, the algorithms less seamless and the data less reliable. In particular there are many issues with data quality and bias, in a world where most data is gathered for specific reasons and in particular economic interests.[47]

An application which generates its own data within a walled garden, such as Amazon, can design the knowledge representation to allow cross-referencing and linking. However, the trade-off is that a walled garden covers only a small part of someone's life in Amazon's case, it will be biased towards commercial interactions. The full power of digital modernity assumes linkage of heterogeneous datasets to create a rich avatar of the individual. This will require a great deal of data cleaning, such as aligning ontologies, assessing relative quality across datasets and so on.[48] The alternative is a walled garden so massive that it takes in social, commercial, governmental and leisure, as with the Chinese app WeChat.[49] It has been argued that China has an advantage in the development of AI technologies because of the relative centralisation of its data.[50] However, the inherent decentralisation of the data infrastructure across different organisations with few incentives for data sharing will tell against the ability of anyone to assemble an overarching picture with ease.

Secondly, 'personalisation' is something of a misnomer, as other chapters in this collection point out. Machine learning can basically perform four operations: clustering (dividing a set of objects into groups, minimising in-group diversity and maximising between-group diversity), association (as in 'people who liked X also liked Y'), feature prediction (suggesting missing values for individuals' attributes) and anomaly detection (such as spotting unusual uses of a credit card). 'Personalisation' is actually classification of the individual based on a retrospective view that will tend to downplay the importance of speculative choices, ignore second-order preferences, maximise social conformity (especially if collaborative filtering is used) and stand in the way of character development; it is not obvious how it could operate differently. As is implicit in the previous section, one would expect it also to suppress autonomy, which is no longer a means to an important end in the subjunctive world of digital modernity.

2.5 PERSONALISATION, HARMS AND CONSTRAINTS

Personalisation, therefore, may be described in other ways – in terms of the classification of the individual against pre-existing behaviours and categories, using data that may be incomplete, inaccurate or biased in certain ways, and algorithms whose power may be hyped. However, another way of critiquing the idea of digital modernity is to consider certain social constructs or practices as they evolve through the pre-modern/modern/digitally modern triad. This provides an alternative perspective on how far digital modernity constitutes a genuine progression, and how far personalisation advances individual well-being (or sacrifices collective benefits).

Let us consider how the values of the three narratives translate into different understandings of harms, discipline (or governance) and remedies. In the premodern era, moral value is often seen as a social phenomenon, and so harm looks like damage to social stability, harmony or cohesion. Discipline is usually couched in terms of prohibitions and rituals, on commandments of what we must do to preserve social harmony. These are not always strict rules, and include etiquette of various kinds, designed to regulate relations with the environment.[51] Finally, remedies tend to revolve around protections where harms can be anticipated, management of common resources, and community help for those in trouble. Protective institutions and practices did not necessarily develop because they were economically efficient, but sometimes as responses to random forces (such as the weather, or the ideas of a king or priest); sometimes in response to cultural beliefs and values; and sometimes following conflict over how resources should be distributed.[52] Much would depend on the power and status of those harmed, whether they themselves would be able to shape the institutions, and whether they were the victims of perceived unfairness (for instance, if the gods were deemed to have been offended by some action or omission). In many circumstances, harm itself can be the evidence for such offence.[53] The creation of protective institutions might be the outcome of conflict, but once in place they promote predictability and reduce perceived risk. Such institutions might resolve conflicts, if not necessarily fairly or justly (consider an institution such as serfdom), and they would often host a nexus of valuable practice and training to reproduce that practice (as with a medieval guild), thereby providing ongoing social benefits as well as a measure of insurance for participants.

The locus of harm under modernity, by contrast, is the self, including the freedom or autonomy of the individual. The classic statement of how to address harm is Mill's harm principle, from *On Liberty*, that 'The only purpose for which power can be rightfully exercised over any member of a civilized community, against his will, is to prevent harm to others.'[54] And because modernity ushered in a notion of universal risk, risk can be pooled using insurance to spread the burden of preparation.[55]

In the subjunctive world of digital modernity, what matters is less the self and its autonomy, than the well-being of the avatar, measured against the data. Harm takes the form of exhibiting risk factors, below-average performance and dragging down national averages. Ethical considerations apply to people as inforgs, who flourish in an information environment (the infosphere), which itself is a moral patient. Information ethics induces a change of perspective, from considering information as epistemological to treating it ontologically.[56] The result is a curious hybrid of the public space where pre-modern societies focused their attention, and the private space of the self where modernity's concerns lie. The constructed 'self' in the digitally modern avatar is created partly from data about the public, rejecting the modern self in impatient terms reminiscent of Richard Sennett: 'Masses of people are concerned with their single life histories and particular emotions as never before; this concern has proved to be a trap rather than a liberation.'[57] Sennett's argument for bringing aspects of a formal public culture into social relations, although it makes little use of technology, sounds a little like the starting gun for digital modernity. Because 'every self is in some measure a cabinet of horrors, civilised relations between selves can only proceed to the extent that nasty little secrets of desire, greed or envy are kept locked up.'[58]

Let us consider an example. In medicine, the behaviour of the overweight, smokers, drinkers and the sedentary is measured against averages, benchmarks and standards in *in silico* models (computer simulations), rather than any parameter directly relevant to them. Targets are used to manage risk. Missing the targets increases the risk of certain events occurring, although the meaning of this is rarely unpacked (or communicated to the patient). The datafication of medicine has been evident for a while, generated by 'the development of such disciplines as probability statistics, increased focus on risk management and health promotion, with recent developments in computer technology as the factor responsible for the escalation seen [since the 1990s]'.[59]

Whether the (mere) improvement of a person's medical data, even given the promise of personalised medicine via genomics, mobile technologies and *in silico* integration of patient-specific data, can realistically, or ought to, be divorced from the subjective experience of the individual, who may create meanings, relationships and ways of life that do raise specific technically defined risks (for instance, going to the pub, or enjoying the camaraderie of a cigarette on the steps outside the office) is surely a moot point.[60] Personalised medicine is designed to afford disease prevention among healthy persons through detection and elimination of risk factors, although this itself creates counter-risk, such as overdiagnosis and overtreatment. Such manipulation of the avatar also takes place in a social context (ranging across the personal goals and habits of the patient, the norms of the social groups of which he or she is a part, the degree of medicalisation in society as a whole, and values which may conflict with the degree of sociotechnical control that personalised medicine implies) which is usually ignored, because it is silent in the data,[61] and the model can be difficult and abstract for the patient to contextualise or convert into action to address health problems.[62] In all, the notion of harm as the exhibition of risk factors in a patient's data is a transformation of, rather than an unalloyed improvement in, earlier notions of illness.

Treatment of such data harms is to manipulate behaviour in order to produce more favourable data. As noted earlier, the best that reality can do according to digital modernity is approach the perfection of the algorithm and the data, but this can lead policymakers to reason that they may legitimately strongarm the physical and social world into providing better data. Because of generally low levels of data literacy,[63] many paternal interventions, such as nudging[64] or setting targets, must therefore go beyond Mill's original principle. Scotland, for instance, has a national walking strategy,[65] while the United Kingdom has a loneliness strategy,[66] policy interventions that would have appeared baffling in the pre-data days when government involvement could not have been judged on the fluctuations of parameters of data.[67] Individuals' decisions about how to get from A to B, or whether, when and with whom to interact, were considered to be their own affair, and not things that could be aggregated into reflections of a population's merit (so that, for example, Scots could beat themselves up because they walk less than Italians or South Africans).

Mill's original principle referred to the harm caused to others by an individual's actions, under the conditions of modernity which assume that the most important harms are to individuals. Under digital modernity, the *avatar* is now the locus of harm, and as social networks and connections are central to the calculation of the well-being of such avatars, one individual, by generating poor value data, can adversely affect the well-being of others. Every person who drives rather than walks drags down total mortality data, and thereby lowers life expectancy of every avatar; the effects of loneliness are apparently equivalent to smoking fifteen cigarettes a day, and thus similarly threaten the length of life predicted for every citizen.[68]

Given this revision of Mill's principle, the maintenance of impressive national statistics showing how well citizens' avatars are flourishing becomes a matter of national policy, however difficult they are to understand in intuitive terms. For example, a recent report in the *Lancet* that South Korean life expectancy was projected to become the highest in the world[69] was taken by many as an important Korean policy success, while also baffling one journalist critical of South Korea's inequalities and poverty.[70] Yet the crunching of the healthcare data led only to adjustment of parameters that are extremely remote from any actual lived experience. The *Lancet* article's headlines were generated, for example, by the discovery that 'There is a 90% probability that life expectancy at birth among South Korean women in 2030 will be higher than 86·7 years ... and a 57% probability that it will be higher than 90 years.' In other words, there is a 57% probability that the mean length of life for the hypothetical cohort of girls born in South Korea in 2030 will exceed 90, if they are all exposed to mortality rates as projected from the present (and, since we do not know the mortality rate for people in the present, since they are all necessarily alive, this parameter itself must be inferred from the mortality rate for even older cohorts). How meaningful this is depends on how seriously one takes risks from, say, climate change, or the continued existence of a fanatically hostile and well-armed state immediately on the Northern border, which could affect mortality rates in highly unpredictable ways. However, under digital modernity, we can see that the actions now, of people with only a remote connection with the 2030 birth cohort, could still drag down life expectancy for that cohort by adversely affecting estimated mortality rates (by smoking, being lonely, driving instead of walking, or other dastardly derelictions of duty to the avatar). The avatars of currently non-existent individuals will have a shorter projected life, and we can see how a version of Mill's harm principle taking into account the harms caused to avatars by adverse data generated by individuals, could indeed legitimise the paternalistic nudging and other interventions discussed above. We start to see the emergence of the 'therapeutic state' predicted by Michael Oakeshott many years ago.[71]

Of course, not all the data that goes into the construction of an avatar is pooled across entire societies in this way (although the avatars of future citizens must surely depend on data about those in the present and past). We might avoid the paternalism of the revised Mill's principle, at least with respect to present citizens, by disaggregating data to produce *personal* risk profiles. However, paternalism does not thereby disappear, because with personalised risk, the pooled insurance model of harm mitigation is less sustainable. Against the principle of equality underlying pooled insurance is placed a principle of merit – the data can show whether you brought illness or accident upon yourself via bad diet, bad driving or bad behaviour.[72] New notions of fairness come into play, depending on whether the data one generates is sufficiently similar to the data generated by others. While policyholders are assumed to be personally in control of their diet or driving style or lifestyle, the data infrastructure provides real-time feedback to disincentivise bad behaviour, so their decisions (e.g. to order extra fries or drive beyond the speed limit) come with a price tag. This illustrates how autonomy looks increasingly irrelevant in the subjunctive world, whatever the balance is between data focused on or generated by the individual, and population data generated by others.

Anti-discrimination laws may attempt to preserve the model of pooled insurance against this neoliberal notion of personal responsibility, but they are not magic bullets; they are likely to come under pressure when they promote arguably unjust outcomes or moral hazard.[73] Actuarial examples in particular are data-driven. It is illegal in the EU to set insurance premiums that are discriminatory on grounds of gender even though, based on the actuarial data, it is cheaper to insure women as they are involved in fewer accidents. There is an associated cost to refusing to discriminate here on grounds of gender, which will ultimately be paid by women, and we may argue about the justice of this outcome, as women are in effect subsidising men's poor driving. In a wider sense, producing fair, accountable and transparent machine learning (FAT-ML, the topic of an already large annual conference supported by the ACM),[74] may have the perverse effect of removing incentives to behave in socially positive ways, such as paying one's debts, taxes or bills, not going to prison, not making insurance claims, and making complex plans for saving and expenditure across decades (such as pensions, mortgages, or paying for children's education), when those positive behaviours (or their opposites) are disproportionately associated with particular social groups, especially those delineated by gender or ethnicity, because of prior structural factors that themselves are discriminatory, and so cannot be discriminated for.

It is also worth noting, finally, that these considerations also apply to aspects of policy that do not rely on personal data, and hence where personalisation does not feature prominently. For example, statements made by Greta Thunberg or Extinction Rebellion[75] about the dangers and catastrophic effects of climate change are characteristically digitally modern in their focus on the effects exhibited by *models* of the global climate system. Their rhetoric concentrates on motivating direct action by supporters on the basis of climate models, eschewing the characteristically modern dilemmas of how to manage the uncertainties contained in such models,[76] and of how to express the advice implicit in such models to policymakers in actionable terms.[77] In the subjunctive world, we *should* work to get carbon emissions down, if only we were acquainted with the relevant models, and our choices that we *should* make about driving, flying or otherwise consuming resources can be read off the model. They are not legitimate choices expressing individuality made in the context of carbon taxes, carbon prices or other economic signals, but rather the model tells us what we should choose.

The characteristics of digital modernity are detectable in this radicalised discourse, with profound consequences for individuals (if Extinction Rebellion's demands, such as reducing greenhouse gas emissions to net zero by 2025, are to be adopted[78]), even though data about individuals is not used for construction of climate models/avatars, and even though there is no personalisation of the choices that individuals should make in this particular policy area, and those demanding action on climate change give little or no thought to the issue of expression of individuality. However, as is usual under digital modernity, the model's health is taken to be the important trigger for action.

It is interesting that in this area, it is rebels and protestors who embrace digital modernity, whereas the state and those in power do not. This is perhaps because of the economic cost of adjusting the global economy to improve the health of the model. In the medical case, it is cheap for authorities to embrace digital modernity, because they have sufficient power and resources to enforce personalisation in medical and other contexts. In the case of the environment, a digitally modern approach tells the state and large corporations something they don't want to hear.

2.6 CONCLUSION

Digital modernity brings with it many benefits, and the democracies that host it are beacons of well-being and tolerance. We should resist the temptation to launch into a jeremiad, although the technology and the narrative are likely to play out differently in societies with less of a tradition of liberty.

However, it seems clear that, while digital modernity preserves the focus on the individual, the sidelining of autonomy and privacy as values, and the decoupling of ideas of harm and remedy from the lived experience of the individual, are both concerning. Many complex social processes are being disrupted and disintermediated by networked technology, with humans being removed from the loop. This may result in an increase in some notion of 'efficiency', but threatens to destroy a lot of social capital, as the world becomes less familiar and navigable.

The shift from choice to personalisation as the mechanism for expressing individuality undermines the individual's control and understanding. Whether the promised delivery of greater benefits in the subjunctive world is sufficient compensation is a moot point. How the shift can be slowed or prevented will require an intense interdisciplinary effort involving law, politics, technology and economics, for several years to come.[79]

NOTES

1 Kieron O'Hara, 'The contradictions of digital modernity' (2020) 35 AI & Society 197, https://doi.org/10.1007/s00146-018-0843-7.

2 Talcott Parsons, 'Evolutionary universals in society' (1964) 29(3) *American Sociological Review* 339.

3 Kieron O'Hara, *The Enlightenment: A Beginner's Guide* (Oneworld 2010).
4 Christopher de Bellaigue, *The Islamic Enlightenment: The Struggle between Faith and Reason: 1798 to Modern Times* (W. W. Norton 2017) xvii.
5 Arif Dirlik, 'Global modernity', *The Wiley-Blackwell Encyclopedia of Social Theory* (2017) https://doi.org/10.1002/9781118430873.est0841.
6 Jürgen Habermas, *The Lure of Technocracy* (Polity Press 2015) 145.
7 Yascha Mounk, *The People vs. Democracy: Why Our Freedom Is in Danger and How to Save It* (Harvard University Press 2018).
8 Edward Shils, *Center and Periphery: Essays in Macrosociology* (University of Chicago Press 1975).
9 David Goodhart, *The Road to Somewhere: The Populist Revolt and the Future of Politics* (Hurst & Company 2017); Jonathan Hopkin, 'When Polanyi met Farage: market fundamentalism, economic nationalism, and Britain's exit from the European Union' (2017) 19 (3) *The British Journal of Politics and International Relations* 465, https://doi.org/10.1177/1369148117710894; Harry Bromley-Davenport, Julie McLeavey and David Manley, 'Brexit in Sunderland: the production of difference and division in the UK referendum on European Union membership' (2019) 37(5) *Environment and Planning C: Politics and Space* 795, https://doi.org/10.1177/0263774X18804225.
10 Anthony Giddens, *The Consequences of Modernity* (Polity Press 1990).
11 Peter Wagner, *Modernity: Understanding the Present* (Polity Press 2012).
12 Ulrich Beck, *Risk Society: Towards a New Modernity* (Sage 1992).
13 Thanks to Jacob Eisler for making this point; I have borrowed some of his words from a personal communication.
14 Zygmunt Bauman, *Liquid Modernity* (Polity Press 2000).
15 Jean-François Lyotard, *The Postmodern Condition: A Report on Knowledge* (Manchester University Press 1984).
16 O'Hara (n 2).
17 Luciano Floridi, *The Ethics of Information* (Oxford University Press 2013).
18 Klaus Schwab, *The Fourth Industrial Revolution* (World Economic Forum 2016).
19 Ray Kurzweil, *The Singularity Is Near* (Viking Penguin 2005).
20 Erik Brynjolfsson and Andrew McAfee, *The Second Machine Age: Work, Progress and Prosperity in a Time of Brilliant Technologies* (W. W. Norton 2014).
21 Paul Mason, *Postcapitalism: A Guide to Our Future* (Penguin 2016).
22 Brynjolfsson and McAfee (n 20).
23 Eric Schmidt and Jared Cohen, *The New Digital Age: Reshaping the Future of People, Nations and Business* (Random House 2013).
24 Ian Ayres, *Super Crunchers: How Anything Can Be Predicted* (John Murray 2007).
25 Viktor Mayer-Schönberger and Kenneth Cukier, *Big Data: A Revolution That Will Transform How We Live, Work and Think* (John Murray 2013).
26 James Barrat, *Our Final Invention: Artificial Intelligence and the End of the Human Era* (Thomas Dunne Books 2015).
27 O'Hara (n 2).
28 Clayton M Christensen, Michael E Raynor and Rory McDonald, 'What is disruptive innovation?' *Harvard Business Review* (Boston, December 2015) 44, https://hbr.org/2015/12/what-is-disruptive-innovation.

29 Martin Curley and Bror Salmelin, *Open Innovation 2.0: The New Mode of Digital Innovation for Prosperity and Sustainability* (Springer 2018)15–25.

30 Joseph Schumpeter, *Capitalism, Socialism and Democracy* (3rd edn, Harper & Row 1950).

31 Massimo Colombo, Chiara Franzoni and Reinhilde Veugelers, 'Going radical: producing and transferring disruptive innovation' (2015) 40(4) *Journal of Technology Transfer* 663.

32 Brian Parkinson and others, 'The digitally extended self: a lexicological analysis of personal data' (2018) 44(4) *Journal of Information Science* 552, https://doi.org/10.1177/0165551517706233; Minna Ruckenstein and Mika Pantzar, 'Beyond the quantified self: thematic exploration of a dataistic paradigm' (2017) 19(3) *New Media and Society* 401, https://doi.org/10.1177/1461444815609081.

33 Jesse M Shapiro, 'Smart cities: quality of life, productivity and the gowth effects of human capital' (2006) 88(2) *Review of Economics and Statistics* 324, https://doi.org/10.3386/w11615.

34 Andrea Zanella and others, 'Internet of Things for smart cities' (2014) 1(1) *IEEE Internet of Things* 22, https://doi.org/10.1109/JIOT.2014.2306328.

35 William Gibson, *Neuromancer* (Ace Books 1984) 69.

36 Floridi (n 17).

37 Immanuel Kant, 'What is enlightenment?' (first published 1784 as 'Answering the question: what is enlightenment?') in Isaac Kramnick (ed), *The Portable Enlightenment Reader* (Penguin 1995).

38 Robert D Putnam, *Bowling Alone: The Collapse and Revival of American Community* (Simon & Schuster 2000).

39 Ralf Caers and Vanessa Castelyns, 'LinkedIn and Facebook in Belgium: the influences and biases of social network sites in recruitment and selection procedures' (2011) 29(4) *Social Science Computer Review* 437, https://doi.org/10.1177/0894439310386567; Mitchell Hobbs, Stephen Owen and Livia Gerber, 'Liquid love? Dating apps, sex, relationships and the digital transformation of intimacy' (2017) 53(2) *Journal of Sociology* 271, https://doi.org/10.1177/1440783316662718.

40 Beate Rössler, *The Value of Privacy* (Polity Press 2005).

41 Samuel D Warren and Louis D Brandeis, 'The right to privacy' (1890) 4(5) *Harvard Law Review* 193.

42 Ramnath K Chellappa and Raymond G Sin, 'Personalization versus privacy: an empirical examination of the online consumer's dilemma' (2005) 6(2–3) *Information Technology and Management* 181, https://doi.org/10.1007/s10799-005-5879-y; Jennifer Golbeck, 'User privacy concerns with common data used in recommender systems' in Emma Spiro and Yong-Yeol Ahn (eds), *Social Informatics: Proceedings of the 8th International Conference SocInfo 2016* (Springer 2016) https://doi.org/10.1007/978-3-319-47880-7_29.

43 Richard Jeffrey, 'Preferences among preferences' (1974) 71(13) *Journal of Philosophy* 377, https://doi.org/10.2307/2025160.

44 Richard Sennett, *The Fall of Public Man* (Alfred A Knopf 1977).

45 Amartya Sen, 'Rational fools: a critique of the behavioral foundations of economic theory' (1977) 6(4) *Philosophy and Public Affairs* 317.

46 Mayer-Schönberger and Cukier (n 25).

47 Ganaele Langlois, Joanna Redden and Greg Elmer (eds), *Compromised Data: From Social Media to Big Data* (Bloomsbury 2015).

48 Xu Chu and others, 'Data cleaning: overview and emerging challenges' (Proceedings of the 2016 International Conference on Management of Data – SIGMOD'16, San Francisco, June 2016) 2201, https://doi.org/10.1145/2882903.2912574.

49 Alexis Bonhomme, 'How to get the most from WeChat' (2017) 5(2) *Journal of Digital & Social Media Marketing* 146.

50 Kai-Fu Lee, *AI Superpowers: China, Silicon Valley, and the New World Order* (Houghton Mifflin 2018).

51 See, e.g., Nurit Bird-David, '"Animism" revisited: personhood, environment, and relational Epistemology' (1999) 40(S1) *Current Anthropology* 40(S1), S67–S91 https://doi.org/10.1086/200061.

52 Sheilagh Ogilvie, '"Whatever is, is right"? Economic institutions in pre-industrial Europe' (2007) 60(4) *Economic History Review* 649 https://doi.org/10.1111/j.1468-0289.2007.00408.x.

53 Cindel White and Ara Norenzayan, 'Belief in karma: how cultural evolution, cognition, and motivations shape belief in supernatural justice' in James M Olsen (ed), *Advances in Experimental Social Psychology Volume 60* (Academic Press 2019).

54 See Ben Saunders, 'Reformulating Mill's Harm Principle' (2016) 125(500) *Mind* 1005 https://doi.org/10.1093/mind/fzv171for a useful reformulation of this in terms of consensual versus non-consensual harm.

55 Ulrich Beck, *Risk Society: Towards a New Modernity* (Sage 1992).

56 Floridi (n 17).

57 Sennett (n 44) 5.

58 ibid.

59 John-Arne Skolbekken, 'The risk epidemic in medical journals' (1995) 40(3) *Social Science & Medicine* 291 https://doi.org/10.1016/0277-9536(94)00262-R.

60 Anna Luise Kirkengen and others, 'Medicine's perception of reality – a split picture: critical reflections on apparent anomalies within the biomedical theory of science' (2016) 22(4) *Journal of Evaluation in Clinical Practice* 496 https://doi.org/10.1111/jep.12369.

61 Sara Green and Henrik Vogt, 'Personalizing medicine: disease prevention in silico and in socio' (2016) 9(30) *HUMANA.MENTE Journal of Philosophical Studies* 105 http://www.humanamente.eu/index.php/HM/article/view/62.

62 Valerie F Reyna and others, 'How numeracy influences risk comprehension and medical decision making' (2009) 135(6) *Psychological Bulletin* 943 https://psycnet.apa.org/doi/10.1037/a0017327.

63 ibid.

64 Richard H Thaler and Cass R Sunstein, *Nudge: Improving Decisions about Health, Wealth and Happiness* (Yale University Press 2008).

65 Scottish Government, *Let's get Scotland Walking: The National Walking Strategy* (Scottish Government 13 June 2014) https://www.gov.scot/publications/lets-scotland-walking-national-walking-strategy/.

66 Department for Digital, Culture, Media and Sport, *A Connected Society: A Strategy for Tackling Loneliness – Laying the Foundations for Change* (HM Government 15 October 2018) https://www.gov.uk/government/publications/a-connected-society-a-strategy-for-tackling-loneliness.

67 Eisler suggests that these types of policy concerns might also suggest the breakdown of prior units of social well-being, the integrity of the community and the flourishing of the individual, and may be inevitable results of digital modernity. I suspect that 'inevitable' is too strong, but the increasing adoption of such targets is surely likely to undermine institutions protective of social well-being.

68 Julianne Holt-Lunstad and others, 'Loneliness and social isolation as risk factors for mortality: a meta-analytic review' (2015) 10(2) *Perspectives of Psychological Science* 227 https://doi.org/10.1177/1745691614568352.

69 Vasilis Kontis and others, 'Future life expectancy in 35 industrialised countries: projections with a Bayesian model ensemble' (2017) 389(10076) *The Lancet* 1323 https://doi.org/10.1016/S0140–6736(16)32381-9.

70 Justin McCurry, 'South Korea's inequality paradox: long life, good health and poverty' *The Guardian* (London, 2 August 2017) https://www.theguardian.com/inequality/2017/aug/02/south-koreas-inequality-paradox-long-life-good-health-and-poverty.

71 Michael Oakeshott, *On Human Conduct* (Clarendon Press 1975).

72 Mikael Dubois, 'Insurance and prevention: ethical aspects' (2011) 32(1) *Journal of Primary Prevention* 3 https://doi.org/10.1007/s10935–011-0234-z; Gert Meyers and Ine Van Hoyweghen, 'Enacting actuarial fairness in insurance: from fair discrimination to behaviour-based fairness' (2018) 27(4) *Science As Culture* 413 https://doi.org/10.1080/09505431.2017.1398223.

73 Ronen Avraham, 'Discrimination and insurance' in Kasper Lippert-Rasmussen (ed), *The Routledge Handbook on the Ethics of Discrimination* (Routledge 2018).

74 See Fairness, Accountability, and Transparency in Machine Learning https://www.fatml.org/ and ACM Conference on Fairness, Accountability, and Transparency (ACM FAccT) https://facctconference.org.

75 Extinction Rebellion, 'The Emergency' https://rebellion.earth/the-truth/the-emergency/.

76 Jonathan Rougier and Michel Crucifix, 'Uncertainty in climate science and climate policy' in Elisabeth A Lloyd and Eric Winsberg (eds), *Climate Modelling: Philosophical and Conceptual Issues* (Palgrave Macmillan 2018).

77 Reto Knutti, 'Climate model confirmation: from philosophy to predicting climate in the real world' in Elisabeth A Lloyd and Eric Winsberg (n 76).

78 Extinction Rebellion, 'Our Demands' https://rebellion.earth/the-truth/demands/.

79 Many thanks to the editors for constructive comments on this chapter.

3

Personalisation, Power and the Datafied Subject

Marc Welsh

It is the actual instruments that form and accumulate knowledge, the observational methods, the recording techniques, the investigative research procedures, the verification mechanisms. That is, the delicate mechanisms of power cannot function unless knowledge, or rather knowledge apparatuses, are formed, organised and put into circulation (Michel Foucault, 2004[1]).

3.1 INTRODUCTION

The collection, storing and analysing of information on the physiological, behavioural, economic and geolocational data of individuals has grown exponentially, amplified since the 1980s by the increasing capacities of networked information technology and the ubiquity of data capture devices. The imperative of data gathering underpins contemporary forms of 'government' ('the conduct of conduct').[2] To bastardise the words of Abraham Lincoln, here liberal forms of government <u>of</u> the people and <u>for</u> the people are a question of power, what might be termed 'biopower': technologies of power that make both the individual (the 'subject') and the group (the 'population') their targets of political strategy. In this framing, biopower marks a 'profound transformation of the mechanisms of power'[3] from a juridico-discursive conceptualisation of power as repressive and negative, to one that exerts a positive influence on life of the body and the people.

This chapter draws upon Foucauldian ideas, to explore how the 'datafication' of modern life might shift the modes of power acting within the social body. At its essence the chapter argues that the construction of the data-self marks a shift in modes of power, revitalising a governmentality centred simultaneously upon intimate knowledge of the individual (subjectivities) and the population, one characterised by corporate rather than state-based forms of government power. Significantly, such personalisation migrates responsibility for 'correct' forms of action or behaviour from the relation between the free (and potentially rebellious) individual and the state to a more closely monitored and constantly intervening type of 'private oversight'.

Through a brief exploration of three banal everyday social practices (driving, health, gambling) that triangulate on the intersection between technology, data and subjectivation (the process by which one becomes a subject), the intent is to reveal some of the ways a 'neoliberal subject' is produced, or more accurately how certain forms of subjectivity are inculcated and internalised by individuals. In their 'everydayness' such data personalisation technologies reproduce discourses of neo-liberalism; atomised, responsibilised, monitored, rational actors empowered through consumption, responsive to the demands of capital, and where the locus of capacity to govern increasingly sits with private capital while the state and the notion of the social body is eroded. Self-evidently there is a normative critique at the heart of this analysis. However, the intent is to reveal processes of change and their power effects rather than judge them. Through such exposure the goal is to provide some analytical purchase, drawing upon Foucauldian insights, to open up space for critical debate and reflection on a rapidly changing world increasingly constituted through algorithmic government.

The philosopher Michel Foucault had a lot to say about 'power', largely by problematising the assumptions of what power is, how it operates and where it is located. His fundamental concern, and a fundamental concern of academic ana-lyses of the operation of data-driven personalisation, was with power/knowledge. Foucault was concerned with how (by what means) is power exercised between 'free subjects' to (re)structure the world. For him power is socially constituted; power relations are rooted in systems of social networks (including law) and therefore unique to the historical formation of a given society. In other words, power is not something possessed or a material thing but only ever an effect of the relationship between individuals. This does not deny the capacity or agency of individuals (to use or resist force for example), but instead draws attention to the multiple, contingent, heterogenous and historically particular systems (or *dispositifs*) through which power relations are structured.

In seeking to explain the contemporary transformation of Western liberal democ-racies, Foucault identifies and traces the emergence and co-existence of different forms of power that coalesce around a new mentality of government concerned with the 'welfare of the population, the improvement of its condition, the increase of its wealth, longevity, health etc.'.[4] In this context *government* relates to the way in which order is produced. It is not confined to the formal state and its apparatus (although 'the state' plays a role in networks of power) but to the array of techniques through which power is exercised, and internalised by individuals, to secure the welfare of the population. For Foucault the liberal modes of governing rely on freedom, on free acting autonomous subjects governed at a distance, notably through the discourse of political economy. Critically for this paper, and technolo-gies of algorithmic government through data personalisation, the nexus between power and knowledge becomes central to debates about the relocation (or appropriation) of personal and population data space by non-state institutions.

To proceed to a problematisation of data personalisation technologies, and their effects upon the social and individual body, this paper of necessity first outlines some of the contributions and analysis Foucault provides that centre on the question of power and its operation through 'the market'. It then identifies algorithmic government and associated technologies as exemplars of Foucault's conception of 'governmentality'; power as productive, exercised through securing and fostering life. Lastly, it considers the relation between the subject and the data through three banal examples of privately mediated algorithmic life. Whether it be monitoring and managing the motion of objects (car insurance), the motions of bodies and the health of populations (the data-veilled Fitbit subject), or human irrationality (the geo-locational tracking of gambling), these examples raise profound questions about algorithmic government, data personalisation, neoliberal subjectivity and the contemporary blurring of the private and public state.

3.2 A FOUCAULDIAN GENEALOGY OF POWER

3.2.1 *Governmental Technologies towards Improving Populations*

Foucault identifies the displacement of sovereign power (crudely qualified 'power over death') that characterised much of European political history, with the emergence in the eighteenth century of two new forms of biopower to 'make life live' – disciplinary power and biopolitics.[5] His analysis reveals power as an array of practices, diffuse and distributed through the social body, and the mechanisms by which these forms of power are co-constituted by types of knowledge. Mechanisms or technologies of power are generative of different types of knowledge that solicit and utilise information on people's activities and presence in the world. The knowledge gathered reinforces the exercises of power that produce it. In this way power and knowledge are mutually constitutive – hence the Foucauldian reference to power/knowledge.[6]

Foucault's project was to provide a history of the present. He sought to identify the antecedents of emergent forms of (neo-)liberal governmentality observable at the end of the 1970s. In particular he focuses upon the way 'the market' becomes the dominant space for the production of 'truth', natural order and natural law in the mid-eighteenth century. The specific combination of Enlightenment ideas and the development of new forms of expertise (medicine, psychiatry, law, demography) and technologies, coupled with industrial capitalism, led to the mass expansion of sites or social realms to be governed. For Foucault this assemblage constructed a new object of government – the population. This he refers to as biopolitics. Disciplines, such as medicine or economics, serve to define subjects, to monitor them through centralised information systems, to act to improve the welfare of the population, and to normalise discourses that reproduce specific forms of subject identity.[7]

Government – conceived as 'the conduct of conduct' (see 'The biopolitical self' below) – sits both in tension and alliance with sovereignty and discipline as a triad of practices of power that have as their primary target the welfare of the population. An array of technologies of power seek to arrange or order the social world so that people, acting in their own self-interest, will act as desired for the welfare of the population. This imperative, to *improve* populations, is reliant on the exercise of a distinct form of governmental rationality to secure the right disposition of things. As Tania Murray Li expands, this 'governmentality' is not normative, it is not directed at a common good, but plural and convenient for each of the things that are to be governed.[8] In describing the shift from modes of power centred on the sovereign (the king) and their power over individual conduct, to the problem of population and security, Foucault argues that the governing rationality of the market emerges as a productive form of biopower.

As he outlines, this 'conception of market mechanism is not just the analysis of what happens. It is at once an analysis of what happens and *a program for what should happen.*'[9] Thus economic theories pave the way to the policies and practices of intervention and regulation of individual conduct. '[I]t is an economics, or a political economic analysis, that integrates the moment of production, the world market, and, finally, the economic behaviour of the population, of producers and consumers.'[10]

3.2.2 *The Biopolitical Self*

The challenge for contemporary government is how to provide for the security of the species through the discourse of freedom for the individual. Foucault's history of the present sought to describe an emerging neoliberal discourse of government in which political power is modelled on the principles of a market economy – one must 'govern for the market rather than because of the market'.[11] Indeed this formed the subject matter of much of his 1979 lecture series on 'The Birth of Biopolitics'.

In this 'genealogy' the modern state is characterised as

> the ensemble formed by the institutions, procedures, analyses and reflections, the calculations and tactics that allow the exercise of this very specific albeit complex form of power, which has the population as its target, political economy as its major form of knowledge, and apparatuses of security as its essential technical instrument.[12]

In the West this ensemble came to pre-eminence over other forms of power (sovereignty, discipline). This form of power he terms 'government', the conduct of conduct. He identifies a number of mechanisms by which behaviour is regulated – prohibition and permission (legal codes), surveillance and correction (discipline), normalisation of optimal actions and acceptable variation (security of populations). Foucault describes law as part of disciplinary modes of power, giving greater definition to the permitted and forbidden, closing in, enclosing spaces where its mechanisms function fully. By contrast he sees apparatus of security as 'centrifugal',[13] expansive, enrolling new elements into ever expanding forms of organisation in which 'freedom' is the means by which the 'liberal arts of government' sustain regimes of power. In this sense, power/knowledge is diffuse and everywhere. Central to this conception is the notion that the current historical era is governed by an explosion of techniques that *simultaneously* operate on the body, on the subjective self and on species-level relations of the population.[14]

We contend that the *construction of the data-self marks a shift in modes of power*, of a revitalised governmentality centred on the growing capacity to simultaneously govern through knowledge of the individual (subjectivities) and of the population (or populations) characterised by corporate rather than state-based forms of government power. Here the current hegemony of neoliberal capitalism as an organising principle, emblematically reflected in the rise of the Big 5 technology companies, might be seen in rather totalising and pernicious terms, the Big 5 taking on state-like capacities and functions. Of course, the emergence of 'the state' historically is intimately entwined with the emergence of the 'big corporation' (obvious examples might be the East India Company,[15] Nederlandsche Handel-Maatschappij,[16] or United Fruit Company[17]), not only in relation to juridical and administrative technologies, but also in relation to their biopolitical practices – concern with security of the population as the object of government. What is distinctive about the current era is less the notion of private entities making both the individual (the 'subject') and the group (the 'population') their targets of political strategy but the use of technology to govern both simultaneously.

The discourse of neoliberalism, in Foucault's terms, was far from an unregulated *laissez-faire* but, as Newheiser describes, a means through which 'freedom functions as the means by which individuals are governed, the counterpart of power rather than its limit'.[18] Normalisation, the construction of universal subjects against which people measure themselves and are measured (for example through statistical analysis of the multitude – census data, medical records, social media feeds), is central to government through freedom.

Some argue that our 'present' is rather different to Foucault's and therefore his analytical tools provide limited insights into the contemporary data-driven world. This is explicitly because another form of power has emerged and acts through 'ceaseless algorithmic assessment' upon the social body and the individual – what Koopman[19] refers to as 'info-power' and Ruckenstein and Dow Shull[20] as 'datafied power'.

In this regard Andrejevic notes that central to analyses of info-power is the recognition of the 'asymmetric relations between those who collect, store and mine large quantities of data and those whom data collection targets'.[21] Governments and commercial corporations are seen as 'data-rich' and individual citizens as 'data-poor' – with gradations of data-poverty (some individuals are 'poorer' than others).

The data-poor voluntarily proffer their data to be monetised by companies who combine it with the data lives of others to produce population-wide correlations and inferences that can be utilised to generate profit or reduce losses through forms of algorithmic government.

The rest of this paper explores some examples of this ceaseless algorithmic assessment. Where we depart from Koopman is not in denying that Foucault's concepts of power are incomplete and therefore provide a limited means for interrogating the political dynamics of data. Rather we argue that algorithmic technology is a technology of governmentality that Foucault could only dream of (one that targets the population and the individual) and that the personalised data subject is Foucault's 'docile subject' *par excellence*: not passive bodies but bodies constituted to be 'useful', receptive to the subtle forms of power that discipline their actions and capacities. As such it might prove fruitful to consider in what ways this algorithmic world constructs physical and virtual places in which subjects assume capacities to care for themselves within broader governmentalities that work to stabilise and secure populations, economies and societies.[22]

3.2.3 *The Algorithmic Life*

Social media and the world of 'big data' have been widely interrogated in relation to Foucauldian ideas of surveillance, surveillance capitalism and security.[23] Pasquale suggests that society is populated by 'enigmatic technologies' that mask the values and prerogative operationalised through those technologies within 'black boxes',[24] a subject to be explored in the next section. David Beer asks in what ways are these calculating devices ordering the social world? Might software 'be taking on some constitutive or performative role in ordering that world on our behalf?'[25]

Such algorithms reflect models of the social world, built upon preceding ideas, categories and means of classification rather than emerging from the ether. They are not neutral but designed with particular outcomes in mind and reflect existing ideologies about the universal subject. Those outcomes, the objects to which the algorithms are applied, are increasingly influenced by commercial interests and agendas (i.e. search engines and their revenue models service capitalist society and ideology[26]) and act outside of, but parallel to, more typical state institutions and modes of governance. In that sense 'big tech' takes on state-like capacities and functions of government, whether intentionally or not. They also have the capacity, and are designed, to create 'truths' about that world – around things like choice, risk, health, desire. Internalising the outputs of the algorithm (e.g. an instruction to 'be healthy') will produce the docile subject; disciplined, transformed and improved. Yet there is a difference between how algorithms are used to frame decision-making and behaviour, to construct the 'regime of truth',[27] and how they are experienced and reacted to. In other words, whilst the technology seeks to influence agency, the target of action (the body, the subject) has capacities to evade or at least distort their effects (e.g. choice of browser, identity politics, lying, or indeed the very construction of a virtual persona – 'we are not our avatars').

The 'power' of algorithmic government is in their relational nature. Algorithms exist in relation to the defined objects/data they refer to. They possess no power, rather power is realised in the outcomes of algorithmic processes.[28] Decisions are presented as neutral, objective, trustworthy, maximising multiple goals. And the algorithm itself serves as an idea that reproduces a wider discourse about contemporary rationality, one based on calculation, competition, efficiency and objectivity as virtues to be inculcated;[29] the algorithmic life promising an objectively quantified, better future.

Writing just before the birth of the virtual world, and of social life mediated by machines, Michel Foucault stated that his 'objective [had] been to create a history of the different modes by which, in our culture, human beings are made subjects.'[30] Here the 'subject' is essential to the operation of the contemporary mode of government. The individual must be constituted as 'a subject whose merits are analytically identified, who is subjected in continuous networks of obedience, and *who is subjectified through the compulsory extraction of truth*'[31] (emphasis added).

Algorithms processing the data subject are enrolled in the governance of the self through simultaneous processes of individualisation and subjectivation (e.g. through discipline and surveillance), and processes of totalisation (the biopolitics of the population). Technologies bundled up in notions of the Internet, social media, smart technology and others forms of algorithmic government render the world iteratively responsive to individual choice or action. So algorithmic government, through monitoring, analysing, reporting and modifying behaviour, inculcates a *plurality* of subjectivities that construct docile subjects fit for a (capitalist) algorithmic world.

In the remainder of this chapter, I want to look briefly at three unexotic data gathering, analysing and personalising technologies with a view to opening up some of the more banal circuits through which new neoliberal subjectivities are produced through interactive algorithms.

3.3 CASE STUDIES IN BANAL PERSONALISING TECHNOLOGIES

3.3.1 *Driving Metrics: Opening the Black Box*

The majority of accidents are a result of driver behaviour. In 2010 the total economic cost of motor vehicle crashes in the United States alone was put at $242 billion. Telematics or 'intelligent transport systems' are increasingly finding a place in the insurance of life.[32] This technology has been used as a simple tracking metric for a number of decades. Attached to accelerometers and algorithms, their ubiquity has grown since 2010.

These are widely understood as the 'blackbox' that gives teenage road racers cheap insurance and parents the security of safer driving (even imposing a 'curfew' to prevent late night revels). Insurance premiums are based on a range of factors, of which age is considered a major determinant of 'risk'. The black box uses GPS and G-Force sensors to map movement and force. Currently it is estimated there are nearly a million such policies in the UK.[33]

The box documents and relays real-time information about where you are, how fast you are going, braking smoothness, time of day, distance travelled, breaks, etc., all connected to a database comparing practice to conditions around you (speed limits, nature of road – blind corners – , traffic jams, no emission zones) to build up a virtual version of your driving self. This 'driver behaviour profiling' generates a 'driving style score' or a category of what type of driver you are. Dependent on which category you are in you 'earn rewards' for safe driving. These might range from extending the miles you can drive in a week to lowering subsequent insurance quotes. They also offer feedback via smartphone apps to help you adapt and self-police driving behaviour. Some, such as Marmalade's system, even point to errors made in particular locations via Google Street View. Through such feedback you can change your driver behaviour profile, and so change your costs.

This is personalised risk assessment. Rather than assessing risk based on how other people with similar characteristics to you drive, it assesses risk based on how you actually drive – but benchmarked against a universal norm of ideal driving behaviour in given situations. So this combination of material technology and algorithm uses personalised data to construct a data self and amend costs and policies accordingly, directing particularly new young drivers to adopt less risky behaviours. It has an element of disciplinary power, but fundamentally is about allying the data self with the physical one and shaping the behaviour of both. Such technology is also productive. Both black boxes and mobile phones are increasingly used to inculcate more desirable or commodified driving identities in a disciplinary mode of power.

Companies with large fleets of vehicles have adopted telematics technology for a number of years. Recently the nature of that use has shifted to metricise labour, logistics planning, fuel efficiencies and safety. For example, the company Quartix (based in Newtown, mid-Wales) is one of a number that concentrate on data profiling of drivers for companies that have large fleets of vehicles in constant motion. They grant the company managers unprecedented levels of real-time insight into the activities of their employees. The software maps movement, routes analysis, speed analysis, fuel usage, provides daily driver briefings (including reviewing incidents of harsh braking or accidents), and of course how long vehicles were on site and between sites – in other words monitoring the performance of staff on the job.

At the other end of the spectrum, the technology allows driver self-monitoring and analysis to give feedback and engender other, more socially progressive, sorts of subjectivities. Driver behaviour remains the major factor in determining fuel consumption for vehicles running at optimal performance. For example, navigation algorithms can improve fuel efficiency through selection of route planning.[34] An early attempt to develop a visual feedback system to alter driver behaviour to achieve environmental goals was developed by 'ecoDriver', an EU-funded transnational research project centred on the University of Leeds. This met the modest but encouraging goal of achieving fuel savings of 'up to 6%' through small nudges, such as suggesting a recommended speed on individual roads.

Driver behaviour can also be modified through the use of smartphones,[35] 'cheaply' turning the consumer into a sensor for monitoring road vehicle traffic whilst also providing data for usage-based insurance of the sort described above.[36] Indeed, Google Maps use data from such mobile technologies to provide almost real-time feedback on vehicle movements, hence its apparently magical ability to identify congestion as it happens. This is based on vast data sets that normalise traffic flow, identifying whether traffic is moving faster or slower than normal for the type of road and number of vehicles on it.

In a similar vein, the Dutch app 'Flo' was developed to run on smartphones; it includes 'gamified' feedback of driving style data, which is connected to insurance data and to eco-driving to incentivise (via insurance premiums) both safety and eco-efficiency. The French greentech startup 'WeNow' similarly nudges people towards carbon-friendly driving, targeting the eco-driving (and financial costs) of vehicle fleets, also incorporating elements of gamification (awards and challenges for fleet drivers) and the measurement of carbon emissions tied to carbon-offsetting projects.

These examples of emergent *productive* uses for personalised data are yet to become ubiquitous in relation to environmental normalisation. They point to further expansion of data personalisation for social goals, as well as its more repressive uses as a means of surveilling labour.

3.3.1.1 Healthy Subjects: The Fitbit Self

Health, being particular types of 'healthy', has become normalised in Western societies as the objective of the responsible citizen. The datafication of health has been widely documented.[37] Indeed, for some, 'big-data' promises answers to questions we do not even know we need answered yet.[38] Trawling through, analysing, hunting for correlations and patterns in the biodatabases of corporate and public health, governmental and increasingly 'consumer lifestyle' and commercially focused institutions offer tantalising solutions to the health challenges of individual and social life. Here the promise is that personalised healthcare mobilised by cross-referencing data from multiple sources (ranging from the epidemiological to so-called 'eHealth' or digital health ICT systems to self-care consumer-driven products) will deliver self-actualising healthy subjects, or at least a means of treating them efficiently and profitably.

While such technologies and their increasing integration enhance the capacity for understanding, monitoring (in real-time), developing treatments for, and addressing the social basis for, ill health, might they also have other consequences for the datafied self? In this section, we focus on the infiltration and intersection between digital tracking tools, the data they collect, the embodied data subject and the social body they monitor, and the types of subjectivities these might be producing. Specifically, we are concerned with what Esmonde and Jette refer to as the 'Fitbit subject' [39] and the biopolitics of the 'quantified self.[40]

Tracking tools such as the ubiquitous 'Fitbit', covering an array of technologies that range from wearable cameras, to nano-sensors monitoring stomach acid or blood pressure, to sleep recording devices, to mobile phone location tracking software and applications like MyFitnessPal, are hugely empowering. They provide a means to gain control over a life that is understood as out of control, through self-tracking and self-correcting. Promising 'self knowledge through numbers' (the motto of the 'Quantified Self' movement), individualised self-tracking practices are increasingly shared and socialised, communal in their production and utility.[41] The clinical gaze of the doctor is to some extent displaced by the all-seeing eye of the disciplinary algorithm. Devices responding to personal behaviours (sufficient 'steps', calories consumed, biceps curled, heart rate raised) encourage both action and self-valorisation through how effectively one responds to their 'recommendations'.

The concerned and time-unlimited subject has always had other ways to self-monitor such actions, but the availability and relatively low prices of self-tracking devices open up the quantified self to powerful algorithms applied in the service of self-actualisation, using data about 'you'. Where such knowledge sat in the realm of the medical professional, the expert, now everyone (with the money) can benefit from expertise provided by responsive algorithms that analyse and advise on your body's data. In this way we internalise a set of discourses about the body, about responsibility to the social body, about the need to counter certain structural factors that affect individual health (trans-fats, sugar, time) through using technology to produce 'a better me'. And, at the heart of this discourse, is... the self-governing individual, in charge of their health, their wellbeing, needing a little nudge to become even better.

For many critical social scientists this 'datafication of health' has a more pernicious effect, in the form of subjectification it promotes.[42] Specifically, a number of studies emphasise how such health-tracking devices promote the withdrawal of the welfare state – a discursive shift from care of the health of the social body to self-care of the neoliberal subject.[43] The consequence is the slow erasure of the communal self, of the social realm: the responsibility of the state to provide for the biopolitic is displaced by a responsibilisation of the subject. Empowerment through knowledge becomes obligation through being known.

In this sense the 'Fitbit subject' is an idealised neoliberal subject, one accepting, and encouraged to accept, the decline in social and health provision by internalising the responsibility for one's own health, by measuring, regulating and collecting biometric data and taking control of their own bodies on a detailed level.[44] It is here that power is most evident.

The atomised nature of neoliberal governance is, in this brave new world, embodied by the self-governing individual, who exists in relation to the thing under attention. Therefore the healthy subject exists in relation to the number of 'kms run' or 'calories consumed', and the proper disposition of such a subject is to be responsible for not being unhealthy.

But while a neoliberal discourse for reducing the form and functions of the state through responsibilising the docile Fitbit subject to serve the interests of capital and the subject themselves, that subject is exceptional, not universal. The data-subject of such 'technologies of the self'[45] must make themselves malleable to the technology, not the other way round. They must become subjects who do not rely on the state, on the social body, to ensure their health or wellbeing, but are responsible consumers of the measurements, benchmarks and instructions to become in perpetuity their better, more productive, selves. In performing their better selves their bodies become the visible marker of shifting beliefs about the 'right' ways to live; certain practices, representations of the healthy body, responsibilities of both the healthy and unhealthy individual, become normalised, inscribing this new subjectivity upon the social body. But what happens to the left-behind, the unmetricised, the unhealthy? Health has social and structural dimensions, dimensions that the healthy algorithms are hard-pressed to capture. Numerous studies of political ecologies and environmental justice reveal that poverty and exclusion are intimately tied to health – an effect of diet, location (pollution), leisure time, sites of activity, access to medical expertise, mobility, etc.[46]

Akin to the black box, the Fitbit subject is one where the health of the individual is increasingly a matter of concern for the corporation. As Christopher Till documents, in relation to Apple Watch and two corporate wellness self-tracking programmes (Global Corporate Challenge, and Virgin Pulse), health, wellness and happiness have been conflated with productivity and hence recast as legitimate objects of intervention by capitalist interests.[47] Employees have demonstrated resistance to direct disciplinary controls, increasingly anticipate 'workplace responsiveness' to their needs, and as neoliberal subjects have internalised the precarity discourse to embrace 'flexiblity'. As the Manpower Group describe, employees have been reimagined as 'consumers of work' who managers need to motivate through emotional and psychological tactics to drive productivity.[48] Corporate Wellness programmes deploy tactics to 'nudge' and discipline the 'well-being' and 'happiness' of workers to improve productivity in an economic system where surplus value (or profits) is associated with cognitive, emotional and symbolic labour.[49]

Evidently this characterisation refers to an emergent workforce, and one situated in particular socio-cultural contexts (the 'creative class'), perhaps rather exceptional ones, rather than a totality of it. Other analyses reveal the opposite, that wearable technology and workplace quantification increases objective and subjective precarity.[50] In this context 'dataveillance'[51] and self-tracking technologies have been mobilised to produce suitably productive subjects. Indeed Amazon infamously patented self-tracking technology that would allow it to not only track warehouse workers' movements, but to use 'haptic feedback' to direct the gaze and hands of the worker – here the body becomes a machine for the algorithm to direct.

This is not to suggest that the Fitbit subjects are simply oppressed subjects, used and abused by capital to simply become better selves, healthier labour providers, active consumers. Rather, the subject of this form of government is one subjectified through the voluntary, rather than compulsory, 'extraction of truth'[52] in a relationship that Tania Murray Li describes as 'convenient for each of the things that are to be governed'.[53] Both the data subject and the data controlled are in a negotiation that delivers them some advantage. All of which begs questions about the relationship between technology, algorithmic government of the self and the healthy subject of neoliberal governance. Some surround the relationship between the responsible subject as a social norm based on particular concepts of that subject (young, active, time rich, financially secure[54]) and the diversity of ages, forms, capacities and histories that constitute the population. How does that play out in the roll-back of state provision of, or marketisation, of healthcare? Others relate to the ownership of data. The corporate collection of intimate details of personal behaviour, willingly given but owned, traded and commodified, by corporate interests, for corporate interests, is surely something worthy of discussion.

3.3.1.2 Gambling on Metrics

'Money won is twice as sweet as money earned' – Fast Eddie Felson, *The Colour of Money*[55]

So, the datafied healthy subject and the streamlined reflexive telematicised driver illustrate a form of productive power, monitored and modifying their behaviour to achieve efficiencies in action and body. They exemplify the responsibilised data subject, a subject fit for a neoliberal environment: productive, individualised/atomised rational actors, choices enacted through market mechanisms, responsible for their own 'fitness', goal directed, responsive to the demands of capital and self-managing their deportment as neoliberal subjects.

What if the responsible neoliberal subject is not rational? How might data personalisation impact upon the irrational subject that makes sub-optimal choices influenced by cognitive biases and mental shortcuts (black boxes) to overcome cognitive limitations of imperfect knowledge and time?

Gambling has been a ubiquitous practice across human societies and eras. Choices are driven by risk, by the sensations obtained through winning against the fear you might lose. Cognitive biases and neurological reward and risk aversion systems (dopamine and serotonin pathways) can dominate behaviour, resulting in compulsive or disordered forms of gambling. As a social practice, gambling reflects *homo irrationalis* rather than the *homo economicus* avatar imagined to sit behind the neoliberal subject.

The way gambling is conceived and its conduct governed has changed in line with a Foucauldian analysis of European history. In the sixteenth century, under the Protestant reformation, gambling was sinful. During the Enlightenment gambling stood in opposition to reason, order, predictability; it was not sinful so much as the embodiment of irrationality, albeit also a template for statistical modelling and probability theory. By the nineteenth century, gambling was reconceptualised as an 'immoral vice', a drain on the key capitalist resource of the era – diligent productive labour – and criminalised by a suite of legislative mechanisms. By the early twentieth century, addictive gambling became the subject of the clinical gaze, a medicalised form of deviance. In addition, in the late twentieth century it was pathologised – problem gambling classified as a disease.

The global gambling market reached $450 billion in 2018. It is expected to achieve revenues of over $565 billion by 2022,[56] with smartphone and tablet penetration and device capability driving much market growth. In 2017, in the United Kingdom, 46 per cent of the population had gambled in the previous four weeks, 18 per cent (and rising) of them online.[57] Around 45 per cent of online gamblers reported that adverts had prompted them to gamble and a surprising 6 per cent of recent gamblers reported that they had 'self-excluded' in the past. In other words, they had had to find a method of preventing themselves from gambling.

In the neoliberal era, such problem gamblers are located as susceptible individuals who struggle to regulate their own behaviour, but who fundamentally are responsible for their situation. Such narratives erase social and structural factors that frame gambling practices. The gambler, in this rendering, is shorn of power relations and reduced to a mere cog in a sociotechnical system.[58] Yet as an industry gambling has been at the forefront of applying research into the psychology of choices to generate revenue. Here data, its processing and personalisation, has proven increasingly key to future revenue growth.

Data personalisation plays out in a number of different settings. Online customers are segmented, their data harvested and traded. Third-party data has become key to expanding the customer base. Targeted marketing, drawing on information about income, credit, marital status, insurance details, etc., allows firms to target ads to particular demographics, with accusations of targeting people on low incomes or lapsed players identified for 'dynamic retargeting',[59] who are enticed back into the gambling habit with offers of 'free bets'.

Artificial intelligence and behavioural analytics have been developed to profile customers and predict their behavioural responses to triggers. As Busby records in *The Guardian*,

Gamblers' every click, page view and transaction is scientifically examined so that ads statistically more likely to work can be pushed through Google, Facebook and other platforms.[60]

Predictive analysis is used to allow promotional offers based on previous activity and interests, or even physical location, to hit customers with content tailored to moments when the customer may be more receptive to the prompt. For example, a customer may have bet on a football fixture and therefore will receive a reminder prior to the rematch, or if they regularly bet on particular events but are identified as 'late' for this one, a 'push notification' may nudge them into action. And the systems are iterative, models and segmentation refined as products are promoted and engaged with, in an ongoing mass population experiment.

The conjunction between spatial and virtual data technologies is perhaps best exemplified in the emergence of geo-locational tracking around gambling. Whilst geo-locational technology, in smartphones for example, has been utilised to market gaming opportunities, or to customise the interaction between gambler and gambling app (e.g. local currency, events or language), it is in the area of regulation that the technology has become particularly cutting edge.

In some jurisdictions, physical location is an essential determinant of whether or not both the gambler and gambling provider are acting within the law. Therefore, in some American states, gambling is restricted to physical spaces (casinos), or classified as illegal – or online gambling is only legal outside of gaming venues. In New Jersey, for example, online betting is legal within the state borders, but not from outside of them. Geolocation software uses location data from a mobile device to determine whether the device is within or outside the political boundaries of New Jersey state ('geofencing'). Such software even caters for physical gambling spaces, preventing online betting within a casino, but not outside; or enabling the directed marketing of events or gaming opportunities to mobile devices within specific areas of the casino ('beaconing'); or targeting gamblers physically located in a rival casino.

Further expanding the scope for data personalisation, the industry is at the cutting edge of applying tracking technology and AI to managing the gaming environment in real-world casinos. In some jurisdictions (e.g. British Columbia, Canada), the rationale is regulatory – surveillance via facial recognition software and AI can be rolled out to keep criminal and addictive behaviour out of casinos. This has been linked in particular to practices of 'self-exclusion', whereby a problem gambler recognises their irrational behaviour and seeks to become 'responsible' by excluding themselves from sites of gambling. The Ontario Lottery and Gaming Corporation is using facial recognition and AI software to manage a self-exclusion programme for 15,000 problem gamblers.[61]

The same technology is reportedly being used in some jurisdictions to manage players, rather than exclude them. Biometric and geo-locational data is increasingly useful for casino operators seeking to manage their sites and security. Bloomberg reported in June 2019 that casino operators in Macau were using hidden cameras, facial recognition technology, RFID tagged poker chips and tables to capture data on players and their style of play. Such data can then be used to segment players by age, gender (clothing, even) and risk profile; to identify the high rollers, the loss escalators (those for whom a loss will trigger an increase in spending), the casual gamers, and ensure both personal attention and perks are offered to keep them playing and to prevent fraud.[62]

Therefore, in this major global industry, data gathering and processing, personalisation of behavioural prompts, AI and geo-locational technology come together to manage the interplay between the irrational (and socially unproductive) and the rational subject of neoliberal governance. The recognised, segmented, known data subject is governed to be made fit for voluntarily risking their finances on the throw of a dice, the turn of a card or the placement of a datafied chip.

3.4 CONCLUSION

Algorithms processing personal data and providing nudges, guidance and instruction are enrolled in the governance of the self through simultaneous processes of individualisation and subjectivation (e.g. through discipline and surveillance) and those of totalisation (the biopolitics of the population). The outputs of such algorithms are designed to produce particular effects. They are situated in a cultural milieu in which government of individuals operates through 'freedom', specifically of free acting autonomous subjects governed at a distance through political economy.

Foucault's 'objective [had] been to create a history of the different modes by which, in our culture, human beings are made subjects.'[63] The key here is 'subjects', plural. Foucault sought to avoid the reduction of people to categories, to resist the universalising vision of *homo economicus*. Here subjectivity is not singular but contextual and relational. In understanding how data personalisation impacts the modern world we must avoid the tendency to see the subject as passive and universalised. Indeed, we would contend that an imaginary of a universal subject is hard wired into much algorithmic government and deployed to discipline and punish resistant subjects. The real-time monitoring and metrics of the population provides a benchmark for aggregating types of ideal subjects against which algorithmic government benchmarks and seeks to transform the individual to be a fit-bit of a neoliberal economic model.

In this chapter we have attempted, through three banal social practices (driving, health, gambling) that triangulate on the intersection between technology, data and subjectivation, to reveal some of the ways a 'neoliberal subject' is produced under conditions of increasing private oversight. The examples have some coercive or regulatory elements (constraining certain actions with the risk of punishment or knowledge of being observed). Yet they also empower, they provide examples of power as productive, or making subjects live, albeit live public lives managed by private corporations to produce docile subjects fit for purpose – to consume, to share their data, to be individually responsible. We argue that such data personalisation technologies are increasingly central to processes of reproduction of neoliberalism and neoliberal subjects. Normatively there is an argument here that seeks to question the hegemony of current neoliberal modes of governance and pose the idea that the neoliberal subject is an outcome of relations between people and machines. This is not an argument for conspiracy or intentionality, though this may be a feature of some of the technologies discussed. It is more an argument for critical engagement with the complex interactions, intersections, effects and unintended consequences of multiple technologies that, through the use of data, make the simultaneous government of individuals and populations their targets of action.

NOTES

1 Michel Foucault, *Society Must Be Defended: Lectures at the Collège de France 1975–1976* (Penguin 2004) 34.

2 Michel Foucault, 'The Subject and Power' (1982) 8(4) *Critical Inquiry* 777, 789: 'The exercise of power consists in guiding the possibility of conduct and putting in order the possible outcome. Basically power is less a confrontation between two adversaries or the linking of one to the other than a question of government'. Here, 'government' refers to the art of governing as 'the conduct of conduct' (see Foucault (n 1) 17 March 1976 Lecture) rather than restricted to political executive and administrative decision making systems of State institutions.

3 Michel Foucault, *The History of Sexuality: 1: The Will to Knowledge* (1990) 136. Translated by Robert Hurley, Pantheon Books: New York.

4 Michel Foucault, 'Governmentality' in Graham Burchell, Colin Gordon and Peter Miller (eds), *The Foucault Effect: Studies in Governmentality* (University of Chicago Press 1991) 100.

5 Biopolitics is theorised by Foucault as a new and specific modern form of exercising power, an alliance of forms of knowledge (science) and technologies of power that render the life of the species the target of political strategy.

6 Thomas Lemke, 'Foucault, Governmentality, and Critique' (2002) 14(3) *Rethinking Marxism* 49.

7 Foucault (n 1) '17 March 1976'.

8 Tania Murray Li, 'Governmentality' (2007) 49(2) *Anthropologica* 275.

9 Michel Foucault, 'Lecture: 18th January 1978' in *Security, Territory, Population: Lectures at the Collège de France 1977–1978* (Michel Senellart ed, Graham Burchell tr, Palgrave 2007) 40.

10 ibid 41.

11 Michel Foucault, *The Birth of Biopolitics: Lectures at the Collège de France, 1978–1979* (Graham Burchell tr, Palgrave 2008) 121.

12 ibid 108.

13 ibid 45.

14 Foucault M. (1976) *The History of Sexuality, Vol 1: The Will to Knowledge*, London: Penguin, p.139-141

15 Stephen Legg, *Spaces of Colonialism: Delhi's Urban Governmentalities* (Wiley-Blackwell 2007).

16 Albert Schrauwers, 'A genealogy of corporate governmentality in the realm of the 'merchant-king': the Netherlands Trading Company and the management of Dutch paupers' (2011) 40(3) *Economy and Society* 373.

17 Diane Nelson, 'Life during wartime: Guatemala, vitality, conspiracy, milieu' in Jonathan Xavier Inda (ed), *Anthropologies of Modernity: Foucault, Governmentality, and Life Politics* (Blackwell 2005).

18 David Newheiser, 'Foucault, Gary Becker and the Critique of Neoliberalism' (2016) 33(5) *Theory Culture and Society* 3, 5.

19 Colin Koopman, 'The power thinker' *Psyche / Aeon Magazine* (Aeon.co, 15 March 2017) https://aeon.co/essays/why-foucaults-work-on-power-is-more-important-than-ever.

20 Minna Ruckenstein and Natasha D Schull, 'The Datafication of Health' (2017) 46(1) *Annual Review of Anthropology* 261.

21 Mark Andrejevic, 'The big data divide' (2014) (8) *International Journal of Communications* 1673.

22 Stephen Legg, 'Subjects of truth: Resisting governmentality in Foucault's 1980s' (2019) 37 (1) *Environment and Planning D: Society and Space* 27.

23 Reuben S Rose-Redwood, 'Governmentality, geography, and the geo-coded world' (2006) 30 (4) *Progress in Human Geography* 469; Louise Amoore, 'Data derivatives: on the emergence of a security risk calculus for our times' (2011) 28(6) *Theory, Culture & Society* 24; Sarah Elwood and Agnieszka Leszczynski, 'Privacy, reconsidered: new representations, data practices, and the geoweb' (2011) 42(1) *Geoforum* 6; Kirstie S Ball and David Murakami Wood. 'Editorial. Political economies of surveillance' (2013) 11(1/2) *Surveillance & Society* 1; Jeremy W Crampton, 'Collect it all: national security, Big Data and governance' (2015) 80 *GeoJournal* 519; Agnieszka Leszczynski and Jeremy W Crampton, 'Introduction: spatial Big Data and everyday life.' (2016) 3(2) *Big Data & Society*; David G Beer, 'The Social Power of Algorithms' (2017) 20(1) *Information, Communication and Society* 1; Tobias Matzner, 'Opening black boxes is not enough – data-based surveillance In *Discipline and Punish* and today'. (2017) 23 *Foucault Studies* 27; Tobias Matzner, 'The human is dead – long live the algorithm! Human-algorithmic ensembles and liberal subjectivity' (2019) 36(2) *Theory, Culture & Society* 123.

24 Frank Pasquale, *The Black Box Society: The Secret Algorithms that Control Money and Information* (Harvard University Press 2016).

25 David G Beer, 'The Social Power of Algorithms' (2017) 20(1) *Information, Communication and Society* 1.

26 Astrid Mager, 'Algorithmic ideology: how capitalist society shapes search engines' (2012) 15 (5) *Information, Communication & Society* 769.

27 Michel Foucault, 'The political function of the intellectual' (1977) 17 *Radical Philosophy* 12, 13 www.radicalphilosophyarchive.com/issue-files/rp17_article2_politicalfunctionofintellectual_foucault.pdf.

28 David G Beer, 'The Social Power of Algorithms' (2017) 20(1) *Information, Communication and Society* 1, 7.

29 ibid 9.

30 Foucault (n 2).

31 Michel Foucault, 'Lecture 7, 22nd February 1978' in *Security, Territory, Population: Lectures at the Collège de France 1977–1978* (Michel Senellart ed, Graham Burchell tr, Palgrave 2007) 183-84.

32 Jair Ferreira Júnior and others, 'Driver behavior profiling: an investigation with different smartphone sensors and machine learning' (2017) 12(4) *PLoS ONE*.

33 Sam Barker, 'Drivers are being caught out by telematics insurance – here's how to beat the boxes' *Daily Telegraph* (London, 10 May 2019) www.telegraph.co.uk/insurance/car/drivers-caught-telematics-insurance-beat-boxes/.

34 Kanok Boriboonsomsin and others, 'Eco-routing navigation system based on multisource historical and real-time traffic information' (2012) 13(4) *IEEE Transactions on Intelligent Transportation Systems* 1694.

35 German Castignani, Raphaël Frank and Thomas Engel, 'An evaluation study of driver profiling fuzzy algorithms using smartphones' (21st IEEE International Conference on Network Protocols ICNP, Göttingen, October 2013); German Castignani and others, 'Driver behavior profiling using smartphones: a low-cost platform for driver monitoring' (2015) 7(1) *IEEE Intelligent Transportation Systems Magazine* 91.

36 Peter Händel and others, 'Smartphone-Based Measurement Systems for Road Vehicle Traffic Monitoring and Usage-Based Insurance' (2014) 8(4) IEEE Systems Journal 1238.

37 Ruckenstein and Schull (n 20).

38 Chris Anderson, 'The end of theory: the data deluge makes the scientific method obsolete' *Wired*, 23 June 2008 www.wired.com/2008/06/pb-theory/.

39 Katelyn Esmonde and Shannon Jette, 'Assembling the 'Fitbit subject': a Foucauldian-sociomaterialist examination of social class, gender and self-surveillance on Fitbit community message boards' (2020) 24(3) *Health* 299.

40 Josh Cohen, 'Quantified Self: The algorithm of life' *Prospect Magazine* (London, 5 February 2014) www.prospectmagazine.co.uk/arts-and-books/quantified-self-the-algorithm-of-life; Btihaj Ajana, 'Digital health and the biopolitics of the Quantified Self' (2017) 3 *Digital Health* 1.

41 Ajana (n 40).

42 Ruckenstein and Schull (n 20).

43 Ajana (n 40); Deborah Lupton, 'The digitally engaged patient: self-monitoring and self-care in the digital health era' (2013) 11 *Social Theory and Health* 256; Natasha D Schull 'Data for life: wearable technology and the design of self-care' (2016) 11(3) *BioSocieties*.

44 Ajana (n 40).

45 Michel Foucault, 'Technologies of the self' in Paul Rabinow and Nicolas Rose (eds), *The Essential Foucault: Selections from Essential Works of Foucault, 1954–1984* (The New Press 2003).

46 Russel P Lopez and Patricia Hynes, 'Obesity, physical activity, and the urban environment: public health research needs' (2006) 5 *Environmental Health*; Julie Guthman, 'Opening up the black box of the body in geographical obesity research: toward a critical political ecology of fat' (2012) 102(5) *Annals of the Association of American Geographers* 951; Paul Jackson and Abigail H Neely 'Triangulating health: toward a practice of a political ecology of health' (2015) 39(1) *Progress in Human Geography* 47; Judy Y Ou and others, 'Self-rated health and its association with perceived environmental hazards,

the social environment, and cultural stressors in an environmental justice population' (2018) 18 *BMC Public Health* 970; Felicia M Mitchell, 'Water (in)security and American Indian health: social and environmental justice implications for policy, practice and research' (2019) 176 *Public Health* 98.

47 Christopher Till, 'Creating 'automatic subjects': Corporate wellness and self-tracking' (2019) 23(4) *Health* 418.

48 ManpowerGroup, 'Human age 2.0: future forces at work' (2016) www.manpowergroup.co .uk/wp-content/uploads/2016/01/humanage2-futureforcesatwork.pdf.

49 Till (n 47).

50 Phoebe V Moore, *The Quantified Self in Precarity: Work, Technology and What Counts* (Routledge 2017).

51 Lupton (n 43).

52 Foucault (n 31).

53 Murray Li (n 8).

54 Self evidently other healthy subjects also exist; the point is each is essentialised to provide a benchmark for 'real people'

55 *The Colour of Money*, directed by Martin Scorsese (1986; Touchstone Pictures)

56 The Business Research Company, 'Gambling global market opportunities and strategies to 2022' (Researchandmarkets.com, May 2019) www.researchandmarkets.com/reports/4773078/ gambling-global-market-opportunities-and, press release Laura Wood, 'Global gambling market to reach \$565 billion by 2022: opportunities & strategies report, 2014 to 2022 – ResearchAndMarkets.com' (Businesswire.com, 6 June 2019) www.businesswire.com/news/ home/20190606005537/en/Global-Gambling-Market-Reach-565-Billion-2022.

57 Gambling Commission (UK), Gambling participation in 2018: behaviour, awareness and attitudes – Annual Report (February 2019) www.gamblingcommission.gov.uk/PDF/survey-data/Gambling-participation-in-2018-behaviour-awareness-and-attitudes.pdf.

58 Marc Welsh and others, 'The 'problem gambler' and socio-spatial vulnerability' in Fernand Gobet and Marvin Schiller (eds), *Problem Gambling: Cognition, Prevention and Treatment* (Palgrave MacMillan 2014).

59 Mattha Busby, 'Revealed: how gambling industry targets poor people and ex-gamblers' *The Guardian* (London, 31 August 2017) www.theguardian.com/society/2017/aug/31/gambl ing-industry-third-party-companies-online-casinos.

60 Mattha Busby, 'Revealed: how bookies use AI to keep gamblers hooked' *The Guardian* (London, 30th April 2018) www.theguardian.com/technology/2018/apr/30/bookies-using-ai-to-keep-gamblers-hooked-insiders-say

61 Anita Elash and Vivian Luk, 'Canadian casinos, banks, police use facial-recognition technology' *The Globe and Mail* (Toronto, 25 July 2011) www.theglobeandmail.com/ news/national/time-to-lead/canadian-casinos-banks-police-use-facial-recognition-technol ogy/article590998/.

62 Jinshan Hong, 'China's big brother casinos can spot who's most likely to lose big' (Bloomberg.com, 25 June 2019) www.bloomberg.com/news/articles/2019-06-25/china-s-casinos-use-ai-to-spot-who-s-most-likely-to-lose-big.

63 Foucault (n 2).

4

Personal Data and Collective Value: Data-Driven Personalisation as Network Effect

Nick O'Donovan

4.1 INTRODUCTION

In today's technologically advanced economies, individuals spend ever more time interacting with one another digitally. We communicate with our friends via messaging platforms such as Whatsapp and Skype, we communicate with our 'friends' via social networks such as Facebook and Instagram, we communicate with taxi drivers via Uber and Lyft, and we communicate with retailers via Amazon Marketplace. We also spend ever more time interacting with the world digitally: we navigate using smartphone maps, we check the weather via our screens rather than our windows, we can program our heating systems, download the latest film, read the news, apply for a loan and even make a coffee with nothing but an internet-enabled device in our hands. As is well known, these interactions generate a stupendous volume of data. Almost every journey we take with our smartphones is logged, as is every transaction, every idle Google search for chess lessons or diet plans or hair-replacement surgery, every whim, neurosis and poorly suppressed longing. All of this data is categorised and preserved – albeit, hopefully, within the bounds of data protection law and user consent.

Data-driven personalisation seems to be one of the more innocuous uses of this trove of personal data (compared to, say, blackmail, or training robots to act as a substitute for my salaried labour, or determining whether or not I have perpetrated any thoughtcrimes of late). Amazon's recommendations alert me to the existence of interesting books that I might not have noticed otherwise. My Google Maps app has learned to highlight the location of the nearest McDonald's by default, saving me the trouble of typing in the full search term. The fact that Netflix suggests shows that I might enjoy, based on my past viewing habits, decreases the chance that I will waste time watching a dud. And I can always ignore or override these recommendations, should I so wish. True, they operate in some sense as nudges, subliminally channelling my thoughts and actions in ways that are not always consciously apparent to me, prompting me to buy more, eat more and watch more junk than might otherwise have been the case – but if that means I do not waste time or money on different junk that I would enjoy less, that is a trade-off I am in all probability willing to make.

Admittedly, data-driven personalisation has a less innocuous side too. An airline might choose to 'personalise' the price of a flight, based on how much I earn, how much I have in the bank and whether a close personal friend or relative of mine is dying. A political movement that I would not normally countenance voting for, were I aware of everything they stand for, might use personalisation to highlight aspects of their platform that might appeal to me, while simultaneously downplaying or actively denying their less savoury (at least to me) ambitions. Similarly, data-driven personalisation might be used, not just by advertisers, but by potential employers, insurers, or mortgage providers, to determine whether I 'fit the profile' of a good employee, driver or borrower.

For the purposes of this chapter, however, I am not going to discuss these more troubling facets of data-driven personalisation in depth. Instead, I will focus on more mundane and apparently inoffensive uses of these techniques – particularly those involving the targeting of content, goods and services to individuals in everyday online activities such as search, social media and e-commerce. Even in these apparently innocuous cases, I will argue, data-driven personalisation generates 'network effects', which can contribute to highly concentrated markets with minimal competition, with implications both for economic dynamism and for the social and political power wielded by a handful of private sector businesses. That today's tech giants benefit from substantial network effects is by now a familiar claim in the literature.[1] Nevertheless, precisely *how* these network effects relate to questions of personalisation has received relatively little attention, and this is the focus of the present chapter.

To this end, we begin by unpacking what a network effect is, before evaluating the extent to which data-driven personalisation satisfies this definition. In so doing, it will become apparent that personalisation differs from many of the more conventional kinds of network effects discussed in the literature. To capture these differences, this chapter distinguishes between first-order network effects, which involve a *quantitative* increase in the number of potential connections between people and the content they create, and second-order network effects, which involve *qualitative* improvements in the way in which people are connected to things they might enjoy (which can include other people and the content they create). For example, as social networks expand, they offer their users ever-greater first-order network effects (allowing users to connect with an increasing number of other users), but also second-order network effects (providing users with better recommendations for content and connections, as the platform accumulates information about who and what different kinds of users will find engaging). This chapter then examines how different business models in the tech sector deploy different combinations of first-order and second-order network effects, and how these effects can interact to create substantial barriers to market entry, stifling competition and innovation. We conclude by sketching some of the implications of this analysis of market structure for public policy: arguing that, where data-driven personalisation contributes to market concentration, governments may need to intervene to ensure that this collectively created value operates in the collective interest.

4.2 NETWORK EFFECTS AND DATA-DRIVEN PERSONALISATION

4.2.1 *Network Effects Defined*

What, then, is a network effect? Network effects arise when adoption of a particular product, standard or platform by additional users makes the product, standard or platform more valuable to other users.[2] A classic example of such effects is the telephone network, whereby each additional household that chooses to connect to the network makes the network a more useful means of communication for every existing telephone-owner, as they can all now contact a larger proportion of the population. Such 'network effects' or 'positive network externalities' are clearly evident in social media platforms, whereby people want to share (or have the option of sharing) content with as many friends and acquaintances as possible, while also having the ability to consume shared content from as wide a social circle as possible too. Similarly, as a consumer seeking a taxi ride or a short-term rental, I will look first at the platform with the most taxi-drivers and accommodation suppliers registered with it; as a taxi-driver or accommodation supplier, I will gravitate towards the platform that attracts the most consumers.[3]

Network effects have serious implications for the level, or even the possibility, of competition within a particular market. Imagine a world with two distinct telephone networks. Users of network A can only dial other users of network A; users of network B can only dial other users of network B. Network A might have cheaper line rental and calling charges than network B, and the service quality might be superior too. Nevertheless, assuming network B is at least tolerably functional and affordable, the main questions I will ask myself when choosing between networks are: which network have people I want to call already adopted, and which network are people I want to call likely to adopt in the future? Assuming a critical mass of my would-be contacts are already on network B, I will gravitate towards it too, despite network A offering a technically superior and cheaper product. As more and more people go through a similar thought process and adopt network B, the more powerful this effect will prove. Network effects can lock-in solutions on account of an early lead in market share, which consumers might find sub-optimal all else being equal.[4]

Network effects have been an integral part of the digital economy since its early days.[5] The ubiquity of Microsoft's MS-DOS (and, subsequently, Windows) on home and office computers attracted developers to Microsoft's operating systems, resulting in an ever-growing range of software applications created for those systems, ensuring that users would continue to gravitate towards Microsoft's operating systems in order to run those applications.[6] These kinds of network effects are clearly visible in the business strategies of many of today's tech giants too.[7] The attraction of social networks such as Facebook, Instagram and LinkedIn lies in the fact that people who I want to connect with are already on the platform, along with the content they have already created and uploaded – and over time other people whom I want to connect with will in all probability be drawn into these platforms too. Two-sided markets such as Uber, Airbnb, eBay and Taskrabbit – where users might be exclusively buyers or sellers of goods or services (or engage in both activities) – also exhibit strong network effects, as consumers are attracted to these platforms by the ready availability of vendors, and vendors are attracted by the ready availability of consumers.

These network effects make it very difficult to challenge large incumbent digital companies. Users must be encouraged to switch from the old platform, which means the new platform cannot just be technically superior or more user-friendly – it must promise people access to the same or better networks too, a hard sell so long as the incumbent is providing a minimally satisfactory service. The challenger business will thus require deep pockets to fund its growth as it tries to achieve sufficient scale to be profitable, including a hefty advertising budget (much of which will ultimately end up in the pockets of today's incumbent tech giants).[8] Consequently, the literature on markets characterised by strong network effects emphasises the importance of early-mover advantage, as well as the tendency of such markets to become highly concentrated, often 'tipping' decisively in favour of one competitor at a certain point in their lifecycle.[9]

4.2.2 *Double-edged Sword of Personalisation Techniques: User Benefit or Profit?*

However, not all successful tech companies are predicated on connecting me to other users of their platform. The dominance of major businesses such as Google Search and Netflix appears to rely on traditional economies of scale, as opposed to network effects in the conventional sense. The design and refinement of the Google Search algorithm, as well as the provision of servers necessary to host this algorithm and the map of the Internet that it produces, appear at first to be fixed costs. Adding additional users simply creates a more attractive proposition for advertisers at near-zero marginal cost to the platform, in much the same way as free-to-view television channels want to offer their advertisers the largest audience possible, thereby generating more revenues to cover the fixed costs that they incur when acquiring or producing programmes.[10] Netflix, too, incurs fixed costs for content creation: additional users do not directly improve the content that existing users consume, they simply provide additional subscription fees that Netflix can choose to reinvest (or not) in acquiring more content for its user-base.

Yet on closer inspection, something akin to a network effect is visible in these businesses' use of data-driven personalisation. The selection of a particular search result or TV programme by a particular user, as well as measures of how satisfied they were with their choice (be that feedback explicit, in the form of a user-written review, or implicit, by dint of how long that show or website maintained their attention and whether or not they looked for an alternative shortly afterwards), provide Netflix and Google Search with insight into how relevant these options were to that user, allowing them to refine their recommendations for future users (whether all future users, or more specifically future users with a similar behavioural profile).[11] As platforms accumulate this data, they should become better and better at making relevant recommendations, which should make them more valuable to their users – minimising user time spent searching for the right product, webpage or TV programme, and connecting them to content, goods and services that will be more relevant and valuable to them. In short, data-driven personalisation techniques mean that platforms will provide a better service to existing users, the more additional users they are able to recruit: the defining characteristic of a network effect.[12]

Nevertheless, many commentators have been reluctant to describe data-driven personalisation as a network effect. Lina Khan, in her influential *Yale Law Review* article on 'Amazon's Antitrust Paradox', suggests network effects arise with regard to Amazon's user reviews, but differentiates such network effects from 'control over data... to better tailor services.'[13] Similarly, in the final report of the UK's Digital Competition Expert Panel, personalisation is presented as an example of the anti-competitive effects of incumbents' 'data advantage', rather than as an example of 'network effects'. Nevertheless, the authors go on to acknowledge that 'user feedback loops' that 'occur when companies collect data from users which they use to improve the quality of their product or service, which then draws in more users... [demonstrate] similar characteristics to network effects.'[14]

The reason for these equivocations is the double-edged nature of personalisation techniques themselves. Conceivably, a platform's algorithm might be configured such that personalisation is solely a matter of connecting users to the goods, services and content that will be of most value to them. For a subscription-based business such as Netflix, commercial imperatives are broadly aligned with the viewer's interest: by recommending things that we will enjoy watching, Netflix helps us to get more out of the service we are already paying for, making it less likely that we will cancel our subscriptions. A social media company that wants to maximise the amount of time that users spend on its platform has an incentive to prioritise content that users will find most relevant and engaging. A search engine that produces relevant responses to a search query is more likely to enjoy repeat visits. In all of these cases, it makes strategic sense for businesses to use personalisation to produce network effects: and the more people use the platform, the better these recommendations should become, from the perspective of the user.[15]

However, the same data can also be used to tailor the user experience in ways that do not aim at delivering user benefit (although they may do so incidentally, to some extent and in some cases). Instead of benevolently seeking to connect users to things that they are most likely to want, data-driven personalisation techniques can also be deployed to draw user attention to products, content and causes that deliver the highest profit margins for the platform in question (because the products in question have high profit margins; because advertisers are willing to pay a high price for delivery of their message). Moreover, data-driven insights into an individual's beliefs and desires can allow platforms and their advertisers to tailor the presentation of said products, content and causes, making it more likely that an individual will devote money and attention to them – even though she might prefer to make other choices, were she better informed about the alternatives available.

Data-driven personalisation techniques can thus be deployed to improve individual experience (generating network effects), *and* to increase profits (by using data-driven insights into consumer behaviour to extract more money from consumers and marketers). These uses of data are not necessarily perfectly aligned. In practice, profit-driven platforms will seek a balance between the two. They will promote goods, services and content that individual users will find sufficiently relevant to maintain their engagement. At the same time, they will also try to prioritise goods, services and content that deliver profits, seeking to tailor the presentation of these goods, services and content to improve the chances of a given user engaging with them.

4.2.3 *Data-driven Personalisation as a 'Second-order' Network Effect*

Even where (and to the extent that) today's tech giants opt to use data-driven personalisation techniques to generate network effects, using the increases in data gleaned from new users to improve the service received by the entire user base, important differences persist between the network effects generated by personalisation and more conventional forms of network effect. In businesses such as social networks, online marketplaces and matchmaking services, additional users primarily create additional value for existing users by enlarging the *quantity* of possible connections between users (including connections to the content, services and/or products that users supply to each other). As the user base increases, each new user makes more inter-user connections possible than the user before them: there is an 'increasing returns' dynamic.[16] The number of new connections a new user makes possible increases with the size of the network – so the third user of Instagram will allow each of the existing two users to make a new connection, whereas the million-and-first user will allow a million users to connect to someone new. To be sure, in reality, increases in the value of the network are not uniform: much hinges on who the new person is, and how much existing users want to engage with them (and the content, goods, or services that they offer).[17] At present, Kim Kardashian generates substantially more online interest than I do. Nevertheless, the point remains that, with conventional network effects, each additional user of a network makes multiple new connections possible.

By contrast, the network effects produced by data-driven personalisation create additional value for existing users by improving the *quality* of the match between an individual user and the content, services and/or products that she may wish to consume (which may or may not be supplied by other users of the same network). These network effects can be described as 'second-order' network effects, to differentiate them from more conventional 'first-order' network effects.[18] In comparison to first-order network effects, second-order network effects display more limited potential for value growth. First-order effects can grow *ad infinitum*, as new connections are facilitated, whereas with second-order effects, there comes a point when it becomes difficult to improve the quality of connection between any given individual and the finite pool of things to which they might be connected.

Where precisely this point lies is a product of both how diverse the user population is (how many or how few relevantly different variables, clusters and sub-clusters the user population can be algorithmically broken down into), as well as how diverse what they are being connected to is. We like to think of ourselves as irreducibly particular – no-one else has had the exact same career history, let alone life experiences, as me – but it may be that the things that we believe individuate us are largely irrelevant for personalisation purposes. In all probability, Netflix can make a decent set of recommendations for me on the basis that I have repeat-watched Hannah Gadsby's *Nanette* and *Breaking Bad*, but failed to make it through an entire episode of *Orange is the New Black*. We are all different, but we may not all be *that* different, and not all differences are relevant to personalising particular choices. In statistical analyses, there are diminishing gains in predictive precision to be had from ever-increasing sample sizes; what matters is how many different clusters and sub-clusters really exist, and how large and how systematic the differences between and within them are.[19] The scope for personalisation also depends on the complexity of what is being personalised. There is a clear limit to the different recommendations that Netflix can make from its 4,000-strong film catalogue.[20] This means there will be many fewer permutations of personalisation possible for that content than there would be for the more than hundred million products available through Amazon.com,[21] or for the hundreds of billions of webpages scanned by the web-crawling routines of Google Search.[22]

Irrespective of the precise configuration of these forces in any given instance of data-driven personalisation, there is still a diminishing-returns dynamic in the case of second-order network effects when compared to conventional first-order network effects. Beyond a certain point, the network effects that additional users can generate for other users through incremental improvements in personalisation will begin to

TABLE 4.1. *Tech sector business models by type of network effect.*

	Second-order network effects	Minimal second-order network effects
First-order network effects	Facebook, Amazon Marketplace, eBay	Uber, Lyft, Google Maps
Minimal first-order network effects	Google Search, Amazon.com, Spotify, Netflix	

subside. Economies of scale may still continue to grow: the cost of servicing additional users might be vanishingly small, compared to the incremental revenue that can be generated from them (whether income received directly from the new user herself, and/or from advertisers seeking to target her). Nevertheless, the network effects produced by data-driven personalisation will display a different growth path to more conventional kinds of network effect. Quite how the value of these effects grows – and quite how relevant such effects are to users in the context of a particular service – is a matter for empirical investigation.

4.3 THE IMPLICATIONS OF NETWORK EFFECTS

4.3.1 *Network Effects, Business Strategy and Market Structure*

First- and second-order network effects can operate in tandem, reinforcing each other. Table 1 shows how a range of different technology businesses employ different combinations of network effect. Some businesses use only first-order network effects, with no or minimal personalisation. Unsurprisingly, this strategy is only readily apparent in sectors where the product offered and/or the users of the platform are largely undifferentiated. Cab firms such as Uber or Lyft ultimately sell all their customers the same product: a journey from one location to another. While they are diversifying somewhat – Uber, for instance, offers different service classes of car, ride-sharing and even electric scooters – the range of products to which users can be connected is still very limited, offering minimal scope for personalisation. It does not take an algorithm to work out that I will almost always prefer the cab that is available soonest, the shortest distance from my pick-up destination, and the same is true for the overwhelming majority of Uber's other customers. Similarly, Google Maps connects me to live travel information culled from other smartphone handsets in motion, providing me with information about any traffic problems on my intended route – but I am connected to this data in aggregate, and the information is linked to the journey proposed, rather than to personal data about my driving habits.[23]

By contrast, businesses which make a wide range of options available to their users (be these options content, goods, or services), but which do not rely on users to provide these options, tend to display second-order network effects but not first-order network effects. As mentioned previously, both Google Search and Netflix exhibit such personalisation effects. These effects can also be seen in Amazon's retail business, at least insofar as the products on offer come from Amazon's own inventory: both search results and unsolicited recommendations can be optimised on the basis of user data, prompting more sales (and, in theory, better-satisfied customers) than would otherwise be the case.[24] However, as discussed above, they can also be optimised to serve different goals, such as prioritising higher-margin products – which may reduce the positive network effect enjoyed by the user.

Finally, some tech businesses deploy both first-order and second-order network effects. This combination is obvious in the case of Facebook, where additional users create value for the existing user base by providing additional content and connections for users to enjoy (a first-order network effect), as well as by training algorithms to improve the matching of that content to existing users (a second-order network effect). Similar dynamics can be seen in the business models of retail portals such as Amazon Marketplace and eBay. Here, in addition to the first-order network effect whereby customers are attracted by the large pool of vendors, and vendors are attracted by the large pool of customers, customers and vendors are also better matched to each other as a result of the second-order network effect of data-driven personalisation.

What are the implications of data-driven personalisation for market structure? Depending on how valuable personalisation is to users of any given service, and how it interacts with any first-order network effects and economies of scale enjoyed by that service, second-order network effects may play an important role in increasing the costs of market entrance, thereby stifling competition. New challenger businesses, who lack the data amassed by incumbents, will struggle to offer a personalised service, and as a result will struggle to attract the user base necessary to develop such an offering. Moreover, stores of personal data and large existing user bases offer incumbents substantial advantages in adjacent sectors, allowing them to imitate and overtake new companies and products.[25] The fact that the Android user base can be effortlessly enlisted for any new Google offering, and that the likes of Google and Facebook already possess a vast compendium of data that can be used for personalisation purposes in new contexts, means that entrepreneurs who might otherwise consider a particular start-up venture may be deterred from doing so. In effect, the first-mover advantages that tech giants enjoy in their existing domains of operation give them an advantage over first-movers in *adjacent* sectors, stifling innovation and restricting consumer choice. Finally, amassing additional users and user data also makes it possible for a platform to tailor services to individual users to generate greater revenues, whether received directly from users themselves (through purchases and subscription fees) or indirectly (from other organisations seeking access to users and their data) – revenues which can be reinvested to further consolidate a platform's advantage over its competitors.

In sum, the competitive advantage conferred by sophisticated data-driven personalisation techniques, coupled with the limited number of businesses with the data required to operationalise these techniques, can contribute to highly concentrated market structures in some parts of the digital economy. Where a single platform dominates, or where a small number of viable rivals deploy similar business models, consumers are deprived of reference points by which to critically assess the kind of personalisation they are receiving, let alone exercise meaningful choice over a range of different options. Absent alternatives, consumers cannot determine whether or not they are receiving recommendations that genuinely enhance their wellbeing, as opposed to recommendations that serve instead to exacerbate their anxieties about missing out, or to maximise the commercial gain of platform owners and their paying customers. Market concentration may also aggravate some of the less savoury features of data-driven personalisation. Consumers' economic powerlessness might force them to support business models that engage in stereotyping, cultivate addiction, or propagate misinformation; lack of choice might limit their ability to veto the sale of their personal data to particular organisations and/or for particular purposes (such as political marketing, credit checks, insurance assessments, recruitment decisions or law enforcement).

4.3.2 *Public Policy of Personalisation and Attendant Market Concentration*

What are the policy implications of understanding the competitive advantage conferred by data-driven personalisation as a matter of network effects, rather than of data? Policy interventions that aim to tackle the negative consequences of market concentration generally fall into two brackets: interventions that seek to increase competition in the market in question, and interventions that seek to mitigate the lack of competition. Markets characterised by strong network effects do not only display a tendency towards concentration; moreover, it is generally *efficient* for these markets to be concentrated, as they operate in effect as natural monopolies. Because users derive benefits from other users subscribing to the same platform or standard, a situation where the user base is fragmented across multiple different platforms or standards is likely to be sub-optimal, from a user perspective. Consequently, policy interventions that attempt to tackle the negative consequences of market concentration by facilitating competition between incompatible platforms and standards may result in products that consumers find less useful, and/or in markets that display only a brief window of contestation before once again 'tipping' in favour of a dominant player. Examples of such policy interventions include efforts to break up monopolistic and quasi-monopolistic companies into competing rivals, preventing mergers and acquisitions that reduce the number of competitors in a particular domain, as well as regulatory measures to facilitate the portability of individual user data across different platforms. Without further efforts to address the structure of markets in which data-driven personalisation plays an important role, such interventions will either fail to tackle market concentration, or do so at the expense of consumer welfare.

A more promising strategy for policymakers trying to increase competition in the face of network effects is to insist upon the interoperability of standards and platforms. Interoperable standards allow members of one network to communicate with members of another network, accessing the goods, services and content that those people have to offer. Such open standards have played a pivotal role in the development of our digital world: email protocols are an example of one such standard, HTML another. Interoperability eliminates the first-order network-effect incentive to join the most popular platform. If I can access my friends' Facebook posts via MySpace, or if I can access all drivers in my vicinity via my local taxi company's ride-hailing app (irrespective of whether said drivers work for Lyft and Uber), then my choice of digital platform will be dictated primarily by convenience and service quality (including the ways in which the platform operator uses my personal data), rather than by the historical choices made by other people.

However, it is harder to see how interoperability might apply in the case of the second-order network effects associated with data-driven personalisation: the scope of the data to be shared might be vast as well as highly personal, and the range of potential recipients ill-defined. I might be comfortable allowing Facebook to transmit my posts to another social network (or to the specific members of that network I want to connect with), but I might be less comfortable about Facebook transmitting personal details about my predilection for chess lessons or diet plans or hair-replacement surgery to any business seeking to develop any product involving data-driven personalisation. One possible solution to these problems is the sharing of anonymised data;[26] but anonymised data is of self-evidently limited value to challenger businesses competing to offer a personalised service to their users.

Given that competition cannot be easily cultivated in markets where data-driven personalisation makes a significant contribution to market concentration, policymakers might instead seek to restrict and channel market power arising from second-order network effects. The most obvious way in which they can do so is through regulation. Particularly with regard to digital services that constitute core components of the infrastructure of modern societies – foundations upon which communal activity is predicated, and without which we cannot participate fully in contemporary economic and social life – regulation may be appropriate to ensure that dominant suppliers do not engage in exploitative pricing, discrimination against individuals,[27] or denial of service to rivals. Such regulation recognises that today's tech giants – most notably, the 'Big Five' of Microsoft, Apple, Google (Alphabet), Amazon and Facebook – play an increasingly inescapable role in everyday interactions, akin to the role played by 'public utilities' such as rail, water, energy and telecommunications.[28] Where data-driven personalisation constitutes a core component of the competitive advantage enjoyed by dominant businesses, regulators might seek to monitor and constrain prices charged to consumers or to other businesses; ensure consumers and businesses enjoy equal access to services, on non-discriminatory terms; as well as mandate and enforce minimum service levels (which might include examining the way in which personalisation is deployed to generate both user benefit and commercial gain).

Another – potentially complementary – way in which market concentration can be made to work for the common good is through taxation. Monopolists generate super-normal profits, over and above what they would be able to earn in competitive markets. In theory, a properly designed excess profits tax could capture some of that value for wider society, without affecting the production and investment decisions of the monopolist. Indeed, there are compelling reasons to believe that governments *should* levy more revenues from businesses engaging in data-driven personalisation. Following international concern about the tax avoidance strategies of multinational companies, there is an emerging consensus that taxation rights should be better aligned with the locations in which value-enhancing economic activity is located.[29] As we have seen, the value generated by data-driven personalisation – both for users, through second-order network effects, and for platforms, who monetise their users and their data – is co-created by users themselves. This implies that the mere fact that a platform has users in a given jurisdiction could be enough to legitimise imposing a tax liability there – even if that platform was conceived, programmed, maintained, marketed, financed and owned elsewhere.[30]

A third policy alternative for mitigating the downsides of monopoly is nationalisation of the industry in question. Nationalisation offers a more direct way of achieving the same aims as regulation and taxation. Rather than regulating dominant private companies, to ensure that they do not abuse the dominance that they enjoy, a state-owned service provider might be directly mandated to behave in ways that are aligned with consumer interests and public values. Rather than attempting to tax the super-normal profits of a private business, state ownership would guarantee that any profits over and above operating and capital costs are returned to the public purse. Against such considerations must be weighed well-known concerns about the governance and economic efficiency of state-owned enterprises, once they are insulated from the disciplining influence of capital markets – concerns that are particularly acute given the ongoing importance of innovation in the digital sector. Moreover, it should also be remembered that bringing user data under collective democratic governance and direction does not prevent it from being used for purposes contrary to any given individual user's interest. Indeed, the prospect of putting the many thousands of terabytes of data held by private companies directly at the disposal of the state – and in particular, its security and law enforcement services – raises serious concerns about privacy, surveillance and liberty. Whatever Facebook's flaws, at least Mark Zuckerberg does not have an army or a police force at his disposal as well.

4.4 CONCLUSION

Data-driven personalisation techniques can provide users with better quality services. But they can simultaneously contribute to market concentration, generating second-order network effects that make rival platforms comparatively less attractive to users, as more and more people join the market-leading network. Such market structures are often efficient, but they may also lead to consumers and other businesses paying excessive prices for poorer services than would be the case under more competitive conditions. Moreover, lack of consumer choice may mean that other negative aspects of data-driven personalisation go unchecked: such as the (often opaque) prioritisation of commercial imperatives above user benefits, loss of privacy, profiling, echo chamber effects, the spread of disinformation and the cultivation of user addiction.

Arguments around the uses and abuses of data-driven personalisation techniques have often been framed in terms of data ownership, emphasising the relationship between the individual and the data that they produce, and the transactional way in which that data might be exchanged with various businesses. On this account, what matters is personal autonomy, as expressed through the choices of atomised consumers operating in a competitive marketplace. Consequently, any harms arising from data-driven personalisation can be mitigated by informed consent around how your data is used and what you are getting in return for it, as well as by broadening the range of outlets to whom you can choose to sell your data. Consumers who dislike the deals on offer can simply withhold their data.

Yet policy interventions premised on this account are unlikely to prove effective in sectors where network effects dominate. Forced competition will fragment networks, thereby making them less valuable to users, restoring competition for a brief window of time before the inherent winner-takes-most structure of these markets reasserts itself. This is because the value created by data-driven personalisation does not reside in individual data, but in the relationship between many individuals' data (as well as in the algorithms used to parse this information). Data-driven personalisation is a network effect, albeit as we have seen, one that differs in important ways from the network effects that have hitherto dominated discussions of the digital sector. Fragmenting this collectively generated value tends to diminish it. Consequently, if policymakers wish to mitigate the harms of market concentration arising from second-order network effects, they must intervene to tax and regulate dominant digital businesses themselves, rather than seeking to impose market discipline by cultivating competition. This is particularly important where withholding data is not a viable option for individuals – namely, where the platforms and services in question constitute vital infrastructure upon which broader social and economic activity is predicated.

One final observation. This chapter has focused primarily on the economic problem of market concentration, rather than the panoply of social, political and cultural harms sometimes associated with data-driven personalisation. This is not because market concentration is necessarily the most problematic dimension of these developments: rather, it is to help us to better define and delineate the range of challenges posed by data-driven personalisation. To what extent would concerns about stereotyping, discrimination, lack of privacy and echo chamber effects be allayed by a wider range of consumer choice? In so far as consumer choice is impractical given the natural structure of markets in which network effects play a significant role, what can substitute for its disciplining effect? Are we worried about private businesses having access to our personal information *per se*, or are we primarily concerned about the volume and granularity of data that can only be amassed by companies whose platforms we interact with and through, by (social) necessity, every day? Although market concentration might not be the most serious problem posed by data-driven personalisation, through addressing market concentration we may yet find that we tackle many of our wider concerns too.

NOTES

1 See, for example, Justus Haucap and Ulrich Heimeshoff, 'Google, Facebook, Amazon, eBay: is the Internet driving competition or market monopolization?' (2014) 11(1–2) *International Economics and Economic Policy* 49 https://doi.org/10.1007/s10368-013-0247-6; José van Dijck, Thomas Poell and Martijn De Waal, *The Platform Society: Public Values in a Connective World* (Oxford University Press 2018); Nick O'Donovan, 'From knowledge economy to automation anxiety: a growth regime in crisis?' (2020) 25 (2) *New Political Economy* 248.

2 Michael L Katz and Carl Shapiro, 'Network externalities, competition, and compatibility' (1985) 75(3) *American Economic Review* 424; W Brian Arthur, *Increasing Returns and Path Dependence in the Economy* (University of Michigan Press 1994); Michael L Katz and Carl Shapiro, 'Systems competition and network effects' (1994) 8(2) *Journal of Economic Perspectives* 93; Nicholas Economides, 'The economics of networks' (1996) 14(6) *International Journal of Industrial Organization* 673. For a survey of more recent literature, see Paul Belleflamme and Martin Peitz, 'Platforms and network effects' in Luis C Corchón and Marco A Marini (eds), *Handbook of Game Theory and Industrial Organization, Volume II: Applications* (Edward Elgar Publishing 2018).

3 Jean-Charles Rochet and Jean Tirole, 'Platform competition in two-sided markets' (2003) 1 (4) *Journal of the European Economic Association* 990; David S Evans and Richard Schmalensee, *The antitrust analysis of multi-sided platform businesses* (National Bureau of Economic Research No w18783 2013).

4 See, in particular, Arthur (n 2). For critical discussion, see Stan J Liebowitz and Stephen E Margolis, 'Path dependence, lock-in, and history' (1995) *Journal of Law, Economics and Organization* 205. Liebowitz and Margolis argue that superior challengers should still be able to emerge and compete successfully for market share; however, they assume agents possess information about other agents' views of the relative superiority of new alternatives, which would make coordination of a network shift relatively easy. In practice, people need both to agree to move, and to agree where to move to – both of which are difficult to assess in a landscape where our primary information about people's desires is the 'revealed' preference of their current network choice.

5 See, for example, Diane Coyle, *The Weightless World: Strategies for Managing the Digital Economy* (MIT Press 1999); Joseph Stiglitz, 'Public policy for a knowledge economy' (Remarks at the Department for Trade and Industry and Center for Economic Policy

Research 1999). For a useful overview of individual case studies of network effects, see David P McIntyre and Mohan Subramaniam, 'Strategy in network industries: a review and research agenda' (2009) 35(6) *Journal of Management* 1494 https://doi.org/10.1177/0149206309346734.

6 Indeed, Microsoft's own window of opportunity to become a platform-provider arose in part when the previously dominant platform-provider, IBM, opted to contract out operating system design in fear of antitrust action from the US government. For an accessible historical account of Microsoft's rise, and of the subsequent antitrust actions against it, see David Warsh, *Knowledge and the Wealth of Nations: A Story of Economic Discovery* (W. W. Norton & Company 2007) 343–369.

7 Reid Hoffman and Chris Yeh, *Blitzscaling: The Lightning-fast Path to Building Massively Valuable Companies* (HarperCollins 2018); David S Evans and Richard Schmalensee, 'Failure to launch: critical mass in platform businesses', (2010) 9(4) *Review of Network Economics* 1.

8 In 2018, Google and Facebook alone accounted for almost 60 per cent of the entire US digital advertising market. See Sheila Dang, 'Google, Facebook have tight grip on growing US online ad market: report' (*Reuters*, 5 June 2019) www.reuters.com/article/us-alphabet-facebook-advertising/google-facebook-have-tight-grip-on-growing-u-s-online-ad-market-report-idUSKCN1T61IV.

9 Stanley M Besen and Joseph Farrell, 'Choosing how to compete: strategies and tactics in standardization' (1994) 8(2) *Journal of Economic Perspectives* 117. It follows that the claim that a given sector is competitive because competition occurred earlier in the sector's lifecycle – found, for example, in Robert H Bork and J Gregory Sidak, 'What does the Chicago School teach about Internet search and the antitrust treatment of Google?' (2012) 8(4) *Journal of Competition Law and Economics* 663 – is not credible.

10 True, in a certain sense, Google Search connects me to content that other people have made available online, in the form of webpages; however, they have not provided that data exclusively to Google, and that content is not exclusively hosted by or made available through Google, hence a network effect does not arise. If you switch from Google Search to Bing or Ask, you can (in theory at least) access exactly the same content as you could before; these search engines may interpret your search terms and rank the results somewhat differently, but they all have access to the same public domain websites that you can access through Google.

Similarly, while the fact that advertisers are attracted to Google Search because of the volume of consumers they can access – which may seem to be a hallmark of a network effect, with users creating value for advertisers – the inverse is not true. It is *not* the case that users are attracted to said platform in order to access more advertising businesses (which differentiates Google Search from two-sided markets such as eBay, Airbnb, Taskrabbit, or even Uber), although obviously advertisers help to fund the service that users do want (as with any traditional ad-carrying media). In the case of Google Search, users are rather attracted by the promise of being able to search online content, irrespective of whether the content-creator has paid Google to advertise it or not. Users are also indifferent as to *how many* different advertisers advertise on Google Search – whereas the attraction of two-sided markets such as Uber and Amazon Marketplace is the possibility of accessing a range of vendors. For a related discussion, see Giacomo Luchetta, 'Is the

Google platform a two-sided market?' (2013) 10(1) *Journal of Competition Law and Economics* 185.

11 Fabrizio Silvestri, 'Mining query logs: turning search usage data into knowledge' (2010) 4(1-2) *Foundations and Trends in Information Retrieval* http://dx.doi.org/10.1561/1500000013.

12 It might be objected that what matters is the data, not the user base: so if a search engine assembled a great deal of historical information, then it could still provide a quality service if it lacked users. However, as Graef notes, some 'types of data, such as the search queries that users have been looking for, are more transient in value and are relevant over a shorter period of time'. Graef goes on to observe that the UK Competition and Markets Authority perceives such transience as a sign that control of data does *not* produce a permanent competitive advantage – see Inge Graef, 'Market definition and market power in data: the case of online platforms' (2015) 38(4) *World Competition* 473, 483. However, data transience does make the possession of an active user base more relevant to competitive advantage: it makes the network that generates data here and now, not the historically accumulated data set, the key resource.

13 Lina M Khan, 'Amazon's antitrust paradox' (2016) 126 *Yale Law Journal* 710.

14 Jason Furman and others, *Unlocking Digital Competition – Report of the Digital Competition Expert Panel* (HM Treasury 2019).

15 Note that 'better' is an ambiguous concept, capable of multiple interpretations. In practice, in making their recommendations 'better' for a given individual, platforms tend to assume that the individual is a rational and atomised vector of their economic impulses – that is to say, that the individual has no higher-order preferences, and no values requiring expression outside their individual consumption activity. Needless to say, both of these assumptions are highly questionable. It is far from clear whether making platforms more engaging to users is truly 'beneficial' for many individuals, as the burgeoning psychological literature on 'fear of missing out' and problematic use of smartphones or social-networking sites makes clear. It is also far from clear whether purely market-based interactions between individuals and platforms properly reflect the broader range of values that individuals hold, and which they might seek to express through collective action rather than individual transaction – for instance, values regarding universality of service provision, security of workers' rights, democratic accountability and responsiveness, and so forth.
On problematic social media usage, see Ursula Oberst and others, 'Negative consequences from heavy social networking in adolescents: the mediating role of fear of missing out' (2017) 55 *Journal of Adolescence* 51; Andrew K Przybylski and others, 'Motivational, emotional, and behavioral correlates of fear of missing out' (2013) 29(4) *Computers in Human Behavior* 1841; Jon D Elhai and others, 'Fear of missing out, need for touch, anxiety and depression are related to problematic smartphone use' (2016) 63 *Computers in Human Behavior* 509. On the conflict between the business models of Big Tech and the wider range of public values that historically applied to sectors in which Big Tech companies operate, see van Dijck, Poell and De Waal (n 1).

16 Arthur (n 2).

17 Allan Afuah, 'Are network effects really all about size? The role of structure and conduct' (2013) 34(3) *Strategic Management Journal* 257.

18 Compare Argenton and Prüfer's use of 'indirect network externalities' to describe the network effects involved in online search, in Cédric Argenton and Jens Prüfer, 'Search

engine competition with network externalities' (2012) 8(1) *Journal of Competition Law and Economics* 73. The present argument goes beyond Argenton and Prüfer's analysis by exploring the unique characteristics of this class of network effects, and also how these effects apply to a broad range of matching/recommender algorithms.

19 See Enric Junqué de Fortuny, David Martens and Foster Provost, 'Predictive modeling with big data: is bigger really better?' (2013) 1(4) *Big Data* 215 for a related discussion. Interestingly, the sparseness of online data sets – the fact that, given the size of the digital world, there is no data either way for most people about most things – means that recruiting additional users does continue to deliver marginal (albeit diminishing) benefits, even for very large data sets (including several million records). This would imply that network effects – and barriers to entry – continue to grow with the size of the user base, potentially indefinitely. See also the discussion of 'tail queries' in Graef (n 12), and discussion of the implications of data retention for search efficacy in Lesley Chiou and Catherine Tucker, *Search engines and data retention: Implications for privacy and antitrust* (National Bureau of Economic Research No w23815 2017).

20 Travis Clark, 'New data shows Netflix's number of movies has gone down by thousands of titles since 2010' (*Business Insider*, 20 February 2018) www.businessinsider.com/netflix-movie-catalog-size-has-gone-down-since-2010-2018-2. Which is not to say the problem is straightforward – for a discussion, see Xavier Amatriain, 'Beyond data: from user information to business value through personalized recommendations and consumer science' (CIKM'13: 22nd ACM International Conference on Information and Knowledge Management, San Francisco, October 2013) 2201 https://doi.org/10.1145/2505515.2514701.

21 'How many products does Amazon sell?' (*ScrapeHero*, April 2019) www.scrapehero.com/number-of-products-on-amazon-april-2019/.

22 'How Search organises information' (Google) www.google.com/intl/en_uk/search/how searchworks/crawling-indexing/.

23 At the time of writing, a Google Maps search for the same journey at the same time on different Google accounts appears to yield identical time predictions; they are not presently tailored to driving habits, such as one's tendency to adhere to speed limits. The introduction of 'Driving Mode' on Android handsets does, however, introduce an element of personalised prediction into the application. See Karissa Bell, 'Google Maps update will automatically predict driving directions' (*Mashable*, 14 January 2016) https://mashable.com/2016/01/13/google-maps-driving-mode/?europe=true.

24 First-order network effects do arise with regard to Amazon's product reviews: users generate content (user reviews and ratings) which attracts other users to the platform. Interestingly, these reviews can also be an input into the computation of personal recommendations for other users, improving the quality of matches between users and products (second-order effect), at the same time as increasing the quantity of user-generated content that other users can access via the platform.

25 Khan (n 13) argues that Amazon's ability to monitor product innovations on its Marketplace platform enables it to ape successful products as part of its own offering; its wealth of consumer data coupled with control over the sales platform itself then allows it to target its in-house products towards would-be consumers, driving the competitor from the market. Sabeel Rahman extends similar arguments to the 'infrastructural power' of Google

and Facebook, too. See K Sabeel Rahman, 'The new utilities: private power, social infrastructure, and the revival of the public utility concept' (2017) 39(5) *Cardozo Law Review* 1621. The stifling of innovation in adjacent markets emerged as a key concern of the UK's Digital Competition Expert Panel, too. See Furman and others (n 14).

26 Argenton and Prüfer (n 18). Anonymised data-sharing also features in the recommendations of the UK's Digital Competition Expert Panel.

27 Alix Langone, 'Amazon will ban you for making too many returns' (*Money*, 23 May 2018) http://money.com/money/5288702/amazon-return-policy-ban/.

28 Rahman (n 25); van Dijck, Poell and De Waal (n 1).

29 Historically, taxation rights were split between 'residence' and 'source' countries, but this 1920s compromise has proven increasingly inadequate in the face of modern business structures, and modern tax avoidance techniques. For a useful summary, see Michael P Devereux and John Vella, 'Are we heading towards a corporate tax system fit for the 21st century?' (2014) 35(4) *Fiscal Studies* 449.

30 In a January 2019 update to its work on the taxation of the digital economy, the OECD announced that it was exploring different approaches to apportioning corporate tax rights between jurisdictions, including a proposal that the role of uncompensated 'user contributions' be factored into consideration. See OECD, *Addressing the Tax Challenges of the Digitalisation of the Economy* (Policy Note, 23 January 2019).

PART II

Themes: Personal Autonomy, Market Choices and the
Presumption of Innocence

5

Hidden Personal Insights and Entangled in the Algorithmic Model: The Limits of the GDPR in the Personalisation Context

Michèle Finck

5.1 THE LIMITS OF THE GPDR

Personalisation is both driven by, and can produce, personal data, and thus it falls within the scope of the General Data Protection Regulation (GDPR).[1] As a consequence, the European data protection framework applies to data-driven personalisation. Yet, whereas there appears to be a general perception that data protection is suitable to function as a general legal framework for AI, it is important to remain realistic regarding both its opportunities and limitations. This chapter examines the application of certain elements of the GDPR to data-driven personalisation. There are hopes that the GPDR can serve as a general legal framework to govern the normative concerns that have emerged in relation to AI. However, as this chapter demonstrates, it is fundamentally inadequate to serve as a 'general AI law'. Whereas the Regulation indeed applies to the processing of personal data, it would be erroneous to frame it as a general 'AI law' capable of addressing *all* normative concerns around personalisation. Most critically, as the GDPR is largely focused on process rather than substance, it only has limited ambitions to impose normative demands on the substantive fairness of data usage.

The examination of select provisions of the GDPR will underline that there are various cross-cutting limitations inherent in the Regulation. First, the GDPR is partly built on the notion of individual self-determination, best illustrated by the fact that data subject consent generally legitimises the use of personal data. There is, however, ample reason to question whether individuals are really in a position to understand contemporary data ecosystems and the implications of their consent. Furthermore, in so far as data analytics also has powerful collective implications by shaping political, economic and social landscapes, the GDPR's focus on individual rights fails to capture these communal repercussions, and the impact of individual consent on the public interest. Second, issues abound regarding enforcement. Indeed, whereas the GDPR is based on the idea that the individual takes a proactive stance in enforcing her rights, in practice individuals rarely do so, and even if they did, the enforceability of their rights would be difficult, if not impossible, to implement, short of removing the entire model in which their data has been fed. Third, the GDPR is based on somewhat outdated understandings of personal data and related analysis practices. These points will be made through the analysis of three separate elements of the GDPR – focusing on the control mechanisms at the time of collection (consent), after collection (deletion and modification), and the power of big data analytics to yield highly sensitive insights about the individuals that an exclusive focus on their own personal data would not.

5.2 'I AGREE' AND THE SHORTCOMINGS OF PERSONAL AUTONOMY

The GDPR recognises different bases that make it lawful to 'process' (that is, 'use') personal data, including where such use is required in a contractual setting (such as for a contract between a bank and its customer).[2] Data subject consent can also legitimise the processing of personal data.[3] Consent appears to be the most frequently used lawful basis for personalisation. It is often needed as personalisation cannot usually be presumed to be included in the original purpose of data processing (the delivery of the service).[4] Indeed, in most cases, the 'collection of organisational metrics relating to service or details of user engagement, cannot be regarded as necessary for the provision of the service as the service could be delivered in the absence of processing such personal data'.[5] As such, consent 'would almost always be required', in particular for direct marketing, behavioural advertisement, data-brokering, location-based advertising or tracking-based digital market research.[6]

Whilst data subjects frequently consent to the use of their personal data for customisation, it is unclear whether they always understand the full implications of that action. Users consent to the collection and analysis of their personal data in accepting a company's terms of service (as they otherwise cannot use that service), or by clicking 'I agree' on cookie notices that pop up when visiting a website.[7] Whereas cookies are governed by the e-Privacy Regulation, the latter adopts the GDPR's standard of consent.[8] For example, in accepting Google's terms of service, users agree that their information is used for customisation such as 'providing recommendations, personalized content, and customized search results' as well as personalised ads.[9] In signing up for Facebook, users agree that their personal data is used 'to personalise features and content (. . .) and make suggestions for you (. . .) on and off our Products'.[10] Thus, by simply using an online service or by clicking away a cookie banner to use a website, users often unknowingly agree that their personal data, including information about their online behaviour on- and off-site, is used to drive personalisation.

Consent is based on the idea of informational self-determination, which is a core facet of privacy and data protection.[11] This goes back to a time when the collection and use of personal data was relatively straightforward, such as when citizens were asked to provide data in a citizen census and were able to understand the nature of the data they were providing, as well as what was being done with that data.[12] It is open to debate whether this can still be the case in light of the complex data ecosystems (which for instance often include third-party cookies to track users off-site) and processing techniques that have been developed over the past decades. There is growing empirical evidence that users of online services fail to grasp the implications thereof. A 2018 UK report revealed that 45 per cent are unaware that their online behaviour is used for targeted advertising, 83 per cent do not realise personal data about themselves is gathered from information shared by third parties (think of someone tagging you in a picture or a location on social media) and 62 per cent are unaware that their social network affects the news they see.[13] Beyond, even when users do read companies' terms of service, they generally fail to understand related implications for privacy and data protection.[14]

This phenomenon is exacerbated by the 'privacy paradox' according to which individuals care about privacy yet refrain from acting upon their preference in privileging data protection friendly services over others.[15] Different explanations have been put forward for this paradox, including general decision fatigue.[16] Indeed, only 6 per cent of UK internet users seem to have taken an active measure to reduce tracking for ends of personalised advertising.[17] This is not surprising given that it has been estimated that just reading all privacy policies the average citizen encounters in a year would take 76 days.[18] These facts underline that there is reason to question the suitability of consent as a legitimation for personal data collection and use.[19] Yet, even leaving aside these overarching concerns, consent may also prove unworkable in personalisation from a practical perspective.

The GDPR imposes a number of conditions on valid consent, which cannot easily be met in customisation contexts. The Regulation requires that consent must be given by a 'clear affirmative act' and be 'a freely given, specific, informed and unambiguous indication of the data subject's agreement to the processing of personal data'.[20] In *Planet49*, the ECJ recently confirmed that consent cannot be said to be actively given through pre-ticked boxes.[21] The practical implementation of these requirements is, however, highly unrealistic if we consider the many different steps and actors involved in the data ecosystems that feed personalisation.

In particular, the requirement that consent be given 'freely' might have far-reaching implications regarding personalisation. For example, can consent be freely given in the absence of a non-personalised alternative? Consent is not treated as freely given 'if the data subject has no genuine or free choice or is unable to refuse or withdraw consent without detriment'.[22] Thus there is no freely given consent if there is no option of choosing 'different personal data processing operations despite it being appropriate in the individual case, or if the performance of a contract, including the provision of a service, is dependent on the consent despite such consent not being necessary for such performance'.[23] It is worth stressing that a higher threshold is applied where consent is sought to legitimise personalisation in a context of data usage within a contractual relationship. So a bank could not rely on its bank-customer contract to offer personalised services to its customers (as personalisation is not necessary for the performance of the contract) and has to obtain additional consent from its clients for it (by making the customer agree to personalisation, e.g. through a pop-up box in a banking app).[24]

Where it is impossible for a user to use a service without consenting to personalisation, 'the user does not have a real choice, thus the consent is not freely given'.[25] There appears to be support for that position in CJEU case law and the practice of national supervisory authorities. In 2013, the CJEU held that consent cannot be used as a lawful basis for fingerprinting in the process of obtaining a passport as people need a passport and there is no alternative option available.[26] The UK Information Commissioner's Office has moreover warned that data controllers ought to avoid making consent a precondition of service as it must imply 'real choice and control' for individuals.[27] The Article 29 Working Party commented that where a mobile app for photo editing asks users to collect GPS location data for the use of its services and behavioural advertising, consent would not be valid if users cannot use the app without consenting to these purposes.[28] Indeed, as neither geo-localisation nor online behavioural advertising is necessary for photo editing and 'go beyond the delivery of the core service provided,' the consent 'cannot be considered as being freely given'.[29] Accordingly it appears that there is a presumption that consent is invalid unless there is an alternative to use the service in a non-personalised way.[30] In turn, this would result in a presumption that data subjects cannot consent to the use of their personal data for personalisation unless a non-personalised alternative is available to them – at least where it is not necessary for the 'core service'. Yet, in practice, service providers generally do not offer non-personalised alternatives to a personalised service.

It follows that consent will often not be the appropriate legal basis to process data for purposes of personalisation. Recent guidance from the EDPB also underlines that contract might not always be a suitable option. On the specific question of using contract as a lawful basis for personalisation, the EDPB opined that it 'may (but does not always) constitute an intrinsic and expected element of certain online services, and therefore may be regarded as necessary for the performance of the contract with the service user in some cases'.[31] Whether this is the case will depend on whether personalisation is an 'intrinsic aspect of an online service', to be determined on the basis of the nature of the service that is provided and the expectations of the 'average data subject in light not only of the terms of service but also the way the service is promoted to users, and whether the service can be provided without personalisation'.[32] These statements underline the difficulties for data controllers to identify a suitable legal basis to process personal data for personalisation purposes. As a consequence, at least some of them are likely to be further looking into the legitimate interest criterion.[33]

The above overview has underlined that consent is often used to legitimise personalisation even where the data subject may have no understanding that they are actually consenting to such processing, or what the implications of processing are. Indeed, the focus on informational self-determination on which consent is based has proven to have serious limitations in today's complex data ecosystems.

5.3 PERSONAL DATA CONTROL MECHANISMS AFTER THEIR COLLECTION

Recommendation algorithms are trained on training data, which is often personal data, before being deployed. This raises the question of how data subjects' rights that involve the modification or deletion of personal data can be reconciled with such characteristics of learning algorithms. There are indeed a number of scenarios in which the GDPR requires that data be modified or no longer processed, including the rights to rectification and erasure as well as the right of the data subject to withdraw consent from the processing of personal data.

Article 16 of the GDPR provides that data subjects have the right to request the rectification of personal data relating to them where such data is 'inaccurate'.[34] Taking account of the purposes of processing, this can be done through the rectification of inaccurate data, for instance by providing a supplementary statement.[35] Where a data subject thus invokes her rights under Article 16 and that claim is well founded, the data controller ought to make sure that the personal data is rectified. The data subject may wish to have data corrected, as it is inaccurate, but also because the personalised recommendations received are based on an erroneous assumption and hence useless. For instance, data subjects may find out that inaccurate data relating to them is processed, such as that they live in Spain whereas in reality they reside in Sweden. That request may be motivated simply by a desire to not have inaccurate data about them circulate or by a desire to stop receiving personalised advertisements for events in Spain.

By the same token, where personal data was collected on the basis of consent rather than one of the other legal bases, that consent is revocable. Thus, for example, where a data subject has consented to the processing of genetic data collected through blood testing for medical purposes, and only realises the implications of that decision later on, the subject has the option of revoking consent. Article 7(3) provides that a data subject 'shall have the right to withdraw his or her consent at any time'. Whereas a withdrawal of consent does not affect the lawfulness of processing based on consent that has occurred prior to withdrawal, it requires the data controller stop processing data once withdrawal has occurred.

Article 17 of GDPR moreover provides that data subjects have, in some circumstances, the right to have their data erased (the 'right to be forgotten'). Where the data subject wants to invoke the right to erasure, an open question is whether Article 17 also applies to observed and inferred data, such as a user's behaviour on a platform. Whereas there is no authoritative answer to that question, it is worth noting that the Article 29 Working Party excluded inferred data from the scope of the right to data portability.[36] However, this was done on the basis of the argument that such data is, contrary to the wording of Article 20 of GDPR, not 'provided by the data subject' – a reasoning that cannot, as such, be transposed to Article 17. Another interesting question is whether a data subject (or group of data subjects) could request the erasure of a model on the basis of the argument that the model itself is personal data. Notably, it has been shown that in some contexts model inversion attacks may allow for the reconstruction of the personal data underlying the trained model.[37]

In each of the above scenarios, data controllers are legally obliged to modify, delete or stop processing personal data. Yet, wherever that data has been used to train the personalisation algorithm, these actions are far from straightforward. Recent computer science research has underlined that solutions to achieve the efficient deletion of individual data points from trained machine learning models are still in their infancy.[38] At present, the complete removal of data could often only be achieved by retraining the model from scratch on the remaining data, which is a computationally intensive exercise and thus neither economical, practical nor environmentally desirable.[39] However, the same research has also shown that alternatives may be possible and deserve further inquiry.[40] The lack of satisfactory mechanisms to remove or modify personal data from a recommender system where needed is particularly problematic, due to the ability in some circumstances to infer personal data from a trained model through a model inversion attack, as mentioned above.[41] The inextricability of personal data from the algorithmic model built upon (big) data sets presents a serious concern about the practical effectiveness and, indeed, technical possibility of GDPR rights. On a more profound level, it also speaks to the very nature of personalisation as occupying an ambiguous and conflictual space between the individual and the group, where relative personal uniqueness only emerges from, and exists against, human commonality – an aspect which data protection law with its singular focus on the individual fails to consider, but which is dramatically enacted through recommender algorithms fed on large personal data sets.

On a related matter, data protection law – with its technical legal jargon applied to technical processes – may also prove tone-deaf to the possibility of varied constructions of 'inaccurate' in the context of Article 16's right to rectification. Again this has been brought out in the personalisation context, especially where it is based on emotional targeting. In emotional targeting, user profiles are created on the basis of a presumed psychological state. For instance, Facebook Australia used to sell advertising data of a user group of presumably psychologically vulnerable teenagers.[42] Facebook sought to determine when teenagers were experiencing a negative emotional state, such as feeling 'insecure' or 'worthless', and share such information with advertisers interested in making use of this vulnerability to sell their products or services.[43] Many other examples exist, such as information on women's moods collected by menstruation tracking apps that share the information with Facebook (which then shares it with advertisers).[44]

In such contexts, information about someone's emotional state is acquired on the basis of self-declaration or through inferences made on the basis of behavioural observations about users. Unlike objective facts (like age or employment status), such classifications operate on a spectrum and can be difficult to assess objectively. This raises the question of the remedies available to parties that have been inaccurately classified. Indeed, if Facebook believes that a user is psychologically vulnerable, would it be sufficient for that user to self-declare that they are not, in fact, psychologically vulnerable in order to obtain the rectification of such data under Article 16 GDPR? There is reason to believe that this is not necessarily the case. In its guidelines issued in the aftermath of *Google Spain*,[45] the Working Party considered that accurate means 'accurate as to a matter of fact'.[46] Whereas these guidelines were adopted in the context of the right to erasure rather than correction, the terminology should arguably be given homogenous meaning throughout the text. This would then leave data subjects with little remedy against wrongful classifications that serve as a basis for personalisation.

Machine learning underlines the tension between data protection law as an individualistic framework, and the fact that systems of computational learning often work with the classification of groups. Data protection law is generally individual-focused (as is the law, and human rights law particularly, in general), but now has to govern an integrated and collective-focused system. The collected data has an undeniably collective dimension, as the data subject is profiled on the basis of data about the behaviour or preferences of other people that have been identified and classified on the basis of training data.[47] For example, if you wished to make a purchase on an e-commerce website and your payment is denied on the basis of other clients in your neighbourhood having a history of insolvency, it matters little if you yourself are not in fact insolvent.[48] This again highlights enforcement difficulties but also that the GDPR's focus on the individual offers little remedy to collective algorithmic harms.

5.4 SENSITIVE INFERENCES FROM NON-SENSITIVE 'PROXY' DATA

The GDPR applies to all personal data but also has a more protective regime for so-called 'special category' or 'sensitive data'. This includes personal data that reveals racial or ethnic origin, political opinions, religious or philosophical beliefs, trade union membership, the processing of genetic and biometric data in view of uniquely identifying a natural person, health data as well as data concerning a person's sex life or sexual orientation.[49] The idea behind this special category is that these matters are of an intensely personal nature and thus should attract heightened protection. Yet, there are many circumstances in which sensitive data is used in the context of recommender systems. For instance, evidence suggests that the Facebook algorithm deciding which ads are shown to a given user takes into account characteristics such as race, gender and religion.[50] As a result, postings for preschool teachers and secretaries were shown to a higher fraction of women, whereas men more often were shown ads for taxi drivers.[51] Already in 2013, Latanya Sweeney highlighted that the Google ad-serving algorithm showed online advertisements of arrest records more often for searches for black-sounding names than white-sounding names.[52] A recently much-discussed example of processing sensitive data through machine learning is facial recognition technologies that classify facial features in pictures or videos in order to identify individuals in previously unseen pictures or videos.[53] In each of these scenarios, data that qualifies as sensitive personal data under the GDPR is used to train machine learning models.

In principle, such data benefits from the special protective regime under Article 9 (1) GDPR which states that its processing is 'prohibited',[54] unless the data subject 'has given explicit consent' or in a number of other scenarios less relevant to personalisation.[55] Whether this special regime applies depends on whether a given data point qualifies as sensitive data – a task that is particularly difficult where computational intelligence is used. Article 9 GDPR assumes that data can be neatly classified into ordinary personal data (subject to the general GDPR regime) and special category data (subject to the more protective sub-regime). However, big data analytics have made such simplicity a thing of the past. Personalisation algorithms may use explicitly sensitive data (such as data regarding sexual orientation where this has been explicitly disclosed, for instance on a dating platform) to classify users according to preferences and often to sell related profiles for advertising purposes as well.[56] However, machine learning can also infer sensitive information from data that is not, ostensibly, sensitive. In this case, 'ordinary personal data' becomes proxy data for sensitive data. For example, researchers have unveiled that Facebook 'friendships' may reveal sexual orientation,[57] just as Facebook 'likes' that are not themselves related to a person's romantic or intimate life may do, too.[58]

As a matter of law, it would appear that proxy data itself amounts to sensitive data under the GDPR, as sensitive data is 'not only data which by its nature contains sensitive information (...) but also data from which sensitive information with regard to an individual can be concluded'.[59] By implication, profiling 'can create special category data by inference from data which is not special category data in its own right but becomes so when combined with other data'.[60] This means that the more data becomes available and the more analytics techniques develop, the easier it will be to infer sensitive attributes from ostensibly non-sensitive data, meaning that potentially any data point may qualify as sensitive personal data.

Yet, as inferences only ever denote a correlation, and not causation, a question that arises is what level of certainty about a sensitive attribute is necessary for an inference to fall under Article 9 GDPR. For example, an analysis of proxy data might indicate that a given individual is politically conservative or diabetic. Yet, the algorithm's loss function (the metric that evaluates how well the algorithm models the data) might indicate that the algorithm only has a certainty of 85 per cent that this is actually the case. Should the information about political orientation and health hence be qualified as sensitive data, although it may not be true and is not based on the analysis of actual personal data relating to health and political inclination? More generally, however, it appears that it is not necessary for information to be correct in order for it to qualify as personal data under the GDPR.

Assuming that proxy data does indeed qualify as personal data, a number of consequences follow. First, the temporal dimension of classification as sensitive data is not clear: should such data be classified as sensitive data from the start, or only after a sensitive attribute has been inferred, and if so, whether this inference needs to be based on a certain level of confidence. Second, data controllers need to comply with the GDPR regime on sensitive data once data is classified accordingly. This, for instance, implies an obligation to carry out a Data Protection Impact Assessment, which is generally required where personal data processing results in a 'high risk' for data subjects.[61] Moreover, the legal obligations in relation to gathering data subject consent as well as the application of Article 22 GDPR are subject to change.

Whilst, as shown above, the threshold for valid consent is high and often not met for personalisation, it is even higher in relation to sensitive data as here the GDPR requires that 'explicit' consent be given. Explicit consent is not defined in the Regulation but has been understood to require compliance with the ordinary criteria for valid consent (it must be specific, informed and unambiguous) and in addition be 'affirmed in a clear statement (whether oral or written)'.[62] Considering the need for such explicit consent – for both the non-sensitive proxy data leading to a sensitive inference and other sensitive source data, which inform a personalised service, it is fair to conclude that many data controllers are not GDPR compliant. Further clarification on these matters is especially imperative for contexts where a fair outcome of the processing of special category data is particularly important.[63] These contexts really highlight the inadequacy and outdatedness of the GDPR's categories of data. Not only are the examples of sensitive information restrictive and they do not capture some of the data that allows for the highly sensitive inferences about an individual, but the application of the current regime may lead to the classification of large quantities of personal data as sensitive data, something that was likely not the legislator's intention.

5.5 OUTLOOK

The examination of the GDPR's provisions on consent, requirements around the rectification and deletion of personal data, as well as special category data in contexts of personalisation driven by machine learning, has revealed some fundamental limitations in the EU data protection framework. The GDPR's focus on informational self-determination stands in tension with the limited ability of individuals to understand the complex contemporary data ecosystems and the various constraints on opting out of a personalisation model, even where such understanding may be present. Furthermore, the GDPR is deeply anchored in the notion of individual rights, whereas data analysis in the personalisation context has a strong collective dimension, which can deliver highly sensitive insights about the individual that would not be apparent to a human observer purely on the basis of her own personal data. This then undermines the value of GDPR categorisation of personal data into more or less sensitive data. The collective dimension also impacts on the enforcement of data protection rights which makes it difficult to 'extract' the individual from the group, or personal data from big data.

The aim of this chapter was to highlight some of the limitations of the GDPR regarding customisation. Further research will be needed to explore them more fully and develop solutions. This should focus in particular on how alternatives of enforcement (compared to the limited leeway of individual data subjects) could be encouraged. Some mechanisms already foreseen in the GDPR in this respect, such as data protection by design and by default, might be used to re-develop the same technical tools that enable personalisation on the offer side to drive personalisation on the demand side. For example, models could 'learn' their users' preferences (such as through an initial Q&A coupled with the monitoring of subsequent behaviour) to, for instance, automatically indicate cookie preferences and select appropriate additional privacy-preserving technology. Similarly, the GDPR's attempt to create a data protection through Data Protection Impact Assessments and certification could be strengthened through additional mechanisms, such as a stronger empowerment of supervisory authorities, NGOs and civil society that would give teeth to existing legal obligations. Beyond this, there may be a need for legislative action (either in the form of new legislation or a revision of the GDPR) to address issues of collective algorithmic harm or other regulatory problems in relation to computational intelligence that are not currently covered by the GDPR.

NOTES

The author wishes to thank Uta Kohl for very helpful comments on an earlier version of this chapter as well as Kai Ebert for excellent research assistance.

1 Regulation (EU) 2016/679 of the European Parliament and of the Council on the protection of natural persons with regard to the processing of personal data and on the free movement of such data [2016] OJ L119/1 (hereafter GDPR). Whereas I limit my analysis to the GDPR, the e-Privacy Regulation or the Law Enforcement Directive may also apply.
2 Ibid. Article 6(1)(b).
3 Ibid. Article 6(1)(a).
4 The principle of purpose limitation in Article 5(1)(b) reads as follows: personal data ought to be 'collected for specified, explicit and legitimate purposes and not further processed in a manner that is incompatible with those purposes; further processing for archiving purposes in the public interest, scientific or historical research purposes or statistical purposes shall, in accordance with Article 89(1), not be considered to be incompatible with the initial purposes'.

5 European Data Protection Board, Guidelines 2/2019 on the processing of personal data under Article 6(1)(b) GDPR in the context of the provision of online services to data subjects (2019) 14.

6 Article 29 Working Party, Opinion 03/2013 on purpose limitation (WP 203) 00569/13/ EN, 46.

7 Cookies are essentially a small piece of data sent from a website and stored on the user's device. They are one of the technical tools used to achieve personalisation as they register users' browsing history, stateful information (such as items added to a virtual shopping bag) and information previously filled into specific fields (such as an address).

8 See further Directive 2002/58/EC of the European Parliament and of the Council of 12 July 2002 concerning the processing of personal data and the protection of privacy in the electronic communications sector (e-Privacy Directive) [2002] OJ L201/37, recital 17.

9 Google, 'Privacy Policy' (15 October 2019) https://policies.google.com/privacy?fg= 1#whycollect.

10 Facebook, 'Data Policy' (19 April 2019) https://en-gb.facebook.com/privacy/explanation.

11 Volkszählungsurteil, BVerfGE 65, 1.

12 Ibid.

13 Catherine Miller, Rachel Coldicutt and Hannah Kitcher, 'People, Power and Technology: The 2018 Digital Understanding Report' (*Doteveryone*, 2018) 6 https:// doteveryone.org.uk/report/digital-understanding/.

14 Omri Ben-Shahar and Carl Schneider, 'The failure of mandated disclosure' (2011) 159 *University of Pennsylvania Law Review* 647.

15 Alessandro Acquisti and Jens Grossklags, 'Privacy and rationality in individual decision-making' (2005) 3 *IEEE Security and Privacy* 26, 29.

16 Kathleen Vohs and others, 'Making choices impairs subsequent self-control: a limited resource account of decision making, self-regulation and active initiative' (2008) 94 *Journal of Personality and Social Psychology* 883.

17 Miller, Coldicutt and Kitcher (n 14) 23.

18 Alexis C Madrigal, 'Reading the privacy policies you encounter in a year would take 76 work days' (*The Atlantic*, 1 March 2012) www.theatlantic.com/technology/archive/ 2012/03/reading-the-privacy-policies-you-encounter-in-a-year-would-take-76-work-days/ 253851/.

19 See further Elettra Bietti, 'Consent as a free pass: platform power and the limits of the informational turn' (2019) *Pace Law Review* (forthcoming).

20 GDPR (n 2) recital 32.

21 Case C-673/17 *Planet49* [2019] ECLI:EU:C:2019:801.

22 GDPR (n 2) recital 42.

23 Ibid. recital 43.

24 Ibid. Article 7(4).

25 Eleni Kosta, 'Peeking into the cookie jar: the European approach towards the regulation of cookies' (2013) 21 *International Journal of Law and Information Technology* 380, 396.

26 Case C-291/12 *Schwartz* [2013] ECLI:EU:C:2013:670, para 32.

27 Information Commissioner's Office, 'Guide to the General Data Protection Regulation (GDPR) – Consent' (*ICO*) https://ico.org.uk/for-organisations/guide-to-data-protection/ guide-to-the-general-data-protection-regulation-gdpr/lawful-basis-for-processing/consent/.

28 The Article 29 Working Party has now been replaced by the European Data Protection Board.

29 Article 29 Working Party, Guidelines on consent under Regulation 2016/679 (WP259 rev.01) 17/EN, 6.

30 Frederik Borgesius and others, 'Tracking walls, take-it-or-leave-it choices, the GDPR, and the eprivacy regulation' (2018) 3 *European Data Protection Law Review* 353, 361 (making this argument in relation to consent for tracking walls on websites).

31 Ibid.

32 Ibid.

33 Pursuant to Article 6(1)(f) GDPR, 'processing is necessary for the purposes of the legitimate interests pursued by the controller or by a third party, except where such interests are overridden by the interests or fundamental rights and freedoms of the data subject which require protection of personal data, in particular where the data subject is a child'.

34 Pursuant to Article 16 GDPR, 'The data subject shall have the right to obtain from the controller without undue delay the rectification of inaccurate personal data concerning him or her. Taking into account the purposes of the processing, the data subject shall have the right to have incomplete personal data completed, including by means of providing a supplementary statement'.

35 GDPR (n 2) art 16.

36 Article 29 Working Party, Guidelines on the right to data portability (WP 242 rev.01) 16/EN.

37 Michel Veale, Reuben Binns and Lilian Edwards, 'Algorithms that remember: model inversion attacks and data protection law' (2018) 376 *Philosophical Transactions Royal Society* A https://royalsocietypublishing.org/doi/10.1098/rsta.2018.0083.

38 Antonio Ginart and others, 'Making AI Forget You: Data Deletion in Machine Learning' (33rd Conference on Neural Information Processing Systems NeurIPS 2019, Vancouver, December 2019) https://arxiv.org/abs/1907.05012v1.

39 Ibid.

40 Ibid.

41 Veale, Binns and Edwards (n 38).

42 Sam Levin, 'Facebook told advertisers it can identify teens feeling "insecure" and "worthless"' *The Guardian* (London, 1 May 2017) www.theguardian.com/technology/2017/may/01/facebook-advertising-data-insecure-teens.

43 Ibid.

44 'No Body's Business But Mine: How Menstruation Apps Are Sharing Your Data' (*Privacy International*, 9 September 2019) www.privacyinternational.org/long-read/3196/no-bodys-business-mine-how-menstruations-apps-are-sharing-your-data.

45 Case C-131/12 *Google Spain v AEPD* [2014] EU:C:2014:317.

46 Article 29 Working Party, Guidelines on the Implementation of The Court of Justice of the European Union Judgment on Google Spain v AEPD C-131/12 (WP 225) 14/EN.

47 As per GDPR (n 2) art 4(4), profiling means 'means any form of automated processing of personal data consisting of the use of personal data to evaluate certain personal aspects relating to a natural person, in particular to analyse or predict aspects concerning that natural person's performance at work, economic situation, health, personal preferences, interests, reliability, behaviour, location or movements'.

48 Particularly if Article 22 GDPR does not apply.
49 GDPR (n 2) art 9(1).
50 Muhammad Ali and others, 'Discrimination through optimization: how Facebook's ad delivery can lead to skewed outcomes' (2019) 3 Proceedings of the ACM on Human-Computer Interaction https://dl.acm.org/doi/abs/10.1145/3359301.
51 Ibid.
52 Latanya Sweeney, 'Discrimination in online ad delivery: Google ads, black names and white names, racial discrimination, and click advertising' (2013) 11(3) *ACMQueue* https://queue.acm.org/detail.cfm?id=2460278.
53 Note, however, that facial recognition is merely one way of identifying in dividuals on the basis of their bodily features.
54 GDPR (n 2) art 9(1).
55 GDPR (n 2) art 9(2)(a).
56 José González Cabañas, Ángel Cuevas and Rubén Cuevas, 'Facebook use of sensitive data for advertising in europe' (2018) Arxiv https://arxiv.org/abs/1802.05030.
57 Carter Jernigan and Behram Mistree, 'Gaydar: Facebook friendships expose sexual orientation' (2009) 14 *First Monday* https://firstmonday.org/article/view/2611/2302.
58 Teo Armus, 'Facebook can tell whether you're gay based on a few "likes", study says' (*NBC News*, 22 Nov 2017) www.nbcnews.com/feature/nbc-out/facebook-can-tell-if-you-re-gay-based-few-likes-n823416.
59 Article 29 Working Party, Advice paper on special categories of data ("sensitive data"), Ref Ares(2011) 444105 – 20/04/2011 6.
60 Article 29 Working Party, Guidelines on automated individual decision-making and profiling for the purposes of Regulation 2016/679 (WP 251 rev 01) 17/EN 15.
61 GDPR (n 2) art 35(1).
62 Information Commissioner's Office, 'Guide to the General Data Protection Regulation (GDPR) – What is valid consent?' https://ico.org.uk/for-organisations/guide-to-data-protection/guide-to-the-general-data-protection-regulation-gdpr/consent/what-is-valid-consent/.
63 Niki Kilbertus and others, 'Blind Justice: Fairness with Encrypted Sensitive Attributes' (2018) 80 Proceedings of the 35th International Conference on Machine Learning 2630.

6

Personalisation, Markets, and Contract: The Limits of Legal Incrementalism

TT Arvind

6.1 INTRODUCTION

This chapter argues that data-driven personalisation poses risks for ordinary individuals which the legal system has largely failed to ameliorate. The legal approach to regulating the gathering and use of data has been shaped by analogies with existing legal norms and the reuse of existing legal concepts and categories – in particular, those associated with 'privacy' and 'consent'. In principle, the heuristic reuse of existing legal categories is both sensible and defensible, in that those categories bring with them a range of legal tools, principles, and evaluative frameworks on which judges or regulators can draw in dealing with a new social problem.[1] Nevertheless, it also has a weakness[2] which is of particular relevance to data-driven personalisation. The reuse of existing categories and concepts to deal with a new social problem implies making an analogy between the new phenomenon and the existing phenomena which the categories were originally devised to cover. There are, however, two reasons why such an analogy might fail, the first relating to its problem-solving power, and the second to its normative power. Both of these apply to data-driven personalisation, as this chapter will show.

Firstly, although legal analogies have considerable problem-solving power, they can divert attention away from matters that are unique to the new phenomenon and have no counterpart in existing phenomena.[3] Legal reasoning, and legal analogies, are shaped by 'exemplars' – paradigmatic instances of the application of a framework to a type of situation.[4] These exemplars underpin and give force to the analogical extension of a legal category such as 'privacy' or 'consent' to a new situation: they claim, in effect, that the new situation is sufficiently like the old one to give privacy and consent the same problem-solving power and normative appeal that they have in their core domain. What, then, if this claim is false, and privacy and consent do not in fact produce outcomes which are satisfactory, once close attention is paid to the context? The second part of this chapter argues that this fatally flaws the privacy-based approach which has become the major regulatory response to data-driven personalisation.[5] This key dimension distinguishing data-driven personalisation from the traditional, 'core' domain of privacy lies in the role contract plays in enabling data-driven personalisation. Contract is largely immaterial to the core domain of privacy. The person infringing the claimant's privacy is rarely, if ever, in a contractual relationship with the claimant.[6] Data-driven personalisation, in contrast, is deeply enmeshed in contractual relationships. Unlike a typical 'offline' infringement of privacy, the initial gathering of data, as well as each of the key steps in its subsequent use, are mediated by contract. This has significant implications for how we think about the process of personalisation and its impact on individuals, as well as for the efficacy of privacy and consent as tools for dealing with the deleterious consequences of this impact.

The second reason why an analogy might fail relates to the implicit assumptions on which a concept or category is based. In the third part of this chapter, I argue that the conceptual apparatus of privacy and contract are built on the assumption that consensual transactions operate to enhance both parties' autonomy. This assumption, however, fails in relation to data-driven personalisation, which creates a new de-relationalised type of personalisation which calls into question not just standard understandings of personalisation, but also important aspects of what are assumed to be the underpinnings of markets and contracting, in ways that erode, rather than enhance, the data subject's autonomy. Neither privacy nor consent offers effective ways of dealing with the issues this poses, in both cases because of their reliance on a particular, ideal-typical image of interaction grounded in the idea of autonomous, freely consenting transactors.[7] The consequence is that the law fails not only to respond to the actual social harm caused by data-driven personalisation, but also to provide evaluative tools that can be used to identify situations where legal action is necessary.

The chapter concludes that dealing with these problems requires reframing the issue, by stepping outside established analogies and considering the phenomenon *de novo*. There is, in particular, a need to grasp the nettle of understanding that the resistance of data-driven personalisation to traditional legal controls is a consequence of the role played by contract in enabling the gathering and processing of data. Dealing effectively with the issue requires using concepts and structures which move beyond the law's traditional reliance on autonomy, and are capable of responding to the complexity of the new context introduced by personalisation.

6.2 RECONCEPTUALISING PERSONALISATION: LAW, DATA, CONTRACT

Legal responses to data-driven personalisation have been shaped in large part by periodic concerns about the underlying technology that enables personalisation.[8] As a result, the law remains grounded in a technological framing, and focuses on three elements of personalisation: firstly, the use of computational means – such as cookies, trackers, and databases – to gather data about internet usage and store it in a manner that creates a detailed historical profile of an individual; secondly, aggregating data about an individual gathered from different sources; and thirdly, algorithmically processing that data to draw inferences about an individual's personal characteristics, and using those inferred characteristics to shape future interactions with that individual.[9]

This focus on the means by which data is collected and analysed explains the role concepts rooted in privacy have played in shaping legislation. There are obvious and tempting parallels between the intrusive surveillance and monitoring of private persons by commercial actors that prompted the early leading cases in privacy,[10] and the intensive monitoring of online behaviour that underpins data-driven personalisation. In consequence, privacy has become the main conceptual framework used in thinking about data-driven personalisation. Other frameworks, when used, have been confined to specific issues peculiar to particular sectors – for example, in relation to insurance where regulators have set explicit limits on what personalisation can and cannot be used for.[11]

The analogy with privacy is, however, at best an imperfect one. The exemplars that shape juristic thinking about privacy are concerned with the non-consensual acquisition of data, typically through surveillance by strangers. *Von Hannover v Germany*,[12] which related to the unauthorised, intrusive, and incessant taking of photographs of the applicant by freelance photographers while the applicant was in a public place, is the paradigmatic example. Data-driven personalisation, in contrast, typically involves the consensual acquisition of data, by parties with whom one has a contractual relationship. The paradigmatic example is an online service such as Facebook or Google, which acquires its right to use and analyse a user's data consensually, in accordance with contractual terms of service which the user has been presented with and accepted.[13]

The contractual underpinnings of data-driven personalisation are not trivial. Data-driven personalisation depends on, and is impossible without, a supportive framework provided by contract. In a naturalistic sense, 'data' is simply an aggregation of knowledge about human action and the preferences, motives, and other characteristics that underlie that action. As a type of knowledge, it is necessarily a public good. Unlike a peppercorn, the same data can be used by multiple persons without the data in any way being harmed or diminished, making their use 'non-rivalrous'. Equally, there is nothing inherent in knowledge or data that requires or facilitates excludability. Data-driven personalisation, in contrast, is predicated on treating data as a private good: a commodity which is capable of being acquired, accumulated, and transferred through market transactions. The transformation of a public good (knowledge) into a private good (data) depends on a legal framework that permits data to acquire the legal properties of a commodity.[14] As Table 6.1 shows, it is precisely this framework that the contractual underpinnings of data-driven

TABLE 6.1. *Personalisation and contract*

Requirements for commercial use of data	Legal support necessary to enable broad use of data	Contractual underpinnings of commercial use of data
Ability to collect data	Endowing data with a quasi-proprietary character	License to gather and store
Ability to accumulate data	Commodification of data, permitting free or qualified transferability	Interfirm agreement to transfer data to partners, user license to aggregate collected data with third-party data
Ability to create and use profiles through algorithmic processing of data	Freedom to exploit information derived from processing data	Generalised terms of service permitting deployment of personalisation tools for unspecified purposes

personalisation provide. Contracts provide, firstly, the means through which data is generated and collected. The right to collect personal data, for example, is typically created through terms of service. Secondly, contracts also provide the means through which data is transmitted and exchanged between different entities. An entity holding data about an individual can and does pass the data on to other parties through a contractual transfer, for which authorisation is sought from the data subject through terms of service. Thirdly, contracts are the instruments through which data-driven personalisation is effectuated, and through which a company acquires the right to use information inferred about an individual, including in a manner which may be in its interests, but not in those of the individual.

Contracts, in this sense, are the conduit through which the ability to gather, analyse, and exploit data is channelled. This results in a sharp, and important, divergence between the empirical reality of data-driven personalisation and the doctrinal structure of privacy. Whereas contracts are an intrinsic part of data-driven personalisation, the exemplars that inform doctrinal thinking about privacy are characterised by the *absence* of contract: even if the personal information that is their subject could have been acquired contractually, it is the fact that it has been acquired without contractual consent that is the causative event underpinning the action.

This makes the sort of transactions that are the subject of data-driven personalisation materially different from the exemplars on which we rely when thinking about privacy. The point of privacy is to set boundaries on self-serving action. The point of contract is to enable it. The structure of contract law, and the underlying logic of party autonomy, means that contracts are lightly regulated. Contracts, in the legal imagination, embed a kind of legitimate ruthlessness. In the common law world, at least, parties to a contract are expected and permitted to act with sole regard to their own interests, and they are expected and permitted to act in ruthless disregard of their counterparties' interests, save to the extent the contract requires them to do otherwise.[15] Courts, too, are reluctant to read things into contracts that are not expressly placed there by the parties. Whilst the law does graft a few 'mandatory terms' onto contracts, where there are no applicable mandatory rules the starting point remains the expectation of self-seeking action.[16]

This has significant consequences for the effectiveness of privacy as a template for responding to data-driven personalisation. Privacy has doctrinally and conceptually come to be closely associated with the absence of consent, rather than the character of the actual use that is made of the data. The choice of privacy as the conceptual framework in which the regulation of data-driven personalisation is situated means that its focus, too, is on regulating consent, rather than regulating data use. The GDPR, for example, contains detailed provisions setting out requirements for consent to be valid.[17] Once consent has been given, however, the actual use that will be made of the data is left almost entirely unregulated by law. Although the law does specify that data can only be used for the specific purposes for which consent was given, this amounts to little more than elevating the requirement of consent from simple consent to informed consent. The actual limitations on the purposes for which data can be used flow from the parties' contract, rather than the law.

The result is problematic, as we see when we move from privacy-centric exemplars to exemplars that are more typical of data-driven personalisation. Consider two, not wholly hypothetical, situations.[18] In the first, a company which runs a social network, or provides a smart home assistant, uses its analysis of the activity of individuals in a relationship to identify moments when the individuals are likely to be at a high risk of breakup. It then uses that information to send them targeted advertisements and offers for services which are likely to be of interest to individuals on the verge of breakup.[19] In the second, a company permits advertisers to target advertisements at users based on a range of characteristics, including race, geographical location, and political disposition.[20] An advertiser places advertisements deliberately geared towards suppressing voter turnout from a particular ethnic group.[21]

Under the privacy-based approach adopted by the GDPR, each of these uses is permissible as long as valid consent has been given: it is the absence of consent, rather than the nature of the use, that forms the basis for legal intervention. Nor does the ordinary law of contract restrain the ends to which data is used. The focus of consumer law is on the fairness of contractual terms per se, rather than on the manner in which they are used in a particular case. It is unlikely that a term permitting a company to analyse and use data will be held to be unfair within the meaning of consumer law, as long as the individual has consented to the analysis and its use in personalisation.[22]

The law, in other words, neither deals with nor embeds any frameworks that can deal with the key problem posed by data-driven personalisation, namely, the use of contract to transform a public good (knowledge) into a private good (data) and create the ability to use that private good in sole pursuit of one's own interest and in disregard of other interests, including the data subject's. It is from the resulting freedom to act to the detriment of the data subject that the risks to which a user is exposed by data-driven personalisation arise.

6.3 DE-RELATIONALISING PERSONALISATION: THE LIMIT OF AUTONOMY

As shown, contract plays a central role not just in enabling data-driven personalisation, but also in creating the risks which data-driven personalisation poses for ordinary individuals. A key factor explaining why contract plays this role is the existence of a distinction between the ideal type of personalisation, which envisages a bespoke offering tailored to the unique situation of each individual, and the actual empirical phenomenon of personalisation through the automated analysis of data.

Personalisation outside the data-driven world – for example, a bespoke suit or a bespoke wardrobe – is grounded in the needs of the user and displays a number of characteristics of a relational contract, in particular, participation in a joint project whose successful completion requires a level of collaboration and commitment exceeding a 'discrete' contract.[23] Data-driven personalisation, in contrast, does not seek to understand the data subject's needs, or create mutual commitment. Its purpose, instead, is to construct a model of the data subject. This model does not seek to accurately represent the data subject as a person, nor is it geared towards the construction of a picture of their individual self. Instead, 'personalisation' in practice refers to a process of categorisation, in which a given individual is treated as a locus of congruence of multiple overlapping categories based on sets of characteristics derived from their observed behaviour. These categories are tailored to suit the ends and purposes which the data holder seeks to pursue through personalisation, rather than the ends and purposes which lead the data subject to engage with the data holder.

There is a clear and obvious distinction between customising services to meet customers' needs, and doing so to enable a company to extract as much value as possible from customers; and it is into the latter category that data-driven personalisation typically falls. This distinction between the ideal type of personalisation and the empirical reality of data-driven personalisation has a number of implications. The most important of these is that data-driven personalisation creates the possibility of a new form of contracting which is simultaneously personalised *and* de-relationalised. This poses significant challenges for contract law. Most models of contracting assume a congruence between personalisation and relationality – assuming, in other words, that personalisation and relationality will either both be present or both be absent in a given transaction – and depend on this congruence to act as a practical check on the ability of either party to exploit the other. Contract law, in consequence, has few tools with which to deal with the consequences of a situation where one (personalisation) is present and the other (relationality) is absent.

Neo-classical contract theory, for example, follows classic economic theories of the market in treating contracts as depersonalised and de-relationalised.[24] The paradigmatic contract consists of the terms of a discrete, one-off transaction between sellers and buyers whose focus is on the exchange rather than their counterparty's needs in and of themselves, and who are indifferent as to the identity of their counterparty. At the other end of the spectrum, relational contract theory treats contracts as both personalised and relationalised: the contract springs from an ongoing and evolving relationship between party and counterparty, and reflects not just generic economic rationality but also the transactional rationality of that specific relationship.[25] In both models, it is this congruence between the presence or absence of personalisation and relationality that restrains the ability of the parties to use the contract as an exploitative or extractive device. The absence of congruence in data-driven personalisation, in contrast, leads to a functional transformation of contract.[26] Rather than conferring opportunities on the subject and enhancing their autonomy, as conventional contract theory assumes, its primary effect is to deprive the data subject of participative opportunities – and, thus, diminish their autonomy – while also leaving the ability of the data holder to exploit the data subject unchecked by either social or market-based factors.

Consider, for example, the contrast between data-driven personalisation and a relational contract. In a relational transaction, the relationship between the parties is one of mutual, two-way dependence, which results in their giving priority to their relationship over the strict legal terms of the agreement.[27] Data-driven personalisation, in contrast, does not depend on a pre-existing relationship, or on a relationship of any sort. It depends simply on the ability to create a large number of categories building on a large number of attributes, and to classify a transactor within those categories. Whilst the transaction between the parties is likely to be of at least medium length, the other characteristics of a relational contract are absent. There is, in particular, no genuine commitment to a joint project – at least, not from the company holding the data, which is likely to be motivated by the need to have a critical mass of users, but to whom individual users are likely to be fungible. From the company's perspective, the contract is neither about 'exchange' in the traditional sense, nor is it about a relationship. Unlike a contract for the sale of goods, where goods can be acquired for personal consumption by the company, data is not typically acquired for consumption. It is, instead, acquired to facilitate transactions between the company and third parties – for example, for the sale of advertisements using information derived from the data it holds on the user – or to facilitate the company's own subsequent dealings with the user or other users. The contract is, in other words, a facilitatory framework, whose primary purpose is to enable the company to transact with others, and its effect is to create a one-way dependence, in which the data holder has the ability to customise and determine the transactional opportunities available to the data subject, without the data subject having any equivalent ability.

The consequences of the failure of assumption of congruence are even clearer if we consider the contrast between data-driven personalisation and a purely discrete transaction, which is wholly de-relationalised and wholly subject to market rationality. In conventional market theory, markets have two purposes. Firstly, they provide price signals to help determine optimal levels of production. Secondly, and more fundamentally, they permit individuals to become more effective market participants through the signals they provide. Market prices provide signals to individual participants about their position in the market. An individual can then act to improve this position by using the means at their disposal to take advantage of the conditions and opportunities made available by the market.[28] Markets, in other words, operate as an information-communication framework, which enables participants to enhance the efficacy of their participation in the relevant market.

In market theory, the ability to improve by learning from price signals and other positional signals is one of the key beneficial properties of markets. It is, however, also a product of the combination of depersonalisation and de-relationalisation. De-relationalisation implies a situation in which there is no broader commitment to a joint project or joint maximisation: the transaction is governed purely by the logic of the market and of individual maximisation, and either party is therefore equally free to walk away at any time because no party is in a position of dependence on the other. Depersonalisation, similarly, implies a situation in which the identity of one's counterparty is a matter of indifference: parties are perfectly fungible, in that equivalent performance can be procured from any other party at any point of time.[29] The cumulative result is a lack of dependence on others,[30] which creates the potential for every individual to improve their position by walking away from counterparties when doing so is to their benefit, and learning from the behaviour and choices of counterparties, including choices not to transact with them.

Markets cease to discharge this function if a person cannot act to improve their position, either because the market fails to communicate the information they need to do so, or because the market's structure means that they lack the ability to influence the opportunities available to them. Both are true of data-driven personalisation. Data-driven personalisation is explicitly directed towards ensuring that the market does not provide the same opportunities to everyone. Equally, it also restricts the ability of individuals to understand why particular opportunities are closed to them, or what they need to do to open the door to those opportunities. The process of categorisation on which data-driven personalisation depends reflects an algorithmic construction of reality, based on categories which do not, and are not intended to, represent reality in its entirety. Instead, they are designed for a particular, narrow function – for example, identifying advertisements to which the data subject is likely to be susceptible, or the highest price the data subject is likely to be willing to pay. Individuals are categorised through processes which impose structure on a set of data, based on detected patterns which the algorithm treats as relevant to determining outcomes. The processes followed are typically stochastic rather than deterministic, and even a skilled user knowing both the inputs and the details of the automated system is unlikely to be able to predict the manner in which their data will be categorised by the automated system in question. Individuals, therefore, have little ability to alter the categories into which they have been placed, or even understand why they have been so categorised.

Data-driven personalisation, in other words, poses a serious challenge to the conception of autonomous action that underpins not just the law of privacy but also the law of contract. In both contract and privacy, the ideal-typical transaction is of two arms-length, autonomous actors dealing with each other in a relationship characterised by symmetric levels of mutual dependence or independence. The network of transactions creating data-driven personalisation, however, challenges this; and far from vindicating the autonomy of both parties, operates to erode the autonomy of the data subject. Against this background, the continued hold exercised by the ideal-typical understanding of autonomous action leaves the law impoverished and unable to conceptually represent important dimensions of the social harm caused by data-driven personalisation.

Article 22 of the GDPR, for example, recognises a right 'not to be subject to a decision based solely on automated processing' if that decision significantly affects the data subject. Processing based on consent is, however, exempt,[31] as is processing necessary for entering into or performing a contract.[32] Although the GDPR requires providing 'meaningful information' about the logic, significance, and envisaged consequences of the algorithmic process, it does not in fact require the data subject to be told the details of the algorithm, or even what the subject must do to be processed differently by the algorithm. All that must be explained are the information on which the algorithmic process is based, why that information is significant, and what the consequences of the decision are.[33] The result is a regulatory failure, caused by the law's reliance on analogies with privacy, and on the ideal type of the autonomous, freely consenting actor. The GDPR accepts an autonomy-based framing of the issue, and in consequence seeks to deal with infringements on autonomy, rather than creating a broader system of protection against the undesirable or exploitative use of data by data holders. Although the GDPR also embeds a rich conceptual framework which, drawing on concepts such as legitimate interests, vital interest, contractual necessity, and the public interest, is capable of offering broader protection, these concepts play a secondary, or subservient, role to consent. Every one of the concepts discussed above is, in the GDPR, simply an additional ground justifying the *use* of data. They neither qualify consent, nor do they restrict what can be done with data as long as consent has been given to its use for that particular purpose. The result, as Table 6.2 shows, is to put the focus on the tools rather than the ends to which they are used.

These issues do not represent a failure of imagination on the part of the drafters of the GDPR. Rather, they reflect the location of the GDPR in privacy, and in the

TABLE 6.2. *Privacy and the use of data*

Underlying issue	Privacy-based perception of issue	Privacy-based remedy
Permitting accumulation of data by endowing data with a quasi-proprietary character	Use of cookies and trackers for gathering, and of databases for storage	Requirement to signify unambiguous consent
Permitting aggregation and transfer of data, through (partially or in full) permitting its commodification	Assembling and aggregating data gathered about the same person from different sources and at different times	Requirement of specific consent
Permitting information derived from processing data to be exploited for purposes chosen by the gatherer or transferee	Use of large amounts of publicly observed data to computationally deduce undisclosed private facts	Requirement of informed consent

autonomy-centric conception of privacy that most Western legal systems have adopted under which consent necessarily acts as a defence to any claim of breach of privacy. Any privacy-based system of regulation will, therefore, inevitably focus on ensuring that consent is informed and freely given. The inadequacy of such a framework arises from the thin conception of consent that the law incorporates.[34] As a concept in law, consent is as concerned with protecting defendants, and associated as much with acting as a 'flak jacket' protecting against legal action,[35] as it is with protecting the data subject's moral autonomy. It is not concerned with ensuring that the acts to which consent has been given reflect the data subject's values, or protect their interests.[36] This is not an issue that can be addressed through merely making consent more informed.[37]

Equally, the GDPR, in failing to set regulatory limits to data use, remains rooted in the framework that has been termed 'market individualism'.[38] At its heart, this assumes that markets are relatively benign and capable of producing balanced terms as long as the law plays an appropriate, adaptive role to support and manage the market. Yet, whilst such a description is certainly true of some markets, as the discussion above has shown it is not true of the market of which data-driven personalisation forms part, whose characteristics resemble markets that are one-sided and have a tendency to produce onerous and extractive patterns of interaction. The issues these markets pose can only be dealt with by setting limits to their use directly, and not indirectly through rights such as privacy.[39]

A similar issue also exists in relation to technology-based regulation. Technical regulation requires, at a minimum, the ability to scrutinise the regulated system, and the regulatory capacity to evaluate situations and processes. The classic works of regulatory theory, and the early examples of regulatory success, dealt with sectors where both these were present. Regulation is considerably less successful where one or both are absent, as they are in relation to data-driven personalisation.[40] Nor, absent a strong statutory scaffold that reframes the issue, is it likely that regulation will move outside the narrow social vision and ideal types that currently underpin the law, but fit uneasily with the empirical reality of data-driven personalisation.

This also affects ethical and normative thinking. There has been a significant push within artificial intelligence research to entrench a more ethically grounded principle of 'explicability', also termed 'transparency' and 'accountability',[41] within algorithmic systems, of which the most prominent is the recent work of the AI4People initiative.[42] Explicability, in the sense it is used in this context, goes beyond the GDPR, representing the 'need to *understand* and *hold to account* the decision-making processes'[43] implicit in the algorithm, in a manner that 'makes the relationship between ourselves and this transformative technology... readily understandable to the proverbial person "on the street"'.[44] Yet there has also been considerable scepticism about whether explicability, transparency, and accountability can be implemented in the context of stochastic algorithms.[45] As an ethical rather than an epistemic principle, explicability is not compatible with current approaches to machine learning which are inherently inexplicable, unlike hard-coded rules where the lack of explicability usually represents a commercial decision rather than a technical limitation.[46] As Robbins has recently argued, in many cases, the only way to achieve explicability will be to abandon machine learning in favour of hard-coded rules.[47] A more feasible approach is to restrict the use of explicability-resistant analytical systems to domains where decisions do not require explanation.[48] Adopting such an approach, however, will require a significant shift away from the analogy with privacy and the reliance on ideal-typical pictures of autonomy, and a more direct focus on the purposes to which data-driven personalisation should and should not be used.

6.4 CONCLUSION: TOWARDS A NEW APPROACH

This chapter has sought to argue that dealing effectively with the challenges and risks posed by the rise of data-driven personalisation requires two shifts in the way we currently think about the issue. The first is that regulation is made necessary by the fact that although the computational analysis of personal data has the potential to have a significant deleterious impact on individuals, it is not a tool we are currently inclined to proscribe because we believe that the technology underlying personalisation has the potential to better our lives. The second is that effective regulation requires a deeper diagnosis of the *legal* structures (and not merely the technological capabilities) that both underpin data-driven personalisation and create the potential for it to have a deleterious effect. Of particular importance are the role played by contract law and the potential it creates for harmful, exploitative use of data. An effective response to the challenge of data-driven personalisation, accordingly, requires legal regulations which take account of the resistance of personalisation to traditional legal controls, and which are explicitly geared towards restricting the processes, struc-tures, and purposes through which and for which personalisation is used.

A starting point is to recognise that, as the second part of this paper has shown, data-driven personalisation is enabled by the law. It is the legal framework provided by contract, and the use of contract law to govern data, that enables private actors to transform a public good (knowledge) into a private good (data). Nevertheless, there must be trade-offs for converting a public good into a private good, in the form – amongst others – of use-restrictions. Similarly, as the third part has shown, there is a need to move beyond the ideal-type of the autonomous, self-regarding actor, and to engage more thoroughly with the functional transformation of contract that data-driven personalisation has brought about. The conceptual apparatus necessary to put in place these restrictions are not difficult to find. Many of the issues identified in this chapter could be dealt with through ideas already present in the GDPR – such as legitimate interests, public interests, and vital interests – freed from the framework of consent to which they are currently subordinated, and used not just as a way of legitimising the use of private data, but also as a way of acting as a check on the use of data in situations where that use exacerbates inequality or vulnerability.

More fundamentally, the experience of data-driven personalisation points to the need to approach the re-use of existing categories, and the application of legal analogies, with a degree of caution. Analogies can obscure as much as they can enlighten, and their use must be tempered by a clearer focus on the nature of the social harm that the law seeks to redress, and on implicit assumptions within existing categories that might, if left in place, contribute to exacerbating rather than ameliorating that harm.

NOTES

I am grateful to Jacob Eisler, Uta Kohl, Daithí Mac Síthigh, Lindsay Stirton, and the participants in the symposium for their helpful comments on earlier versions of this piece.

1 See M Eisenberg, *The Nature of the Common Law* (Harvard University Press 1988) 83–96; CR Sunstein, 'On analogical reasoning' (1993) 106 *Harvard Law Review* 741.

2 For another discussion of the limitations of analogies with the physical world as a starting point for regulating digital phenomena, although with a focus on property rather than contract, see DJ Harvey, *Collisions in the Digital Paradigm: Law and Rule Making in the Internet Age* (Hart Publishing 2017) chs 2, 3, 5.

3 For a discussion of the potential problems this creates, see E Sherwin, 'A defence of analogical reasoning in law' (1999) 66 *Chicago Law Review* 1179. Sherwin concedes that this turns analogical reasoning into an 'unscientific practice with imperfect results', but nevertheless defends it as a mode of judicial reasoning. The factors she identifies in its favour do not, however, apply to its use in legislative or regulatory action, which are the primary concern of this chapter.

4 The language of exemplars is taken from the work of Thomas Kuhn. T Kuhn, *The Structure of Scientific Revolutions* (3rd ed., University of Chicago Press 1996) 187–91. For a fuller discussion of their role in legal adaptation, see TT Arvind, 'Paradigms Lost or Paradigms Regained? Legal

Revolutions and the Path of the Law' in S Worthington, A Robertson and G Virgo (eds.) *Revolution and Evolution in Private Law* (Hart Publishing 2018) 63–65, 70–71.

5 Privacy has been the primary tool used to regulate online data-gathering from the early days of regulatory intervention. One of the first European-level actions, for example, was the Directive on privacy and electronic communications of 2002, popularly known as the ePrivacy directive (Council Directive 2002/58/EC of 12 July 2002 concerning the processing of personal data and the protection of privacy in the electronic communications sector [2002] OJ L201/37), which was explicitly grounded in a privacy-based framework. But the link between privacy and the regulation of data processing is far older, and can be seen in the (now repealed) Data Protection Directive of 1995 (Council Directive 95/46/EC of 24 October 1995 on the protection of individuals with regard to the processing of personal data and on the free movement of such data [1995] OJ L281/31). See, for example, art 1(1).

6 Indeed, the absence of a contract has been an important factor in leading cases involving breaches of privacy. See *Douglas v Hello! Ltd* [2007] UKHL 21, [2008] 1 AC 1. This fits with a more general move in the law of privacy. The action for breach of privacy has largely abandoned the relational considerations that were (and remain) a central aspect of breach of confidence, in favour of a wrong-centric conceptualisation of the basis of the action. As subsequent sections of this chapter discuss in more detail, the result is that consent (or its lack) has come to occupy centre stage in privacy, displacing the idea of abuse of relational power (or exploitation of relational vulnerability) that is central to breach of confidence.

7 The terminology of ideal types is used here in its Weberian sense. See D Sheehan and TT Arvind, 'Private law theory and taxonomy: reframing the debate' (2015) 35 *Legal Studies* 480, 490–92.

8 The EU's response to the concern about the risks to individuals posed by the increased potential for data gathering and analysis, for example, took the form of the 'Cookie Directive' (Council Directive 2009/136/EC of 25 November 2009, [2009] OJ L337/11), which amended the ePrivacy Directive (n 5). The directive was expressly created to deal with the issues which new technologies pose for individuals. Its recitals list the various technological measures of data gathering – including IP address tracking (Recital 52), RFID (Recital 56), and spyware (Recitals 65–66), data analysis (see, e.g., recital 53 on the processing of traffic data) and data use (see, e.g., recitals 67–68 on unsolicited marketing) which it seeks to regulate in the interests of end-users.

9 This trifold structure also informs the approach taken under the General Data Protection Regulation (Regulation (EU) 2016/679 of the European Parliament and of the Council of 27 April 2016 on the protection of natural persons with regard to the processing of personal data and on the free movement of such data, and repealing Directive 95/46/EC (General Data Protection Regulation) [2016] OJ L119/1, hereafter 'GDPR'), which expands the older principle of consent to collection contained in the ePrivacy Directive (n 5) with a much broader principle of consent to processing and to specific uses of the information derived through processing.

10 For example, *Campbell v Mirror Group Newspapers Ltd* [2004] UKHL 22 which played an important role in the emergence of privacy as a cause of action in the United Kingdom.

11 See J Davey, 'Insurance and price regulation in the digital era' in TT Arvind and J Steele (eds.), *Contract Law and the Legislature: Autonomy, Expectations, and the Making of Legal Doctrine* (Hart Publishing 2020); R Stirton, 'Insurance, genetic information and the future of industry self-regulation in the UK' (2012) 4 *Law, Innovation and Technology* 212.

12 [2004] ECHR 294.

13 It is worth stressing that online terms and conditions will typically be treated as enforceable contracts, as long as the requirement of consideration (that is, that both sides must provide something of economic value) is met. The provision of access to content will typically meet this bar. It is only in exceptional circumstances, where the service-provider undertakes absolutely no obligations whatsoever, that there will be no contract. See *Spreadex Ltd v Cochrane* [2012] EWHC 1290 (Comm).

14 For a fuller discussion, see G Azam, 'La connaissance, une marchandise fictive' (2007) 29 *Revue du MAUSS* 110, 122.

15 See, for example, the comments of Lord Bingham in the Court of Appeal decision in *Edmonds v Lawson*[2000] EWCA Civ 69, [25], pointing out that a key dimension of contract is that obligations are not undertaken as a purely altruistic exercise, but have a strong element of self-interest. See also the observations of Lord Ackner in *Walford v Miles* [1992] 2 AC 128 (HL) on the centrality of individualism to English contract law.

16 See R Brownsword, 'After investors: interpretation, expectation and the implicit dimension of the "New Contextualism"' in D Campbell, H Collins, and J Wightman (eds.), *Implicit Dimensions of Contract: Discrete, Relational and Network Contracts* (Hart Publishing 2003) and especially 125ff, where Brownsword draws on the decision in *Baird Textile Holdings v Marks and Spencer plc* [2001] EWCA Civ 274 to highlight the prioritisation in English contract law of individualism over cooperativism.

17 GDPR (n 9) arts 7, 13.

18 For further examples from the retail sector, see J Turow, *The Aisles have Eyes: How Retailers Track Your Shopping, Strip Your Privacy, and Define Your Power* (Yale University Press 2017).

19 Research by a Facebook engineer has suggested that it is technically possible, with a reasonable degree of accuracy, to identify the likelihood that a relationship will break up, based on Facebook activity. L Backstrom and J Kleinberg, 'Romantic Partnerships and the Dispersion of Social Ties: A Network Analysis of Relationship Status on Facebook' [2013] arXiv 1310.6753v1 [cs.SI] https://arxiv.org/abs/1310.6753. By using this as a working example, I do not mean to suggest that Facebook has any intention of carrying out such an analysis on a routine basis, or of using the information to target ads at its users. My point relates, rather, to whether the law can and should do anything to restrain data-driven personalisation from being used to these ends, given that it is technically possible for an entity with access to a sufficient amount of data to do so.

20 Although the GDPR prohibits the processing of personal data 'revealing racial or ethnic origin' or 'political opinions' (GDPR (n 9), art 9(1)), it also creates an exception if the data subject 'has given explicit consent to the processing of those personal data for one or more purposes' (GDPR (n 9), art 7(2)(a)). Member States and the EU may specify situations in which consent may not be given, but there are no general restrictions in the GDPR which restrict the purposes for which the data can be used.

21 There is some suggestion that external actors believed to have been linked to Russia did in fact do this through Facebook's promoted posts system during the 2016 US presidential election, with a view to suppressing African-American turnout. Senate Select Committee on Intelligence, *Report on Russian Active Measures Campaign and Interference in the 2016 US Election* (S Rep 116-XX, 2019) vol 2, 38–41. Although the advertisements do not appear to have in fact reduced turnout, the broader point is that, firstly, micro-targeting is

enabled by the aggregation and analysis of data that underpins data-driven personalisation (and, hence, is appropriately seen as one manifestation of data-driven personalisation) and, secondly, that the use of micro-targeting for political purposes is both widespread and successful, even if it was not successful in this specific instance. For a general discussion, see F Liberini and others, 'Politics in the Facebook Era: Evidence from the 2016 US Presidential Elections' (2018) 389 CAGE Working Paper Series.

22 This flows from the fact that the requirements of unfairness under s 62(4) of the Consumer Rights Act 2015 – that the term cause a 'significant imbalance' in the parties' rights and obligations to the detriment of the consumer, and that it be 'contrary to the requirement of good faith' – have been interpreted cumulatively, and the requirement of good faith has been read largely in procedural terms as requiring fair and open dealings. See *West v Ian Finlay* [2014] EWCA Civ 316. Given the nature of the test set out in that case, it is unlikely that a term which meets the GDPR's requirements for consent would ever fail to meet the procedurally oriented element of good faith (and, thus, that it would ever be classified as being 'unfair').

23 David Campbell has argued that all contracts have an element of relationality, and that there is therefore no such thing as a 'purely' discrete contract. See D Campbell, '*Arcos v Ronaasen* as a relational contract' in D Campbell, L Mulcahy and S Wheeler (eds.), *Changing Concepts of Contract: Essays in Honour of Ian Macneil* (Palgrave Macmilan 2013). The distinction I seek to make in this chapter, however, relates not to contracts as such, but to legal models of contracting, in particular, distinguishing between models that treat contracts as being grounded in general market rationality, as opposed to specific transactional rationality.

24 For a defence of this approach, see J Morgan, *Contract Law Minimalism: A Formalist Restatement of Commercial Contract Law* (Cambridge University Press 2013).

25 See I Macneil, 'Values in contract: internal and external' (1983) 78 *Northwestern University Law Review* 340; I Macneil, 'Reflections on relational contract' (1985) 141 *Journal of Institutional and Theoretical Economics* 541.

26 The language of functional transformation is taken from Karl Renner, *The Institutions of Private Law and their Social Functions* (A Schwarzschild tr, Routledge & Keegan Paul 1949). Renner gives the example of how the contract of employment altered the relationship between producer and merchant. In the world of independent artisans, property rights gave producers control over their labour and its products, which contracts supported and sustained. The employment relationship upended this by transforming the relationship from one of exchange to one of unfettered command – a direct consequence of the power conferred by recoding means of production (tools of trade) from chattel to capital (in the form of capital equipment) whilst also hindering the development of doctrines fettering that power of command. The parallel between the functional transformation discussed by Renner and those that are the subject of this chapter are obvious and striking, with both showing a functional shift towards amplifying rather than limiting powers.

27 S Macaulay, 'The real and the paper deal: empirical pictures of relationships, complexity and the urge for transparent simple rules' (2003) 66 *MLR* 44.

28 IM Kirzner, *Market Theory and the Price System* (Van Nostrand 1963) 2.

29 TT Arvind and A McMahon, 'Commodification, control, and the contractualisation of the human body' in E Bertrand, MX Catto and AD Mornington (eds.), *The Limits of the Market: Interdisciplinary Perspectives* (Mare & Martin 2020).

30 G Simmel, *The Philosophy of Money* (T Bottomore and D Firsby trs, 2nd ed., Routledge & Keegan Paul 1978).

31 GDPR (n 9) art 22 (2)(b).

32 Ibid. art 22 (2)(a).

33 Ibid. art 13(2)(f).

34 A Robertson, 'The limits of voluntariness in contract' (2005) 29 *Melbourne University Law Review* 179.

35 See *Re W* [1994] 4 All ER 627 (Lord Donaldson MR).

36 BA Brody, 'Making informed consent meaningful' (2001) 23 *IRB Ethics and Human Research* 1.

37 For a critical analysis of the limitations of informed consent as a regulatory tool, see TT Arvind and A McMahon, 'Responsiveness and the role of rights in medical law: lessons from *Montgomery*' (2020) 28 *Medical Law* Review "https://doi.org/10.1093/medlaw/fwaa006".

38 JN Adams and R Brownsword, 'The ideologies of contract' (1987) 7 *Legal Studies* 205.

39 On these transaction types, see generally TT Arvind and J Steele, 'Remapping contract law: four perceptions of markets' in Arvind and Steele, *Contract Law and the Legislature* (n 11).

40 See TT Arvind and J Gray, 'The limits of technocracy: private law's future in the regulatory state' in K Barker, K Fairweather and R Grantham (eds.), *Private Law in the Twenty-first Century* (Hart Publishing 2017).

41 IEEE, *Ethically Aligned Design Version 2* (2017), standards.ieee.org/content/dam/ieee-standards/standards/web/documents/other/ead_v2.pdf .

42 L Floridi and others, 'AI4People – An ethical framework for a good AI society: opportunities, risks, principles, and recommendations' (2018) 28 *Mind and Machines* 689. Given the limitations of basing responses to computational analysis on analogies with practices in other areas which this chapter has highlighted, it is somewhat relevant to note that the main recommendations of the AI4People initiative are based on an analogy with bioethics and, in particular, the four principles of biomedical ethics identified by Beauchamp and Childress: autonomy (an individual's right to make their own choices), beneficence (a doctor's duty to act with the patient's best interest in mind), non-maleficence (a doctor's duty to do no harm above all), and justice (fairness among individuals); see TL Beauchamp and JF Childress, *Principles of Biomedical Ethics* (7th ed., Oxford University Press 2013). Yet little attempt is made to defend the substantive rationality behind the analogy with biomedical ethics, beyond asserting that it 'closely resembles' digital ethics, and that its principles 'adapt surprisingly well' to the challenges posed by artificial intelligence (Floridi and others (n 42) 696).

43 Ibid. 700.

44 Ibid.

45 S Robbins, 'A misdirected principle with a catch: explicability for AI' (2019) 29 *Mind and Machines* 495.

46 F Pasquale, *The Black Box Society: The Secret Algorithms That Control Money and Information* (Harvard University Press 2015).

47 Robbins (n 45) 508.

48 Ibid. 511.

7

'All Data Is Credit Data': Personalised Consumer Credit Score and Anti-Discrimination Law

Noelia Collado-Rogriguez and Uta Kohl

7.1 INTRODUCTION

Bank credit is essential for individuals in modern society. It gives people access to a wide variety of essential goods – housing, higher education, health care and transport, among others. Obtaining a mortgage, a credit card or a line of overdraft credit is not about living a life of affluence, but rather grants basic financial stability and enables a life of security, opportunity and dignity. It also often functions as 'grease for economic mobility'.[1]

Personalisation is nothing new in access to credit. It has long been controlled by score-based assessment systems that feed on the personal data of the consumer assessed against actuarial risk models trained on data sets derived from various groups of borrowers. Fair, Isaac and Co [FICO] was one of the first analytical companies in the USA, and has offered retail credit scoring since 1956. Similar risk assessment drives the insurance market. Both types of contracts tend to be 'personal' in so far as the attributes or history of the particular consumer shape the terms on which the provider will enter into the contract, if they are willing to do so at all. This use of personal information addresses the *prima facie* asymmetrical negotiating position. The customer has (personal) information that the provider lacks that is relevant to the risks associated with the transactions – in the case of credit transactions, predicting the future likelihood of default in the repayment. The credit score system addresses this informational asymmetry by facilitating the collection of financial facts of the consumer, turning them into variables with an assigned weight, which are then processed in line with the adopted model in order to deliver a quick decision on the consumer's likely future capacity or propensity to repay the loan. Credit checks have been a key tool for lenders to reach decisions about granting credit, and also reflect their particular preferences and level of risk aversion.[2]

Notwithstanding that personal data has long been a key raw material in credit markets, the big data phenomenon – 'a new generation of technologies and architectures, designed to economically extract value form very large volumes of a wide variety of data, by enabling the high velocity capture, discovery and/or analysis'[3] – creates opportunities for intensified personalisation in credit assessments and products. First, it gives lenders access to a much larger volume of data points from a wider range of data sources,[4] and many are not obviously connected to the financial standing of the customer – on the broad assumption that 'all personal data is credit data.'[5] Such non-traditional data are often drawn from a borrowers' online behaviour and activities, that are transformed into 'credit insights'. For example, Zest AI considers how quickly the potential borrower scrolls through terms of service; similarly, LendUp examines how quickly the user scrolls through its site.[6] Demyst Data, Earnest and Kreditech observe a borrower's social media behaviour (online social footprint, online profile data and social graphing, respectively).[7] Kreditech also evaluates a borrower's behavioural analytics (on which features the user clicks, and the time spent on the webpage), e-commerce shopping patterns and even device data (what is the operating system or the apps downloaded).[8] A borrower's credit score may be affected by not carefully reading the online terms and conditions of the credit contract as a proxy for responsibility;[9] or by having 'Friends' on social media with problematic credit histories.[10] Thus emerging credit score models do not just draw on 'hard' facts about a borrower's past and current financial status but also on a range of soft behavioural facts and network-derived insights, which – By analysing the totality of available information through complex algorithms[11]and taking advantage of 'a continuous feedback loop that adjusts the weighting coefficients and the cut-off score'[12] they deliver more fine-tuned or personalised predictions about a consumer's future payment behaviour.[13] This 'micro-segmentation' approach is also becoming prevalent for other financial services and products, notably insurance policies with personalised premiums or usage-based models, such as pay-as-you-go auto-insurance, and bank accounts and investment services.[14]

A second and related point is that big data does not just increase the volume, source and type of data available to lenders, but also their subsequent usage. For lenders it creates opportunities beyond making more fine-tuned assessments about the risk associated with the borrower's financial and other characteristics through credit scoring and the resultant risk-based pricing.[15] It allows them to engage in 'price discrimination' which refers to a lender offering the same product, to consumers with the same risk factor, at different prices, that is regardless of the cost structure,[16] but depending on an assessment of the maximum price they may be willing to pay for a certain product.[17] (Chapter 10). Price discrimination has existed for some time in various industries, including credit markets.[18] A common example is where new customers are being offered lower interest rates on the same loans than existing customers, whose higher rates are effectively cross-subsiding the lower ones. The big data phenomenon opens up the possibility of lenders being able to make more granular judgments about an *individual* customer's willingness to pay a particular price for a financial product – depending on the relative urgency of their need for credit (i.e., desperation), their willingness to shop around or their relative impulsiveness or caution.[19]

Both risk-based pricing and price discrimination lead to price disparities among consumers that arise in the first case from the perceived risk faced by the lender and in the second from the market forces of supply and demand. Some disparities in the price and terms of the credit transactions are legitimate. A poor credit history ought to result in harsher credit terms, or new customers may be appropriately enticed by below-cost interest rates. It may be the case, however, that some disparities that result from profit-maximising decisions by lenders – including disparities enabled by the use of big data – ought to be stopped or limited by regulatory intervention. In particular, where a lender relies on a borrower's social network as a proxy for her likely behavioural patterns and ultimately (un)creditworthiness or willingness to pay more, the result may be worse commercial terms for individuals (particularly from vulnerable or marginal groups) for reasons wholly beyond their control. The question is whether the law can and should intervene to limit such practices.

This chapter asks whether anti-discrimination imposes limits on the extent to which lenders may use big data analytics in arriving at risk-scores and differential credit products. Are price disparities based on big data analytics that profile individual consumers socially and psychologically based on their online behaviour fundamentally different from traditional pricing models based on, for example, poor repayment history or the newness of the customer, and if so, why?

7.2 SOCIAL NETWORK DATA AS INPUT DATA FOR CREDITWORTHINESS – AND ANTI-DISCRIMINATION LAW

Research has provided extensive evidence that shows that data derived from customers' online networks and behavioural patterns can predict an individual's financial behaviour and likely future repayment default with the same or even higher accuracy than traditional models. In an early experiment using data from the online peer-to-peer lending marketplace prosper.com, Lin and others showed that P2P lenders judged the creditworthiness of borrowers by the quality of their 'Friends', and were right to do so, especially when these 'Friends' had within the market place 'roles and identities that are more likely to signal better credit quality'.[20] Thus social capital underscored creditworthiness. More recently, De Cnudde and others have explored whether Facebook data may yield meaningful credit scores in the microfinance setting, and found greater similarity in creditworthiness between Facebook Look-a-Likes (those sharing interests, i.e. liking or commenting on the same posts, even if not connected) than Facebook Best-Friends-Forever (those interacting with one another) who in turn outperformed mere Facebook Friends.[21] There is also a growing body of literature – using large overlapping telecom and lender data sets – that identify mobile network data as a source for credit scoring. Óskarsdóttir and others have shown that 'how people use their phone [i.e. who they call] can be used as the sole data source when deciding whether they should be given a loan or not.'[22] This is guilt (or innocence) by association: the likelihood of a customer defaulting on a loan can be predicted with reference of financial behaviour of their phone contacts. Their research builds on literature about types of social behaviour such as homophily (or the strong tendency to associate with others who are perceived as similar in some ways) and network-mediated social influencing; and corroborates the predictive capacity of phone networks in other contexts, for example, cancellations of telecom subscriptions.[23]

The idea of using call data for credit score models is premised on the assumption that individual call networks are a 'good proxy for their lifestyle and economic activity'[24] – in the same vein, that these networks can also predict many characteristics such as 'age, gender, ethnicity, economic factors, geography, urbanization. . .'[25] For creditworthiness, none of these personal characteristics need to be identified as explicit variables within the credit score system, but they often hover just under the surface. Significantly, many of these are also protected attributes under anti-discrimination law and have been singled out for constitutional or fundamental rights protection. For example, Art. 21 of the European Union Charter of Fundamental Rights prohibits '[a]ny discrimination based on any ground such as sex, race, colour, ethnic or social origin, genetic features, language, religion or belief, political or any other opinion, membership of a national minority, property, birth, disability, age or sexual orientation. . .'[26] The prohibition of discrimination has long been extended to some horizontal, or private legal, relationships. Typically, the Gender Equal Access to Goods and Services Directive[27] or Race Equality Directive[28] expressly require equal treatment of men and women or of members of racial or ethnic minorities, in the provision of goods and services, including banking, insurance and other financial services. Still, there have been studies to show that, for example, ethnic groups experience higher loan denials and pay higher interest rates than white Europeans.[29]

Similar evidence is also available for the USA, where anti-discrimination prohibitions have largely failed to shield protected minorities from discrimination in credit markets.[30] According to a study in the 1990s, protected groups suffered disproportionate credit rejection.[31] Current evidence also suggests that protected groups are charged higher interest for credit than non-protected groups with a similar creditworthiness level.[32] This is despite the fact that the US federal statute known as the Equal Credit Opportunity Act 1974[33] specifically targets discriminatory treatment on the grounds of race, colour, religion, national origin, sex or marital status, or age.[34] This statute has been used by consumers to fight lending decisions based on *overt discrimination or disparate treatment* (with focus on formal equality), or *disparate effect or impact* (with focus on substantive equality) – albeit with low effectiveness given the complexity of proving either.[35] An example of disparate treatment (or direct discrimination) would be a traditional credit score model that attached different weighting to a particular address/suburb or the language used in the application form, either of which could be challenged as a variable that acts as a proxy for ethnicity.[36] In contrast, discrimination based on disparate *effects* (or indirect discrimination) focuses on whether a neutral rule or practice has a worse impact on members of a minority as group-members.

7.3 INDIRECT DISCRIMINATION – CAUSATION, CORRELATIONS AND TRANSPARENCY

In the EU, the concept of indirect discrimination is defined as an 'apparently neutral provision, criterion or practice'[37] [or PCP], that in its application has a disproportionately adverse impact on a protected group. With its focus on 'subtle and unintentional mechanisms which work to the disadvantage and exclusion of [certain] groups,'[38] indirect discrimination would seem ideal for challenging discriminatory effects of complex credit score models based on multifaceted personal digital footprints, precisely because the prohibition focuses on effects, rather than the internal logic of the decision-making process.

In *Essop and Naeem* [2017][39] the UK Supreme Court held that it did not matter *why* a much higher proportion of black and minority ethnic (BME) and older candidates failed the Core Skills Assessment which is a prerequisite to be eligible for promotion in the civil service. In Lady Hale's words, there could be a wide range of reasons, which in themselves may neither be unlawful nor even under the control of the alleged discriminator: 'They could be genetic, such as strength or height. They could be social, such as the expectation that women will bear the greater responsibility for caring for the home and family than will men. They could be traditional employment practices...'[40] What mattered was that the practice affected a minority disproportionately, and this should be established by statistical evidence to show a correlation, *not* causation, between the practice and its comparative disparate impact on the minority.[41] As a matter of practicalities, this is done by comparing 'the impact of the PCP on the group with the relevant protected characteristic and its impact upon the group without it.'[42] In *Essop and Naeem*, '[t]he BME selection rate was 40.3% of the White selection rate and there was a 0.1% chance that this could happen by chance. For older candidates the rate was 37.4% with again 0.1% risk that this could happen by chance.'[43]

With this effect-focused approach, indirect discrimination provides a perfect match, first, for algorithmic decision-making processes with machine learning capabilities – used in numerous commercial and legal contexts, including credit score systems. Here the internal logic of the decision-making process is not just complex to start with, but continually adjusted to optimise results in light of feedback loops running on large data sets. These self-learning systems – known as black boxes – are outside the understanding of their programmers, let alone their users, such as the institutions and customers who rely on credit scores.[44] Whilst Lady Hale was referring to subtle social complexities that can create 'hidden barriers which are not easy to anticipate or to spot,'[45] black box systems create additional indeterminacies as their decision-making processes are neither known nor, arguably, knowable. Yet, regardless of whether the decision-making process is a traditional one or powered by AI, ultimately the causes of indirect discrimination lie in the ambivalent region where the 'apparently neutral provision, criterion or practice' meets social reality. It is here that the disparate effect manifests itself and sometimes, as in *Essop and Naeem*, for reasons that are unknown. Indirect discrimination looks out for (discriminatory) correlations. Such identification of correlations is also the engine of big data. Big data technology works by observing meaningful patterns without the need to explain their underlying logic or moral value. Thus there is a neat symmetry: credit score models that correlate networks, digital footprints and general online behaviours to creditworthiness can be reviewed through a legal mechanism that is equally attentive to correlations, only this time discriminatory ones. Neither system depends on underlying causal explanations. Second, the focus of indirect discrimination on effects, as opposed to the reasons for the discriminatory decision, makes it also an excellent match for credit scoring models which tend to be shrouded in secrecy. In the USA they are often developed by companies other than the banks that use them, and protected as trade secrets, which puts their variables and the relative weight attached to them *prima facie* beyond the review of the banks, their borrowers or regulatory authority.[46] So for the purposes of this discussion, discriminatory impacts of otherwise neutral criteria or practices which cannot be explained or are hidden behind trade secrets, are not without precedents; anti-discrimination law has reviewed them by studying their differential impact. The traditional mechanism to prove indirect discrimination effectively circumvents the lack of transparency, or informational opacity, for which big data algorithms are frequently castigated.

In contrast, data protection law, notably the General Data Protection Regulation[47] [GDPR], purports to address that opacity. A data subject is entitled – in respect of important automated decision based on personal profiling – to human oversight[48] *and*, in connection with that, to 'meaningful information about the logic involved, as well as the significance and the envisaged consequences... for the data subject.'[49] For credit assessments, this might require disclosure of variables and their relative weight (how the algorithm has been trained and what consumer's personal data may be used[50]) but it does not entitle the evaluated customer to an explanation for the reasons behind an adverse decision as such. Furthermore although credit assessments are principally included within the right to human review,[51] the right itself can be surrendered through consent, and is displaced where the assessment is necessary for the contract. Even then the customer must be able to contest the decision.[52] In all, the GDPR's approach to transparency is half-hearted in scope and in its obligatory nature: it imposes a limited disclosure requirement in the first place which can, in the second place, be set aside by the contractual context or the consent of the customer in need of credit, but which then creates another obligation. Given the 'natural' opacity of automated processes and the 'natural' reluctance of lenders to reveal their credit score systems, the effect-focused mechanism of indirect discrimination holds more promise for uncovering systemic unfairness and discrimination than the much touted need for transparency. Still, for the individual customer who is 'merely' poor or vulnerable, but not within a protected group, anti-discrimination law offers no remedy at all, as will be discussed in the next section. Even for those individual consumers who fall within a protected group, establishing relevant discriminatory correlations would also not offer an easy and feasible route to challenge a negative outcome.

The contrasting approaches by anti-discrimination law and data protection law on the appropriate point of oversight go hand in hand with the varying faith each places in the fairness of human versus automated judgments. For data protection law, human oversight provides a much-needed safeguard against the rigidity of automated technocratic decisions; within anti-discrimination law, the presence of broad human discretion to override rule-based automated processes raises a red flag that signals likely human bias and prejudice.[53] These different attitudes are, at least in part, a function of the different eras and contexts when these bodies of law emerged. But they also serve as a useful reminder that automated and human judgments each have their weaknesses and neither provides the panacea to all ills in decision-making.

7.4 INDIRECT DISCRIMINATION – 'OBJECTIVE JUSTIFICATION', PERSONALISED ACCURACY AND THE POOR

7.4.1 The Limits of 'Indirect Discrimination' Protection

The starting point for any case of indirect discrimination is the absence (or lack of evidence) of direct discrimination, whether overtly or by proxy. The argument is that formal equality, or equality of treatment, was (or may have been) present but had an adverse impact on a protected group due to some hidden barrier and thus failed to deliver a level playing field, or equality in outcome. The concept of indirect discrimination is ambitious as it tries to address structural disadvantages that persist even where formal equality is respected (and indeed often because of it).[54] Indirect discrimination undertakes a difficult balancing act considering that rules and practices invariably have differential impacts on individuals and groups, and their value lies precisely in treating everyone – despite individual or group differences – alike. It goes to the heart of formal justice and the rule of law which, as a general matter, is characterised by *neutral* arbitration. Formal equality also has an important communal dimension, as Frederic Schauer eloquently puts it:

> If we are not a community of equals, perhaps we are equals because we are community. The affinity between community and equality stems from our recognition of the real bite of the idea of equality. That bite emerges not from the fact of

descriptive equality, but... from the fact that most of the interesting exemplars of equality exist against the background of important inequality. Rather than being important because it treats like cases alike, equality becomes important precisely because it treats unlike cases alike... To abstract away from our differences to bring us closer together and to generate focus on similarities. When we ignore or abstract away from our differences, we necessarily increase our emphasis on shared standards and equal treatment.[55]

The law on indirect discrimination is thus saddled with an inherently paradoxical task: it must respect formal equality – as being essential for its normative dimension and for fostering affinities despite profound differences – and still critique that formal equality for failing to address those differences. This paradox is legally embodied in the defence to indirect discrimination in the form of 'objective justification': indirect discrimination is lawful if it is *objectively justified* by a *legitimate aim* and the means of achieving that aim are *appropriate and necessary*.'[56] The 'business necessity' test provides a comparable exception to the 'disparate impact' basis under the US Equal Credit Opportunity Act.[57]

This defence means that even where a credit score model based on social media data sets adversely affects a protected group, through, for example, credit rejections (credit-rationing) or higher interest rates (risk-based pricing, whereby higher risk results in higher rates), it is still lawful as long as it can be shown to reliably predict likely defaulting behaviour and thereby to further the legitimate aim of protecting the lender's business. Where those or similar data sets are used to offer different prices to consumers with the *same* credit score, a lender may still argue that such differential pricing is needed to ensure the profitability and survival of its business, even if in this instance it is arguably a less defensive measure, and thus less necessary, than in the case of credit checks. Thus the difference between these two aims is one of degree, not kind. Regulatory expectations that lenders act 'honestly, fairly, transparently and professionally, taking account of the rights and interests of the consumers'[58] may, however, restrict some exploitative price discrimination practices that use behavioural data to exploit vulnerabilities (e.g. depression) to charge higher prices.

So what 'indirect discrimination' gives with one hand, the 'objective justification' defence takes away with the other, and this could not be otherwise. If creditworthiness *is* demonstrably lower amongst a protected group (likely due to structural disadvantages), then a prohibition of indirect discrimination would make credit checks impossible. It would forbid a finding of the very matter that a check is designed to reveal. Of course, not all indirect discrimination can be justified on the basis of being a legitimate financial prognosis.[59]

7.4.2 Accurate and Objective?

Yet, it has been objected that risk-score models based on the credibility or standing of a borrower's Facebook Friends or Look-a-Likes cannot be accurate or fair when they infer scores for individuals from shared group characteristics – rather than from her *individual* financial history.[60] This objection is based on a misunderstanding of actuarial risk assessment models, which are always comparative and probabilistic.[61] This applies as much to recent models drawing on data sets of online behaviour, as it does to traditional ones: an individual borrower's financial history is only insightful against a model trained on comparable financial behaviour by others. That the new models can extract the same intelligence about a borrower's future financial behaviour from data of his personal networks or online behavioural patterns does not alter the inherent comparative and probabilistic nature of the actuarial risk assessment. Indeed, with the benefit of more diverse data sets and more frequent feedback loops, such credit score models would allow for more personalised predictions, as they can draw on a wider and more subtle range of stereotypes against which a borrower can be compared, and thereby ultimately promise to make more accurate predictions. Where a credit score model is based on fewer variables (i.e. the borrower's income, employment history, credit card history or any prior exclusion from the credit market[62]), each variable assumes greater weight and may thus unreasonably skew the final outcome. For that reason, it has also been argued that the move to online or mobile network data sets can open up credit markets to many who might be excluded from the markets by traditional models, for example, due to a lack of a prior credit history.[63] Whether these scores could, in principle and in practice, be used in way that only works to the advantage of otherwise excluded individuals remains to be seen.[64] In any event, under the 'objective justification' defence which looks both to the legitimate purpose for which a test is used and its grounding on some rational basis, any model that improves the accuracy of the individual prediction is bound to be more 'objectively justified' than those that are less accurate.

In fact, it is the increased personal accuracy[65] wherein lies the promise *and* weakness of score models relying on non-traditional sources. The micro-segmentation of big data credit scores implements a heightened user pay model: each customer only gets or pays 'exactly' what they individually deserve. Whilst such precise price differentiation based on 'just desert' is underwritten by liberal notions of individualistic fairness, it implicitly rejects the idea of communal solidarity inherent in more broad-brush models where lower risk borrowers within a risk sub-group effectively carry the costs of higher risk borrowers within the same group through equal treatment within the sub-group. In other words, a lack of individualised precision is built upon and furthers communal solidarity.

Credit score models that draw on a customer's social media or mobile network to judge her financial reliability (i.e. an unexpected correlation) lay bare how the online world, despite its apparent diversity and openness, perpetuates social, economic and cultural stratification.[66] They also make visible that the structural (dis)advantages that impact on individuals – as manifested in their personal networks, digital footprints and behavioural choices – are further perpetuated, and amplified, by 'equal treatment' in commercial and legal contexts and certainly through predictive judgements. By predicting a customer's likely future financial behaviour the score pre-empts, at least in certain circumstances, the future it predicts; it becomes the very vehicle of the future it is only meant to forecast. Assessing an applicant as uncreditworthy pre-empts not just likely defaulting behaviour, but also the possibility, however small, of them proving their financial reliability. The higher the actual or assumed accuracy of the model, the less justification and incentive there is to override a prediction to give an applicant an opportunity to defy the odds. In this respect, models of heightened accuracy strengthened the apparent conclusiveness of the empirical calculations (how likely *is* the customer to default) and hide the fact that the normative judgement (whether a customer *ought* to get a loan) is not reducible to such calculations, and imbued with a whole range of other considerations.

The technocratic nature of the decision-making process, its grounding in empirical (personal) facts and statistical analysis, and its legal protection under the umbrella of 'objective justification' – all disguise the fact that credit score models are steeped in the commercial interests of the lender, and the final credit decisions vary depending on a lender's risk appetite.[67] Whilst credit risk assessment models are capable of making more or less accurate decisions about a borrower's likely future financial behaviour, those predictions by themselves cannot deliver a decision on whether someone ought to get a loan, or its terms. For example, some lenders have responded to high-risk borrowers not by denying them credit, but by giving them credit with higher interest rates which they could ill afford.[68] In the lead-up to the 2008 economic crisis, US borrowers who were granted a subprime mortgage, at a high interest rate, were eight times more likely to default than people with a prime loan.[69] Thus the evaluation of a customer's creditworthiness (and the terms of the credit) raises commercial and normative questions that no actuarial assessment can by itself answer. Yet neither is the defence of 'objective justification' liable to discipline discriminatory market practices by finding that a lender's commercial risk assessment was *not* 'objectively justified' particularly in so far as it is oriented towards the legitimate aim of maximising profits.[70] There is, however, regulation to prevent some exploitative practices. In the EU, for example, the Mortgage Credit Directive prevents lenders granting loans where the probability of repayment is too low.[71]

7.4.3 'All Data is Credit Data': An 'Appropriate' Data Use?

Even if the aim of protecting a lender legitimises otherwise unlawful indirect discrimination, arguably the use of datasets that capture a prospective borrower's digital footprint is neither 'appropriate nor necessary' to fulfil that aim. This objection rests on concerns of informational privacy and the principle that data sets should be used for the purposes for which they were reasonably expected to be used – as reflected in the 'purpose limitation' principle of data protection law (e.g., Art 5(1)(b) of the GDPR) and wider concepts of reasonable privacy expectations that are embedded in privacy and data protection jurisprudence,[72] as well as specific credit protection regulation.[73] This principle seeks to prevent 'function creep' and preserve the functional separation of different (data generating) spheres, so that behaviour in one sphere, such as on social media or on mobile phones, need not be inhibited by the fear of its possible consequences for other spheres, such as credit, employment, health or insurance, that are on their face functionally unconnected with the former.

Helen Nissenbaum's privacy construct of 'contextual integrity' draws on this concern by arguing that incursions into privacy can be explained with reference to norms of appropriateness and to norms of flow of distribution.[74] Both sets are anchored in the idea that different spheres are governed by context-specific norms about the propriety of revelations within those spheres or relationships, but even more so across to other spheres. According to *norms of appropriateness*, people should be able to 'maintain different relationships with different people... [Thus a] person can be active in the gay pride movement in San Francisco, but be private about her sexual preferences vis-à-vis her family and coworkers in Sacramento.'[75] Nissenbaum thus concludes 'appropriating information from one situation and inserting it in an another can constitute a violation.'[76] For the *norms of flow of distribution* Nissenbaum builds on Michael Walzer's theory of justice,[77] according to which 'complex equality, the mark of justice, is achieved when social goods are distributed according to different standards of distribution in different spheres and the spheres are relatively autonomous.'[78] Thus in a 'just society, we would see "different outcomes for different people in different spheres."'[79] For example, a lack of buying power in the market (one sphere) should not impact on access to education or healthcare (another sphere).

In light of both sets of norms, the maxim 'all data is credit data' presents the archetypal example of a violation of privacy. First, it does not honour the context-sensitivity of information shared or collected in one sphere that makes it *inappropriate* for it to be used in another context. Letting data from social media seep into credit scores, is as intrusive as assuming that a participant in the gay pride movement would not mind for their sexual preference to be revealed to their employer or family. Second, 'all data is credit data' is also liable to throw individuals in a single box for all purposes and all social goods by whitewashing the differences between different social spheres; it thereby violates Walzer's theory of justice and complex equality, which Nissenbaum's contextual construction of privacy upholds through insisting on the relative autonomy of different informational domains.

At the extreme end of the seemingly random tapping into the data of a functionally distinct domain lies the consolidation of *all* personal data sets to be used for *all* purposes – as is broadly the underlying design of the Chinese social credit score system.[80] As a system designed for strong social control,[81] it manifests the domination and oppression that result from the concentration of data and universality of function. This oppression is also implicitly present, albeit as a milder version, in big data credit score models,[82] and in a growing body of other commercial and legal applications. This objection belongs, in its generality, to data protection and information privacy law; yet given that the parasitic use of data across functional domains may also be tied up with indirectly discriminatory practices, anti-discrimination law may usefully intervene. After all, less oppressive avenues for judging creditworthiness are frequently available.

7.4.4 *Particularisation of Profiling v. the Broad Brush of Anti-discrimination Law*

A final question that remains to be raised (if not fully answered) is whether the use of big data analytics in credit score models and many other commercial and legal contexts negates altogether the possibility of a finding of indirect discrimination. Although personalised risk assessment models may draw their intelligence from the data of personal networks that are likely to replicate structural disadvantages of protected groups, they are arguably – in process *and* outcome – insensitive to the presence of the protected attributes. Yet, it is group disadvantage within nine or so large categories, upon which discrimination law builds. In *Essop and Naeem*, Lady Hale observed:

> there is no requirement that the PCP [ie the criterion or practice] in question put every member of the group sharing the particular protected characteristic at a disadvantage. The later definitions cannot have restricted the original definitions, which referred to the proportion who could, or could not, meet the requirement…The fact that some BME or older candidates could pass the test is neither here nor there. The group was at a disadvantage because the proportion of those who could pass it was smaller than the proportion of white or younger candidates. If they had all failed, it would be closer to a case of direct discrimination (because the test requirement would be a proxy for race or age).[83]

Indirect discrimination does not require for every member of the group to be adversely affected, but only a proportion. Still, it identifies the disadvantage with membership of the group; the disadvantage arises *because of* being a member of the group. By implication it must be delimited to certain groups, however broadly defined, for example, BME or older candidates. Risk assessment models that draw on big data facilitate greater granularity, or micro-segmentation, than traditional models – both in terms of an analysis capable of absorbing more individual particularities, and in terms of a more fine-tuned outcome that reflects those particularities. For example, a credit score that draws on a borrower's online purchase habits can reveal far more individual particularities than his postcode or even occupation. It puts the individual under a financial microscope, which arguably fits uneasily with the broad brush discrimination that anti-discrimination law envisages and seeks to redress. Even assuming that members of protected groups are still more adversely affected by the process, if the adverse outcome ultimately cuts across protected groups and other non-protected vulnerable individuals and demographic groups, it is likely to reflect, first and foremost, 'disadvantage due to socio-economic status'[84] rather than due to membership of any particular protected group. Although the concept of 'indirect discrimination' has never been insistent on a definitive match between the protected group and the adverse impact of the practice, the personalised approach further blurs the boundaries between groups, and thereby hides continuing deep structural (dis)advantages.

7.5 CONCLUSION

Credit-score models provide one of the many contexts through which the big data micro-segmentation or 'personalisation' phenomenon can be analysed and critiqued. This chapter approached the issue through the lens of anti-discrimination law, and in particular the concept of indirect discrimination. Despite its initial promise based on its focus on impact, 'indirect discrimination' ultimately is unlikely to deliver a mechanism to intervene and curb the excesses of the personalised service model. The main reason for its failure is disconnected from the big data transformation and simply lies in the fact that credit markets are dependent on knowing and absorbing many of the attributes that are also the basis of the structural disadvantages anti-discrimination law seeks to redress.

The anti-discrimination context nevertheless offers some insights that are useful beyond its own disciplinary boundaries. For example, the opportunities for oversight and review based on correlations within outputs rather than analysis of inputs are fundamentally at odds with the current trend that demands greater transparency in AI, but may after all be more practical and realistic considering the AI's 'natural' opacity and businesses' 'natural' secrecy. Similarly, the anti-discrimination approach, which is wary of human judgment when a rule-based automated process is available, is at odds with the contemporary insistence on human oversight of AI-managed decision-making. In each case, anti-discrimination law offers a refreshing perspective on the opportunities and threats of AI that have so far been dominated by the data protection lens.

Finally, the credit risk score context provides a low-key yet powerful illustration of the oppressive potential of a world in which individual behaviour from any sphere or domain may be used for any purpose; where a bank, insurance company, employer, health care provider or indeed any government authority can tap into our social DNA to pre-judge us, should it be considered appropriate and necessary for their manifold legitimate objectives.

NOTES

1 Christian E Weller, 'Credit access, the costs of credit and credit market discrimination' (2009) 36 *The Review of Black Political Economy* 7.

2 Loretta J Mester, 'What's the point of credit scoring?' (1997) *Business Review – Federal Reserve Bank of Philadelphia* 3; Mikella Hurley and Julius Adebayo, 'Credit scoring in the

era of big data' (2017) 18(1) *Yale Journal of Law and Technology* 148, 162f; Cassandra Jones Havard, 'On the take: the black box of credit scoring and mortgage discrimination' (2011) 20 (2) *Boston University Public Interest Law Journal* 241, 261ff.

3 John Gantz and David Reinsel, 'Extracting value from chaos' (2011) *IDC iView* 1,6.

4 Matthew Adam Bruckner, 'The Promise and Perils of Algorithmic Lenders' Use of Big Data' (2018) 93(1) *Chicago-Kent Law Review* 3, 14.

5 Rob Aitken, 'All data is credit data': constituting the unbanked' (2017) 21(4) *Competition & Change* 274, 283.

6 Hurley and Adebayo (n 2) 166.

7 Hurley and Adebayo (n 2) 166.

8 Hurley and Adebayo (n 2) 166.

9 Hurley and Adebayo (n 2)164. See also Bruckner (n 3) 15.

10 Mingfeng Lin, Nagpurnanand R Prabhala and Siva Viswanathan, 'Judging borrowers by the company they keep: friendship networks and information asymmetry in online peer-to-peer lending' (2013) 59(1) *Management Science* 17.

11 Bruckner (n 3) 15ff.

12 Federal Deposit Insurance Corporation, 'Fair lending implications of credit scoring systems' (Summer 2005) *Supervisory Insights* 23 www.fdic.gov/regulations/examinations/supervisory/insights/sisum05/sisummer05-article3.pdf.

13 Hurley and Adebayo (n 2) 151–64.

14 European Securities and Markets Authority, *Joint Committee Discussion Paper on the Use of Big Data by Financial Institutions* (2016) JC/2016/86, 29 www.esma.europa.eu/press-news/consultations/joint-committee-discussion-paper-use-big-data-financial-institutions.

15 Michael Staten, 'Risk-based pricing in consumer lending' (2015) 11 *Journal of Law Economics & Policy* 33, 34f.

16 Akiva A Miller, 'What do we worry about when we worry about price eiscrimination – the law and ethics of using personal information for pricing' (2014) 19(1) *Journal of Technology Law Policy* 41, 44.

17 The definition of price discrimination corresponds to one of the three types observed by economic scholars: the first-degree or perfect price discrimination. Hal R Varian, 'Price discrimination' in (1987) *Center for Research on Economic and Social Theory Working Paper* 2; see also Laura Drechsler, Juan Carlos Benito Sánchez, 'The price is (not) right: data protection and discrimination in the age of pricing algorithms' (2018) 9(3) *European Journal of Law and Technology*.

18 Drechsler and Sánchez (n 17).

19 Miller (n 16) 45f; see also Richard Steppe, 'Online price discrimination and personal data: a General Data Protection Regulation perspective' (2017) 33(6) *Computer Law & Security Review* 768, 669f.

20 Lin, Prabhala and Viswanathan (n 10).

21 Sofie De Cnudde and others, 'What does your Facebook profile reveal about your creditworthiness? Using alternative data for microfinance' (2019) 70(3) *Journal of the Operational Research Society* 353.

22 María Óskarsdóttir and others, 'The value of big data for credit scoring: enhancing financial inclusion using mobile phone data and social networks analytics' (2019) 74 *Applied Soft Computing* 26.

23 Wouter Verbeke, David Martens and Bart Baesens, 'Social network analysis for customer churn prediction' (2014) 14 *Applied Soft Computing* 431.

24 Óskarsdóttir (n 22).

25 Ibid.

26 2000/C364/01. See also Art 10 of Treaty on the Functioning of the European Union, Art 14 of the European Convention of Human Rights, as well as the constitutions of various EU Member States.

27 Council Directive 2004/113/EC of 13 December 2004 implementing the principle of equal treatment between men and women in the access to and supply of goods and services [2004] OJ L 373/37.

28 Council Directive 2000/43/EC of 29 June 2000 implementing the principle of equal treatment between persons irrespective of racial or ethnic origin [2000] OJ L 180/22.

29 Lina Aldén and Mats Hammarsted, 'Discrimination in the credit market? Access to financial capital among self-employed immigrants' (2016) 69(1) *Kyklos* 3.

30 Douglas S Massey and others, 'Riding the stagecoach to hell: a qualitative analysis of racial discrimination in mortgage lending' (2016) 15(2) *City & Community* 118, 134f; Alan M White, 'Borrowing while Black: applying fair lending laws to risk-based mortgage pricing' (2008) 60 *South Carolina Law Review* 677, 679ff; Ira Goldstein and Dan Urevick-Ackelsberg, 'Subprime lending, mortgage foreclosures and race: How far have we come and how far have we to go?' (2008) *Reinvestment Fund* 4ff. According to Havard (n 2) 249, lenders have 'shifted from the credit rationing practice of red-lining to a credit access policy of risk-based pricing.'

31 Alicia H Munnell and others, 'Mortgage lending in Boston: interpreting HMDA data' (1996) 86 *American Economic Review* 25; Anya Prince and Daniel Schwarcz, 'Proxy discrimination in the age of artificial intelligence and Big Data' (2020) 105 *Iowa Law Review* 1257.

32 Havard (n 2) 249.

33 The Regulation that implements Act is 12 CFR, Part 202 (Regulation B).

34 See 15 USC para 1691 (a).

35 Hurley and Adebayo (n 2) 192. Note, the US Supreme Court held in *Washington v Davis* 426 US 229 (1976) that the prohibition of indirect racial discrimination is not grounded in the US Constitution, even if it is prohibited by statute, as first established by *Griggs v Duke Power Co* 401 US 424 (1971). To fall within the constitution, the practice must have been adopted for a racially discriminatory purpose.

36 *United States v Associates National Bank* (D. Del.), discussed in Federal Deposit Insurance Corporation (n 12) 25. For a recent UK decision on direct proxy-based discrimination, see *R (on the application of Coll) v Secretary of State for Justice* [2017] UKSC 40. Although traditionally discrimination based on proxy identifiers of a protected attribute has been considered (intentional) direct discrimination, the use of AI and its search for characteristics to predict a target variable means it is inevitably looking for proxy identifiers, that may then give rise unintentional 'disparate effects' on different groups. So discrimination by proxy may fairly be said to occupy both categories, but plays no direct role in establishing indirect discrimination.

37 For example, Art 2(b) of the EU Gender Equal Access to Goods and Services Directive 2004/113/EC.

38 Titia Loenen, 'Indirect discrimination: oscillating between containment and revolution' in Titia Loenen and Peter R Rodrigues (eds.), *Non-Discrimination Law: Comparative Perspectives* (The Hague 1999) 201.

39 *Essop & Ors v Home Office* (UK Border Agency) [2017] UKSC 27 [*Essop and Naeem*].

40 *Essop and Naeem* [26].

41 *Essop and Naeem* [28].

42 *Essop and Naeem* [41], see also s19(2)(b) of the UK Equality Act 2010.

43 Home Office (UK Border Agency) v Essop & Ors [2015] EWCA Civ 60 [7].

44 Prince and Schwarcz (n 31) 1274.

45 *Essop and Naeem* [25].

46 Hurley and Adebayo (n 2) 166ff, 179. Loren Henderson and others, 'Credit where credit is due?: Race, gender, and discrimination in the credit scores of business startups' (2015) 42(4) *The Review of Black Political Economy* 459, 460.

47 Regulation (EU) 2016/679 of the European Parliament and of the Council of 27 April 2016 on the protection of natural persons with regard to the processing of personal data and on the free movement of such data [2016] OJ L 119.

48 Art 22(1).

49 Art 13(2)(f), Art 14(2)(g), Art15(1)(h) and Recital 63.

50 Prince and Schwarcz (n 31) 1311.

51 Art 22(1) and Recital 71.

52 Art 22(2) and (3).

53 Federal Deposit Insurance Corporation (n 12) 25, but see also Manju Puri, Joerg Rocholl, and Sascha Steffen, 'Rules versus discretion in bank lending decisions' (2011) Working Paper, ESMT Berlin https://ssrn.com/abstract=1786831. More broadly on discretion versus rules, see Frederick F Schauer, *Profiles, Probabilities, Stereotypes* (Harvard University Press 2006) 52ff.

54 For a description of some of the reasons for structural disadvantages, see Weller (n 1).

55 Schauer (n 53) 296f.

56 Art 2(b) of Gender Equal Access to Goods and Services Directive 2004/113/EC.

57 This goes back to the first US indirect discrimination case of *Griggs v Duke Power Co* 401 US 424 (1971), where the Supreme Court held that to justify a racially neutral practice that has a disproportionate impact on minorities, Duke Power had to show business necessity and job relatedness.

58 Art 7 of the Mortgage Credit Directive 2014/17/EU. The Consumer Credit Directive 2008/48/EC only states that the lender must promote responsible practices during all phases of the credit (Rec 26).

59 Henderson (n 46).

60 Contrast to the discussion by Stephanie Bornstein, 'Antidiscriminatory algorithms' (2018) 70(2) *Alabama Law Review* 519, 540ff, where the author argues that antidiscrimination law requires 'individualized treatment even *within* one protected group.' This does not mean that stereotyping per se is outlawed, as occurs in all personalized online offering, where targeting is based on comparability of preferences of different groups.

61 Jonathan Simon, 'The ideological effects of actuarial practices' (1988) 22(4) *Law and Society Review* 771.

62 Hurley and Adebayo (n 2), where the authors note that FICO model in the US, which is one of the most widespread ones (ninety percent of the credit assessments were made using this model in 2010), does not consider borrowers' characteristics such as their salary or employment history. Their assessment just evaluates aspects related to the borrowers past credit history. If there is no such past credit history, there is a higher probability of loan denial.

63 Óskarsdóttir (n 22).

64 Ibid.

65 See Chapter 15 where Konstantinos Katsikopoulos queries whether complex big data models at present can be assumed to outperform simpler models.

66 Yannick Leo and others, 'Socioeconomic correlations and stratification in social-communication networks' (2016) 13 (125) *Journal of the Royal Society Interface* 1.

67 Havard (n 2) 265f.

68 Hurley and Adebayo (n 2) 167f, 173ff. See also Alex Rosenblat and others, 'Data & civil rights: consumer finance primer' (2014) *Data & Civil Rights Conference* 1, 3 https://datasociety.net/wp-content/uploads/2014/10/Finance.pdf.

69 Reflects the practice of risk-based pricing: Michael Staten, 'Risk-based pricing in consumer lending' (2015) 11(1) *Journal of Law, Economics and Policy* 33.

70 A lender's assessment of a borrower's credit risk stopped being entirely discretionary for consumer credit in 2008 (Rec 26 of the Consumer Credit Directive 2008/48/EC) and for mortgage credit in 2014 (Art. 18(2) of the Mortgage Credit Directive 2014/17/EC).In a legal action regarding the consumer creditworthiness assessment, the burden is upon the lender to prove the propriety of the assessment, *CA Consumer Finance SA v Ingrid Bakkaus and Others* C-449/13 (CJEU 18 December 2014). Lenders must also document the processes behind the creditworthiness decision in both mortgage and consumer credit.

71 Art 18(5)(a) of the Mortgage Credit Directive.

72 Art 6(1)(f) and Recital 47 of the GDPR, as interpreted in *Case C-13/16 Valsts policijas Rīgas reģiona pārvaldes Kārtības policijas pārvalde v Rīgas pašvaldības SIA "Rīgas satiksme"* [2017] (CJEU 4 May 2017); see also *Katz v United States* 389 US 347 (1967) on the concept of 'reasonable expectation of privacy' within the Fourth Amendment to the US Constitution. See also Roger Brownsword, 'Knowing me, knowing you – profiling, privacy and the public interest' in Mireille Hildebrandt, Serge Gutwirth (eds.), *Profiling the European Citizen* (Springer 2008) 345.

73 The US Fair Credit Reporting Act 1970 seeks to ensure fairness in consumer credit reporting (by requiring that the consumer can access scores, correct mistakes and understand how personal data is used) and consumer privacy (by limiting how a consumer's credit data can be used). For a critique, see Alexandra P Everhart Sickler, 'The (Un)fair Credit Reporting Act' (2015) 28 (2/3) *Loyola Consumer Law Review* 256.

74 Helen Nissenbaum, 'Privacy as contextual integrity' (2004) 79 *Washington Law Review* 119.

75 Ibid. 139f, quoting Ferdinand Schoeman (internal marks omitted).

76 Ibid. 140.

77 Michael Walzer, *Spheres of Justice: A Defense of Pluralism and Equality* (Basic Books, 1984)

78 Nissenbaum (n 74) 141.

79 Ibid.
80 Daithí Mac Síthigh and Mathias Siems, 'The Chinese social credit system: a model for other countries?' (2019) 82(6) *Modern Law Review* 1034.
81 Simon (n 61).
82 Bart van der Sloot, 'A new approach to the right to privacy, or how the European Court of Human Rights embraced the non-domination principle' (2018) 34 *Computer Law & Security Review* 539.
83 *Essop and Naeem* [27].
84 Jamie McLoughlin, 'Proposal to make 'disadvantaged socio-economic status' a prohibited ground of discrimination under Irish Law' (13 March 2018) *Oxford Human Rights Hub*, https://ohrh.law.ox.ac.uk/proposal-to-make-disadvantaged-socio-economic-status-a-prohibited-ground-of-discrimination-under-irish-law/, where the author discuss the Equality (Miscellaneous Provisions) Bill 2017, which failed to become law due to time lapse. See also Weller (n 1), who recommends that addressing specific structural differences, for example, providing for easier access to professional information, will narrow the credit gap between protected groups and others.

8

Sentencing Dangerous Offenders in the Era of Predictive Technologies: New Skin, Same Old Snake?

David Gurnham

8.1 INTRODUCTION

Questions about how the state might and ought to respond to former offenders believed to pose a continuing danger are rarely very far from the public agenda.[1] There may be no serious doubt that public protection must be part of that response and has a role to play in sentencing alongside other important aims. However, given the practical and moral implausibility of handing out indeterminate or life sentences to all potential re-offenders, indecision and disagreement persist about precisely what that role is.[2] Technologies that use data for purposes of risk assessment and for predicting re-offending arguably have an important contribution to make on this account, and indeed such technologies already play a role in jurisdictions including England and Wales. For example, in the UK the Offender Assessment System (OASys) has since 2002 been producing algorithmic risk scores by combining various data collected about offenders. The system is now used across the criminal justice system to inform risk-based decisions regarding bail, sentencing and parole as well as offender-management in prisons and in the community.[3] However, public protection and risk considerations also provoke countervailing concerns about ensuring proportionality in sentencing and about preventing unduly draconian, stigmatising and marginalising impacts on particular individuals and communities. These concerns are enduring, and principally philosophical and socio-legal in nature. Indeed, that they are not fundamentally altered by the advent of new and more sophisticated predictive technologies is the chief focus of discussion in this chapter.

The chapter contends therefore that prior to, and more fundamental than, any issues about the transparency,[4] fairness[5] and accountability[6] of predictive technology are questions about whether sentencing informed by risk and future offending can be countenanced *at all* in light of liberal justice values such as desert and moral agency. Liberal notions of just punishment are built upon the principle that the individual offender, as a one time and future potential member of the moral community, should be able to understand his punishment as the communication of moral censure for the injury done by the crime to that community as a whole. This is an essential principle from a liberal retributivist standpoint because it ensures that the offender himself 'owns' his punishment: by being made to take responsibility both for the harm he did to the community and for the penitential debt that he consequently and uniquely must repay in order finally to re-join it.[7]

Such a principled approach does make room for future-oriented considerations about the amount of punishment (typically in terms of time to be served in gaol) necessary for the message of censure to be fully understood and to enable reconciliation to take place. However, committing to this principled approach becomes difficult and problematic as soon as we bring to the fore the very different set of priorities represented by the desire to protect the public, and furthermore make the public *feel* protected from the danger of future crimes that convicted offenders *might* commit after their release. As we shall see, these are considerations that pull in entirely different directions: if we are to take seriously the principle of individualised justice as desert in the liberal retributive sense, then we face serious (potentially intractable) difficulties in justifying *any* sort of role for predictive risk profiling and assessment, let alone sentencing based on auto-mated algorithms drawing on big data analytics. In this respect, predictive technologies present us, not with genuinely new problems, but merely a more sophisticated iteration of established *actuarial* risk assessment (ARA) techniques.

This chapter describes some of the reasons why principled and social justice objections to predictive, risk-based sentencing make so elusive any genuinely syn-thetic resolution or compromise. In this arena, the choice for legal experts is not about whether to be a *facilitator* for, or a *brake* on, the application of predictive technology to sentencing, since both of these roles suggest that any legitimacy problems that arise may be overcome by adjusted expectations or differently framed legal or ethical parameters. The question is rather how it might even be possible to conceive such a thing without seriously undermining fundamental principles of justice and fairness. The chapter leaves the well-known socio-technical issues of transparency, accountability, fairness and accuracy to one side, since these are in any case ably discussed elsewhere in this book. Section 8.2 begins by describing the relevant legal and technological context, before Section 8.3 moves on to outline the principled liberal philosophical and social justice objections to predictive profiling and risk assessment having any role to play in criminal justice sentencing. The chapter concludes with a brief reflection on what the irresolution of these objections means for productively advancing discussion.

8.2 SENTENCING DANGEROUS OFFENDERS: THE LEGAL AND TECHNOLOGICAL CONTEXT

The Criminal Justice Act (CJA) 2003 provides the legal framework for sentencing dangerous offenders in England and Wales, albeit now in a form revised and amended numerous times since its original inception.[8] Under the current laws the assessment of offender risk makes provision for the use of algorithmic risk assessment systems without explicitly mandating it. Judges sentencing offenders convicted of certain 'specified offences' (generally serious offences of a violent or sexual nature) apply statutory extended sentencing provisions 'for the purpose of protecting members of the public from serious harm'.[9] In designating the dangerous provisions as applying only to certain very *serious* offences but also that any period of extension to the basic sentence reflects *public protection* priorities, the legislation seeks to promote both retributive (desert-based) and incapacitative (risk-based) principles at the same time.

In order to determine the level of potential danger posed by an offender convicted of a 'specified offence', the CJA 2003 directs that the court (a) '*must* take into account all such information as is available to it about the nature and circumstances of the offence', (b) '*may* take into account any information which is before it about any pattern of behaviour of which [the specified offence] forms part', and, presumably in order to catch anything that might yet escape notice, also (c) 'any information about the offender which is before it'.[10] These provisions afford some considerable latitude as to how any information relating to the offender's risk status may be generated and presented to the court. A psychiatrist may be called upon to give expert evidence after having made a clinical assessment of the offender, or it may be algorithmically produced (OASys, referred to above). The algorithm generates a risk score based on both static variables (age, sex, previous convictions) and dynamic ones (given to change over time).[11] It considers, amongst other things, 'social and economic factors in relation to the offender including accommodation, employability, education, associates, relationships and drug or alcohol abuse; and the offender's thinking, attitude towards offending and supervision and emotional state'.[12]

In assessing the impact of the use of OASys as a system through which algorithmic prediction is already allowed to contribute to sentencing decisions, there are two things that must be noted at this point. The first of these is that there are reasons to believe that its impact on how sentencing courts go about their business has so far been rather modest and undramatic. In the first place, even where OASys is used to inform a sentencing decision, a clinical expert may in any case be called to give oral testimony to the court as to the correct interpretation of the risk score so produced.[13] Furthermore, research by the Law Commission carried out after the introduction of OASys found that judges in England and Wales seemed still to be highly confident in their own innate, instinctual ability to determine risk – a confidence apparently undimmed by the availability of algorithmic risk assessment.[14] On the other hand however, Hannah-Moffat has published research suggesting (albeit relating to a different jurisdiction) that judges see algorithmically derived sentencing decisions as a way for them to minimize the risk to themselves of being blamed for being too lenient or too harsh[15] – as a reputational safeguard and for seeming to be responding to the public's fear of crime.[16]

The second point is that OASys and other systems used by criminal justice agencies around the world for assessing offender risk are in some significant ways different from the more truly automated *personalisation* technologies used in marketing and other commercial contexts. The latter class of systems take fuller advantage of ever-increasing computer processing power, the volume of data that can be handled and the variety of applications to which this can be put[17] to scrape massive quantities of information about an individual created by his or her online presence and activity. By contrast, the data that OASys collects is limited to particular pre-selected variables and gathered by old-fashioned methods such as surveys and interviews conducted in prisons. These variables are then fed into and manipulated by an automated algorithm, but (at least as things currently stand) their inclusion is the result of deliberate human design, choices and labour rather than artificial intelligence.

Both of the points referred to in this section (the impact of algorithmic risk assessment on judicial decision-making and the degree to which the systems used in criminal justice truly exploit automation and available data) warrant scrutiny in their own right. Significant change on either of these fronts would indeed take us into new and uncharted territory. However, this chapter is concerned with what automated risk assessment and predictive systems in criminal justice actually look like now, and as we shall see those already in use pose a major challenge to liberal principles of just punishment.

8.3 OLD ARGUMENTS WITH A NEW URGENCY: TWO PRINCIPLED OBJECTIONS TO PREDICTIVE TECHNOLOGY

We have described in broad terms the relevant legal and technical landscape for dangerous offender sentencing in England and Wales. We are now in a position to examine how, as regards the most important challenges they pose, predictive systems are actually not really new at all, but merely a more sophisticated iteration of established *actuarial* techniques for assessing risk. In this section, therefore, we turn to these hitherto intractable matters relating to the principled basis of risk assessment in criminal justice.

The techniques currently available (and described above in relation to OASys) for automating risk-assessment represent a particular chapter within a larger penological cultural paradigm-shift that took place across a number of jurisdictions (including England and Wales) from the 1970s. This period of criminal justice history saw concerns about punishing and rehabilitating individual offenders giving way at least in part to considerations of how arrays of data might help to develop a more efficient, informed, rational and cost-effective system of managing dangerous populations and public sensitivities towards risk. This paradigm-shift was famously announced by Feeley and Simon as the 'new penology', and was made possible by the development of actuarial techniques and technologies for recording and processing population, demographic and socioeconomic data and using it to predict the risk of offending behaviours.[18] In England and Wales as in other jurisdictions around the world, these techniques have long informed risk-based decision-making in a wide variety of contexts including bail decisions, non-custodial dispositions, offender management and parole, decisions to recall to prison an offender out on licence and civil preventive orders as well as pre-sentence reports for sentencing judges.[19]

The use of predictive algorithms in sentencing may represent something new and different in the sense that much greater quantities of data can be processed more quickly than previous technologies allowed, and that the potential for further advances seems now to be more profound as AI systems become more capable and sophisticated. However, these systems are nevertheless fundamentally a species of the already-established practice of actuarial risk assessment (ARA), and thus share both the principled foundations, and also the objections to which that practice has long been exposed.[20] The key philosophical and socio-legal objections to using actuarial or algorithmic techniques to inform risk-based sentencing are that this is incompatible with fundamental principles of just punishment as a response to individual wrongdoing, and that it leads to sentencing decisions for offenders that are arbitrary, marginalising and socially unjust. We turn to those objections now, and to implications these have for the justifiability of a role for predictive technologies.

8.3.1 *Public Safety versus Individual Liberty, Responsibility and Autonomy*

Liberal notions of justice in the first place regard punishment as necessary in order to acknowledge that a wrong was committed by an individual offender against the community as a whole. They also recognise and accept that the state has a legitimate interest in protecting its citizens from individuals who it has reason to consider pose a severe public risk *if a way can be found to do so justly*.[21] The 'if' is important, because neither the proven justifiability of punishing the offender following conviction, nor the potential risk of his future re-offending provides a justification for punishments that are indeterminate or indefinite. The sentence itself requires justification as a 'deserved response' to lawfully proven crime,[22] and for liberal retributivists desert represents the only good and reliable reason for displacing the usual assumptions about a person's harmlessness and their entitlement to liberty.[23]

If we agree then that public safety and individual liberty are *both* important aims of a liberal criminal justice system, then we must be able to explain how the state can pursue a public safety agenda in a way that does not involve disproportionate treatment of the individual or unjust deprivation of liberty.[24] Proportionate sentencing thus means having regard to the costs that criminal justice measures impose on individual liberty, as well as to the positive value of eventual reconciliation between offender and society.[25] Hence, principles of liberty and proportionality in combination assert themselves as a counterweight to the state's inclination to 'err on the safe side' by keeping the offender in gaol and away from *potential* victims. Principles of liberty and proportionality serve to remind that punishing an offender more than is justified by the seriousness of the crime actually committed imposes *known* burdens and costs upon him, and that by contrast any future offending is always a quantity as yet essentially *unknown* and yet to materialise.[26]

At the level of holding offenders responsible for their wrongdoing, liberal retributive rationales for punishment place considerable weight on the function of punishment as a communicative act that recognises an individual's moral responsibility and autonomy. As matters of principle derived *a priori* rather than empirically, moral responsibility and autonomy serve to justify putting an individual on trial in the first place. They also give sense to the idea of punishment as a moral message of censure from the community (via the criminal justice state) to the offender.[27] From a liberal standpoint, that punishment can be understood as a sort of communicative act is important because it underlines the idea that the punishment serves a justified and principled end: that the infliction by the offender of an injury against the community is something that *he or she can be held responsible for*, and that through his or her punishment he or she can repay a unique debt that has the power to regrow the bond thus severed between offender and the community.

None of this is to deny that there are hoped-for prospective consequential gains to be made during the period of punishment. Punishment that 'works' in a liberal sense is one in which the offender is brought to understand the injury he or she has caused, to accept responsibility for having inflicted it, and to complete his or her penitential and rehabilitative journey back to society. How much of an offender's sentence is eventually spent inside a prison and how much of it may be spent outside and subject to parole or licence conditions may be determined in part by considerations such as progress during the term of incarceration. But the key point is that the assessment about how much punishment is necessary *in total* is retrospective (i.e. desert-based), not prospective (risk-based). Only questions of seriousness and desert for the instant offence may legitimately determine that total measure. Prospective assessments of that total measure of punishment cannot be conceived within the liberal retributivist perspective, since the offender is necessarily unable to take responsibility for an offence he or she has not (yet) committed and may never commit. In other words, the offender's established guilt for the offence he or she was convicted for does not entitle the state to assume that he or she is *already* guilty of a further, future offence. To say otherwise is to undermine the moral premise of punishment itself: that the offender is to be credited as an autonomous individual capable of *choosing not* to reoffend.[28]

This insistence on a desert-based, retrospective calculation of punishment may not prohibit calculations of risk and predictive technologies for decisions about parole or indeed offender management, but there are clearly some serious problems when it comes to setting an overall sentence. At the most basic level, a liberal retributive approach and a risk-based one look in two very different, indeed opposed, directions. On the one hand, liberal retributivism as a philosophy of justice based on individual moral responsibility assumes as a matter of principle that the future is a fundamentally dark continent. Advocates of risk assessment and re-offending predictions in criminal justice on the other hand deny the unknowability of the future; they instead propose that, with sufficient quantities of suitably high-quality and reliable data, sensible predictions about future offending can be made and punishments (as well as other criminal justice interventions, such as policing) determined at least in part on that basis. As we have seen in the previous section, the 'dangerousness' sentencing provisions of the CJA 2003 try to accommodate both of these principles at the same time.

Can this gulf between these approaches to doing justice be bridgeable somehow? In cases involving (say) very great harm and also very little prospect of the offender becoming less of a risk (for example a perpetrator of mass murder who remains convinced of the rightness and necessity of his cause and actions), it would seem that the requirements both of retribution and public protection point in the same direction. In such a case, the problems described above are arguably obviated since a very long sentence would be justifiable by both retributive *and* public protection aims working together, or at least in parallel. This was effectively the reasoning of Lord Steyn in the House of Lords' landmark ruling in *Hindley* that confirmed that 'whole life' tariffs for the most serious cases were lawful and justifiable.[29] At a political level, it is not uncommon to find retribution and public protection fused together as the components necessary to ensure public confidence, for example as in the December 2019 Queen's speech.[30]

The problem with that sort of approach however is that it is entirely contingent on the facts of particular cases, and provides no assistance in instances in which retributive and public protection priorities pull in *different* directions, such as in the case of the convicted terrorist murderer who genuinely and permanently renounces his extreme cause, or the petty arsonist who, unrelatedly, happens to be a committed (say) anti-Semite and harbours a strong desire to kill Jews.

A more generally applicable (and more explicitly utilitarian) defence of using predictive risk assessment in sentencing to promote public safety from future offences is to argue that in cases involving dangerous offenders, ordinary retributive principles might be displaced for the 'greater good', and that this is in the interests of all those people who have *not* committed any crime and may be threatened by the offender's release.[31] This 'choice of principles' has obvious attractions from a public policy point of view, but it is also problematic from a principled one in that it denies the *a priori* status of the dangerous offender as a responsible moral agent and as such the possibility of his reconciliation with the society he has injured.

8.3.2 *Can Predictive Risk-Based Sentencing ever Satisfy Objections about Arbitrariness, Marginalisation and Social Injustice?*

In addition to the concerns about compatibility with philosophical principles of individual justice, critics of predictive technologies point out that serious social justice problems flow from its reliance on actuarial risk assessment (ARA) techniques. It is true that systems for predicting future potential reoffending rely not only on information about the offender's *own* past and present behaviours, attitudes and health (e.g. past offending, hostility to law enforcement or other people, alcohol or drug-dependency), but also on data about the re-offending rates amongst communities sharing the same demographic attributes and socio-economic status as the offender.[32] The problematic implications for policy and social justice have been explored by other scholars (for example, the chapter by Pamela Ugwudike in this book), but this chapter emphasises that the use of demographic information to inform individual punishment is intrinsically morally problematic. In the first place, the use of such data is suggestive, not of *individual* justice, but of a judgement about dangerous populations and communities more generally. For this reason, a sentencing decision so based arguably further undermines the idea of punishment as an expression of censure issued from the community to an individual responsible offender.[33] In the case of both 'dynamic' variables (such as drug use, place of residence and attitudes, that the offender might be able to do something to change over time) and static ones beyond any intervention, (e.g. sex and age),[34] the actuarial approach adopted by OASys and systems like it that calculate risk according to how populations of *other* people with particular characteristics and histories have generally behaved leaves it prone to two particular objections.

The first of these objections is that of *arbitrariness*, since the individual offender could in effect be any number of people who happen to share the same demographic characteristics and historical or current circumstances.[35] The second is that it *exacerbates social inequality*, since an individual offender categorised within a marginalised and vulnerable population is more likely to produce a high risk score than an offender who is not so categorised.[36] This means that a policy of imposing longer sentences on account of a higher risk score will tend also to punish more harshly, for offending of equal seriousness, individuals who are socially and economically disadvantaged. For the same reason, harsher sentences may be expected to follow those with family and mental health-related problems[37] and furthermore carry negative implications about communities that may already be stigmatised or marginalised due to perceptions of dangerousness.[38]

There are four rejoinders to these objections. Assessing predictive risk-assessment systems in their best light (i.e. assuming good quality data and the removal from consideration of any variables that are insignificant or known to be corrupted by bias), these are plausible enough to entertain. However, they are ultimately unpersuasive since they fail to counter the underlying moral objection that actuarial and predictive technologies undermine individualised liberal justice principles.

First, advocates of predictive risk assessment contend that its alleged arbitrariness is tolerable so long as it 'works' in the sense that it can be shown to be generally more accurate than alternative predictive techniques: in that case penal resources can be directed accordingly, and public safety promoted in a rational way.[39]

Second, because it works by deciding in advance which variables to factor in (as opposed to the more truly automated 'big data-scraping' algorithms that we noted above are increasingly utilised in marketing and other commercial contexts), the actuarial principles upon which systems like OASys are built can ensure that cases that are relevantly alike can be treated alike. This ensures that no one offender is treated more leniently or harshly on account of variations in the application of, and weight given by, different judges to the available risk variables.[40]

Third, demographic data can be and is in fact combined with a more individualised assessment of the offender. There is no reason why demographic information should not be used in conjunction with personal information or indeed clinical assessment, and indeed as we have seen above, OASys and the dangerousness sentencing provisions in England and Wales do accommodate both such approaches.[41]

Fourth, in response to the accusation that predictive risk assessment exacerbates social inequality, it might be suggested that there is nothing *intrinsic* to the correlation between high-risk scores and socio-economic marginalisation and vulnerability. In practice, social harm is not inevitable, since a penal policy can be pursued that determines that a low-risk score will be treated as a reason to reduce a sentence rather than a high-risk score as a reason to increase it.[42] In any case, there is no reason why sentencing judges should be obliged (*de jure* or *de facto*) to follow the algorithmically produced risk assessment if there are reasons to take a different view in a particular case, again as noted above in the England and Wales context.

All four rejoinders, however, provoke further objections, all of which suggesting that the problems are not so easily overcome. To take the first one described above (that the arbitrariness of actuarial predictive technologies is tolerable so long as it is more accurate than the alternative), we may observe that testing the accuracy of any given prediction is complicated by contingencies such as the particular impact of the sentencing disposition (say, a prison sentence) on the individual offender. In studies that have nevertheless sought to test the accuracy of re-offending predictions based on actuarial assessments, these have never been shown to get it right more than about 70 per cent of the time. This has remained the case in the era of OASys and other comparable systems with their many co-mingled variables.[43] It is of course possible that future predictive systems that are truly automated and algorithmic in the selection of variables and collection of data might in time prove more 'accurate', but it remains to be seen if indeed such a system could be applied at all in the context of sentencing. In any case, because risk labels as generated in systems now in use represent a *group*-level probabilistic forecast, the re-offending prediction is not subject to proof or falsification by the individual offender.

This is very much a principled objection to prediction. Even putting aside the question of whether the offender is in prison or on release, it is necessarily impossible for that person to show that, after all, it was wrong to label him or her 'high risk' since the risk label itself indicates only what *proportion* of people sharing those characteristics may be expected to commit further crimes, not that *he or she* will.[44] Short of a prediction of either zero or 100 per cent certainty of re-offending, this can never be disproved at an individual level. It is also a matter of some debate as to whether the crime-reduction achieved by the greater incapacitation (and the at least theoretical possibility for rehabilitation) effected by longer sentences for dangerous criminals outweighs the unintended consequences of such a policy.[45] It is plausible to suspect that at least in some cases, offenders will only be further hardened or damaged by having to endure an extended prison term. In these cases, the longer sentences for dangerous offenders may have some value in terms of incapacitation, but they may also serve to *increase* the risk of reoffending after eventual release.[46]

Regarding the second rejoinder (predictive risk assessment enables courts to treat like cases alike), a question may be raised with respect to what constitutes a 'relevant' variable and what justifies us in concluding that 'Case A' is relevantly *like* 'Case B' but *unlike* 'Case C'. If the variable that separates offender C from offenders A and B is a socio-economic one such as indebtedness or employment status (and hence not one relating to the offender's own *criminal* responsibility), then to insist that he therefore be treated differently is no less unjust than the more 'haphazard' variations of treatment between different judges attaching weight inconsistently to the relevant factors, or even applying wholly divergent factors. If anything, the automated approach is almost certainly the more unjust, given that harder treatment of the economically disadvantaged offender is systematically and deliberately embedded in the algorithm.

As for the third rejoinder (group-level risk-factors can be strengthened by being combined with individual ones), it is indeed true that in many cases factors relating to the offender's personal profile and characteristics may appear to lend supporting weight to a calculation of risk otherwise based on demographic or socio-economic data. But what is it that the group-level data actually tells us about *the individual being sentenced*, such that this information can meaningfully be *combined* into the sentencing decision? That an offender may have a string of past relevant convictions arguably bears relevantly on the risk that he or she may re-offend. Notwithstanding that it is not part of the offence for which the offender is being asked in the instant case to take responsibility for, past offending nonetheless at least affords information about how the offender him or her*self* has exercised or failed to exercise moral agency in the past. On the other hand, the fact that the offender may happen to share with a certain section of the population characteristics such as being of a relatively low socio-economic status, does not so reference that individual's moral agency at any point at all. Rather, it simply identifies the offender with a certain number of *other* people, and asks how those other people have behaved in the past. Consequently, that latter set of characteristics cannot simply be welded onto considerations about the individual being sentenced without sacrificing the principles of individual justice and moral autonomy.[47]

Regarding the fourth rejoinder (that social injustice is not inevitable, depending on the policy framework adopted), we may accept that innovative sentencing policy can potentially go some way to countering the socially divisive implications of algorithmically produced assessments. However, it remains the case that if high risk correlates positively with socioeconomic marginalisation and vulnerability (which it generally does) then the *contribution* of such data to sentencing considerations will be to provide a reason to punish marginalised, vulnerable people more harshly.[48] It is after all the principled basis for predictive technology that concerns us here. In any case, we know that in sentencing jurisdictions where such technology is used in the interests of public safety, high risk *does* generally mean a longer sentence, which makes the argument that policy *might in theory* reverse this state of affairs at best disingenuous, and at worst cynical. In England and Wales, there is nothing in the CJA 2003 to prompt judges to treat the marginalising impact for socio-economically disadvantaged offenders of longer sentences as a mitigating factor. Furthermore, experience in this jurisdiction of the ill-fated Indeterminate Sentence for Public Protection (IPP) between 2009 and 2012 (during which time sentencing judges readily exercised their statutory discretion to impose an indeterminate sentence for public protection) suggests that it would be unwise to expect judges to exercise their discretion to make good this lack even if permitted to do so.[49] Both in principle and in practice then, it is legitimate to worry that risk-based sentencing tends to be divorced from broader considerations of the social impact of punishment, namely the vulnerability of those on which it falls most heavily.[50]

8.4 CONCLUDING REMARKS: PROBLEMS WITH NO SOLUTION?

The ever-present demand for efficient ways to allocate limited carceral resources and to offer protection to the public from dangerous offenders means that there will likely always be a demand for smart systems that aid decision-making by making use of available data. By extension, it may be anticipated that there will also always be a role for legal and other relevant experts who can supply a figurative bridge between a rapidly evolving technology, problems of transparency, openness, fairness and bias thrown up by its application and routes to socio-technical solutions and legitimating normative and legal frameworks.[51] But as discussed above, the apparent progress enabled by this marriage of legal, ethical and technical expertise and policy has not resolved some of the most obstinate difficulties facing the justifiability of algorithmic predictive technologies and the risk-based sentencing they support.

Those difficulties are no mere matters of academic scruple, since they engage fundamental principles concerning the basic relationship between the offender and the state: about the basis on which the former's hard treatment and deprivation of liberty by the latter is justifiable at all, how much of that treatment can legitimately be meted out without further justification, and the broader social costs that follow it. At the same time, it would be difficult to overstate the problems involved in actually overcoming this impasse, since the liberal principles in question – retrospective and responsibility-based – are quite separate from, and run directly counter to, those prospective and probabilistic principles of risk assessment.

On the one hand then, this chapter has identified some significant and important problems regarding the justifiability of predictive risk assessment as a source of information for sentencing dangerous offenders. On the other hand, laying out a 'solution' to this, even assuming such a thing exists, is a much larger task for another time and place. I conclude therefore with a plea to colleagues who may be keen to use their legal expertise to assist the development and application of new and apparently world-changing technologies not to lose sight of the issues discussed above: either the core liberal-philosophical principles underlying individual justice or the social justice and marginalisation implications. The nature of these concerns provides compelling evidence that any solution we might come to is unlikely to be found through technological advances. For, if by 'advances' we mean further automation at the data-collection end in order to feed into the process a greater quantity and variety of information, this would inevitably mean undermining the extent to which our current offender risk-assessment systems do guard against bad quality, misleading or discriminatory data. Leaving aside for now those more distant challenges, we may say that data-driven risk-based sentencing is not a source of truly novel problems, but merely a new skin for an old snake whose dimensions and character are already well known.

NOTES

1 See Jamie Doward, 'Usman Khan was freed. Then he went on a killing spree. How did this happen?' *The Guardian* (London, 1 Dec 2019) www.theguardian.com/uk-news/2019/dec/01/khan-attack-will-put-sentencing-and-release-of-terrorists-under-scrutiny.

2 Indeterminate sentences for Public Protection (IPP) were introduced by the Criminal Justice Act 2003 but then abolished by the Legal Aid and Sentencing of Offenders (LASPO) Act 2012. See Harry Annison, *Dangerous Politics* (Oxford University Press 2015).

3 See Home Office, *First-tier Tribunal bail: completing the bail summary* (20 January 2020); HM Prison Service Order, *Offender Assessment and Sentence Management - OASys* (Prison Service Order 2205, 20 April 2005).

4 Lyria Bennett Moses and Janet Chan, 'Using Big Data for legal and law enforcement decisions: testing the new tools' (2014) 37(2) *University of New South Wales Law Journal* 643; Emre Bayamlıoğlu and Ronald Leenes, 'The "rule of law" implications of data-driven decision-making: a techno-regulatory perspective' (2018) 10(2) *Law, Innovation and Technology* 295, 311; Kelly Hannah-Moffat, 'Actuarial sentencing: an "unsettled" proposition' (2013) 30(2) *Justice Quarterly* 270, 284–7; Vincent Chiao, 'Fairness, accountability and transparency: notes on algorithmic decision-making in criminal justice' (2019) 15 *International Journal of Law in Context* 126, 134–5.

5 See Bernard E Harcourt, 'Risk as a proxy for race: the dangers of risk assessment' (2015) 27(4) *Federal Sentencing Reporter* 237, on the history of criminal justice (focusing on US experience).

6 Caryn Devins and others, 'The law and Big Data' (2017) 27 *Cornell Journal of Law and Public Policy* 357, see especially 363–5, 370–85; Bayamlioglu and Leenes (n 4) 303–7, 307–9.

7 RA Duff, *Punishment, Communication, and Community* (Oxford University Press 2000).

8 The most significant changes for present purposes being introduced by the Criminal Justice and Immigration Act 2008 and the LASPO Act 2012. The Counter Terrorism (Sentencing and Release) Bill and the Sentencing Bill set out in the December 2019 Queen's Speech will bring about further changes to the CJA dangerousness provisions (Prime Minister's Office, 2019)https://assets.publishing.service.gov.uk/government/uploads/system/uploads/attachment_data/file/853886/Queen_s_Speech_December_2019_-_background_briefing_notes.pdf.

9 Schedule 15 CJA 2003 (as amended) lists the relevant 'specified' offences. Quoted section: s226A(7), as added by LASPO, s124.

10 s 229(2) subsections (a), (b) and (c). Emphases added.

11 Prison Reform Trust, *Offender Management and Sentence Planning* (2019) www.prisonreformtrust.org.uk/ForPrisonersFamilies/PrisonerInformationPages/OffenderManagementandsentenceplanning.

12 CPS, 'Sentencing dangerous offenders' (06 November 2019) www.cps.gov.uk/legal-guidance/sentencing-dangerous-offenders.

13 Lucia Zedner, 'Erring on the side of safety: risk assessment, expert knowledge, and the criminal court' in GR Sullivan and Ian Dennis (eds.), *Seeking Security: Pre-Empting the Commission of Criminal Harms* (Hart Publishing 2012).

14 Law Commission, The Admissibility of Expert Evidence in Criminal Proceedings in England and Wales: A New Approach to the Determination of Evidentiary Reliability (Law Com Consultation Paper 190, 2009) 43–6. For commentary, see Zedner (n 13) 240 who suggests that the LC research undermines claims to AI-assisted sentencing being particularly 'scientific'.

15 Kelly Hannah-Moffat, 'The uncertainties of risk assessment: partiality, transparency, and just decisions' (2015) 27(4) *Federal Sentencing Reporter* 244.

16 Kelly Hannah-Moffat (n 4) 270. See also Annison (n 2) ch 8 on populism and penal policy.

17 Kelly Hannah-Moffat, 'Algorithmic risk governance: Big Data analytics, race and information activism in criminal justice debates' (2019) 24(4) *Theoretical Criminology* 453, 456–7; Moses and Chan (n 4) 650–1.

18 Malcom M Feeley and Jonathan Simon, 'The new penology: notes on the emerging strategy of corrections and its implications' (1992) 30(4) *Criminology* 449.

19 Andrew Ashworth and Lucia Zedner, *Preventive Justice* (Oxford University Press 2014) 127–29.

20 Kelly Hannah-Moffat and Paula Maurutto, 'Re-contextualizing pre-sentence reports: risk and race' (2010) 12(3) *Punishment and Society* 262; Sonja B Starr, 'Evidence-based sentencing and the scientific rationalization of discrimination' (2014) 66 *Stanford Law Review* 803; John Monahan and Jennifer L Skeem, 'Risk assessment in criminal sentencing' (2016) 12 *Annual Review of Clinical Psychology* 489. For a review of its use internationally, see Gwen van Eijk, 'Socioeconomic marginality in sentencing: the built-in bias in risk assessment tools and the reproduction of social inequality' (2017) 19(4) *Punishment and Society* 463, 465–6; Annison (n 2) ch 8.

21 Indeed, states have a general duty to take steps to promote citizens' Article 2 rights (ECHR).

22 Duff (n 7) 170.

23 Ashworth and Zedner (n 19) ch 6.

24 Andrew von Hirsch and Andrew Ashworth, *Proportionate Sentencing* (Oxford University Press 2005) 56; Ashworth and Zedner (n 19) 120, 162.

25 Duff (n 7) 166. See also von Hirsch and Ashworth (n 24).

26 Zedner (n 13) 220–1. See also Ashworth and Zedner (n 19) 150.

27 Duff (n 7).

28 Ashworth and Zedner (n 19) 149–50.

29 *R v Secretary of State for the Home Department ex parte Hindley* [2000] All ER (D) 430 per Lord Steyn: 'there are cases where the crimes are so wicked that even if the prisoner is detained until he or she dies it will not exhaust the requirements of retribution and deterrence.'

30 Harcourt (n 5) 66. The first of two purposes of the proposed Sentencing Bill are to: 'Ensure that the most serious violent and sexual offenders spend time in prison that matches the severity of their crimes, protecting victims and giving the public confidence.' For discussion of the combination of retributive justice and incapacitation in punishment, see von Hirsch and Ashworth (n 24).

31 J Floud, 'Dangerousness and criminal justice' (1982) *The British Journal of Criminology* 22, 213–28.

32 See Feeley and Simon (n 18). Again, it must be emphasized that the data referred to here concerns past data about the re-offending risk of particular sections of the population, *not* personalised data about the individual's own past behaviours.

33 Duff (n 7) 171.

34 Ibid. The availability of such treatment programmes that would enable a prisoner to reduce his level of risk during the course of his incarceration is not a given however, and indeed it was on account of the poor provision of such services that the UK was found to be in breach of its Article 5 duties in *James, Wells and Lee v UK* (2012) 56 EHRR 159; for further discussion, see Ashworth and Zedner (n 19) 163.

35 Starr (n 20) 842; Eric Silver, 'Actuarial risk assessment: reflections on an emerging social-scientific tool' (2000) 9(1/2) *Critical Criminology* 123, 134–7.

36 On actuarial risk assessment techniques consistently reporting correlation between 'high risk' and high levels of vulnerability and marginalisation, see van Eijk (n 20).

37 See, e.g., Alison Leibling and Shadd Maruna (eds.), *The Effects of Imprisonment* (Routledge 2013); Marie Hutton and Dominique Moran (eds.), *The Palgrave Handbook of Prison and the Family* (Palgrave Macmillan 2019).

38 See Bernard E Harcourt, 'Against Prediction: Sentencing, Policing, and Punishing in an Actuarial Age' (University of Chicago Public Law & Legal Theory Working Paper No 94, 2005) on the problem of the self-fulfilling prophecy and the impact of the symbolic message in targeting populations.

39 Anthony W Flores, Kristin Bechtel and Christopher T Lowenkamp, 'False positives, false negatives, and false analyses: a rejoinder to machine bias: there's software used across the country to predict future criminals. and it's biased against blacks' (2016) 80(2) *Federal Probation* 38.

40 Chiao (n 4) 131–2.

41 Ric Simmons, 'Quantifying criminal procedure: how to unlock the potential of Big Data in our criminal justice system' (2016) *Michigan State Law Review* 947, 984–96.

42 See Richard Couzens, 'Evidence-based practices: reducing recidivism to increase public safety; a cooperative effort by courts and probation' (Cow County Judges Institute, Administrative Office of the Courts Education Division 2011) 10 www.courts.ca.gov/part ners/documents/may11-04-evidence.pdf.

43 See Julia Dressler and Hany Farid, 'The accuracy, fairness and limits of predicting recidivism' (2018) 4(1) *Science Advances* https://advances.sciencemag.org/content/4/1/ eaao5580.full.

44 Ashworth and Zedner (n 19) 232–33.

45 See A Ashworth, *Sentencing and Criminal Justice* (Cambridge University Press 2010) 207.

46 See Starr (n 20) who adapts Harcourt's notion of 'elasticity' to argue that calculations of the incapacitatory effect of imprisonment needs to be weighed against the damaging effects on prisoners (and their risk of re-offending) actually brought about *by* extended sentences. We return to the observation that imprisonment is itself a source of social harm below.

47 As accepted by Monahan and Skeem (n 20).

48 Starr (n 20) 840–1.

49 Ashworth and Zedner (n 19) 162; Annison (n 2).

50 Starr (n 20) 839.

51 Research on AI technologies and their application for government and criminal justice is listed as one of a limited number of key strategic priorities for the Strategic Priorities Fund, UKRI. UK Research and Innovation, 'The Strategic Priorities Fund' (*UKRI.org*) www.ukri .org/research/themes-and-programmes/strategic-priorities-fund/.

PART III

Applications: From Personalised Medicine and Pricing to
Political Micro-Targeting

9

'P4 Medicine' and the Purview of Health Law: The Patient or the Public?

Keith Syrett

9.1 'p4', 'personalised', 'stratified' or 'precision' medicine?

Data-driven personalisation in medicine has been viewed by its most enthusiastic proponents as possessing the capacity to shift the paradigm of twenty-first century healthcare.[1] If such profound change is indeed underway, it will also become important to critically interrogate our understandings of the framework through which contemporary healthcare is legally regulated: that area of academic study and legal practice variously described as 'health law', 'health care law', or (in the United Kingdom, most commonly) 'medical law'. This exercise is an especially worthwhile one given, as will subsequently be discussed, that questions as to the scope and nature of this relatively young sub-discipline continue to occupy scholarly attention in any event. This chapter seeks to proffer some reflections on this matter with particular reference to the UK, although the analysis also has broad applicability to other jurisdictions.

An important approach to personalisation in medicine is the concept of 'P4 medicine', which is associated most closely with the work of Leroy Hood, a US biologist who was involved with the Human Genome Project from its inception in 1985, and who established a Department of Molecular Biotechnology at the University of Washington in the early 1990s, with financial assistance from Bill Gates, who shared an interest in uniting computer technology and biological research and utilising the results for medical research. Hood pioneered a systems approach to biology, especially through the vehicle of the non-profit Institute for Systems Biology, founded in 2000.

This approach uses computational and modelling methodologies to analyse complex biological systems, notably the human body: 'The defining feature of systems medicine is the collection of diverse longitudinal data for each individual. These data sets can be used to unravel the complexity of human biology and disease by assessing both genetic and environmental determinants of health and their interactions.'[2] Hood and his followers have referred to these as 'personal, dense, dynamic data clouds,'[3] arguing that these 'will surround each patient and that we will have computational tools to reduce that enormous data dimensionality to simple hypotheses about health and disease, and to sculpt these phenomena, with exquisite specificity, for each individual.'[4]

A systems approach to biology – coupled with the 'digital revolution' which has allowed for the management and analysis of big data; enabled the development of personal health-monitoring devices; and resulted in the development of patient-driven social networks[5] – is given its clinical manifestation through what Hood has labelled 'P4 medicine'. This is described as 'employ[ing] the tools of systems medicine for quantifying wellness and demystifying disease for the well-being of the individual.'[6] The terminology refers to medicine which is predictive, preventive, personalised and participatory. It is *predictive* in the sense that it will enable longitudinal measurements to be taken throughout a lifetime, 'immediately identifying any transitions from health to disease, sending alerts early on and suggesting preventive measures such as changes in dietary or exercising habits';[7] *preventive* in that it entails identification of genetic and other risks for disease, enabling these to be planned for in advance; *personalised* in so far as it rests upon 'data clouds' which are unique to the individual, enabling treatments to be tailored more effectively to particular genomic sequences; and *participatory* in that it allows for the active engagement of patients in their own care. Overall, Hood has argued that adoption of P4 medicine will signal that 'the objective of twenty-first century medicine will be to understand deeply and optimize wellness, to understand disease and its progressions, and to identify and reverse the earliest transitions between the two.'[8]

P4 medicine may be regarded as a particular manifestation of that which has variously been termed *personalised*, *stratified* or *precision* medicine, all of which 'broadly refer to the possibilities that are opened up by the translation of emerging modes of data-intensive biomedical research to the context of medical practice and health care delivery'.[9] Erikainen and Chan convincingly demonstrate that these terms possess slightly distinct nuances of meaning, and that 'each positions patients and citizens differently with respect to health and biomedicine as well as in relation to governance and the state.'[10] To aid in understanding, these will now be briefly outlined.

'Personalised' medicine is the most commonly used label, with particular currency within Europe. It has been argued that this 'term best reflects the ultimate goal of effectively tailoring treatment based on an individual's "personal profile", as determined by the individual's genotype and phenotype data,'[11] and it has become associated with patient-centred approaches to health care delivery, including greater control over one's own health. However, it has been criticised in so far as it might be said that all medicine is to some degree, and has always been, personalised;[12] and (in partial contrast) in that the goal of 'tailoring treatment' is practically infeasible or 'overambitious',[13] since the best that can be achieved is to categorise patients into more closely defined subgroups.

The terminology of 'stratified medicine' seeks to respond to this latter point: this has been defined as 'the grouping of patients based on risk of disease or response to therapy by using diagnostic tests or techniques.'[14] Yet, while seemingly more modest in its ambition, this label is also problematic in that it is relatively inaccessible to the public, and carries connotations of social division, for example, based upon ethnicity or socioeconomic status.[15]

Finally, 'precision medicine' is the term in predominant use in the United States, especially in light of the launch of the 'Precision Medicine Initiative' by President Obama in his State of the Union address in January 2015. This has been defined as

> an approach to disease treatment and prevention that seeks to maximize effectiveness by taking into account individual variability in genes, environment, and lifestyle. Precision medicine seeks to redefine our understanding of disease onset and progression, treatment response, and health outcomes through the more precise measurement of molecular, environmental, and behavioural factors that contribute to health and disease.[16]

This closely resembles the European 'personalised medicine' terminology – and draws similarly on concepts of patient-centredness[17] – but seeks to avoid the perceived over-ambition of the former, as well as the divisive connotations of stratification.[18] A report published by the World Health Organization further differentiates the latter by identifying stratification as a technique for assessing the benefit-risk profile of a medicine within a subgroup of the population, with 'precision medicine' referring to 'the *clinical consequences* – a better treatment'.[19]

The lexical complexity which is evident here is reflective, as Erikainen and Chan emphasise, of 'struggle over what a desirable and realizable future does and does not, and should and should not look like. Each term taps into different interests and links to future imaginaries that can then be used to gather support for and investment in emerging research activities.'[20] Given limitations of space, rather than engaging in detail with the 'particular associations, connotations, "hopes" and "truths"' which are engendered by these various terms,[21] this chapter utilises the single term of 'P4 medicine' as shorthand. It is submitted that this is also helpful in that, first, it connects this form of medicine more closely to the data-rich systems biology approach which Hood and colleagues have espoused – and thus to the subject-matter of this book; and second, that it serves to underline that 'personalisation' is only one dimension of this development, albeit a central component.[22]

9.2 FROM MEDICAL PATERNALISM TO PATIENT CHOICE

9.2.1 *The Hegemony of 'Autonomy' in Contemporary UK Medical Jurisprudence*

In order to understand how these developments in medical treatment might intersect with our understandings of 'health law' (or cognate terms), it is necessary first to outline the prevailing trend of contemporary medical jurisprudence in the UK, even though this story will be familiar to those working within this sub-discipline.

The overall direction of travel can be clearly identified by way of brief consideration of the 2015 UK Supreme Court decision of *Montgomery v Lanarkshire Health Board*,[23] which (in common with the development of P4 medicine) has been viewed by some as representing a 'paradigm shift'.[24] Here, the Court articulated a revised test of informed consent in relation to the disclosure of the risks of medical treatment to a patient, holding that 'an adult person of sound mind is entitled to decide which, if any, of the available forms of treatment to undergo, and her consent must be obtained before treatment interfering with her bodily integrity is undertaken.'[25] Underpinning the adoption of this test were various social and legal developments outlined by the Court, which were said to have impacted on the character of the clinician–patient relationship. These include greater availability of information, the status of patients as rights-holders, the growth of consumerism in health care and the impact of the Human Rights Act 1998, especially the right to respect for private and family life under Article 8 ECHR. The Court opined that these:

> point away from a model of the relationship between the doctor and the patient based upon medical paternalism. They also point away from a model based upon a view of the patient as being entirely dependent on information provided by the doctor. What they point towards is an approach to the law which, instead of treating patients as placing themselves in the hands of their doctors... treats them so far as possible as adults who are capable of understanding that medical treatment is uncertain of success and may involve risks, accepting responsibility for the taking of risks affecting their own lives, and living with the consequences of their choices.[26]

This passage clearly corroborates Arvind and McMahon's observation that 'few areas of law illustrate the judicial shift away from paternalism and deference, and the growing importance of patients' rights, as well as the law in relation to informed consent,'[27] although these authors note also that any change in paradigm in this regard has been a gradual rather than abrupt process.[28] Underpinning the 'rights-based' approach to the issue of provision of information upon risks, and consequent consent to medical treatment which the Supreme Court adopted in *Montgomery* is the foundational concept of *autonomy*, which may now be said to represent the preeminent ethico-legal value in medical law in the UK.[29] The matter is clearly articulated in a leading textbook:

> the undoubted fact [is] that autonomy is by far the most significant value to have influenced the evolution of contemporary medical law, at least in the context of the therapeutic relationship. The concept which has dominated the control of medical practice more than any other in the last half-century is the insistence that individuals should have control over their own bodies, should make their own decisions

relating to their medical treatment, and should not be hindered in their search for self-fulfilment. The acknowledgement of autonomy has served to discredit medical paternalism in almost all its forms and has led to the promotion of the patient from the recipient of treatment to being a partner, or even client, in a therapeutic project – and this change has been reflected in the rapid development of the legal and political regimes by which medical treatment is now regulated in the United Kingdom.[30]

It will be noted that mention is made here of the political environment within which regulation of medical treatment takes place. Obliquely referenced by the Supreme Court in *Montgomery*, an important contemporary trend has been measures instituted by government, especially within the English NHS, to give effect to patient choice and to patient-(or person-) centred care.[31] These include, *inter alia*: the availability of 'personal health budgets' for those with complex care needs,[32] and statutory duties placed upon clinical commissioning groups (which bear primary responsibility for the commissioning of health services in England) to promote the involvement of patients in decisions relating to prevention or diagnosis of illness and care and treatment, and to enable patients to make choices with respect to aspects of health services provided to them.[33] There is also secondary legislation which requires providers to design care or treatment with a view to achieving service users' preferences and ensuring their needs are met, to understand care or treatment choices and to discuss the balance of risks and benefits involved in any particular course of treatment, and to enable and support participation in decision-making on care or treatment to the maximum extent possible.[34] Finally, the Department of Health acknowledges as a 'guiding principle' that 'the patient will be at the heart of everything the NHS does. It should support individuals to promote and manage their own health. NHS services must reflect, and should be coordinated around and tailored to, the needs and preferences of patients, their families and their carers.'[35]

In concluding this short survey, I would note that it is not my intention to offer detailed analysis of the *meaning* attached to 'autonomy' in its role as the pre-eminent value in contemporary medical law and ethics in the UK.[36] In any event, as Coggon has observed, 'there is not. . . one generally accepted definition of the concept or the limits of its validity', and it is rarely exposed to rigorous philosophical analysis in case-law.[37] It will suffice for the purposes of the further argument made in this chapter to state that it is clear that a fundamental dimension of the concept is the notion of self-rule, or the capacity to govern oneself: 'one must be in a position to act competently based on desires (values, conditions, etc.) that are in some sense one's own.'[38]

9.2.2 *P4 Medicine and Autonomy: Choice and 'Responsibilisation'*

From the preceding outline, it is possible to discern a clear association between the trend of contemporary UK medical jurisprudence towards the centrality of the autonomous patient and the aims and character of P4 medicine, even if the latter development did not receive specific mention in the Supreme Court's account of the contextual factors underpinning the altered paradigm which it identified in *Montgomery*.

In order to achieve full self-rule, individuals must possess *information* to enable them to make choices which correspond to their desires and values. This, of course, lies at the heart of the approach adopted by the UK Supreme Court in *Montgomery*, and it is central also to P4 medicine in three respects. First, P4 medicine provides a source of 'personalised' information deriving from unique 'data clouds' surrounding individuals which can serve to quantity the health of that individual. Secondly, that information can be used 'predictively' so that the individual is alerted to potential or actual changes in their personal health status, and consequently, and thirdly, to enable them to exercise control over their own lives either by making 'preventive' choices (e.g. over lifestyle or diet) which might reverse or delay the transition from wellness to disease, or merely to adapt and plan their lives in accordance with the information received.

However, as Coggon and Miola have observed,[39] mere provision of information alone does not ensure genuine autonomy. It is also necessary for the individual to *understand* that information so that s/he can choose whether to act upon it (or not) in a manner which accords with personal desires and values. In this respect, the fourth 'P' of P4 medicine, participation, is particularly germane. The proponents of this model envisage:

> newly activated and networked patients and consumers. Collectively, they will constitute a vital new stakeholder... that is very different from the passive recipients of expert advice characteristic of pre-digital medicine. Activated and networked consumers will do more than demand more effective health care – they will help direct the changes to achieve it.[40]

These consumers are seen as 'educated',[41] although it is conceded that such education will present 'an enormous challenge'.[42] Nonetheless, advocates of P4 medicine argue that this challenge can be surmounted, primarily through engagement with digital social networks,[43] particularly familial networks in which certain individuals are especially active 'in setting familial health-related standards and in caring for members with health problems'.[44] This will 'allow P4 medicine to systemically and more effectively deal with the reality of the social context in which patients and consumers are embedded and which largely determines how they eat, exercise and sleep'.[45]

There is considerable correspondence between this vision of participatory medicine,[46] and some of the contextual factors outlined by the UK Supreme Court in *Montgomery*, albeit that the latter are (unsurprisingly) fleshed out in less detail. For example, both utilise the discourse of 'consumerism'[47] which connects closely to the rhetoric, and accompanying policy initiatives, of 'choice' which have been prevalent in recent reforms to the NHS in England.[48] Similarly, the P4 vision of 'networked and activated consumers as active participants in health care, as opposed to passive recipients of expert advice'[49] chimes closely with the Supreme Court's observation that 'patients are now widely regarded as persons holding rights, rather than passive recipients of the care of the medical profession'.[50]

In sum, therefore, the P4 approach can be seen as fully congruent with the model of the informed and active consumer-patient articulated in *Montgomery*, and – more broadly – with a trend towards autonomy as a pre-eminent ethical and jurisprudential value.

Before moving on to outline the significance which this might hold for possible readings of the reach and remit of the connected academic sub-discipline, there is one further implication of P4 medicine which warrants particular consideration with reference to the manner in which 'autonomy' has been given practical realisation within health care in the UK (again, especially within the NHS in England) in recent times.

Erikainen and Chan note that an important dimension of the personalisation of medicine is the 'responsibilisation' of health,[51] a matter discussed in a 2010 report of the Nuffield Council of Bioethics. Simply stated, this refers to 'policies that combine increased autonomy with increased obligations'.[52] The Council explains:

When it comes to health care, responsibilisation is a theme that has been taken up in various ways in recent years. The practice of involving patients in the choices to be made over their treatment and shared decision making, rather than presenting them with take-it-or-leave-it options, is a common feature of modern professional health care, and one that illustrates the double-edged character of such developments – on the one hand individuals are accorded more power to choose, on the other, they are obliged to take a share of the responsibility for that choice and its outcomes.[53]

P4 medicine connects to responsibilisation in the manner previously outlined: the predictive dimension offers information on potential changes in health status which provide 'alerts' to the individual, and – in so far as s/he is able – the individual can prevent a transition from wellness to disease by taking certain 'remedial' actions in response to those alerts. It is merely a short – but ethically and politically significant – distance from having the *capacity* to prevent ill health, to possessing an *obligation* to do so. This prospect, that 'patients may feel increased pressure to take control and manage their conditions, which seems just a small step away from demanding that patients have a moral responsibility to become well',[54] has been acknowledged by the proponents of P4 medicine. They have, however, dismissed the notion that the P4 approach should not be followed because it will give rise to onerous obligations to become, and stay, well, by arguing that such a claim 'boils down to the irrefutable assertion that technological capabilities can be misused. Our challenge as a society is to use them appropriately – a challenge we cannot avoid without turning our back on scientific and technological progress altogether.'[55]

Yet, as the Nuffield Council on Bioethics observes,[56] normative obligations to manage one's health have recently become discernible in the UK.[57] The primary manifestation of these is contained within the NHS *Constitution for England* which, while it does not impose legally binding obligations upon individuals, exhorts patients and the public to 'please recognise that you can make a significant contribution to your own, and your family's, good health and wellbeing, and take personal responsibility for it.'[58] The accompanying handbook fleshes out this responsibility in more detail, noting that the fact that 'the NHS belongs to all of us' 'means doing everything we can to keep ourselves and our families healthy and to reduce our risks of developing the avoidable long-term conditions that not only stop us living a full and active life, but place extra demands on the NHS, reducing its ability to provide vital and life-saving support to others.'[59] It further identifies a healthy diet, taking regular exercise, and the avoidance of smoking or excessive consumption of alcohol as 'the best ways to make sure that you live a full and active life for as long as possible'.[60]

The autonomous patient-consumer is thus conceptualised as one who not only possesses rights in respect of health care, but who also bears responsibilities. The *Constitution* and other recent policy discourse do not explicitly make the connection to the personalisation of medicine, but the latter development can certainly be viewed as further reinforcing the evolution of obligations (albeit presently moral and political, rather than legal)in respect of one's own health status.[61]

9.3 P4 MEDICINE AND READINGS OF 'HEALTH LAW': INDIVIDUAL AND POPULATION PERSPECTIVES

In his book *The Jurisdiction of Medical Law*, Kenneth Veitch notes the 'inexorable expansion' of this area in recent years, and observes that this has been accompanied by 'much reflection on the nature, or what might be called the constitution, of medical law – what defines it; which principles constitute its essence; what distinguishes it from other legal sub-disciplines.'[62] One might identify various reasons for this concern. First, the field is a relatively new one: in the UK, it certainly dates back no further than 1958,[63] and arguably can be more clearly traced to the late 1970s or early 1980s.[64] Second, as Veitch notes, the subject has grown substantially in scope over the passage of time, from its initial foundation in the law of tort (specifically, medical negligence); and thirdly and relatedly, it draws from a variety of other legal sub-disciplines, especially tort and criminal law, but also family law, property law, public law and regulation, and jurisprudence (shading into ethics), which might mean that 'it does not presently possess a sufficiently mature framework and conceptual basis to lay claim to independence in its own right.'[65]

While others have argued that 'the subject [is] now past any growing pains'[66] there continues to be debate as to its nature and scope.[67] One such debate concerns nomenclature. Jonathan Montgomery, one of the leading contemporary scholars in the field, has argued that it should be styled 'health care law', to signify that it 'embraces not only the practice of medicine, but also that of the non-medical health care professions, the administration of health services, and the law's role in maintaining public health.'[68] Elsewhere, the term 'health law' is preferred,[69] including by the present author. One reason for so doing is that identified in the preceding quotation from Montgomery's text: it allows for the clear extension of the field to embrace *public health law*, which might be defined as 'a field of study and practice that concerns those aspects of law, policy and regulation that advance or place constraints upon the protection and promotion of health (howsoever understood) within, between, and across populations'.[70] This field, while of venerable history, has garnered increasing scholarly interest over the past two decades, stimulated by Lawrence Gostin's work in the United States and on a global scale,[71] and more recently articulated in a UK context.[72] Furthermore, in light of the COVID-19 pandemic of 2020, it seems certain that public health, and the legal regulation thereof, will sit squarely at the forefront of academic analysis in this area for some time to come.

The development of P4 medicine seems clearly to underscore a particular vision of this subject area which might be described as 'traditional' medical law. The latter term is defined in another leading text in the field, as being 'essentially concerned with the relationship between doctors... and patients.'[73] As Montgomery observes, 'this approach... sees the clinical interaction between doctor and patient as the paradigm. This view influences both the content of the subject, individualising its focus, and its underlying conceptual coherence, emphasising the application of ethical principles' – of which, as previously analysed, autonomy is paramount.[74] For sure, there are certain points of distinction which are worthy of note: as observed above, there is an increased emphasis on individual responsibility for health within the P4 model which might diminish the role (and claim to authority) of the clinician; furthermore, there is a preventive orientation to P4 medicine which is usually viewed as more characteristic of public health than clinical medicine (which has tended to focus on sickness rather than wellness). However, at base, P4 medicine is fundamentally concerned with the health of a particular patient as distinct from the health of a collective entity such as a population, and it thus corresponds closely to the individualised focus which has predominantly characterised this area of legal enquiry and practice since its birth.

There is a danger, therefore, that while it parallels contemporary jurisprudential and ethical trends in the respects previously outlined, a focus on P4 medicine insufficiently aligns with other developments in scholarship and policy in this area, or that, at best, it presents us with an incomplete picture of the role which law might properly play in respect of health by largely overlooking its function at population level. Comparable concerns – albeit not phrased as a matter of legal discourse – have been expressed by critics of the P4 approach. For example, Bayer and Galea, writing of Obama's 'Precision Medicine Initiative', observe forcefully as follows:

[T]here is now broad consensus that health differences between groups and within groups are not driven by clinical care but by social-structural factors that shape our lives. Yet seemingly willfully blind to this evidence, the United States continues to spend its health dollars overwhelmingly on clinical care... Research undertaken in the name of precision medicine may well open new vistas of science, and precision medicine itself may ultimately make critical contributions to a narrow set of conditions that are primarily genetically determined. But the challenge we face to improve population health does not involve the frontiers of science and molecular biology. It entails development of the vision and willingness to address certain persistent social realities, and it requires an unstinting focus on the factors that matter most to the production of population health.[75]

From a legal perspective, the worry is that unthinking commitment to a P4 approach, and the consequent focus on individual autonomy and the clinician–patient relationship, risks neglecting the capacity of legal intervention to ameliorate, and also potentially to exacerbate, the social determinants of the health of a population, such as housing, sustenance, education, employment, income, gender, social exclusion and discrimination, etc.[76] These factors are now widely acknowledged to have a significant impact on health status and outcomes.[77]

9.4 CONCLUSION

This chapter has sought to show that data-driven personalisation in medicine – focusing by way of illustration on the P4 approach articulated by Leroy Hood and colleagues – is consonant with a particular reading of the role of law in respect of health, and with the dominant ethical principle of autonomy which underpins this. While this mirrors contemporary jurisprudential developments in the UK, as exemplified by *Montgomery*, it offers an incomplete account of law's potential role and function in this area and, in addition, the scope of this legal sub-discipline as a scholarly enterprise.

The claim that law is best understood, and studied, within its social, economic, cultural, political and, one might add, techno-scientific, context is now so familiar as to scarcely warrant repeating.[78] However, the issue explored in this chapter demonstrates that a broad, holistic, understanding of the meaning of 'context' is needed. Focusing on a particular aspect of the environment in which law sits, such as the emergence of personalised medicine, risks overlooking other, equally significant, contextual developments which might pull in a different direction – in this instance, the impact of social factors on health, which has been the subject of considerable recent policy interest and academic research. In short, we would do well to temper talk of personalisation constituting a 'paradigm shift' in medicine with a reminder that the latter is merely one part of what might be needed to achieve both individual and population health, and that it therefore also represents only one dimension of the appropriate remit of law in this field.

NOTES

1 See, for example, Andrea Weston and Leroy Hood, 'Systems biology, proteomics, and the future of health care: toward predictive, preventative, and personalized medicine' (2004) 3 *Journal of Proteome Research* 179; Leroy Hood and others, 'Systems biology and new technologies enable predictive and preventative medicine' (2004) 306 *Science* 640; Leroy Hood, Rudi Balling and Charles Auffray, 'Revolutionizing medicine in the twenty-first century through systems approaches' (2012) 7 *Biotechnology Journal* 992.

2 Nathan Price and others, 'A wellness study of 108 individuals using personal, dense, dynamic data clouds' (2017) *Nature Biotechnology* 747, 747.

3 Ibid.

4 Leroy Hood, quoted in David L Chandler, 'Leroy Hood's systematic approach' (*IEEE Pulse*, 17 April 2014), www.embs.org/pulse/articles/leroy-hoods-systematic-approach/.

5 See Leroy Hood and Mauricio Flores, 'A personal view on systems medicine and the emergence of proactive P4 medicine: predictive, preventive, personalized and participatory' (2012) 29 *New Biotechnology* 613.

6 Ibid., 616.

7 Hood, Balling and Auffray (n 1) 996.

8 Leroy Hood, 'Big Data, complexity, wellness and disease' ('Measurable man', Swedish Collegium for Advanced Study and Uppsala Biomedical Centre inaugural symposium, Uppsala, October 2019).

9 Sonia Erikainen and Sarah Chan, 'Contested futures: Envisioning "personalized", "stratified", and "precision" medicine' (2019) 38 *New Genetics and Society* 308, 308.

10 Ibid., 309.

11 European Commission, Advice for 2018–2020 of the Horizon 2020 Advisory Group for Societal Challenge 1, "Health, Demographic Change and Well-being" (European Commission 2016) 19.

12 See, for example, Fintan Steele, 'Personalized medicine: something old, something new' (2009) 6 *Personalized Medicine* 1.

13 Susanne Vijverberg and Anke-Hilse Maitland-van der Zee, *Priority Medicines for Europe and the World "A Public Health Approach to Innovation": Update on 2004 Background Paper 7.4, Pharmacogenetics and Stratified Medicine* (World Health Organization, 2013) 8.

14 Academy of Medical Sciences, *Stratified, Personalised or P4 Medicine: A New Direction for Placing the Patient at the Centre of Healthcare and Health Education* (2015) 4.

15 Ibid., 18.

16 Precision Medicine Initiative (PMI) Working Group Report to the Advisory Committee to the Director, NIH, *The Precision Medicine Initiative Cohort Program – Building a Research Foundation for Twenty-first Century Medicine* (2015) 1.

17 Ibid.: 'Coincident with advancing the science of medicine is a changing culture of medical practice and medical research that engages individuals as active partners – not just as patients or research subjects'.

18 Erikainen and Chan (n 9) 320.

19 Vijverberg and Maitland-van der Zee (n 13) 8. Emphasis added.

20 Erikainen and Chan (n 9) 326.

21 Ibid.

22 See Hood, Balling and Auffray (n 1) 992, arguing that 'personalised medicine' 'fails to reflect the enormous dimensionality of this new medicine'.

23 [2015] UKSC 11.

24 See, for example, Luke Sizer and Philip Arnold, 'The changing paradigm of the doctor-Patient relationship: *Montgomery v Lanarkshire Health Board* and Developments in the "Duty to Warn"' (2016) 129 *New Zealand Medical Journal* 71; RS Chauhan and SP Chauhan, 'Montgomery v Lanarkshire Health Board: a paradigm shift' (2017) 124 *BJOG: An International Journal of Obstetrics and Gynaecology* 1152. Note also reference to *Montgomery* as a 'landmark case': see, for example, Philippa White, 'Consent after *Montgomery*: what next for healthcare professionals?' (2016) 22 *Clinical Risk* 33; George Buttigieg, 'Re-visiting *Bolam* and *Bolitho* in the light of *Montgomery v Lanarkshire Health Board*' (2018) 86 *Medico-Legal Journal* 42. But see (n 28).

25 *Montgomery v Lanarkshire Health Board* [2015] UKSC 11 [87].

26 Ibid. [81].

27 TT Arvind and Aisling McMahon, 'Responsiveness and the role of rights in medical law: lessons from *Montgomery*' (2020) 28 *Medical Law Review* 445.

28 Ibid. The Supreme Court itself noted in *Montgomery* (n 25) [75] that 'it had become *increasingly clear* that the paradigm of the doctor–patient relationship implicit in the speeches in that case [*Sidaway v Board of Governors of the Bethlem Royal Hospital and the Maudsley Hospital* [1985] AC 871] has ceased to reflect the reality and complexity of the way in which healthcare services are provided, or the way in which the providers and recipients of such services view their relationship' (emphasis added). For further discussion of the gradual evolution of the law on informed consent up to *Montgomery*, see, e.g., Rob Heywood, 'RIP *Sidaway*: patient-oriented disclosure: a standard worth waiting for?' (2015) 23 *Medical Law Review* 455; Jean McHale, 'Innovation, informed consent, health research and the Supreme Court: *Montgomery v Lanarkshire* – a brave new world?' (2017) 12 *Health Economics, Policy and Law* 435.

29 See John Coggon and José Miola, 'Autonomy, liberty and medical decision-making' (2011) 73 *Cambridge Law Review* 523, 524, who describe autonomy as having 'attained a supreme status'.

30 Graeme Laurie, Shawn Harmon and Edward Dove, *Mason and McCall Smith's Law and Medical Ethics* (11th ed., Oxford University Press 2019) [1.20].

31 See, for example, Department of Health, 'Choosing Health—Making Choices Easier' (2004); Department of Health, 'Choice Matters' (2007); NHS Choices, 'NHS Choices: Delivering for the NHS' (2008); Department of Health, *Equity and Excellence: Liberating the NHS* (Cm 7881, 2010); Department of Health, *Liberating the NHS – Greater Choice and Control – Consultation* (2010); Department of Health, 'Liberating the NHS: No decision about me, without me' (2012). For critical discussion, see Christopher Newdick, 'From Hippocrates to commodities: three models of NHS governance' (2014) 22 *Medical Law Review* 162.

32 See NHS England and NHS Improvement, *Guidance on the legal rights to have personal health budgets and personal wheelchair budgets* (2019).

33 National Health Service Act 2006, ss 14U, 14V, inserted by Health and Social Care Act 2012, s 26.

34 The Health and Social Care Act 2008 (Regulated Activities) Regulations 2014, SI 2014/2396, cl 9.

35 Department of Health, *The NHS Constitution for England* (2015) 3.

36 For more extensive theoretical discussions of the concept in general, see, for example, Gerald Dworkin, *The Theory and Practice of Autonomy* (Cambridge University Press 1988); Onora O'Neill, *Autonomy and Trust in Bioethics* (Cambridge University Press 2002).

37 John Coggon, 'Varied and principled understandings of autonomy in English law: justifiable inconsistency or blinkered moralism?' (2007) 15 *Health Care Analysis* 235, 236.

38 John Christman, 'Autonomy in moral and political philosophy', *The Stanford Encyclopedia of Philosophy* (Spring ed., 2018) https://plato.stanford.edu/archives/spr2018/entries/autonomy-moral/. See also Coggon and Miola (n 29) 524.

39 Coggon and Miola (n 29) 535.

40 Hood and Flores (n 5) 619.

41 Ibid.

42 Ibid., 620.

43 It is also suggested, perhaps more fancifully, that education could be facilitated by production of a *CSI*-type television programme to 'bring knowledge of P4 medicine to the average viewer' and by the use of computer game-like strategies: Ibid. 621.

44 Ibid., 620.

45 Ibid.

46 See further Leroy Hood and Charles Auffray, 'Participatory medicine: a driving force for revolutionizing Healthcare' (2015) 5 *Genome Medicine* 110.

47 In respect of *Montgomery* (n 25) [75], note especially the following: 'They [patients] are also widely treated as consumers exercising choices: a viewpoint which has underpinned some of the developments in the provision of healthcare services'.

48 See sources (n 31).

49 Hood and Flores (n 5) 620.

50 *Montgomery* (n 25) [75].

51 Erikainen and Chan (n 9) 314.

52 Nuffield Council on Bioethics, '*Medical profiling and online medicine: the ethics of 'personalised healthcare' in a consumer age*' (2010) [2.13]. The concept derives from social science literature, see, for example, Nikolas Rose, *Powers of Freedom: Reframing Political Thought* (Cambridge University Press 1999) 74; Rik Peeters, 'Manufacturing responsibility: the governmentality of behavioural power in social policies' (2019) 18 *Social Policy and Society* 51.

53 Nuffield Council (n 52) [2.14].

54 Eric Juengst and others, 'After the revolution? Ethical and social challenges in "personalized genomic medicine"' (2012) 9 *Personalized Medicine* 429, 435.

55 Mauricio Flores and others, 'P4 Medicine: How systems medicine will transform the healthcare sector and society' (2013) 10 *Personalized Medicine* 565, 574.

56 See Nuffield Council (n 52) [2.14].

57 See further Karen Jochelson, *Paying the Patient: Improving Health Using Financial Incentives* (King's Fund 2007) 2: 'individual responsibility for health and self-care are key themes in recent health policy documents in England'.

58 Department of Health (n 35) 11.

59 Department of Health & Social Care/Public Health England, *Handbook to the NHS Constitution for England* (2019), www.gov.uk/government/publications/supplements-to-the-nhs-constitution-for-england/the-handbook-to-the-nhs-constitution-for-england#patient-and-public-responsibilities.

60 Ibid.

61 But see John Coggon, Keith Syrett and AM Viens, *Public Health Law: Ethics, Governance, and Regulation* (Routledge 2017) 170–73, for an analysis of this responsibility as a form of 'self-regulation'.

62 Kenneth Veitch, *The Jurisdiction of Medical Law* (Ashgate 2007) 1.

63 The date of publication of Glanville Williams, *The Sanctity of Life and the Criminal Law* (Faber & Faber 1958). John Keown, *The Law and Ethics of Medicine: Essays on the Inviolability of Human Life* (Oxford University Press 2012) 23 states that this book is 'widely regarded as its [i.e., medical law's] foundation stone (at least in the United Kingdom)'.

64 Two milestones in this period were a paper delivered by Ian Kennedy at Middlesex Hospital Medical School in 1979, later published in Ian Kennedy, *Treat Me Right: Essays in Medical Law and Ethics* (Clarendon Press 1988), which is cited by Veitch (n 62); and the first edition of J Kenyon Mason and Alexander McCall Smith, *Law and Medical Ethics* (Butterworths 1983).

65 Veitch (n 62).

66 José Miola, 'Book Review: The Jurisdiction of Medical Law' (2009) 17 *Medical Law Review* 113, 118.

67 For a recent example, see John Harrington, *Towards a Rhetoric of Medical Law* (Routledge 2017) 2, which 'proposes a different method for analysing medical law... the standard model of scholarship rests on an oversimplified model of legal argumentation'.

68 Jonathan Montgomery, *Health Care Law* (2nd ed., Oxford University Press 2003) 4.

69 See, for example, Lawrence Gostin, *Global Health Law* (Harvard University Press 2014); Tamara Hervey and Jean McHale, *European Union Health Law: Themes and Implications* (Cambridge University Press 2015).

70 Coggon, Syrett and Viens (n 61) 72.

71 See Lawrence Gostin, *Public Health Law: Power, Duty, Restraint* (1st ed., University of California Press 2000); Gostin (n 69).

72 Coggon, Syrett and Viens (n 61).

73 Andrew Grubb, *Medical Law* (3rd ed., Butterworths 2000) 3.

74 Montgomery (n 68) 1.

75 Ronald Bayer and Sandro Galea, 'Public health in the precision-medicine era' (2015) 373 *New England Journal of Medicine* 499, 500. For similar arguments, see, for example, Juan Pablo Rey-López, Thiago Herick de Sá and Leandro Fórnias Machado de Rezende, 'Why precision medicine is not the best route to a healthier world' (2018) 52 *Revista de Saúde Pública* 12; for a less sceptical view, see, for example, Nikolaos Evangelatos, Kapaettu Satyamoorthy and Angela Brand, 'Personalized health in a public health perspective' (2018) 63 *International Journal of Public Health* 433.

76 For a recent, important, analysis of the capacity of law to impact upon the social determinants of health, see Lawrence Gostin and others, 'The legal determinants of health: harnessing the power of law for global health and sustainable development' (2019) 393 *Lancet* 1857.

77 The most notable contribution is Commission on the Social Determinants of Health, *Closing the Gap in a Generation: Health Equity through Action on the Social Determinants of Health. Final Report* (World Health Organization 2008). See also the work of Michael Marmot, for example, *Status Syndrome: How Your Social Standing Directly Affects Your Health* (Bloomsbury 2005); *The Health Gap: the Challenge of an Unequal World* (Bloomsbury 2015).

78 For discussions, see, for example, William Twining, *Law in Context: Enlarging a Discipline* (Clarendon Press 1997); Philip Selznick, '"Law in context" revisited' (2003) 30 *Journal of Law and Society* 177.

10

Personalised Pricing: The Demise of the Fixed Price?

Joost Poort and Frederik Zuiderveen Borgesius

10.1 INTRODUCTION

On 15 May 2020, J. C. Penney filed for bankruptcy. This legendary department store founded in 1902 by John Cash Penney, with approximately 850 locations across the USA,[1] had become famous for various retail innovations and a company policy it summarised as the 'golden rule': to treat others as you would like to be treated. One of the innovations J. C. Penney introduced was to offer the goods for low but fixed prices, at a time when haggling was the standard in stores. Is the bankruptcy of J. C. Penney just an example of the creative destruction that drives innovation and capitalism, in this case spurred by the COVID-19 crisis? Or does it signify the end of an era: the demise of the fixed price?

In our current data-driven world, an online seller or platform is technically able to offer every consumer a different price for the same product, based on information it has about the customers. For example, a seller can classify consumers according to their assumed wealth, or rather their price sensitivity, and charge those who are presumed to be less price sensitive higher prices. This chapter synthesises our previous findings on such online price discrimination,[2] a concept defined as differentiating the online price for identical products or services, based on the information a company holds about a customer.[3] We give examples of online price discrimination, discuss its underlying basis in economic theory, and its popular perception. The chapter argues that the General Data Protection Regulation (GDPR) applies to the most controversial forms of online price discrimination, and not only requires companies to disclose their use of price discrimination, but also the prior consent by the customer to it. Industry practice, however, does not show any adoption of these two principles – for reasons explored below. Price discrimination may also invoke the operation of anti-discrimination law (see Collado-Rodriguez/Kohl, Chapter [X]),[4] competition law[5] or consumer protection law,[6] which are not further considered here.

10.2 ONLINE PRICE DISCRIMINATION AND THE UNDERLYING ECONOMIC THEORY

Many internet users will recognise the experience that after looking at shoes, a hotel room or a flight, they are followed around the web by advertisements for those products for weeks. This is an example of *behavioural targeting*. In this marketing technique, companies track consumers' online behaviour and use the information collected to display their targeted ads.[7] If companies can tailor ads to what they know about consumers, they can also tailor prices. 'Just as it's easy for customers to compare prices on the Internet, so is it easy for companies to track customers' behavior and adjust prices accordingly', consultants at McKinsey & Company wrote already in 2001, and added '[t]he Internet also allows companies to identify customers who are happy to pay a premium.'[8] Whether consumers are 'happy' to pay a premium is debatable; some evidence suggests otherwise. In an early incident, Amazon attracted criticism[9] when its customers, upon deleting the cookies from their browsers, would see the prices for DVDs drop. Amazon appeared to be charging higher prices to existing customers, or – put differently – appeared to be trying to attract new customers with lower prices. In response to the exposure, Amazon stated that it had tested different prices, but not adjusted prices to customer profiles based on their demographics,[10] and refunded affected customers.

The techniques of such discrimination have become more precise and innovative with time. In 2012, researchers evidenced online price discrimination by some US web stores based on their customers' neighbourhoods,[11] as revealed by the IP address of their computers. For example, the office supply store Staples charged lower prices if the website visitor was in a place where there was a competing brick-and-mortar-store within a 20-mile radius. This pricing strategy makes sense from the seller's perspective, as most consumers will not drive an hour to save a few dollars on a box of printer paper. But if a consumer can buy printer paper in a shop just around the block, she will do so if the price in the online store is too high. This pricing strategy also had the unintended effect that, on average, customers on lower incomes paid higher prices. Similar research has also shown that a hotel room in Los Angeles can be 14 per cent more expensive for someone with a Dutch IP address than for someone with an American IP address.[12] Online stores could also adjust prices based on the surfing behaviour of customers, as revealed by the cookies placed in their browsers.

If online price discrimination is possible, profitable and legally permissible, one would expect it to be pervasive. However, at this stage its prevalence appears to be limited,[13] for which there may be several explanations. First, some providers may refrain from price discrimination because they fear negative responses from consumers. Second, others may lack sufficient data or technology to adapt prices with sufficient precision, which would be remedied with easier and cheaper access to relevant technology. Finally, price discrimination may occur without in fact being noticed, as sellers can adapt prices in ways that are hard to detect, for example, when a provider advertises one price on its website but emails each consumer a different discount coupon. Many commentators expect that price discrimination will become more common as data-driven technology advances.[14]

While data-driven personalisation technology has provided new possibilities for price discrimination, it is not a new phenomenon. Classic examples are a lower conference rate for students than for corporate participants, or a reduced rate for children for theatre, cinema or flight tickets. According to underlying economic theory, three conditions must be fulfilled for price discrimination to work effectively: (i) the seller must be able to distinguish customers to know what price to charge to whom; (ii) the seller must have a sufficiently strong market position to be able to set prices above marginal costs and (iii) resale must be impractical, costly or prohibited in order to avoid arbitrage between customers.[15]

For online sales, these conditions are often met. Companies can distinguish between customers with increasing precision. Some providers, for example Amazon.com and Booking.com, have a strong market position and stimulate customer lock-in, which is likely to allow them to achieve higher margins. Finally, reselling is also often impossible (as, for example, in the case of plane tickets or hotel rooms), difficult or expensive. In combination with the fact that prices can be adjusted with ease and unnoticed, the online environment provides a highly fertile ground for the proliferation of price discrimination.

As a matter of background, economists distinguish between first-, second- and third-degree price discrimination.[16] In *first-degree price discrimination*, each consumer is charged an individual price equal to his maximum willingness to pay. In practice, despite the rise of big data analytics, such an extreme form of price discrimination is still unlikely to occur, as sellers are unlikely to know each buyer's exact willingness to pay. Rather, first-degree price discrimination serves as a stylised benchmark to evaluate other pricing schemes. *Second-degree price discrimination* refers to situations where the price of a good or service depends on the *quantity* purchased, for example, through quantity discounts. In the cinema, for example, popcorn is often cheaper per gram if you buy a larger box. For second-degree price discrimination, the seller does not need information about the buyer, because buyers themselves choose the price by choosing the quantity. Loyalty programmes are also sometimes characterised as second-degree price discrimination, which is correct to the extent that such programmes involve a quantity discount over time: past purchases give a discount on future purchases.

By creating customer profiles, providers can also use loyalty programmes for personalised prices, which qualifies as third-degree price discrimination. In the case of *third-degree price discrimination*, prices differ between groups of buyers. Discounts for students, children or the elderly are well-known examples. The distinction can also be geographical as, for example, when medicines and textbooks are sold at lower prices in developing countries. For third-degree price discrimination, it is not necessary to recognise individual buyers. Sellers only need to know the characteristics of the customer that are used to base the price differences on. Nevertheless, sellers often use unique identifiers to distinguish different types of buyers, such as a student card with a student number and photo or even a formal ID card. This unique identification of customers helps to meet two of the most important conditions for price discrimination: differentiating between buyers and preventing arbitrage.

Online price discrimination usually works similarly. An online provider identifies a customer based on, for example, an IP address or login details, as a means to distinguish between groups of customers. However, compared to distinguishing students based on a student card, an online profile can be much more detailed and allow for much more sophisticated price discrimination. In this way, online third-degree price discrimination can shift towards the holy grail of perfect first-degree price discrimination, under which all consumer surplus is extracted for the benefit of the seller. For instance, an online provider could at the same time adjust prices based on past purchasing behaviour of a consumer depending on: whether she landed from a competitor's website; whether she lives in a poor or a rich neighbourhood (information which can be deduced from her IP address); whether she uses an Apple or a Windows device and whether she uses a mobile device or a laptop.

Another pricing strategy widely used on the Internet is *dynamic pricing* or *time-based pricing*. With dynamic pricing, a company (automatically) adjusts prices based on market conditions concerning supply and demand. For example, an airline will increase the price of tickets if a flight is almost fully booked. The airline will also charge higher prices on popular times and days, for example, for tickets to beach destinations during school holidays. Taxi platform Uber is also notorious for its dynamic prices.[17] Dynamic pricing is often mistaken for online price discrimination when, for example, the potential customer returns to the website and sees that the airline ticket has become more expensive. In this situation, the change in price may be due either to the departure date being closer or the aircraft being fuller (dynamic pricing), or the fact that the airline has seen that the customer looked at the ticket before and is therefore probably serious about a purchase (third-degree price discrimination).[18]

Economists are generally positive about price discrimination (and dynamic pricing). Price discrimination can benefit both buyers and sellers, leading to an increase of both consumer and producer welfare.[19] Price discrimination can help the seller to recoup his fixed costs without losing many potential customers and make a good or service accessible to buyers with a smaller purse, even if it will lead to higher prices for other customers. For the latter, however, price discrimination deprives them of consumer surplus. The more sophisticated the pricing scheme used by the seller, the more this will be the case, because a more accurate price discrimination scheme will extract more additional value from those willing to pay more. While this may improve efficiency and allow the seller to widen the scope of the market to marginal consumers, such benefits are 'financed' by the additional squeezing of higher prices from those willing to pay more. In addition, as the example of Staples charging higher prices to those far from competing retailers demonstrates, price discrimination may reinforce economic inequality by unintendedly leading to higher prices for poorer customers: not because they are poor, but as a by-product of other variables, such as the proximity of competing suppliers. Thus price discrimination can contribute to a cycle of economic inequality.

There is a large body of literature on the welfare effects of price discrimination under different assumptions about consumer demand, the information available to consumers and suppliers, etc. The impact of price discrimination on the average price of goods and services and thereby on total consumer welfare is not always clear.[20] The total welfare effects of consumers and producers combined are ambiguous too. Price discrimination may lead to a net welfare loss, when the loss by consumers who pay higher prices (based on price discrimination) is greater than the net gain by producers. And even sellers themselves may suffer a net welfare loss, if price discrimination intensifies competition for price-sensitive consumers. Thus, the short answer to the question about the welfare effects of price discrimination is: it depends. To increase welfare, price discrimination must lead to a significant increase in total output by serving markets not previously served. However, even then, less price-sensitive consumers will often be worse off from price discrimination because they will, on average, pay higher prices.

The more price discrimination becomes personalised, the more welfare will generally shift from consumers to suppliers. The reason for this is that personalising prices more, entails placing consumers in smaller, more homogeneous segments and charging them a price that can be closer to their willingness to pay. For example, in the analogue world, prices may be differentiated between students and other consumers, based on the idea that the average student has less disposable income. However, within the student population, there will be poor students and rich students. In the digital world, suppliers may further differentiate within this student population, based on, for instance, the neighbourhood where they live and the type of device they use to navigate the Internet. By doing so, sellers can charge richer students a premium.

10.3 POPULAR PERCEPTIONS OF PRICE DISCRIMINATION

Despite several sporadic pieces of evidence of online price discrimination in practice, it is largely unknown at what scale it is actually taking place. Nevertheless, it is relevant to know what the popular perceptions of price discrimination are, for instance to inform policy makers. This section provides empirical evidence regarding why personalisation might be concerning, especially as it expands its reach and power. To investigate consumer attitudes towards different forms of price discrimination and dynamic pricing, we conducted two surveys among a representative sample of the Dutch population of 18 years and older.[21]

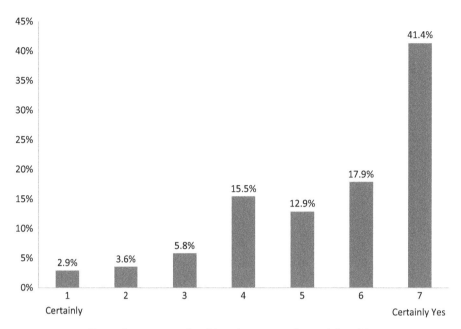

FIGURE 10.1. 'According to you, should such practices be prohibited?'
(N = 1233)

10.3.1 *Survey 1: General Experiences and Views*

The first survey was conducted in April 2016 and had a response rate of 1,233 (81.0 per cent). The questions focused on consumers' experiences with online price discrimination and their attitudes towards it. In the questions, the term 'price discrimination' was not used because it could have a normative connotation. The survey described personalised pricing as follows:

> Web stores can adjust prices on the basis of data about an Internet user, such as the country where the user is based, or the time the user visits the web store. This makes it possible that two Internet users, who visit the same web store at the same time, see different prices for the same product.[22]

After this introduction, respondents were asked how often they had experienced this themselves. Fifty-seven per cent said they had never experienced online price discrimination, while 4 per cent said they experienced it often or very often. Around 40 per cent asserted that they experienced online price discrimination rarely or occasionally.[23] Next, respondents were asked to indicate on a scale of 1–7 whether they think such practices should be prohibited. Figure 10.1 shows that a large majority is in favour of a ban: 72 per cent choose 5, 6 or 7.

Asked whether online price discrimination is acceptable and fair, more than 80 per cent indicate that they find it unacceptable and unfair to a certain extent,

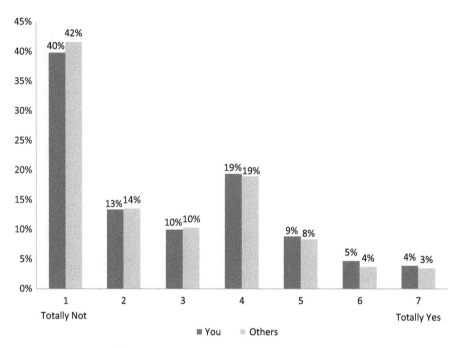

FIGURE 10.2. 'Would you find it acceptable if a web store gives a discount to you/others based on your/their online behaviour (such as the websites you/they have visited before)?' (N = 1233)

while only a few per cent indicate they find it acceptable. The differences in outcomes between 'acceptable' and 'fair' are minimal, which suggests these concepts are closely linked in the perception of respondents. Figure 10.2 shows that if online price discrimination is framed as a personalised *discount*, acceptance increases slightly, but about 65 per cent still find price discrimination unacceptable. Surprisingly, popular opinion hardly depends on whether the price discrimination favours themselves or others.

Finally, to find out *why* consumers do or do not agree with online price discrimination, we presented respondents with three propositions. Almost 80 per cent agree with the statement that web stores should be obliged to inform customers about online price discrimination. And 56 per cent are to some extent concerned about paying more than others, while 65 per cent are worried about not noticing price adjustments.

10.3.2 *Survey 2: Specific Examples*

The second survey asked respondents for their opinion on specific examples. Fifteen examples were presented to them and, as in the first study, they were asked to indicate on a 7-point scale to what extent they considered them acceptable. This survey was conducted in November 2016 and had a response rate of 1202 (82.2 per cent).

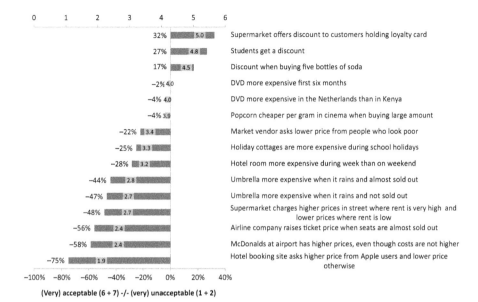

FIGURE 10.3. Net acceptability of different forms of price discrimination and dynamic pricing (N = 1,202)

Figure 10.3 summarizes the answers to all fifteen questions by presenting the 'net acceptability'. We define net acceptability as the difference between the percentage that indicates 6 or 7 (acceptable or very acceptable) and the percentage that indicates 1 or 2 (unacceptable or very unacceptable). If 40 per cent of respondents find an example (very) acceptable and 30 per cent (very) unacceptable, the net acceptability is therefore 40% – 30% = 10%. In Figure 10.3, this net acceptability is sorted from high to low. The number within the bars gives the average of the scores: this ranges from 5.0 to 1.9 (4 is neutral) and strongly correlates with the net acceptability.

In general, Figure 10.3 illustrates that consumers reject many forms of price discrimination and dynamic pricing: for nine out of fifteen examples, the average score is below 4 and the net acceptability is well below 0 per cent. Only three examples are regarded as predominantly acceptable: a supermarket offering discounts to customers with a loyalty card, a student discount and a quantity discount on bottles of soft drinks. Those surveyed reacted neutrally to three other examples, but found some examples unacceptable, even though such practices have been around for decades, such as airlines that raise their prices when the seats are almost sold out, and holiday homes that are more expensive during school holidays.

10.3.3 *Analysis of the Results: Fairness, Transparency and Choice*

These results show that a majority of the population finds price discrimination consistently unfair and unacceptable. Why do most consumers feel so uncomfortable with the practices of online price discrimination and dynamic pricing? Figure 10.2 shows that acceptance hardly depends on whether the price discrimination favours respondents themselves or others. There are also some (albeit inconclusive) trends in the answers to the second survey and the characteristics of the examples.[24] Respondents find volume discounts (second-degree price discrimination) relatively acceptable, while the picture for third-degree price discrimination is mixed, for example, the supermarket loyalty cards are acceptable, but varying hotel prices based on the consumer's computer brands are not.

One key to understanding varying consumer sensitivity lies in the wording in which the price discrimination is framed. It is more acceptable if it is presented as a *discount* (or if the words 'cheaper' or 'lower price' are used) and less if it is presented as 'higher prices' or 'more expensive'. Behavioural economics has long shown that 'losses loom larger than gains'[25] and so the aversion to price discrimination can also be linked to an aversion to *loss* or *regret*.[26] Having said that, most consumers reject online price discrimination even when framed as a discount. Perhaps this is because many understand that there will be no gains without losses and that not receiving a discount resembles paying a premium.

Another key to understanding popular perception to price discrimination is that consumers appear to react more positively to price discrimination if it is more transparent. Student discounts and quantity discounts in supermarkets, for example, are generally transparent, whilst airline prices are opaque for most consumers. As mentioned, a majority of consumers worry that price adjustments may go unnoticed. On the other hand, discounts in the supermarket for customers with a loyalty card, the most accepted strategy in Figure 10.3, can be personalised and opaque; customers rarely see the size of the discount of other customers, although they might assume equality of treatment. By the same token, it is transparent that holiday homes are more expensive during school holidays, but consumers still do not like it.

A third key to making sense of consumer reactions to price discrimination is choice; a lack of real choice undermines the perceived legitimacy of price discrimination as, for example, 'trapped' customers behind the customs of an airport who are met with inflated prices for food and drinks while waiting to board their planes, parents with young children and holiday prices during the school vacations. In contrast, anyone can get a loyalty card from a supermarket to qualify for discounts, and someone can decide to go for a quantity discount and buy several bottles of soda or a large bucket of popcorn.

Finally, the relationship between respondents' responses and demographic factors suggests that price discrimination is most accepted by young, highly educated men in higher-income groups, while older, less educated women in lower-income groups are the least accepting.[27] It is likely that the link with education is driven by a better understanding of the underlying logic or even the positive effects that such strategies can have on allocation and welfare. The positive correlation between acceptance and income could be seen as unexpected, because higher income groups will in most cases be the 'victims' of price discrimination and pay higher prices. It is tempting to conclude that the perceived fairness transcends self-interest here. An alternative explanation is that it simply makes less of a difference to richer consumers, or that they benefit indirectly because without price discrimination – for instance, for holiday cottages – they would more often be crowded out by less wealthy consumers.

10.4 THE GDPR AND ONLINE PRICE DISCRIMINATION

In Europe, there are no specific rules on price discrimination, and thus *prima facie* it is allowed. Contractual freedom implies that price discrimination is generally legitimate; economic actors are, in principle, free to decide with whom to contract and on what terms, including the price. A seller may choose a price for a product or service, and if a consumer consents to that price, there is no problem, at least from the perspective of contractual freedom.

However, online price discrimination whereby prices are adjusted to individual consumers generally invokes the operation of the GDPR, as such price discrimination typically involves the processing of personal data.[28] The GDPR tries to ensure that the processing of personal data happens fairly, lawfully and transparently, and grants rights to individuals whose data is processed ('data subjects'), and imposes obligations on organisations that process personal data ('data controllers'; we also speak of 'companies' for ease of reading).[29] Independent Data Protection Authorities monitor compliance. The GDPR applies when 'personal data' is 'processed' which practically refers to everything that could be done with personal data.[30] The GDPR defines personal data as 'all information about an identified or identifiable natural person...'[31] which in turn is defined in this way:

> an identifiable natural person is one who can be identified, directly or indirectly, in particular by means of an identifier such as a name, an identification number, location data, an online identifier or one or more elements characterising the physical, physiological, genetic, mental, economic, cultural or social identity of that natural person.[32]

The definition of personal data is thus broad in scope and includes data that can be used for online price discrimination, such as tracking cookies, IP addresses and similar identifiers.[33]

For example, suppose Alice is a regular customer of an ecommerce site, and logs in with her email address. The online store sees that Alice uses an expensive smartphone, and also knows that she often buys the most expensive brands. Thus, the store concludes that Alice is not price conscious, and charges Alice 10 per cent extra on all purchases. The store recognises Alice when she logs in with her email address and a password. Her email address is personal data, because Alice can be identified from her email address. The GDPR's processing definition applies to recognising someone from her email address and adjusting the prices for that person. There is also Bob who is not a customer yet, but the online store recognises him by means of a tracking cookie that a partner company has placed on his computer, that collects (personal) data about Bob's browsing activities. The provider gives Bob a 5 per cent discount, without telling him, in the hope that he will become a customer.

In both cases the online store processes personal data, which invokes the operation of the GDPR. The fact that the GDPR applies does not mean that the use of personal data is *per se* prohibited, but rather that an organisation, such as the online seller, must meet the GDPR's requirements, which in fact reflect some of the consumer expectations identified above.

10.4.1 *Transparency Obligations Resulting from the GDPR*

The principle of transparency is one of the main principles of the GDPR.[34] The GDPR provides a detailed list of the information to be disclosed. For example, a company must provide information about its identity and the 'purposes of the processing' and must provide more information when necessary to ensure fair processing.[35] Thus a company must inform its customers if it processes personal data to personalise prices. Transparency about price discrimination could reduce the current information asymmetry and would allow consumers to choose web stores that do not personalise prices (provided there is sufficient competition), or delete their cookies if that gives them a better deal.

For that very reason, it is likely that companies prefer not to tell customers about personalised prices, especially if they charge higher prices, considering the empirical evidence presented in the last section, which showed that most consumers find online price discrimination unfair and reject it. Hence, consumers could be expected to react negatively and look for 'fairer' prices elsewhere. Currently there does not seem to be any website that tells their customers that they are personalising prices. Perhaps companies that fall within the ambit of the GDPR do not personalise their prices, or perhaps some do but fail to comply with the GDPR.

Alternatively, some companies may try to comply with the GDPR with a sentence such as: 'we use personal data to offer our customers better personalized services.' However, the GDPR requires companies to formulate and disclose a 'specified' and 'explicit' purpose for the collection of data and thus a general statement as above is unlikely to meet that requirement.[36] European Data Protection Authorities have emphasised that 'a purpose that is vague or general, such as for instance "improving users' experience" [or] "marketing purposes"... will – without more detail – usually not meet the criteria of being "specific".'[37] In short, the GDPR requires transparency and obliges companies to inform their customers about the personalisation of prices explicitly and clearly.

10.4.2 *The GDPR and the Requirement for Legal Basis*

Another core principle of data protection legislation is the requirement that companies that use personal data must have a legal basis for doing so. The GDPR provides an exhaustive list of six possible principles for the processing of personal data. The three legal bases that are most relevant to the private sector are consent, necessity for contractual performance and legitimate interest.[38]

First, a company may have a basis for processing personal data if the data subject has given consent to the processing of his or her personal data for one or more specific purposes.[39] The requirements for valid consent are strict. The GDPR requires a 'freely given, specific, informed and unambiguous indication of the data subject's wishes by which he or she, by a statement or by a clear affirmative action, signifies agreement to the processing of personal data relating to him or her.'[40] However, given the aversion of most consumers to price discrimination, it seems unlikely that many would give their consent. It is possible, however, that many users would click 'I agree' without reading the privacy notice.[41]

A second possible basis is that the 'processing is necessary for the performance of a contract to which the data subject is party or in order to take steps at the request of the data subject prior to entering into a contract.'[42] For example, if someone buys a book online, his or her address, which is personal data, would be required to deliver the book. The use of the address would be 'necessary for the performance of the contract', that is the delivery, but not for personalised pricing. 'Necessity' has a high threshold and is interpreted restrictively,[43] and thus the fact that a company might consider using personal data useful or profitable to price discriminate, does not make such use 'necessary'.[44]

Third, the data controller's 'legitimate interest' can sometimes provide a valid basis for using personal data in the absence of consent. A controller can rely on this legal basis when personal data usage is necessary for the controller's 'legitimate interests' and those interests are not 'overridden by the interests or fundamental rights and freedoms of the data subject which require protection of personal data'.[45] This legal basis seeks to strike a fair balance between the company's interests (i.e. profit) and the consumer's interests (e.g. privacy, or low or fair prices). The legal basis is appropriate for standard business practices, such as marketing one's own products to existing customers. However, the legal basis does not seem appropriate for price discrimination, since this can hardly considered 'necessary'. Moreover, in the case of price discrimination, the consumer's interests would generally weigh heavier than the controller's interests. Indeed, Data Protection Authorities have declared that price discrimination is an example of a practice that cannot usually be based on the provider's legitimate interests.[46]

In conclusion, consumer's consent appears to be the only available legal basis for price discrimination based on personal data.[47] Yet, as mentioned above and in light of the survey results, consumers are unlikely to give their consent to such practices.

If, regardless of this requirement of consent, online providers use personal data for price discrimination, Data Protection Authorities could enforce the GDPR and impose serious fines, of up to 20 million Euro or up to 4 % of a company's worldwide turnover.[48]

10.5 CONCLUSION

While personalised pricing is far from a novel tool for sellers to appeal to different audiences, the explosion of online shopping has enabled much more precise price discrimination. Online stores can offer *each* consumer a different price based on detailed histories and profiles (unless those consumers take often elaborate and conscious steps to minimise their online footprint). Such new forms of price discrimination exacerbate concerns regarding the fairness, morality and regulation of price discrimination.

One regulation that seems to offer a potential lever against the power that price discrimination grants to sellers, is data protection law. The GDPR applies when companies personalise prices and obliges them to inform customers about the purpose of processing their personal data and ask for their consent before using their personal data to personalise prices. The fact that we do not know of any companies requesting such permission may imply several things: either that websites are not yet engaging in price discrimination using personal data, or that they do so without complying with the GDPR on this point. If a Data Protection Authority suspects that a web store is personalising prices, it could start an investigation, and impose fines for non-compliance with the GDPR. Such investigations are, however, slow, costly and cumbersome. Nevertheless, at least in principle, the GDPR seems to be the most useful legal instrument to regulate online price discrimination.

Alternatively, specific rules for online price discrimination could be introduced to address its various controversial issues. That would require an answer from the legislator to questions such as: is price discrimination fair if it leads to higher prices for richer customers, and lower prices for poorer ones? Is 'fairness' the appropriate yardstick for regulation? Is price discrimination only problematic if it leads to illegal discrimination, for example, on the basis of ethnicity, or should some forms of price discrimination be banned altogether?

Our surveys suggest that, were it decided by consumers, online price discrimination would be banned. Consumers tend to be critical and suspicious of online price discrimination. Most consider online price discrimination unacceptable and unfair, and are in favour of a ban. When stores apply online price discrimination, most consumers think they should be informed about it. To many, the lack of transparency which often surrounds online price discrimination seems to violate the 'golden rule' as advocated by J. C. Penney, to treat others as you would like to be treated. And yet J. C. Penney went bankrupt, while dynamic pricing is rampant on the Internet, and companies are continuing to experiment with different kinds of price discrimination.

NOTES

1 JC Penney Newsroom, "About JCPenney" (*JCPennyNewsroom.com*) www.jcpnewsroom
.com/about-company-info.html.

2 Parts of this chapter are based on J Poort and FJ Zuiderveen Borgesius, 'Does everyone
have a price? Understanding people's attitude towards online and offline price discrimination' (2019) 1 *Internet Policy Review* 1; FJ Zuiderveen Borgesius and J Poort, 'Online price
discrimination and EU Data Privacy Law' (2017) 40 *Journal of Consumer Policy* 347; FJ
Zuiderveen Borgesius, 'Algorithmic decision-making, price discrimination, and European
non-discrimination law' (2020) 31(3) *European Business Law Review* 401. The authors
thank Claes de Vreese, Natali Helberger, Sophie Boerman and Sanne Kruikemeijer for
their input for the survey.

3 The word 'identical' is crucial here, because it excludes price differences resulting from
differences in the cost of serving different customers. Think for example of different
shipping costs or different risk profiles in insurance and credit markets. Based on demographics or a person's past, he or she may be more likely to cause a traffic accident, fall ill,
become unemployed or default on a loan. As a result, the cost of providing insurance or
credit will differ. These cost differences justify price differences that most authors would
not consider price discrimination. In fact, one could argue insuring different people
entails different products. Different versions of a product sold with different margins also
fall outside the scope of this chapter. An economically more profound definition of price
discrimination by Stigler is 'the sale of two or more similar goods at prices which differ in
relation to marginal costs'. GJ Stigler, *Theory of Price* (4th ed., Macmillan 2003) 210.
Under that definition, price differences which merely stem from cost differences do not
constitute price discrimination. Versions may qualify as a result of the rather vague word
'similar'.

4 See also Zuiderveen Borgesius (n 2).

5 Inge Graef, 'Algorithms and fairness: What role for competition law in targeting price
discrimination towards end consumers?' (2018) 24(3) *Columbia Journal of European
Law* 541.

6 T de Graaf, 'Consequences of nullifying an agreement on account of personalised pricing'
(2019) 8.5 *Journal of European Consumer and Market Law* 184.

7 FJ Zuiderveen Borgesius, *Improving privacy protection in the area of behavioural targeting*
(Kluwer Law International 2015) http://hdl.handle.net/11245/1.434236.

8 W Baker, M Marn and C Zawada, 'Price smarter on the net' (2001) 2 *Harvard Business
Review* 122.

9 See for instance P Krugman, 'Reckonings; What price fairness?' *New York Times* (New
York, 4 October 2000) www.nytimes.com/2000/10/04/opinion/reckonings-what-price-
fairness.html.

10 Amazon News Room, 'Amazon.com issues statement regarding random price testing'
(27 September 2000) http://phx.corporate-ir.net/phoenix.zhtml?c=176060&p=irol-newsArticle_
PrintandID=502821.

11 J Valentino-Devries, J Singer-Vine and A Soltani, 'Websites vary prices, deals based on
users' information', *Wall Street Journal* (New York, 23 December 2012) http://online.wsj
.com/article/SB10001424127887323777204578189391813881534.html.

12 M Rose and M Rahman, 'Who's paying more to tour these United States? Price differences in international travel bookings' (*Technology Science*, 11 August 2015) https://techscience.org/a/2015081105.

13 See for instance T Badmaeva and J A Hüllmann, 'Investigating personalized price discrimination of textile-, electronics- and general stores in German online retail' (14th International Conference in Wirtschaftsinformatik, Siegen, February 2019) https://aisel.aisnet.org/wi2019/specialtrack01/papers/1/. See also: A Leibbrandt, 'Behavioral constraints on price discrimination: experimental evidence on pricing and customer antagonism' (2020) 121 *European Economic Review*. This study acknowledges that we know relatively little about the actual use of online price discrimination. In an experimental setting, it finds that sellers tend to overprice low value customers to avoid antagonising high-value customers but that customers do not generally reject price discrimination.

14 See for instance A Odlyzko, 'Privacy, economics, and price discrimination on the Internet' (2003) *Proceedings of the 5th International Conference on Electronic Commerce (ACM)* 355.

15 See, for example: HR Varian, 'Price discrimination', in R Schmalensee and RD Willig (eds.), *Handbook of Industrial Organization, Volume I* (Elsevier 1989).

16 AC Pigou, *The Economics of Welfare* (Macmillan 1932).

17 See L Chen, A Mislove and C Wilson, 'Peeking beneath the hood of Uber' (2015) *Proceedings of the 2015 Internet Measurement Conference* 495.

18 See about dynamic prices and flight tickets: T Vissers and others, 'Crying wolf? On the price discrimination of online airline tickets' (7th Workshop on Hot Topics in Privacy Enhancing Technologies (HotPETs 2014), Amsterdam, July 2014) https://hal.inria.fr/hal-01081034/.

19 For an illustration of this, see Zuiderveen Borgesius and Poort 2017 (n 2) 353–4.

20 See, for an overview, for instance Varian (n 15); M Armstrong, 'Recent developments in the economics of price discrimination' in R Blundell, W Newey, and T Persson (eds.), *Advances in Economics and Econometrics, Theory and Applications: Ninth World Congress* (CUP 2006).

21 Both studies were carried out within the Liss-panel (Longitudinal Internet Studies for the Social Sciences). This is a panel for academic research purposes, administered by CentERdata (Tilburg University, The Netherlands). The panel consists of 4,500 households, comprising 7,000 individuals. It is based on a true probability sample of households drawn from the population register by Statistics Netherlands (CBS). Households that could not otherwise participate are provided with a computer and internet connection.

22 All surveys were in Dutch; questions have been translated into English for this chapter.

23 More details about the questions and outcomes of this survey are provided in Poort and Zuiderveen Borgesius 2019 (n 2).

24 Poort and Zuiderveen Borgesius 2019 (n 2).

25 D Kahneman and A Tversky, 'Prospect theory: an analysis of decision under risk' (1979) 47 *Econometrica* 263.

26 G Loomes and R Sugden, 'Regret theory: an alternative theory of rational choice under uncertainty' (1982) 92 (368) *The Economic Journal* 805.

27 See Poort and Zuiderveen Borgesius 2019 (n 2).

28 Regulation (EU) 2016/679 of the European Parliament and of the Council of 27 April 2016 on the protection of individuals with regard to the processing of personal data and on the free movement of such data and repealing Directive 95/46/EC (General Data Protection Regulation), L 119/1 (GDPR).

29 The official term for an organisation that processes personal data is 'controller'. See Article 4(7) GDPR. For ease of reading, we speak of 'company' in this chapter.

30 Article 4(2) GDPR.

31 Article 4(1) GDPR.

32 Article 4(1) GDPR.

33 Recital 30 GDPR.

34 Article 5(1)(a) GDPR.

35 Articles 13 and 14 GDPR.

36 Article 5(1)(b) GDPR.

37 Article 29 Working Party, Opinion 03/2013 on purpose limitation (WP 203) 00569/13/EN, 16.

38 See for the six principles: Article 6(1) GDPR.

39 Article 6(1)(a) GDPR.

40 Article 4(11) GDPR.

41 A Acquisti, Alessandro, L Brandimarte, G Loewenstein, 'Privacy and Human Behavior in the Age of Information' (2015) 347(6221) *Science* 509; FJ Zuiderveen Borgesius, 'Behavioural sciences and the regulation of privacy on the Internet', in AL Sibony and A Alemanno (eds.), *Nudge and the law – what can EU law learn from behavioural sciences?* (Hart Publishing 2015).

42 Article 6(1)(b) GDPR.

43 Case C-524/06 *Huber v Germany* [2008] ECLI:EU:C:2008:724, para 52.

44 Article 29 Working Party, Opinion 06/2014 on the notion of legitimate interest of the controller under Article 7 of Directive 95/46/EC (WP 217) 844/14/EN, 20.

45 Article 6(1)(f) GDPR.

46 Article 29 Working Party, Opinion 06/2014 on the notion of legitimate interest of the controller under Article 7 of Directive 95/46/EC (WP 217) 844/14/EN, 39.

47 Steppe comes to a similar conclusion: R Steppe, 'Online price discrimination and personal data: a General Data Protection Regulation perspective' (2017) 33(6) *Computer Law and Security Review* 768.

48 Article 83 GDPR.

11

Data-Driven Algorithms in Criminal Justice: Predictions as Self-fulfilling Prophecies

Pamela Ugwudike

11.1 INTRODUCTION

Data-driven predictive algorithms known as risk assessment tools are increasingly used in criminal justice systems to inform procedures liable to deprive individuals of their freedom. They have found applications in a variety of penal contexts, including bail decisions, sentencing, probation revocation investigations and parole board hearings. The extant scholarship on the harms caused by applications of such algorithms focuses mainly on technical problems such as those that occur when biased data generates biased algorithmic outputs, and thus relate to differential validity, and predictive accuracy in general.[1] Whilst this scholarship focuses primarily on the criminal justice implications of the algorithms, sufficient attention has not been paid to social justice implications such as the truth-producing or epistemic power with which the algorithms impose risk labels that can constitute and also trigger a self-fulfilling prophecy.

This paper draws on Foucauldian analysis of the epistemic power of discourse to show how predictive technologies can operate as mechanisms of epistemic domination and to problematise the epistemic privilege through which they generate risk labels that fuel social injustice. In the focus on criminal justice ideals of accurate profiling and risk classification, this structural dimension pertaining to social justice has been ignored warrants attention. Admittedly, criminal justice and social justice problems often crosscut, particularly when biased criminal justice decisions initiate or reproduce structural inequalities, causing social injustice. Nevertheless, a nuanced analysis of how both dimensions of justice intersect when algorithmic predictive technologies are applied is lacking in the literature, which focuses primarily on criminal justice technicalities to do with the nexus of biased data and algorithmic accuracy.

The discussion here deviates from this trend and advances the current scholarship on data-related harms by unravelling the capacity for biased data to provoke outcomes that not only produce adverse criminal justice implications, but also point to broader social injustices. This paper sheds light on the tendency of profiling algorithms to generate labels that counterproductively evoke a self-fulfilling prophecy and foment future criminalisation. This outcome exposes affected risk subjects to social injustice, not least because of the stigmatising and exclusionary effect of criminal justice labels such as 'criminal' or 'offender'. The chapter critiques the fairness of predictive algorithms and their broader social outcomes. It proposes fairness constructs rooted in social justice ideals and thus directed towards normative conceptualisations of fairness quite unlike the descriptive constructions based on 'algorithmic accuracy'.

11.2 TRENDS IN PENAL PREDICTIVE ALGORITHMS AND SCHOLARLY CRITIQUES

11.2.1 *Increased Reliance on Predictive Analytics in Penal Systems*

Data-driven profiling in penal systems relies on the application of predictive algorithms that analyse aggregate data including criminal justice datasets, such as police and probation records of their decision making, in order to predict risk of reoffending. Data provenance in this context is frequently unclear.[2] Whilst earlier actuarial risk assessment tools relied primarily on smaller scale administrative data from within the criminal justice system, the more advanced algorithms, particularity those with machine-learning functionality, now also rely on 'big data' sourced from an array of vendors, but data provenance issues mean that exact sources are not always known.[3] These can comprise information on credit history, employment records, health data, and other datasets culled from real-time activities across digital spaces and platforms.

Regardless of the data source, algorithms make statistical inferences from patterns in the data in order to allocate risk scores to individual risk subjects on the basis of the characteristics they share in common with other people who, most critically in this context, have reoffended in the past, according to the data.[4] Creators of these algorithms rely on several constructions of reoffending. Their definitions range from rearrest, probation revocation, and recall to prison, to reconviction or some other criminal justice outcome.[5] If a risk subject shares similar characteristics with others in the datasets who have offended or reoffended, the predictive algorithm generates a higher risk of reoffending score. A lower risk score is similarly generated when a risk subject has a similar profile with others who have had lower risks of reoffending in the past. These predictions then inform adjudications and this approach to risk-focused decision-making has been central to sentencing and penal practice (in probation and prison) in the form of actuarial risk assessment since the evidence-based policy approach became formalised across Western and other jurisdictions in the 1980s–1990s.[6]

More than 150 predictive algorithms are now applied in penal systems across the world, including 'low- and middle-income countries'.[7] Some are specialist tools in the sense that they are used for predicting the likelihood of general offences that are violent and/or sexual in nature. An example is the Violence Risk Approval Guide-Revised (VRAG-R).[8] This and other specialised algorithms are applied in forensic settings and typically supplement generic risk prediction tools.[9] One example of tools in this category is the Correctional Offender Management Profiling for Alternative Sanctions (COMPAS) tool applied in some parts of the US.[10]

Some rely on statistical algorithms to automate data and compute risk scores, while others rely on algorithmic models with Machine Learning (ML) functionality, making them part of the 'smart justice' innovations currently informing criminal justice decision-making.[11] In their description of what qualifies as ML predictive algorithms, Brennan and Oliver state that 'supervised learning' ML methods are used for allocating probationers to 'preestablished risk levels', and such ML systems can draw on data to learn new ways of categorising cases.[12] Unfortunately, such optimisation does not benefit those already categorised by the ML systems. 'Unsupervised learning' ML systems perform data analytics to identify patterns, themes and other similar features in complex data. Examples are: 'types of drunk drivers, varieties of sociopathic offenders, and offender developmental pathways'.[13] This information then informs penal decision-making.

To conduct risk assessments using these tools, the forensic practitioner, for example a probation officer, typically holds an interview with the risk subject and collects information on demographic attributes, criminal history, personality, attitudes, and personal circumstances including family background, associates/peers, level of education and employment history.[14] This information, known collectively as risk predictors or risk factors is fed into the algorithm, which then calculates the risk score based on the number of risk predictors the risk subject shares with others in the data set. Structured risk assessment technologies allow practitioners to influence this process by ensuring that the risk subject's specific circumstances inform risk categorisations.

As the foregoing suggests, data-driven algorithms proceed on the assumption that information about others in data sets, such as those who have been involved in the justice system, is generalisable to the individual risk subject. Thus risk technologies 'personalise' risk and its management by comparing the data of the risk subject with the data drawn from populations; they profile the risk subject through generalisations made on the basis of historical data from others. Meanwhile, a growing scholarship on data-related harms is now demonstrating that the data sets that algorithms rely on to make predictions, expose minorities and socioeconomically marginal groups to overprediction, considered in the next section.[15]

11.2.2 *Trends in Scholarly Critiques: The 'Garbage In, Garbage Out' Fixation*

Central to the scholarship on data-related harms is the view that biased data sets generate flawed risk predictions which in turn inaccurately categorise risk subjects as more or less risky than others. Some of this scholarship is reductionist in its exclusionary focus on 'algorithmic accuracy' and the criminal justice implications. It ignores broader questions and problems such as the criminogenic quality of algorithmic risk labels and their wider social implications. Instead, it focuses on how biased data undermines the accuracy of the tools: in this context, this typically refers to measures of differential validity and captures the extent to which the tools are biased against minorities.[16] Within this scholarship, the legitimate concern is that the historical datasets on which algorithms rely are imbued with biased criminal justice decisions, such as racially biased arrests, and the algorithms then generate predictions that replicate those systemic biases. This occurs when the algorithms infer from patterns in such data that racial minorities may be more prone to arrests than others and are therefore more deserving of higher risk labels, even if in some individual cases that risk label is in fact misplaced. As algorithmic risk prediction is only ever probabilistic, there will always be prediction errors, but the errors may disadvantage certain groups more than others and benefit other groups. For example, a racially biased algorithm may give a white offender the benefit of the doubt not afforded to a black offender, even where both offenders are otherwise similarly positioned. On this basis the scholarship on data-related harms posits that biased data generate higher error rates for affected risk subjects, making the algorithms unfair.[17] Proponents of algorithmic profiling similarly highlight technical dimensions in their analysis of predictive algorithms and their impact[18]. Thus both proponents and opponents of predictive algorithms prioritise in their arguments the criminal justice aims of predictive accuracy and efficient risk classification. Questions relating to deeper structural concerns are often ignored.

In particular, debates about technical accuracy and efficiency overlook the truth-producing or epistemic power with which the algorithms impose the label of risky on some more than others. Also ignored is the reality that criminal justice labels can be criminogenic and can create a self-fulfilling prophecy by exposing affected risk subjects to further criminalisation and accompanying structural disadvantage resulting in social injustice. In what follows, I draw upon Foucauldian analysis of the epistemic power of discourse to bring to the fore the epistemic dominance exerted by algorithmic profiling and its manifestations through criminal justice labels. I also discuss the wider social justice implications of algorithmic risk labels as informed by labelling theories.

11.3 BEYOND A CRIMINAL JUSTICE PERSPECTIVE

11.3.1 *Predictive Technologies as Structural Mechanisms of Epistemic Domination*

A Foucauldian 'epistemic domination' take on predictive algorithms shows how these algorithms feed into the construction of risk labels as forms of individual and population control. Indeed, predictive algorithms may be described as ideal mechanisms of epistemic domination, given their role as technologies that generate risk labels which are then ascribed to risk subjects to determine the appropriate level of penal intervention. The construction of these algorithms as scientific, evidence-based tools enables them to dominate criminal justice discourses about risk and riskiness.[19]

From a Foucauldian perspective, the concept of epistemic domination refers to the capacity to exert epistemic power by constructing discourses that evolve into accepted knowledge of social problems such risk and riskiness.[20] Algorithmic profiling technologies – rooted as they are in psychological, criminological, and other human science theories and methods – exert this form of power and dominance in their role as knowledge producers. In this role, they exercise epistemic privilege by dominating the discourse about who is and who is not risky, with ramifications for management and control of individuals. This strongly resonates with Foucault's view of the human sciences as capable of exercising power 'through [their] ability to categorise individuals as normal or abnormal depending on assessments of the individual's level of conformity with, or deviation from, the norms of behaviour set by the disciplines.'[21] The knowledge they produce about norms of behaviour becomes an instrument of control, serving as a means of controlling not only those labelled as deviant and placed in penal and other institutions, but also the rest of society.[22] Foucault observed in relation to 'the repetitive discourse of criminology' and other disciplines:

> [B]y solemnly inscribing offences in the field of objects susceptible of scientific knowledge, they provided the mechanisms of legal punishment with a justifiable hold not only on offences, but on individuals; not only on what they do, but also on what they are, will be, may be.[23]

This description provides a close fit for predictive algorithms, including their apparent power to define risk, foretell the future, and pre-empt undesirable futures. On this reading, algorithmic governance extends the purpose and evolution of human science disciplines in seeking to identify, label, and control 'risky' populations.

The algorithms exert epistemic domination in several ways that are vital to our understanding and critiques of these technologies. First, they exert epistemic domination by using opaque and unchallengeable decision-making processes to generate risk scores and shape constructions of risk, which in turn obscure the systemic biases and structural inequalities embedded in data and replicated in risk scores. As noted above, by relying on data sets imbued with biased criminal justice decision-making, algorithms inflate risk scores of affected groups and in doing so, attach the risk labels more frequently on them. Second, their grounding in scientific theories and methods means that they are ostensibly objective knowledge producers: the apparent basis of algorithmic technologies in pure fact and science has the effect of entrenching their epistemic privilege in so far as it silences critics and depicts algorithmic labels of riskiness as scientific truth.

The view that algorithms are scientific or evidence-based ratifies the veracity of their risk labels which, as we shall see, can produce profound social injustice, and validates their apparent legitimacy. Yet, this overlooks the reality that design choices are influenced by the values of the developers of technologies generally and predictive algorithms specifically, as well as by theoretical orientation.[24] This includes data choices and predictor construction. Indeed commonly used socio-economic predictors are underpinned by crime theories and some of these theories ignore structural factors that may explain the presence of socioeconomic risk predictors in a risk subject's profile.[25] The predictors may also be insensitive to cultural diversity and are rooted primarily in Western conservative norms, particularly in relation to education, employment, family background and composition (the two-parent family being the norm).[26] Groups who are acculturated to different norms or unable to conform to Western norms, sometimes due to blocked access to relevant resources, may consequently be more vulnerable to higher risk scores than others.

In the 2018 case of *Ewert v Canada* the plaintiff, a member of the indigenous Métis tribe in Canada, objected to the use of five actuarial risk assessment tests, that is, data-driven profiling tools, to assess his risk of reoffending, on the basis that the tools were arguably based on Western norms and as such culturally inappropriate for indigenous groups.[27] The argument was that the Correctional Service of Canada (CSC) should have provided evidence of the tools' accuracy for indigenous people. The trial court's ruling that the tools required further validation to enhance their cultural sensitivity before they could be applied was upheld by the Supreme Court of Canada. It held that the CSC had breached its statutory obligation in failing to verify the accuracy of the disputed tools for indigenous people. This case draws attention to the reality that the Western norms on which predictive algorithms are trained and based may collide with norms prevailing in other socio-structural contexts, with adverse consequences for affected subjects. Such cultural insensitivity could mean that minorities may be misidentified as high risk and labelled as such because their profile is inconsistent with those norms.

The foregoing suggests that problematising the epistemic privilege or truth-producing power of predictive algorithms must occur on two levels. In the first place, the capacity of the algorithms to produce 'accurate results' or truths about risk needs to be questioned. In particular, it is important to ask whether data sets and embedded risk predictor variables are biased and expose minorities and socioeconomically marginal groups to overprediction. In the second place, it needs to be recognised that predictive algorithms currently generate labels that classify some groups as riskier than others, and that by doing so the profiling algorithms do not simply create a 'record' of reality but construct and constitute it, echoing the Foucauldian take on reflexiveness between power and discourse.[28] The next section continues this structural analysis of algorithmic predictive technologies.

11.3.2 *Predictive Technologies as Structural Mechanisms of Self-fulfilling Prophecies*

A fast-growing body of literature regarding the quality of the data sets on which predictive algorithms rely, and on data-related harms, has emerged from diverse disciplines including law,[29] criminology,[30] computer and data science.[31] What unites these studies is an understanding that the data sets (such as arrest data and probation revocation data) informing algorithmic predictions tend to be imbued with biased decision-making of criminal justice officials. The scholarship on data-harms provides rich insights by highlighting the link between biased data and biased outputs, but is arguably insufficiently focused on structural concerns, such as the epistemic domination of risk tools. Instead, criminal justice imperatives of minimising bias and enhancing accuracy to achieve efficiency are afforded greater priority. However, a nuanced analysis that goes beyond criminal justice aims is needed to demonstrate the wider structural impact of algorithmic risk prediction. Such broader structural impact occurs when a prediction is made about an individual, and factors extrinsic to that individual converge to fulfill it. Algorithmic risk labels operate as such an extrinsic factor towards the fulfilment of a negative prediction. In other words, as a label that predicts future criminality, the prediction activates extrinsic processes which eventually lead to the prediction becoming a reality. In this way, algorithmic risk labels generate self-fulfilling prophecies.

Below, I explain how these occur by using the example of the systemic biases affecting racial minorities. In such cases, the process of creating a self-fulfilling prophecy occurs in two phases, both of which call into question the scientific basis of the technologies. The first phase is triggered by racial profiling, which contaminates the criminal justice data sets on which algorithms rely for prediction. This phase begins even before data sets are analysed by the algorithmic technologies. It starts when criminal justice decisions, such as arrests, are made on the basis of the underlying belief that minorities possess high criminal propensity and are more likely to offend or re-offend than others. This belief renders the group vulnerable to overexposure to certain interventions, such as arrests. Administrative data comprising historical records of criminal justice decisions would then show a pattern of high arrest rates or similar adverse outcomes for racial minorities. Subsequently, when algorithms process the data imbued with biased arrest decisions, although race is not included as a risk predictor, the algorithms statistically infer from the data that racial minorities are riskier than others because they have worse criminal justice outcomes, even if the outcomes are in fact due to the biased overexposure. The implication of this algorithmic inference is that minorities will be ascribed labels in the form of higher risk scores far more frequently. In this way, algorithms fulfill the initial prophecy made at the initial profiling stage. Further, it can trigger a self-fulfilling prophesy which according to Robert Merton, one of the chief architects of the concept, refers to 'a false definition of the situation evoking a new behaviour [or extrinsic factor] which makes the originally false conception come true.'[32] In the case of an algorithmic prediction of high risk, the algorithm becomes the 'extrinsic factor' that fulfills the initial prophecy, regardless of the fact that the profiling on which it is based rested on false beliefs. As labelling theories posit, negative labels have harmful effects regardless of whether or not the labels are spurious. By the same token, studies showing that the commonly applied algorithms which rely on administrative data generate higher risk scores for minorities than warranted, expose the capacity of algorithmic risk labels to provoke a self-fulfilling prophesy and, by implication, also problematise the scientific claims underpinning predictive algorithms. The studies demonstrate that algorithmic risk labels are man-made artefacts, not objective scientific truth generators. For example, Jimenez and colleagues tested whether the LS/CMI applied in a probation area in the USA was a strong predictor of probation recidivism for minority probationers.[33] They analysed the records of 19,344 probationers and found evidence of racial difference in the way the LS/CMI predicted recidivism: 'Minorities scored higher on seven of eight risk domains on the LS/CMI.'[34] The researchers assessed whether this racial disparity could be attributed to the personal biases and prejudices of the probation officers administering the tool, but this was not the case. In fact, it was the data on which the tool was relying for predictions that generated the observed disparity. Initial beliefs at the profiling stage may have been embedded in the prediction data, prompting the algorithm to generate high-risk labels for minorities, thus replicating and confirming the initial beliefs. Reinforcing this, Angwin and Larson's analysis of COMPAS found that the tool tended to record a higher percentage of false positives[35] for black people.[36] The algorithm generated unfounded high-risk labels at a greater rate for minorities, which confirmed earlier profiling decisions (embedded in prediction data) about the group's criminal propensity.[37] Hao and Stray have since devised a tool that uses the datasets from Angwin and Larson's study to demonstrate how algorithms that rely on biased data sets expose minorities who are typically affected by such biases to overprediction or artificially inflated risk scores.[38]

Algorithmic inferences from biased data can also produce a self-fulfilling prophecy in another way. This occurs after the label of high risk confirming the initial prediction made at the profiling stage is imposed on the risk subject. Labelling theories suggest that when negative labels are imposed (deservedly or undeservedly) a combination of social and psychological factors can drive the labelled subject to adopt the label and act accordingly, exposing themselves to further criminalisation. This perspective on the impact of deviant labels is primarily associated with the work of neo-Chicagoan sociologists of deviance, notably Howard Becker, who argued that negative labels pose adverse psychological and social implications that may provoke future deviance and criminality.[39] In terms of the psychological impact of criminal justice labels, for example a high-risk score, labelling theorists such as Becker maintained that these labels can alter the individual's self-identity. They can foment a negative self-identity whereby those affected start to perceive themselves as deviant and to act accordingly. Regarding the social impact of deviant labels, Becker and others argued that, as noted above, the individual may experience public stigmatisation and exclusion.[40] Thus, risk labels can trigger a combination of social and psychological problems that converge to block access and opportunities required for a law-abiding lifestyle. Deviance and further criminalisation then occur, confirming the original prediction. The label thus becomes the prophecy that fulfills itself irrespective of the (original) inclination of the labelled. Studies have indeed shown that negative labels, whether they are real or erroneously imputed, can trigger future criminalisation. A longitudinal study of pathways into and out of crime sampled approximately 4,300 young people in Edinburgh.[41] The study found that interactions at an early age with agents of social control such as the police or social workers, corresponded with 'amplified contact' with these agencies later in life.

11.3.3 *Predicting Technologies from a Social Justice, and Not Just Criminal Justice, Perspective*

In so far as algorithmic inferences based on biased data trigger self-fulfilling prophecies, the algorithms that produce these inferences are unfair over and beyond adverse criminal justice outcomes and extend to their social justice implications. Yet, as noted above, within the large body of work on the fairness of algorithms in the penal context, critics and proponents similarly explore fairness concerns about the accuracy and efficacy of risk tools, reflecting prevailing criminal justice imperatives. That said, a key difference between the critics and proponents is that proponents of algorithmic assessments adopt definitions of fairness that minimise problems, such as the racial bias, that contaminate data sets and algorithmic outputs. For instance, in their refutation of the study by Angwin and Larson which concluded that the COMPAS algorithm was biased against minorities, Skeem and Lowenkamp tested the predictive accuracy of the PCRA, a similar algorithm, to demonstrate its fairness.[42] Their study relied on violence arrest data as its measure of recidivism, ignoring the fact that racial bias could be embedded in such data. Instead the researchers described the data as 'the most unbiased criterion available'. Using their data set containing arrest data, they analysed whether the PCRA accurately predicted the re-arrest of their study sample. Much like the COMPAS study, they found disparities in risk scores across racial groups; the scores were higher for minorities. But they argued that the observed racial disparities reflected real differences in risk of recidivism, not any biases that could be attributed to the PCRA. Critics would reject this conclusion and rightly point to the potential for criminal justice data to bias algorithmic outputs. The authors also maintained that the PCRA algorithm is rooted in scientific theories and methods which ensure the accuracy of its predictions. As shown above, the scientific basis of the epistemic domination or truth-producing power of predictive algorithms can be challenged on several grounds.

Nevertheless, both critics and proponents of predictive algorithms have debated algorithmic fairness on technical issues to do with scientific accuracy, particularly differential validity.[43] From this perspective, fairness is achieved if risk technologies have strong differential validity and other forms of validity and reliability. For the proponents, this is the case even if social problems such as racial biases contaminate data sets and thereby reinforce deep-rooted inequality and prejudice. The premise seems to be that the task of predictive technologies is to predict risk accurately, not to solve social problems.[44] Thus, a focus on technical dimensions of fairness comes at the expense of broader social justice concerns about the potential for the algorithms to embed the social and economic status quo. In contrast, fairness constructs that proceed from a social justice perspective would emphasise considerations that go towards redressing inequities and inequalities, discrimination and prejudice. A clear distinction can therefore be made between technical fairness which typically complements the criminal justice imperative of systemic efficiency, and substantive fairness based on social justice ideals. The former is depicted by its supporters as the important empirical measure of fairness. In contrast, a social justice perspective goes beyond this to emphasise adverse structural consequences, including the self-fulfilling prophecy of algorithmic risk labels. This perspective therefore draws attention to the need for laws and regulations that focus on a normative conceptualisation of fairness in its application to predictive algorithms.

11.3.4 The Perceptual Character of Fairness and Its Role in Algorithmic Risk Prediction

A social justice perspective on algorithmic fairness also concerns itself with the perceptual character of fairness, with attention being paid to the views of those affected by biased algorithmic predictions. Arguably, prevailing definitions of fairness have paid insufficient attention to this dimension. Nevertheless, it is important because it concerns the level of trust risk subjects invest in the inferences made by predictive tools and the scientific basis of their risk labelling. Some critiques of predictive algorithms emphasise their lack of transparency and as such, touch upon fairness in so far as such opacity prevents an assessment of the fairness of the algorithmic output. But those critiques rarely have the risk subject in mind as the relevant observer and evaluator, but rather the legal expert, advocate, or law enforcement officer. This exclusion of the perspective of the risk subject about algorithms and their inferences instantiates once more the concept of epistemic domination. Still, the fairness of the predictive technology, as seen through the eyes of the risk subject, is critical for its perceived legitimacy as well as the perception of the procedural justice accorded to her and, by implication, is also critical for her future compliance with the law, with the police and other criminal justice officials.[45]

In the justice system, procedural justice refers to the fairness of the decisions made by criminal justice officials during their interactions with citizens. The legitimacy of risk assessments is undermined if risk subjects are unable to assess the procedural fairness of the decision affecting them. This occurs when they are unable to follow the inferences of opaque and unchallengeable decision-making processes.[46] There is now significant evidence from criminological,[47] sociopsychological,[48] and legal[49] perspectives that when citizens interact with criminal justice officials, such as probation officers and the police, they evaluate the processes of decision-making. Studies show that they are more likely to believe that the process is fair if they have been given the opportunity to have their say or to have their voice heard and taken into account when a decision is made. Conversely, perceived procedural unfairness provokes negative attitudes towards authority, with adverse implications for the perceived legitimacy of the entire criminal justice system.[50] There is also evidence that criminal justice systems require a degree of public legitimacy for their survival.[51] Without such legitimacy, they have to rely on costly and somewhat unsustainable deterrent and retributive measures to enforce cooperation and compliance with the law.[52] By the same token, as Harcourt notes in a critical study of predictive algorithms, outcomes that disproportionately profile a particular population can 'have a delegitimizing effect on the criminal justice system that may lead disaffected members of the profiled group to greater disregard of the criminal law in a kind of backlash against perceived or real prejudice.'[53] In line with labelling theories, one of the social implications of disaffection with exclusionary societal systems is that it drives affected individuals towards criminality and further criminalisation.

Last but not least, the opacity of algorithmic decision-making also undermines the ability of affected groups to challenge a decision that substantially affects their lives and liberty, based on the unfairness of the decision-making process. For that reason, risk prediction tools lacking in transparency are arguably in violation of the human right to a fair trial, enshrined in Article 6 of the European Convention on Human Rights, and Article 47 of the Charter of Fundamental Rights of the European Union, as well as constitutional due process rights of citizens.[54] Yet, in the US case of *Loomis v Wisconsin*, the Wisconsin Supreme Court held that the defendant's inability to access and examine the COMPAS software that assigned him a risk score which in turn contributed to determining the length of his sentence (six years) did not violate the US constitutional right to due process.[55] As COMPAS is a privately owned software licensed to the state, its workings are protected by proprietary rights and trade secret law. Thus Northpointe (now rebranded as Equivant), the creator of the software, could validly refuse to disclose, to the defendant and the court, how COMPAS scores were computed or how the risk predictors were weighed. This makes it difficult to subject the predictive analytics used for risk prediction to rigorous independent evaluation to assess their accuracy and to examine whether they make racially or otherwise biased decisions.[56] Thus algorithmic decisions are not always amenable to rebuttal, which aligns with the idea of them as factual and scientific outputs that are in fact not amenable to argument. So apart from denying them a voice in the decision making process, algorithmic predictive technologies can deny affected risk subjects the opportunity to challenge the process and its outcomes.

In the UK there have been calls to grant data subjects and others affected by algorithmic decision-making the right to scrutinise and challenge algorithmic decision-making processes.[57] Key official reports also advocate official oversight to ensure transparency and enhance accountability.[58] Meanwhile, denying risk subjects the opportunity to scrutinise algorithmic decision-making and rebut decisions reinforces the ability of the algorithms to operationalise the epistemic privilege that allows them to construct unchallengeable risk labels – thereby provoking self-fulfilling prophecies with profound social justice implications.

11.4 CONCLUSION

The paper sought to expand the parameters of the scholarship on data-driven predictive algorithms in penal systems by arguing that algorithmic constructions of risk can become self-fulling prophecies. Thus profiling technology does not simply deliver an account of 'reality' as a neutral bystander, but reflexively interacts with it and changes the very subjects under its purview, and – along a Foucauldian reading of normalising discourses – society at large. Where such profiling technology is directed towards measuring the relative level of risk individuals pose to society, not only will such algorithms necessarily find, on a spectrum of risk, some individuals and groups 'riskier' than others, but the biases and prejudices that the tool, including its data sets, brings to the profiling will be reinforced through the profiling as a matter of finding what one looks for (i.e. overexposure of minorities) and through setting penal interventions into motion that mould the subject to fit their underlying assumptions. Thus, the discussion sought to demonstrate that it is essential for critiques of predictive algorithms to move beyond a narrow focus on criminal justice implications, taking a wider social justice perspective that helps to illuminate these broader structural consequences of predictive technologies and directs attention to the need for normative fairness constructs.

Arguably in contrast to their current standing in the penal system, risk prediction technologies look back to noble beginnings. Their emergence was motivated by the concern to counter the decline of rehabilitative approaches following the 'nothing works for offenders' ideology that dominated much of the 1970s and 1980s.[59] In the late 1980s and the early 1990s, researchers in Western jurisdictions including the USA, the UK, and Canada challenged this ideology.[60] They conducted meta-analytic reviews of rehabilitation programmes and found that certain practice principles could be linked to rehabilitation.[61] One of the principles was the risk principle, according to which risk assessments should be conducted to target for rehabilitative intervention.[62] This principle in turn led to the creation of generic risk technologies which are now used for selective incapacitation. However, the researchers who developed the risk principle and whose work informed the creation of most of the currently applied generic tools have long made it clear that predictive technologies should not focus on penal control aims, such as selective incapacitation, but are best applied for the more humane purpose of rehabilitative intervention, preferably in community-based settings.[63] This background offers a number of useful concluding perspectives for the above discussion. For a start, it humanises algorithmic risk prediction tools by linking them to their analogue histories. Despite their big data, machine learning, AI, black box credentials that appear to lift algorithmic tools beyond human critique, their grounding in statistical methodology brings them back onto a more familiar terrain that makes them more blatantly fallible and certainly a possible and necessary subject of deliberation and contestation. Their idealistic beginnings also humanise profiling algorithms in that they serve as a reminder of possible progressive uses of statistical profiling. Their current capture as 'public safety' vehicles within a risk-averse society – regardless of the wider social injustice brunt borne by already disadvantaged minorities – is neither their only nor greatest potential.

NOTES

1 See Karren Hao and Jonathan Stray, 'Can you make AI fairer than a judge? Play our courtroom algorithm game' (*MIT Technology Review*, 17 October 2019) www.technologyreview.com/s/613508/ai-fairer-than-judge-criminal-risk-assessment-algorithm/.

2 Jessica M Eaglin, 'Constructing recidivism risk' (2017) 67(1) *Emory Law Journal* 59.

3 Kelly Hannah-Moffat, 'Algorithmic risk governance: Big Data analytics, race and information activism in criminal justice debates' (2018) 23(2) *Theoretical Criminology* 453.

4 Eaglin (n 2); Seena Fazel and others, 'Use of risk assessment instruments to predict violence and antisocial behaviour in 73 samples involving 24,827 people: systematic review and meta-analysis' (2012) 245 *British Medical Journal* 1; Phillip D Howard and Louise Dixon, 'The construction and validation of the OASys Violence Predictor: advancing violence risk assessment in the English and Welsh correctional services' (2012) 39 *Criminal Justice and Behaviour* 287.

5 Sarah L Desmarais and Jay Phoenix Singh, *Risk Assessment Instruments Validated and Implemented in Correctional Settings in the United States* (Council of State Governments Justice Centre 2013).

6 Readers interested in finding out more about how the approach originated and evolved in the UK and beyond can refer to Ronen Ziv, 'The evidence-based approach to correctional rehabilitation: current status of the Risk-Need-Responsivity (RNR) Model of offender rehabilitation' in Pamela Ugwudike and others (eds.), *Routledge Companion to Rehabilitative Work in Criminal Justice* (Routledge 2019).

7 Fazel and others (n 4).

8 Grant T Harris, Marnie E Rice and Vernon L Quinsey, 'Violent recidivism of mentally disordered offenders: the development of a statistical prediction instrument' (1993) 20 *Criminal Justice* 315.

9 Grant T Harris, Marnie E Rice, Vernon L Quinsey and Catherine Cormier, *Violent Offenders: Appraising and Managing Risk* (3rd ed., American Psychological Association 2015).

10 Tim Brennan, William Dieterich and Beate Ehret, 'Evaluating the predictive validity of the COMPAS risk and needs assessment system' 2009) 36 *Criminal Justice and Behavior* 21.

11 Tim Brennan and William Oliver, 'The emergence of machine learning techniques in criminology: implications of complexity in our data and in research questions' (2013) 12 *Criminology & Public Policy* 551.

12 Ibid. 552.

13 Brennan and Oliver were, at the time of their publication, affiliated to Northpointe, Inc, the company that created COMPAS and which later rebranded itself as Equivant.

14 For more on the risk predictors on which algorithms rely, see Sarah L Desmarais, Kiersten L Johnson and Jay Phoenix Singh, 'Performance of recidivism risk assessment instruments in US correctional settings' (2016) 13 *Psychological Services* 206.

15 See generally, Julia Angwin and Jeff Larson, 'Bias in criminal risk scores is mathematically inevitable, researchers say' (*ProPublica*, 30 December 2016) www.propublica.org/article/bias-in-criminal-risk-scores-is-mathematically-inevitable-researchers-say; Eaglin (n 2); Hao and Stray (n 1).

16 Compare Angwin and Larson (n. 19) and William Dieterich, Christina Mendoza and Tim Brennan, COMPAS Risk Scales: Demonstrating Accuracy Equity and Predictive Parity: Performance of The COMPAS Risk Scales in Broward County (Technical Report, Northpointe Inc 2016).

17 Ibid.

18 Jennifer Skeem and Christopher Lowenkamp, 'Risk, race, & recidivism: predictive bias and disparate impact' (2016) 54(4) *Criminology* 680, 685.

19 See also Eaglin (n 2).

20 See Pamela Ugwudike, *An Introduction to Critical Criminology* (Policy Press 2015).

21 Ibid.

22 Michel Foucault, *Discipline and Punish: The Birth of the Prison* (Penguin 1977).

23 Ibid 18–19.

24 Paula Maurutto and Kelly Hannah-Moffat, 'Assembling risk and the "restructuring of penal control"' (2005) 46 *British Journal of Criminology* 438.

25 Pamela Ugwudike, 'Digital prediction technologies in the justice system: The implications of a 'race-neutral' agenda' (forthcoming) *Theoretical Criminology*.

26 Maurutto and Hannah-Moffat (n 27).

27 *Ewert v Canada* (2018) SCC 30.

28 Ugwudike (n 23).

29 Eaglin (n 2); Sonja B Starr, 'Evidence-based sentencing and the scientific rationalization of discrimination' (2014) 66 *Stanford Law Review* 803.

30 Hannah-Moffat (n 3); Ugwudike (n 28).

31 Hao and Stray (n 1).

32 Robert K Merton, *Social Theory and Social Structure* (New York Press 1968) 477.

33 Alisha Caldwell Jimenez and others, 'Validation and application of the LS/CMI in Nebraska probation' (2018) 45(6) *Criminal Justice and Behaviour* 863.

34 Ibid., 875.

35 False positives occur when people who are given a high-risk score do not reoffend and false negatives occur when those given lower risk scores reoffend.

36 Angwin and Larson (n 19).

37 See also Julia Dressler and Hany Farid, 'The accuracy, fairness and limits of predicting recidivism' (2018) 4(1) *Science Advances* http://advances.sciencemag.org/content/4/1/eaao5580.full.

38 Hao and Stray (n 1).

39 Howard Becker, *Outsiders: Studies in the Sociology of Deviance* (Free Press 1963).

40 See for example CC Lemert, 'Whatever happened to the criminal? Edwin Lemert's Societal Reaction' in CC Lemert and MF Winter (eds.), *Crime and Deviance: Essays and Innovations of Edwin M. Lemert* (Rowman & Littlefield 2000).

41 Lesley McAra and Susan McVie, 'Youth crime and justice: Key messages from the Edinburgh Study of Youth Transitions and Crime' (2010) 10(2) *Criminology and Criminal Justice* 179.

42 Skeem and Lowenkamp (n 22).

43 See also *William Dieterich, Christina Mendoza and Tim Brennan, COMPAS Risk Scales: Demonstrating Accuracy Equity and Predictive Parity: Performance of The COMPAS Risk Scales in Broward County (Technical Report, Northpointe Inc 2016).*

44 Skeem and Lowenkamp (n 51).

45 But see Pamela Ugwudike, 'Applications of risk prediction technologies in criminal justice: the nexus of race and digitised control' in Ugwudike and others (n 6).

46 Ibid.

47 Ibid.

48 Tom Tyler, *Why People Obey the Law* (Princeton University Press 2006).

49 AJ Wang, 'Procedural justice and risk-assessment algorithms' (2018) SSRN https://ssrn .com/abstract=3170136.

50 Gwen Robinson and Pamela Ugwudike, 'Investing in 'toughness': probation, enforcement and legitimacy' (2012) 51(3) *The Howard Journal of Criminal Justice* 300.

51 Tyler (n 56).

52 Robinson and Ugwudike (n 58).

53 Bernard E Harcourt, *Against Prediction: Profiling, Policing, and Punishing in an Actuarial Age* (University of Chicago Press 2007) 29.

54 Article 47 of the Charter of Fundamental Rights of the European Union [2012] OJ C 326/ 391 provides that 'Everyone whose rights and freedoms guaranteed by the law of the Union are violated... is entitled to a fair and public hearing within a reasonable time by an independent and impartial tribunal previously established by law'.

55 *Loomis v Wisconsin* 881 NW2d 749 (Wis 2016); Editor, 'Wisconsin Supreme Court requires warning before use of algorithmic risk assessment in sentencing – *State v. Loomis*, 881 N.W.2d 749 (Wis 2016)' (2017) 130 *Harvard Law Review* 1530.

56 Another way of doing it is by testing the outputs.

57 Wendy Hall and Jérôme Pesenti, *Growing the Artificial Intelligence Industry in the UK* (independent review, Department for Digital, Culture, Media & Sport and Department for Business, Energy & Industrial Strategy 2017).

58 House of Commons (UK) Science and Technology Committee, 'Algorithms in decision-making' (HC 2017-19, 351).

59 Don Andrews, James Bonta and Robert D Hoge, 'Classification for Effective Rehabilitation: Rediscovering Psychology' (1990) 38(7) *Criminal Justice and Behaviour* 19.

60 Ibid.

61 Ibid.

62 Ibid.

63 James Bonta and Don Andrews, *The Psychology of Criminal Conduct* (6th ed., Routledge 2016).

From Global Village to Smart City: Reputation, Recognition, Personalisation, and Ubiquity

Daithí Mac Síthigh

12.1 INTRODUCTION

'Smart city' projects today range from a proposed (and now abandoned) redevelopment of a waterfront site in Canada, infused with sensors and automated systems, to 'pilot cities' in China, utilising the rating of citizens as a key tool of governance, to multiple cities in the UK that are, as part of 'city deals' with central and devolved governments, building testbeds, innovation districts, and digital strategies. Across these and other projects, and distinguishing current developments from an earlier wave with more of a focus on city operations, new ways of delivering personalised services to people, including residents, are being explored. But what are the guiding principles governing these initiatives, and what motivates their proponents?

How the *individual* navigates and engages with the smart city has long been a concern in science fiction. Philip K. Dick's *The Minority Report*, a mid-twentieth-century short story, was the basis for a turn-of-the-century film of almost the same title, containing production designer Alex McDowell's vivid depictions of facial and retina identification, and – famously – personalised (and contextual) advertising utilising audio, video, holographic projections, and interactivity of various sorts.[1] More recently, a 2016 episode of the series *Black Mirror* imagined a world where we rate every interaction we have with other people, and how this information, overlaid on our view of the world, in the style of augmented reality, would drive our social standing, our access to markets, and even our freedom.[2]

Presently, we see cities around the world trying to set standards for their digital agendas, and constructing smart city 'roadmaps'. They confront a set of shared challenges: whether to emphasise the power of aggregate data or the delivery of personalised services; whether to seek the most innovative technology or focus on interventions with the greatest impact on quality of life; whether to prioritise improving the work that public authorities already do, or facilitate experimentation and the emergence of new products and services, or a new role for the private sector.

I explore these tensions in this chapter, taking stock of emerging approaches that seek to apply or supplement existing rules on privacy and data protection and to sustain public confidence and support in the face of innovation and change. First, I situate this work in the context of new waves of smart city projects, and the growing critical literature, in law, planning, and other fields, that seeks to identify the nature and implications of these initiatives, beyond the promotional language of 'smart'. With these developments highlighting important tensions between public and private sector approaches, I then highlight the work of Sidewalk, a Google-affiliated company, which articulated various iterations of its masterplan for a site in Toronto, engaging in significant debates on data ownership, surveillance, and intellectual property, and of the Los Angeles Department of Transportation, which developed a new and influential approach to mobility data (data associated with ridesharing, 'micromobility' such as e-scooters, and in time autonomous vehicles), responding to technological and market change in a field with significant environmental, quality of life, and privacy implications.

Then, I explore two facets of urban technology that relate to (and ultimately enable) the delivery of personalised services by public authorities and others. The first is ratings and reputation, where I highlight Chinese cities deploying aspects of the emerging 'social credit' systems, building upon the prevalence and acceptability of reputation measurement that dates back to credit scoring. Indeed, reputation is at the heart of many features of Western digital markets, including online auctions and the sharing economy, but is taking on a new role, supported by the pervasiveness and interconnectedness of surveillance, in service delivery. The second is facial recognition, which is currently being reviewed in light of data protection law, human rights requirements, public policy concerns, and discrimination; the ability to recognise individuals in this way, without a conventional and more deliberate identification (e.g. supplying a name, entering a password, or older biometric systems such as fingerprint scanning), is a key part of many proposed personalised services.

12.2 EVOLVING CONCEPTS OF THE SMART CITY

It is expected that two-thirds of the world's population will live in a city by 2050.[3] In planning for this, public authorities (and their private sector partners) are already addressing increasing urban populations, the delivery of services at scale, changing patterns of living (multi-occupancy units, 24-hour activity), conflicts over natural resources and shared spaces, and more. So, work that falls under the broad 'smart city' label, especially that which seeks to manage the relationship between the responsible authority and individual residents or other users (visitors, workers, etc.) is happening in a context where new technologies can and should be assessed in terms of how well they address these existing and increasingly urgent questions of policy and planning.

These plans and innovations in urban planning often aim to address the most salient problems facing society, globally and locally. For example, as plans and strategies have proliferated, an emphasis upon (environmental) efficiency and sustainability has emerged. So, for example, the 2017 Digital Strategy adopted by the Scottish Government takes as a working definition for smart cities that they encompass 'a way of using digital technologies to manage resources and infrastructure in a sustainable way, making our cities more efficient and greener places to live and do business'.[4] This, of course, builds upon long-standing visions of how the use of digital technologies and services affects the relationship between the citizen and the city:

> Imagine life for the citizen of the smart city: you awake in your sustainably built home … eating breakfast, you scan the flat screen, fed by maximum bandwidth internet, where the special, easy click local neighbourhood menu allows you to compare your daily energy use with other houses in the area, confirm your webcam appointment with your doctor, top up the balance of your all-purpose travelcard, order your groceries and leave messages for your child's teacher.[5]

This particular depiction, dating from 2010, is found in some of today's cities (and has become more familiar in 2020 on account of restrictions on movement imposed in response to Covid-19).[6] Yet as vision becomes reality, for better or for worse, the complexities of the citizen–city relationship in a technological context still need to be addressed. In particular, the possibility of using information, and either the digital delivery of that information to the individual, or its use in the background in order to present a different path to said individual, is likely to be controversial. As Cobbe and Morison put it in discussing informational asymmetries, bodies (including local government) seek to 'influence behaviour… according to the rationalities of efficiency, sustainability, and participation' through everything from personalised or differentiated pricing to sending notifications to smartphones, and (at macro level) routing and movement control. They therefore summarise life in the smart city, for the citizen who is also conceived of as a consumer, as 'a process of perpetual choice-making'.[7]

Twenty-first-century innovations, both in urban renewal more generally and in media and information industries, often address 'pseudo-public' spaces.[8] Examples include open squares constructed within private developments, city centre revitalisation projects, online communities, and search engines. In these 'pseudo-public' spaces, it is particularly likely that the rights of and basis for authority over individuals are ambiguous, or that there is a tension between the presentation of the space and the prevailing legal conditions. For instance, various aspects of contract or property law may be the basis for broader governance of behaviour.

Smart city initiatives encapsulate this ambiguity by creating a 'smart' urban space, likely to be a hybrid of virtual and material,[9] and so deserving of analysis that goes beyond parallels or analogies between, for example, a town square and an online discussion board. Edwards observes that some of these new spaces are *pseudo-private*, where what is historically and unquestionably public is becoming 'privately operated or at least full of privately operated sensors with the data collected held in private databases'.[10] Similarly, Green emphasises how the 'smart city is a dream come true' for those who have perfected online data collection, but see new opportunities in physical space.[11] So, the types of regulatory measures (including user rights) available will vary across new schemes and services in cities – and so the starting points and doctrinal 'homes' for oversight of personalised services will vary as well.

Brauneis and Goodman, writing about the Toronto project discussed below, ask questions of the governance models, identifying the importance of access to and ownership of data and the analysis thereof, control over physical infrastructure, and so 'whether public entities will be able to take control of the informational and physical assets should they wish to end the relationship with the private company'.[12] Even in contexts where private sector activity is the subject of a general regulatory regime, as under EU data protection law, the emergence of projects like in-store tracking highlights the varying relevance of legal safeguards that only impact some classes of actors, as well as the potential ineffectiveness of the mitigation measures that might be deployed in other contexts (e.g., privacy-enhancing technologies or 'do not track'-style settings).[13]

These questions about understanding the regulatory constraints on components of the smart city, also bring us back to the role of data analytics in the delivery of personalised services.[14] Yeung's distinction between 'static nudges' and 'hypernudges' helps us to understand these implications.[15] While the typical static nudge – a fashionable and controversial aspect of twenty-first-century public policy – is based on the organising party's ability to design an intervention in order to deploy it for a particular end[16] (e.g. the spatial organisation of a cafeteria in order to promote healthy choices), hypernudges are formulated in light of data analysis and, in particular, 'continuously updated'.[17] The allure of such approaches is clear. For instance, research conducted regarding social media use showed how the consideration of behaviour (i.e. reading history) and network analysis (i.e. shared interests) provided 'better performance' than allowing users to customise their own settings.[18] On the other hand, particular types of targeting may raise a version of the famous 'uncanny valley' problem in robotics,[19] whereby a certain measure of automation is convenient and appealing, but a particular level of 'imitation' of human behaviour can provoke distrust and even fear or disgust. So where a city proposes or facilitates a new relationship with individuals (such as the project in Nice to provide customised advice on skin protection in light of skin type and real-time UV data[20]), feasibility and lawfulness are accompanied by important discourses of acceptability and impact.

Many of these interventions benefit from being understood not just as new ways of gathering and using data, but as 'social mediation technologies' – other examples of which include clocks, cars, and mobile phones.[21] These technologies cannot be understood as only concerning personal choices, given their implications for others and in the organisation of social life. So, for instance, the use of a mobile phone does not just affect the user – it reshapes their social interactions with their contacts (everything from whether to set a meeting time and place to how decisions, including those with legal implications, are made), as well as the obvious changes in shared physical spaces when disparate individuals bring or use the devices.

The link between the opacity of some of the technological developments and services mentioned in this section, and their implications for individuals and for social relations, is appropriately highlighted in a broader context by Bridle. He identifies a proclivity to think computationally and so consider new technologies as 'inherently emancipatory'.[22] Similarly, Morozov describes the 'solutionism' applied by technology companies, and their admirers in public service, to long-established social and economic problems.[23]

Having outlined some of the dilemmas and challenges facing developers of innovative projects in cities more generally, we can now illustrate these by considering a specific (and very controversial) project in one city (Sidewalk Toronto), followed by an initiative developed in another city but being adopted elsewhere (the Los Angeles 'Mobility Data Specification'). These debates highlight a crucial challenge for data-informed and data-driven approaches to city governance – developing against a backdrop of a quarter-century of public–private partnerships and other administrative developments[24] – of how to proceed in contexts where ownership and control spans the public and private sectors.

12.3 SMART CITIES AND THE PUBLIC/PRIVATE DIVIDE

12.3.1 *Sidewalk Toronto*

The planned *Sidewalk Toronto* development, which was discontinued in May 2020, can be understood as a good illustration of the implications of planned 'smart city' development. Sidewalk Labs is a subsidiary of Alphabet (Google's holding company), and followed some initial projects based around specific technologies with a larger and more ambitious project – a demonstrator or examplar urban neighbourhood of the future, to be built on a parcel of land held by the waterfront redevelopment authority in the Canadian city of Toronto. On what a newspaper called 'twelve acres of unsightly, soggy Toronto waterfront real estate',[25] Sidewalk sought to put into practice its mission statement of 'reimagining cities to improve quality of life', but faced multiple and sustained criticisms on issues including privacy, data control and ownership, and the use of public spaces and public resources.[26] The key documents in the Sidewalk Toronto project, relevant to the present analysis, include a 'master innovation and development plan' (2018–19),[27] reports from Waterfront Toronto's 'digital strategy advisory panel' (2019–20),[28] and a 'digital innovation appendix' (late 2019)[29] setting out specific approaches to questions such as data protection.

What was first proposed for Sidewalk – making it, in its own phrase, 'the most measurable community in the world'[30]– represents what Hollands called the *ubiquitous city*, with technology, especially sensors for data collection, embedded in its fabric.[31] A subsequent assessment of breakthrough technologies published in the MIT Technology Review described Sidewalk as an example of the 'sensing city'.[32] Indeed, the early plans for Sidewalk Toronto included a proposed 'data layer', combining an established trope in twentieth-century utopian and urban renewal design, of rethinking the city through its vertical layers (e.g., separating utilities from pedestrians from traffic, as in famous twentieth-century projects ranging from university like the University of East Anglia to the unbuilt Experimental City in Minnesota)[33] with the centrality of layering to internet infrastructure.[34]

Reports on the plans understandably emphasised the significance of the data layer to the achievement of the project's goals. One report by writer Laura Bliss, who followed the project closely through its development, utilised footfall, building occupancy, energy use, and the contents of rubbish bins as examples, making an explicit link to Sidewalk's own correlation of measurement with better management, and the above-mentioned 'most measurable community' goal.[35] In their detailed analysis of Sidewalk's documentation and negotiations, Goodman & Powles identified the technologies planned for deployment, and how they would interact with the delivery of services, and utilise 'hypernudge' approaches in order to regulate land use and resident behaviour in an effective fashion.

In the later stages, Sidewalk emphasised 'quality of life' as the key innovative contribution of the project, highlighting features like streetscapes that adapted to weather conditions (including matters dear to the Torontonian's heart, like paving slabs that would detect and melt snow where appropriate).[36] In a 2019 update, Sidewalk emphasised aggregation (e.g. tracking footfall) and improving services at the general level (e.g. 'self-driving' refuse bins), noting that a majority of services would not engage with personal data, and swearing off the use of facial recognition.[37]

Yet the difference between 'normal' urban space and what Quayside would look like has been part of the debate, and the governance implications of such pseudo-public and pseudo-private spaces are significant. As one headline from the Canadian public broadcaster put it, echoing a familiar objection to digital and online services: 'Welcome to the neighbourhood; have you read the terms of service?'[38] For Goodman and Powles, proposals like the 'smart chutes' in apartment buildings (which would differentiate between recyclable waste on one hand and refuse destined for landfill on the other) call into question control over data (which would be collected through Sidewalk's infrastructure). From this, they ask whether innovation of this nature relates to or potentially marginalises the broader role of competent public authorities, who might wish to take data-driven approaches to their functions but would rely upon the private sector for access to key data.[39]

As the project developed, we can note how the responsible authority (Waterfront Toronto) began to articulate the public policy goals that technological innovation would address more clearly. In its 2018 'priority outcomes' it explained its desired outcomes as employment and economic development, affordable housing, sustainability, mobility, and urban innovation.[40] Sidewalk itself subsequently explained its plans under these headings,[41] though Waterfront Toronto's digital strategy advisory panel thought that the plan contained too much 'tech for tech's sake'.[42] This is consistent with Cobbe and Morison's identification of the recurrent themes found in the 'goals' of smart city projects, or the 'problems' that they seek to address: competitiveness, efficiency, sustainability, and (challenging) top-down governance.[43] The governance questions in relation to Sidewalk – especially whether it would perform functions in substitution for local government, or be beyond scrutiny – drew particularly sustained objections.[44] One question left unanswered (echoing the Morozov critique of solutionism) is whether criticism of the project can be characterised as an objection to the selection of problems, or an acceptance of the problems while being dissatisfied with the solutions. As such, even though the systems will not be built (at least not in Toronto), the record of adaptation and reframing on the part of the various partners, and the way in which objectives and use cases were, over time, documented in more detail, is of enduring significance.

12.3.2 *Mobility Data*

The role of the individual in the networked or ubiquitous city is called into question in the case of new transport or mobility services. Here, too, we see the articulation of a problem and the presentation of solutions aided by new technologies. Tackling congestion and associated environmental harm has long been a key goal for planners and those concerned with future cities,[45] and visually represented, or at least imagined, in everything from jetpacks[46] to hoverboards[47] – and, in *Minority Report*, autonomous cars. For 'smart mobility' to have a positive impact, it is essential – as Docherty and co-authors have argued – to address questions of governance, so as to avoid a situation where new technologies are deployed in a way that makes the problems worse rather than better.[48]

Of particular relevance in this chapter is the fact that new forms of mobility, including ridesharing, 'micromobility' (e.g. electric scooters), and in time autonomous vehicles of various sorts, have a set of data flows built into their design; this facilitates location and pricing, in the first instance, but offers the potential for dynamic management of how spaces (including roads) are used, as well as providing better, real-time 'multimodal' information on transport and other options to individuals.

Building upon the experiences of regulating the sharing economy (ridesharing in particular), and schemes such as docked or dockless bike rentals (as well as, in some cases, established procedures whereby commercial activity or the placing of property in public spaces requires permission), many US cities are now operating systems whereby scheme operators must obtain a licence or permit from city authorities. Increasingly, such systems also seek to address data issues. This is illustrated by an influential, open-source Mobility Data Specification (MDS), first developed by the City of Los Angeles, and now managed by a broader Open Mobility Foundation, with a number of industry participants.[49] The use of MDS is a requirement of permits to operate e-scooter rental schemes in Los Angeles and a number of other US cities.

In early iterations, the focus was on API-enabled transfer of data from service providers to the city, though it now also includes certain functionality for data going in the other direction. MDS has provoked a broad discussion of the appropriateness of data sharing and of the implications of any decision on data for the future of mobility and city planning. There has been criticism of MDS and of data sharing requirements, including from some of the companies providing services, often citing the privacy of users as a concern; this has included challenges to the lawfulness of city-imposed requirements for data sharing.[50] In response, city officials have collaborated on good practice guidance for mobility data,[51] although legislative change (which would allow cities to require some data, but only in accordance with said legislation) is under consideration in some US states.[52]

The management of mobility data thus addresses this theme of how conventionally understood public functions, especially in terms of relationships with individuals, come under challenge. The initial relationship, for instance, may be between the person who rents an e-scooter for ten minutes, or calls a rideshare car through an app as part of their commute, and the relevant service provider or platform. But the job of the city, or a public transport authority, includes managing use conflicts, understanding footfall and traffic, and – potentially – directing users in real time, providing neutral and comprehensive options on different modes, or coordinating the activities of disparate service providers.

So, as in other areas, we see the actual 'service', as narrowly defined, being delivered by private actors in a regulated market. But in the specific case of mobility, we also ascertain a broader concept of a relationship between the individual and the city that begins to feel like a service (possibly but not necessarily personalised). Commitments to 'mobility as a service' (MaaS) in a number of strategies underline these trends.[53] Making this work is very likely to require data sharing in various ways. Yet, the issues regarding personal data are significant, but a remedy of aggregation and decontextualisation may only facilitate certain uses (e.g. research, trends) and not others (e.g. trip planning, interoperability, integration with other public services).[54]

12.4 CHALLENGES IN PERSONALISED SERVICES

12.4.1 *Ratings and Reputation*

The infamous Social Credit System (or systems) currently under development in China represents an elaborate illustration of the coming to prominence of rating and reputational systems utilising digital information and a wide range of infrastructure, and so the associated legal and other controls that would govern the calculation and utilisation of, and challenges to, 'scores', blacklists, and other initiatives.[55]

Reputational systems have developed over the course of centuries, facilitated by technological developments (such as the ability to link databases), the presence or absence of legal measures, and commercial practices. So there is a thread running from the development of consumer credit rating (which has a significant reputational dimension) as capitalism expanded west in the United States in the nineteenth century, to how computers standardised and expanded this in the twentieth century, to the significance of trust to the success of eBay, the centrality of ratings to the sharing economy business models, and the exploration of alternatives to conventional credit scoring that is still going on today (such as taking signals from social media history and/or networks as an indication of creditworthiness) – not to mention unusual projects like a dating service based around credit scores.[56] Indeed, we are increasingly reliant upon rating or reputational measures, for example, in ecommerce or sharing economy markets with unfamiliar sellers or service providers – but there are significant questions regarding data protection law, the power of platforms, and discrimination.[57]

Meanwhile, the Chinese government has sought to build what has been termed a 'Social Credit System'. While a number of systems operate under this label, they have in common attempts to measure and 'score' sincerity, honesty, integrity, and compliance, and have some association with the regulation of individual behaviour and freedom (often through integration with existing legal measures, such as prioritisation in access to services). They resemble, but go beyond, more established rating and reputational systems by taking into account a wider range of factors (or, to put it differently, drawing upon more datasets) and by operating across contexts; the involvement of the state, and therefore the potential for systems to be all-encompassing without the ability to opt out, is also more significant than many earlier systems developed in the (Western) private sector for use with existing customers.

The most relevant instances for this chapter are where social credit systems manage the relationship between the individual and, say, the public authority responsible for managing city life. Social credit systems in China include China-wide blacklists, compliance scores by pilot cities, and social credit scores issued by financial institutions.[58] The first of these is a readily understandable list of those who have not complied with court judgments, though has been expanded and is particularly noteworthy when it involves co-operation with financial institutions. The second is more closely tied to surveillance, and is found in systems such as that in Rongcheng where 'points' are added and subtracted on account of behaviour, with implications for access to public services as well as public shaming through billboards. The third is perhaps the closest variant on credit scoring, though considerably more innovative, and involves the 'big three' of the Chinese IT industry – Baidu, Alibaba, and Tencent, albeit with some doubt in more recent times as to continued cooperation with the People's Bank of China and with public authorities.

We may think of conventional credit scoring – and indeed the current fascination with league tables, rankings, and measuring everything that moves[59] – as quintessentially reductive, and in some respects the opposite of 'personal'. Yet the centrality of reputation to the 'sharing' economy, and the rapid developments of new systems and services in China, indicate (albeit in different ways and with varying implications) an important realignment of the relationships in how people participate in markets and (in the Chinese examples) the relationship between state and citizen. In some ways, this echoes earlier rationales for systematised credit scoring, in that it allowed each borrower to be dealt with in light of their specific circumstances, eschewing the use of rank or family.[60] But while this was true to an extent, proxies (including in relation to character) never disappeared, and computerisation in the twentieth century supported the use of broader (statistical) measures of risk.[61]

In present-day China, then, we see an old story of character and trustworthiness, but in a new context of commercial and physical access to, for example, transport and accommodation.[62] The emerging importance of the sharing economy to city life – and the involvement of major information industry players in smart city projects – in the Western world could deliver, through less direct means, similar results.

12.4.2 *Facial Recognition Technologies*

Even a fair and transparent system using reputational information (or information supporting customisation more generally) is of little use without an extremely reliable way of associating individuals with the correct data. Credit scoring in the USA, for instance, was transformed by the use, across organisations, of social security numbers (issued by the US government, but not initially for this purpose).[63] In smart city projects, facial recognition technologies (FRTs) have emerged as one possible equivalent. FRTs are thus part of many smart city projects, and indeed, of a number of the social credit pilots.[64] In Toronto, Sidewalk made a new and explicit commitment, in the later stages of discussion, *not* to use FRTs, addressing criticism from privacy advocates.[65] Moreover, the desire to deliver efficient and customised services is a key driver of research and development in FRTs, especially as they offer the prospect of delivering personalised services in public spaces, or without the more conventional registration or authentication functions that are suitable in certain areas of service delivery (e.g. library borrowing, managing one's tax or property affairs) but less so in others. But as these technologies reach the stage of being more widely deployed, especially for real time or 'live' use, it has become apparent that their use by public or private sector bodies is provoking controversy – ranging from the concerns over surveillance that have also been aired in relation to CCTV, number-plate recognition, and the like, to criticism of the accuracy of FRTs (including the differential performance of systems in terms of gender and race).[66]

This has now become one of the higher profile debates regarding law and technology, both in terms of broad (and sometimes normative) proposals but also the specific application of existing measures, especially in data protection law. The two are connected: see for instance the UK Information Commissioner's support for a statutory code of practice, echoing the creation of a Surveillance Cameras Commissioner and associated code under the Protection of Freedoms Act 2012.[67] This recommendation is made as part of the ICO's analysis of police use of FRTs, which goes beyond an initial assessment of the lawful basis required under data protection law for the use of FRT, and sets out a broader concern regarding whether the current combination of laws and codes provides a robust regulatory regime for these technologies.

Judicial and legislative attention is also apparent. In *R (Bridges) v Chief Constable of South Wales Police*[68] the Court of Appeal in England and Wales will consider the lawfulness of the use of FRTs by South Wales Police (the national 'lead' for FRT trials, which has been funded by central government to this end). At first instance, the High Court did not find that anything unlawful was taking place: common law police powers in particular were engaged, and Article 8 of the European Convention on Human Rights was not violated, though it was accepted – against the submissions of the police force – that various aspects of data protection and human rights legislation were engaged. A Private Members' Bill has been introduced by a member of the House of Lords,[69] and a general debate on the subject took place in the House of Commons in January 2020.[70] A number of US cities (including the northern Californian cities of San Francisco and Oakland) have already adopted various prohibitions.

There has been an understandable focus, in media commentary, on what were said to be proposals, from the European Commission, to place a moratorium on the use of FRTs in certain locations. The final version of the Commission's paper (on artificial intelligence more generally, published February 2020) noted the need for a specific and proportionate legal basis under data protection law, and, 'in order to address possible societal concerns relating to the use of AI for [FRT] purposes in public places', called for a 'broad European debate on the specific circumstances, if any, which might justify such use, and on common safeguards'.[71] If a moratorium of some sort becomes law, it is quite possible that there will be some exclusions (i.e. situations where the tightly regulated use of FRTs is lawful), but will this include the delivery of personalised services, or will the emphasis be on security e.g. counterterrorism? If so, which other means of working with individuals on a customised basis will be technologically and commercially feasible?

As other contributors to this volume have commented, there are close links between personalisation and the detection of identity.[72] In relation to personalised services, then, the resolution of current debates on FRTs is important. One immediate issue will be the scope of any restriction. For instance, the US city of Portland is currently considering whether to focus on police and public authority activity or seek to constrain private sector use of FRTs. More broadly, the use (or disavowal of using) FRTs may be a factor in public reactions to smart city projects, as has already emerged in Toronto.

12.5 CONCLUSION

The argument that a smart city is a 'more efficient and greener place to live and do business' is echoed across the projects discussed in this chapter – though with the efficiency and environmental rationales being emphasised to different degrees throughout. Despite the different contexts of each, they all challenge – through the adoption and deployment of various technologies or approaches to data – a twentieth-century understanding of the role of public authorities. Many obviously municipal services have been delivered in an undifferentiated way, subject in some cases to democratic oversight, and indeed still pursuing environmental and efficiency goals. What we see in this century, though, is a more personalised or customised relationship between states and individuals, driven in some cases by persistent connections and the continuous analysis and combination of data, and often mediated by the relevant technology companies. This amended relationship, then, becomes part of the promise that the green, efficient city is one that knows its people and deals with them, whether directly or through hypernudges and other means, as individuals.

As such, facial recognition technologies, sensors embedded in flagstones and flagposts, and the traces of scooters and drones flying in three dimensions around a crowded city, all contribute to the reliability of these inchoate personalised interactions. FRTs allow the individual to be recognised – and so to be denied access. Sensors replace inefficient monitoring (or worse, sampling) – but bring the best and worst of the internet environment into the neighbourhood, street, and even apartment. Mobility data allows cities to do air traffic control on the ground and deliver the best possible advice – if it can be gathered in a way that works across public/private boundaries and with respect for individuals. A city interested in any of these three, or (as is increasingly the case) some combination thereof, must understand how existing laws delimit what is possible, and engage in reasoned debate on new governance arrangements.

Even so, objections to, for instance, FRTs are not just about an analysis of the specific affordances and use cases of how an image is captured and processed. There is a clear sense of a certain level of unease with the balance of power, with mission creep, and with the ways in which change comes about. The travails of Sidewalk Toronto, for one, serve as an illustration of the centrality of vision and mandate, but also the proper role for public authorities and private companies. And even the best-intentioned debates may result in temporary bans or self-denying ordinances, focused on specific iterations rather than the whole. If we debate FRTs or reputational scores as inherently good or bad, without attending to the contexts in which they are used (such as personalised services), we run the risk of avoiding more challenging questions about the shape of the future city.

In this chapter, I have sought to show how success in the smart city depends not just on the development of new technologies, but the careful identification of relevant goals (e.g., sustainable forms of mobility), the trade-offs that might be necessitated, and the governance mechanisms that must be put in place (whether the project is delivered by a public body or otherwise). Compliance with data protection or privacy law is part of that route to success, but compliance alone does not bring public confidence – let alone provide the conditions for a genuine debate on how technology, and the collection of personal and non-personal data, can be used to improve quality of life.[73] Predictions about the future are notoriously unreliable – especially in relation to urban living – but expectations and objectives can engage residents in a debate about how personal they want their interactions with public authorities to be, and how data can be properly managed. Such debates can and should encompass technologies not currently on the mass market (e.g. autonomous vehicles) and systems that are at an advanced stage of development in different political contexts (e.g. the Chinese social credit systems). At a time when a healthy scepticism regarding the turn-of-the-century apparent consensus on the liberating power of technology and the Internet has come to prominence, a return to urbanist utopian thinking of earlier decades, regarding the shape of the city rather than the technology, with municipalities and their understanding of the public good as a key voice, might allow personalised services to emerge and command trust and legitimacy, unlocking the efficient and sustainable city of the future.

NOTES

1 *Minority Report* (dir. Stephen Spielberg) (20th Century Fox, 2002); for the original story, see Philip K Dick, 'The minority report' (1956).
2 'Nosedive' (S3E1).
3 Robert Kunzig, 'Rethinking cities' (2019) 235(4) *National Geographic* 70.
4 Scottish Government, 'Digital strategy evidence discussion paper' (2017) 11 www.gov.scot/publications/scotlands-digital-strategy-evidence-discussion-paper/.
5 Terry Kirby, 'City design: transforming tomorrow' *The Guardian* (London, 8 September 2010).
6 Aamer Baig and others, 'The COVID-19 recovery will be digital' (*McKinsey*, 14 May 2020) www.mckinsey.com/business-functions/mckinsey-digital/our-insights/the-covid-19-recovery-will-be-digital-a-plan-for-the-first-90-days.
7 Jennifer Cobbe and John Morison, 'Understanding the Smart City: framing the challenges for law and good governance' in Jean Bernard Auby, Émilie Chevalier and Emmanuel Slautsky (eds.), *Le futur du droit administratif / The Future of Administrative Law* (LexisNexis 2019).

8 Daithí MacSíthigh, 'Virtual walls? The law of pseudo-public spaces' (2012) 8 *International Journal of Law in Context* 394.

9 See, for example, Hilton's argument, after Carlo Ratti, that the availability of ubiquitous computing influences the design of physical spaces: Steve Hilton, *More Human: Designing a World Where People Come First* (Ebury 2015) 269. For a more fundamental argument (on spatial approaches to software), see Rob Kitchin and Martin Dodge, *Code/space: Software and Everyday Life* (MIT Press 2011); for an application of the code/space theory in a smart city context, see, for example, Rob Kitchin, 'From a single line of code to an entire city: reframing the conceptual terrain of code/space' in Rob Kitchin and Sung-Yueh Perng (eds.), *Code and the City* (Routledge 2016).

10 Lilian Edwards, 'Privacy, security and data protection in Smart Cities: A critical EU law Perspective' (2016) 2 *European Data Protection Law Review* 28.

11 Ben Green, *The Smart Enough City: Putting Technology in Its Place to Reclaim Our Urban Future* (MIT Press 2019) 99.

12 Robert Brauneis and Ellen Goodman, 'Algorithmic Transparency for the Smart City'(2018) 20 *Yale Journal of Law and Technology* 103.

13 Vasilios Mavroudis and Michael Veale, 'Eavesdropping whilst you're shopping: balancing personalisation and privacy in connected retail spaces' Living in the Internet of Things: Cybersecurity of the IoT https://ieeexplore.ieee.org/document/8379705.

14 See further Sofia Ranchordás and Abram Klop, 'Data-driven regulation and governance in Smart Cities' in Vanessa Mak, Eric Tjong Tjin Tai and Anna Berlee (eds.), *Research Handbook in Data Science and Law* (Edward Elgar2018).

15 Karen Yeung, '"Hypernudge": Big Data as a mode of regulation by design' (2016) 20 *Information, Communication & Society* 118.

16 Richard Thaler and Cass Sunstein, *Nudge: Improving Decisions about Health, Wealth, and Happiness* (Yale University Press 2008); Muireann Quigley, 'Nudging for health: on Public Policy and Designing Choice Architecture'(2013) 21 *Medical Law Review* 588; Christopher McCrudden and Jeff King, 'The dark side of nudging: the ethics, political economy, and law of libertarian paternalism' in Alexandra Kemmerer and others (eds.), *Choice Architecture in Democracies, Exploring the Legitimacy of Nudging* (Hart 2016).

17 Yeung (n 15) 122.

18 Tuck Siong Chung, Michel Wedel and Roland Rust, 'Adaptive personalization using social networks'(2015) 44 *Journal of the Academy of Marketing Science* 66.

19 Ashesh Mukherjee, *The Internet Trap: Five Costs of Living Online* (University of Toronto Press 2018)51; for the original, see Masahiro Mori, Karl MacDorman and Norri Kageki, 'The uncanny valley' (2012) 19 IEEE Robotics & Automation 98; for recent applications in legal and policy contexts, see, for example, Jeannie Suk Gersen, 'Sex lex machina' (2019) 119 *Columbia Law Review* 1793; Sulaf Al-Saif, 'Animal healthcare robots: the case for privacy regulation' (2019) 14 *Washington Journal of Law, Technology & Arts* 77; EricGerson, 'More gore – video game violence and the technology of the future note' (2010) 76 *Brooklyn Law Review* 1121.

20 Marie Veltz, Jonathan Rutherford and Antoine Picon, 'Smart urbanism and the visibility and reconfiguration of infrastructure and public action in the French cities of Issy-les-Moulineaux and Nice' in Andrew Karvonen, Federico Cugurullo and Federico Caprotti (eds.), *Inside Smart Cities: Place, Politics and Urban Innovation* (Routledge 2019) 141.

21 Richard Seyler Ling, *Taken for Grantedness: The Embedding of Mobile Communication into Society* (MIT Press 2012).

22 James Bridle, *New Dark Age: Technology and the End of the Future* (Verso 2018) 3–4.

23 Evgeny Morozov, *To Save Everything, Click Here* (Penguin 2013) ch 1.

24 Rob Kitchin, 'Data-driven urbanism' in Rob Kitchin, Tracey Lauriault and Gavin McArdle (eds.), *Data and the City* (Routledge 2018) 51.

25 Josh O'Kane, 'Sensor city: Google project triggers debate over data' *The Globe and Mail* (Toronto, 24 February 2018) B1.

26 This is well documented in a number of recent publications, including Ellen Goodman and Julia Powles, 'Urbanism under Google: lessons from Sidewalk Toronto' (2019) 88 *Fordham Law Review* 457; Sofia Ranchordás and Catalina Goanta, 'The New City Regulators: Platform and Public Values in Smart and Sharing Cities' (2019) 20 *Computer Law & Security Review*; Green (n 10) ch 7.

27 In multiple volumes; for the overview, see https://storage.googleapis.com/sidewalk-toronto-ca/wp-content/uploads/2019/06/23135500/MIDP_Volume0.pdf.

28 For the 2019 preliminary report, see https://waterfrontoronto.ca/nbe/wcm/connect/water front/30c682ff-8172-49dc-bf63-09b2a2f1845a/DSAP+Preliminary+Commentary+-+September+10%2C+2019.pdf; see also the supplementary report at https://waterfrontoronto.ca/nbe/wcm/connect/waterfront/521b1d08-3499-4a49-9d2c-b5fc34990ce5/DSAP+Report+%2B+Appendices.pdf.

29 https://storage.googleapis.com/sidewalk-toronto-ca/wp-content/uploads/2019/11/15093613/Sidewalk-Labs-Digital-Innovation-Appendix.pdf.

30 Tom Knowles, 'Google sets sights on Toronto as its city of the future' *The Times* (London, 27 November 2018).

31 Robert Hollands, 'Critical interventions into the corporate Smart City'(2015) 8 *Cambridge Journal of Regions, Economy and Society* 61.

32 *MIT Technology Review* (January/February 2018).

33 John Sutton, *Gridlock: Congested Cities, Contested Policies, Unsustainable Mobility* (Taylor & Francis 2015) 137ff (concept); Basilio Tobias, 'Urban Projects and Megastructures: Modernist Campuses' in Carmen Díez Medina and Javier Monclús (eds.), *Urban Visions: From Planning Culture to Landscape Urbanism* (Springer 2018) (campus design); Peter Dormer and Stefan Muthesius, *Concrete and Open Skies* (Unicorn 2001) 74 (East Anglia); *The Experimental City* (dir. Chad Freidrichs) (Unicorn Stencil, 2017) (Minnesota).

34 Lawrence Lessig, *Code v 2.0* (Basic Books 2006) ch 4.

35 Laura Bliss, 'How smart should a city be? Toronto is finding out' (*CityLab*, 7 September 2018) www.bloomberg.com/news/articles/2018-09-07/what-s-behind-the-backlash-over-side walk-labs-smart-city.

36 Ibid.

37 Moira Warburton, 'Sidewalk Labs' Toronto smart city to feature self-driving garbage cans, apartment noise monitors' *National Post* (Toronto, 16 November 2019); Digital Innovation Appendix (n 2).

38 Matthew Braga, 'Welcome to the neighbourhood. Have you read the terms of service?' (*CBC News*, 16 January 2018) www.cbc.ca/news/technology/smart-cities-privacy-data-per sonal-information-sidewalk-1.4488145.

39 Goodman and Powles (n 26) 487.
40 Waterfront Toronto, 'Realising the waterfront's potential' (December 2018) https://quaysideto.ca/wp-content/uploads/2019/04/Evaluation-and-Objectives_Draft_Dec82018.pdf.
41 MIDP (n 27) 162ff.
42 Digital Strategy Advisory Panel, preliminary commentary (n 28); cf Amy Fleming, 'The case for ... making low-tech 'dumb' cities instead of 'smart' ones' *The Guardian* (15 January 2020) www.theguardian.com/cities/2020/jan/15/the-case-for-making-low-tech-dumb-cities-instead-of-smart-ones.
43 Cobbe and Morison (n 7).
44 Goodman and Powles (n 26) pt IIB.
45 See for instance Sutton (n 33); though as Bertaud notes, there was no golden age, and Roman authors bemoaned recognisable challenges in the ancient city: Alain Bertaud, *Order without design: how markets shape cities* (MIT Press 2018) 158.
46 Daniel Wilson, *Where's My Jetpack? A Guide to the Amazing Science Future that Never Arrived* (Bloomsbury 2007).
47 *Back to the Future: Part II* (dir. Robert Zemeckis) (Universal Pictures, 1989); see also Jonah Engel Bromwich and Daniel Victor, 'Why a "Back to the Future" hoverboard never took off', *New York Times* (New York, 21 October 2015) www.nytimes.com/2015/10/22/business/why-a-back-to-the-future-hoverboard-never-took-off.html.
48 Iain Docherty, Greg Marsden and Jillian Anable, 'The Governance of Smart Mobility' (2018) 115 *Transportation Research Part A: Policy and Practice* 114.
49 Ashley Hand, 'Urban mobility in a digital age: a transportation technology strategy for Los Angeles' (2016) https://static1.squarespace.com/static/57c864609f74567457be9b71/t/57c9059b9de4bb1598eeee49/1472793280502/Transportation+Technology+Strategy_2016.pdf; for the specification itself, see https://github.com/CityOfLosAngeles/mobility-data-specification/wiki; for the new governance model adopted in 2019, see https://www.openmobilityfoundation.org.
50 Center for Democracy & Technology, 'Comments to LADOT on privacy & security concerns for data sharing for dockless mobility' (29 November 2018) https://cdt.org/insight/comments-to-ladot-on-privacy-security-concerns-for-data-sharing-for-dockless-mobility/; Aarian Marshall, 'Why Uber is fighting cities over data about scooter trips' (*Wired*, 13 May 2019) www.wired.com/story/why-uber-fighting-cities-data-about-scooters/; Alfred Ng, 'Uber in talks with Los Angeles as scooter location data lawsuit looms' (*CNET*, 30 October 2019) www.cnet.com/news/uber-in-talks-with-los-angeles-as-scooter-location-data-lawsuit-looms/.
51 For instance, the National Association for City Transportation Officials (NACTO, a North American organisation) principles on 'managing mobility data', identifying core principles (data as a public good, data protection, purposeful collection, and portability), and advising cities to reserve the right to 'share data with third-party researchers/organisations to fulfill planning, research, regulatory, or compliance needs', but also emphasising the importance of treating geospatial trip data as personally identifiable information with appropriate safeguards: NACTO, 'Managing mobility data' (2019) https://nacto.org/wp-content/uploads/2019/05/NACTO_IMLA_Managing-Mobility-Data.pdf; NACTO, 'Guidelines for regulating shared micromobility' (2019) 31 https://nacto.org/wp-content/uploads/2019/09/NACTO_Shared_Micromobility_Guidelines_Web.pdf.

52 Joe Fitzgerald Rodriguez, 'State bill taking aim at city bikeshare, scooter regulations stalls in Senate' *San Francisco Examiner* (San Francisco, 3 July 2019) www.sfexaminer.com/the-city/state-bill-taking-aim-at-city-bikeshare-scooter-regulations-stalls-in-senate/.

53 Department for Transport, *Future of Mobility: Urban Strategy* (2019); House of Commons Transport Committee, *Mobility as a Service* (HC 590, 2017–19).

54 See further Teresa Scassa, 'Navigating legal rights in spatial media' in Rob Kitchin, Tracey Lauriault and Matthew Wilson (eds.), *Understanding Spatial Media* (Sage 2017).

55 I draw here upon my own earlier work (with Mathias Siems), in which we explore the SCS, and rating and reputational systems in more detail: Daithí Mac Síthigh and Mathias Siems, 'The Chinese social credit system: a model for other countries?' (2019) 82 *The Modern Law Review* 1034; on China, see also Kai Strittmatter, *We Have Been Harmonised: Life in China's Surveillance State* (Ruth Martin tr, Old Street 2019) ch 9; Rogier Creemers, 'China's social credit system: an evolving practice of control' (2018) https://dx.doi.org/10.2139/ssrn.3175792; Fan Liang and others, 'Constructing a data-driven society: China's social credit system as a state surveillance infrastructure' (2018) 10 *Policy & Internet* 415.

56 See Josh Lauer, *Creditworthy: A History of Consumer Surveillance and Financial Identity in America* (Columbia University Press 2017) (19th and 20th century consumer credit scoring and rating); Rachel Botsman and Roo Rogers, *What's Mine is Yours: How Collaborative Consumption is Changing the Way We Live* (Collins 2011), Michael Fertik, *The Reputation Economy: How to Optimise Your Digital Footprint in a World Where Your Reputation Is Your Most Valuable Asset* (Little, Brown 2015) (both regarding consumer markets); Arun Sundararajan, *The Sharing Economy: The End of Employment and the Rise of Crowd-Based Capitalism* (MIT Press 2016) (Uber, Airbnb, etc.); Jessica Silver-Greenberg, 'Perfect 10? Never mind that. Ask her for her credit score' *New York Times* (New York, 26 December 2012) A1 (dating). For detailed analysis of new developments in credit markets, and the intersection with anti-discrimination law, see Noelia Collado-Rogriguez and Uta Kohl, '"All data is credit data": Personalised Consumer Credit Score and Anti-Discrimination Law', this volume [[page number]].

57 Donncha Marron, *Consumer Credit in the United States: A Sociological Perspective from the Nineteenth Century to the Present* (Palgrave Macmillan 2009) 133, 157; Mac Síthigh and Siems (n 55) 1061–4.

58 Kevin Werbach, 'Panopticon reborn: social credit as regulation for the age of AI' (2020) http://dx.doi.org/10.2139/ssrn.3589804; Mac Síthigh and Siems (n 55) 1048ff.

59 Jerry Muller, *The Tyranny of Metrics* (Princeton University Press 2018); Geoffrey C Bowker and Susan Leigh Star, *Sorting Things Out: Classification and Its Consequences* (MIT Press 1999) 324ff; Wendy Nelson Espeland and Michael Sauder, 'Rankings and reactivity: how public measures recreate social worlds' (2007) 113 *American Journal of Sociology* 1.

60 Lauer (n 56) 26.

61 Ibid., 172, 183.

62 Mac Síthigh and Siems (n 55) 1053.

63 Lauer (n 56) 198–9.

64 Mac Síthigh and Siems (n 55) 1050.

65 Moira Warburton, 'Sidewalk Labs' still facing questions over data use in Toronto smart city project proposal' *National Post* (Toronto, 28 February 2020). For evidence of Sidewalk's earlier interest in FRTs, see, e.g., Goodman and Powles (n 26) 491.

66 E.g,. Kashmir Hill, 'Face scan app inches toward end of privacy' *New York Times* (New York, 19 January 2020) A1; Steve Lohr, 'Facial recognition is Accurate, if you're a white guy' *New York Times* (New York, 9 February 2018); Madhumita Murgia, 'The face race' *Financial Times* (London, 20 April 2019) Magazine 26; Robert Draper, 'They are watching you' (2018) 232(2) National Geographic 30; Woodrow Hartzog, *Privacy's Blueprint: The Battle to Control the Design of New Technologies* (Harvard University Press 2018) ch 7.

67 Opinion 2019/01, 'The use of live facial recognition technology by law enforcement in public places' https://ico.org.uk/media/about-the-ico/documents/2616184/live-frt-law-enfo rcement-opinion-20191031.pdf.

68 *R (Bridges) v Chief Constable of South Wales Police* [2019] EWHC 2341 (Admin).

69 Automated Facial Recognition Technology (Moratorium and Review) Bill [HL] 2019–20.

70 Hansard HC (6th series) vol 670 cols 647-556 (27 January 2020).

71 COM (2020) 65.

72 See Marc Welsh, 'Personalisation, power and the datafied subject', this volume [[page number]]; see also Shoshana Zuboff, *The Age of Surveillance Capitalism: The Fight for a Human Future at the New Frontier of Power* (Profile 2019) 251–3.

73 In this regard, I share the reservations as to the ability of legal measures protecting privacy to do the task of regulating markets, set out this volume: TT Arvind, 'Personalisation, markets, and contract: The limits of legal incrementalism', this volume, part III.

13

Micro-targeting in Political Campaigns: Political Promise and Democratic Risk

Normann Witzleb and Moira Paterson

13.1 INTRODUCTION

Political parties, movements and candidates increasingly rely on personalised communication informed by sophisticated profiling techniques to target potential voters. Social media platforms are central to such data-driven campaigning because they are the medium for such communications as well as the custodians of the data that enables profiling. Profile-based communication with voters exploits vast troves of personal data held by social media platforms to infer individuals' political views and craft messages to which targeted persons are expected to be particularly receptive. The Facebook/Cambridge Analytica scandal has revealed some of the darker practices of political micro-targeting and its actual and potential effects on democratic processes. The (now defunct) political consulting firm, Cambridge Analytica, had used a Facebook app to harvest the personal data of up to 87 million Facebook users without their consent,[1] and claimed to have developed models for sophisticated 'psychographic' profiling that allowed political parties to target potential voters with specifically tailored advertisements.[2] These revelations dramatically increased the concerns that had first arisen in relation to the role of data analytics in the Trump election and Brexit referendum results.[3]

The Cambridge Analytica scandal, as well as related concerns about the rise of 'fake news' in social networks,[4] had a substantial legal and political fallout. In many countries, regulatory investigations and parliamentary enquiries sought to assess the scale of problematic practices in political campaigning and to strengthen the regulatory regimes of the digital influence industry. The most detailed and significant enquiries at national level occurred in the United Kingdom, where the House of Commons Digital, Culture, Media and Sport (DCMS) Committee found that Facebook intentionally and knowingly violated data privacy and anti-competition laws.[5] The Committee recommended greater regulatory control of social media companies through a compulsory Code of Ethics to be enforced by an independent regulator, reforms to electoral communications laws and improved transparency. After a wide-ranging investigation into the use of social media platforms for micro-targeting by UK political parties and consultations into a draft framework code of practice, the UK Information Commissioner's Office (ICO) also published guidance for the transparent and lawful use of personal data in political campaigns.[6] Other reports, by the UK Electoral Commission, have looked into broader issues of digital campaigning and campaign financing.[7] At the European level, major online platforms including Facebook, Google, Microsoft and Twitter, as well as online advertising companies, adopted a self-regulatory Code of Practice on Disinformation, as part of a strategy developed in an EU Commission action plan.[8]

The Cambridge Analytica scandal revealed significant gaps in the scope and enforcement of data protection laws.[9] However, even in the absence of unsavoury or illegal practices, micro-targeting in political campaigns raises thorny issues that go to the heart of the democratic process. The personalisation of political communication is its core virtue but also its vice: political micro-targeting has the potential to awaken and strengthen the political engagement of voters who are otherwise hard to reach. These messages appear on voters' preferred media channels and are crafted to appeal to their individual interests, leanings and preferences. But these personalised interactions also carry the risk of fragmenting political debates and open the door to voter manipulation. Rather than seeking exchange with, and convergence in, the narratives of the 'opposing' sides, these interactions have the potential to polarise political communications and to reinforce personal bias in filter bubbles and echo chambers.[10]

This simultaneity of the beneficial and the harmful in micro-targeting typifies the 'personalisation' trend that is becoming so prevalent in various social domains. Yet, its application in the political context has particular significance, in so far as it infects the very processes designed to control political and economic power. Furthermore, micro-targeting also epitomises the problematic link of private and public power in harvesting and analysing personal data. The same personal data gathered by online platforms is as valuable to platforms and other businesses seeking to sell goods and services, as it is for political parties and political interest groups seeking to 'sell' their programs, ideas and ideologies. In both contexts, personalisation amplifies the power asymmetry between the information intermediaries and the providers of the personalised product, on the one hand, and private citizens, who are both data subjects and consumers of the personalised services, on the other hand.

Against this background, the chapter explores whether data protection law may be strengthened to moderate (in both senses of the word) micro-targeting towards stronger democratic accountability. Yet, this discussion needs to be mindful of the inherent limitations of data protection law given its prime focus is on the 'input side' of personal information processing. By regulating the collection, use and storage of personal data for profiling and targeting specific voters, it is insensitive to the 'output side', that is, the content of political communication. Other measures, such as campaign financing regulation or rules mandating accuracy in political advertising, may be required to address unfair advantages in political communication or inappropriate voter manipulation. Nevertheless, as personalised political communication is dependent on profiling, data protection is the logical starting point for its regulation. Profiling and targeting utilises personal information collected not just from individuals who deliberately provide their information to receive targeted communications (e.g. by signing up to a party or candidate newsletter). It also utilises information that is extracted from many other contexts in far less consensual (new) ways and then repurposed for unanticipated objectives. That 'repurposing' of personal information, which may occur in the absence of consent or by stretching existing consent, is a privacy harm that data protection law can and should effectively redress.

A second limitation of data protection law (and information privacy more generally) lies in its focus on the individual that generates a blind spot with regards to the collective interests engaged in politics and strongly affected by micro-targeting.[11] Big data analytics relies on a strong nexus between group and individual profiling, with each reflexively informing the other. Yet, data protection law, with its rationale grounded in the values of human dignity and personal autonomy, has traditionally focused on the individual rather than on group interests. Personal autonomy, in turn, is deeply challenged in an environment in which information about the individual is extracted in the form of micro data that is by itself fairly meaningless, but can be used to construct highly insightful individual and group profiles. This intelligent transformation occurs through big data analytics, which looks for correlations between data points in large data sets consisting of huge amounts of micro data. The treacherous distance between individual consent to the collection of *insignificant* data, often provided in wholly unrelated contexts, and its *profound* power in 'understanding' or 'knowing' individuals and groups is a concern not limited to the political context, but yet again amplified in it.

Drawing on some of the themes above, the chapter explores how micro-targeting of campaign communications is simultaneously a virtue and a vice of contemporary politics, and explores how data protection currently negotiates this tension and could be reformed to do so better. In law, the tension to which micro-targeting gives rise is expressed through the complementary and competing rights of freedom of (political) expression, both in terms of the right to communicate and the right to receive information, on the one hand, and of information privacy, on the other hand.

13.2 THE VICES AND VIRTUES OF MICRO-TARGETING

In John Dunn's words, 'the power and appeal of democracy comes from the idea of autonomy – of choosing freely for oneself'.[12] Free elections enable democratic self-governance, as citizens express their interests and preferences through voting

(typically through selecting representatives but occasionally through direct refer-
enda). Both privacy and freedom of political communications are essential to free
and legitimate elections. Traditionally, the imperative of autonomous decision-
making has translated into privacy protections at the point of voting, in particular
the secrecy of ballots, designed to facilitate free political choices.[13] Privacy has also
acted in support of political communications, for example, through the (contested)
possibility of making anonymous campaign donations or allowing anonymous
pamphlets.[14] So privacy *and* free communication between candidates and the
electorate have traditionally been seen as complementary in support of political
participation, and only occasionally as competing. Prior to big data analytics,
contemporary liberal democracies had established regimes that accommodated both
privacy and freedom of political communications,[15] and settled points of conflict
generally by protecting freedom of political communication over personal privacy,
as demonstrated, for example, by the disclosure thresholds for campaign contributions. Equally, in the political arena, data protection law has often been taken out of
the equation by releasing political parties and actors from the general data protection obligations, as further discussed below. In a number of jurisdictions, political
parties – as not-for-profit bodies – are allowed to collect and use data about their
members and other regular contacts[16] without the typical level of regard for privacy
required of other entities.

The rise of big data analytics and the possibility of data-driven political micro-
targeting has altered the existing dynamics. Because the ability to harvest and deploy
data by political entities is now closely aligned with the goal-directed profiling
effected by private entities, the less demanding data protection standards for parties
are arguably no longer suitable.

13.2.1 *Vices of Political Micro-targeting*

Micro-targeted political communications are significantly different from those that
existed prior to the big data analytics revolution. In contrast to conventional political
broadcasts in mass media, campaign speeches and strategic door-knocking, modern
political communication is 'much more precise, and "knowing"'[17] about its recipients. Harnessing the power of artificial intelligence, they can be designed, based on
the profiling of individual traits, to maximise the emotional and psychological
impact on their recipients. Significantly, those individual traits are not necessarily
concerned with political leanings per se, but might include anxieties, concerns or
vulnerabilities into which a particular political message can tap. As discussed in
Chapter 5 of this volume, big data analytics allows such vulnerabilities to be
deduced from otherwise mundane, non-sensitive personal data. Official inquiries
in the aftermath of the Cambridge Analytica scandal[18] have highlighted the wide-
scale manipulation and deception of voters by domestic and foreign actors, consisting of 'intentionally and covertly influencing [voters'] decision-making, by targeting

and exploiting their decision-making vulnerabilities'.[19] This type of political messaging is a far cry from the liberal assumption underlying democratic processes that has a rational and well-informed citizenry freely deliberate on past governing records and alternative political manifestos.[20] Whilst the exploitation of prejudice, bias and anxieties in political campaigning is not a novel phenomenon (consider, for example, the long-standing use of xenophobia to exploit material insecurities), the ability to fine-tune communications to the individual level *is* novel. Such subtle personalised communications also make it infinitely harder to identify the manipulation and guard against it.

Along the same lines, political campaigning based on access to a wide range of personal data of prospective voters also makes it easier to mislead them. For example, a party may represent to each audience that it stands only for one or more specific issues that are of concern to them.[21] Taking it a step further, political micro-targeting provides a perfect vector for the dissemination of 'fake news', that is the deliberate spreading of distorted or false versions of events, and other 'computational propaganda'.[22] Confirmation bias means that we tend to be drawn to messages that confirm our existing beliefs.[23] This is particularly problematic in light of studies into indirect news consumption on social media such as Twitter which found that false news diffuses faster and broader than true news.[24] Disinformation does not just diminish trust in the integrity of political processes or actors, but also affects personal autonomy per se. The three pillars upon which liberal democracies are built are – the '*self*' or autonomous individual whose 'free will' leads her to choose to participate as a member of a *civil society or body politic* in which she and others in that civil society have the *ability to influence political actors and actions* in ways that are consistent with their preferences.[25]

Disinformation in its various forms is harmful because it has the potential to disrupt our individual capacity for self-authorship and, as a consequence, our communal capacity for self-government.

Although neither manipulative nor misleading political campaigning is new, micro-targeting *is* an unprecedented tool in political campaigning because it removes the common platform upon which disagreement can and should take place: '[it] makes it increasingly difficult to have a public argument when there is no "basis for a common conversation about … political decision[s]"'.[26] Yet, shared public discourse about what each party and candidate stands for is fundamental to processes of reasoned decision-making and accountability in liberal democracies.[27] The dwindling of a shared political arena goes hand in hand with the creation of filter bubbles or echo chambers, and these in turn are linked to the polarisation of the political spectrum:

> '[I]n the end, all you might get is your own opinions reflected back at you. This causes social polarization, resulting in the formation of separate groups that no longer understand each other and find themselves increasingly at conflict with one another.'[28]

Andrejevic and Volcic have argued that, in the mass customised media environment, the real challenge to democratic deliberation is 'not the narrowing of content and perspectives available on social media platforms, but the combination of their indefinite proliferation with the erosion of the social preconditions for adjudicating between them'.[29] The multiplication of echo chambers with increasingly sound-proof walls poses a political dilemma, but is not easily redressed by legal interventions, primarily because these echo chambers are, at least partially, the result of autonomous decision-making by the individual voter. Filter bubbles are comfortable. In this respect, political micro-targeting highlights one of the key conundrums of data-driven personalisation: the personalised message is not simply imposed on individuals against their will by corporate or political actors but may well be accepted and welcomed by individuals. This means that if political micro-targeting was on balance considered harmful and therefore subject to legal intervention, the device of consent is unlikely to prove an effective moderator.

While consumers increasingly rely on algorithmic personalisation to provide them with news content that aligns with their preferences, the effect that recommender systems have on news diversity and quality is difficult to measure.[30] Similarly, there is as yet insufficient evidence that online audiences are indeed more fragmented than offline audiences.[31] Meta studies suggest, however, that digital platforms have assumed an important role in filtering and curating the increasing quantity of news and that, depending on their design, algorithms can both increase or narrow the range of views available to consumers.[32] The fact that social media companies and news aggregators wield increasing influence over both news production and news consumption has led to calls for greater transparency and accountability of digital intermediaries to protect consumer autonomy and choice,[33] as will be further discussed below.

Finally, the phenomenon of micro-targeting in political campaigns with its inherent capacity for manipulation, deception and filter bubbles must also be understood against recent profound structural changes in the political landscape that have reduced the influence and coordinating roles played by political parties, parliament and elections.[34] Digital platforms have become a primary outlet for civic engagement and decision-making. Margetts demonstrates how digital activism through 'tiny acts of political participation',[35] such as liking, following or tweeting about a political event or movement, gives ordinary citizens arguably more direct political influence than in the pre-social media era. The potential of direct political activism to reduce the role of political parties and elections suggests a shift from representative to deliberative democracy, which in itself is hardly undesirable. However, the rise of online campaigning has the further consequence that political actors are becoming increasingly dependent on digital intermediaries. The corporate actors operating in this domain are reluctant to disclose the methods and technologies they use for data-driven personalisation.[36] Even more disconcertingly, it has been shown that technology companies have lent their superior expertise to political parties and interest groups in the expectation of promoting their own political or commercial objectives.[37]

13.2.2 *Virtues of Political Micro-targeting*

Although the above suggests an overwhelmingly negative impact of using micro-targeting in political communications, the overall picture is more mixed. Political scientists have for some time identified downward trends for four key indicators used to measure the health and well-being of representative democracies: voter turnout, party membership, trust in politicians and interest in politics.[38] In essence, these indicators all relate to different aspects of voter engagement, which representative democracies depend upon for their functioning and legitimacy. Increased personalisation of political messaging has the potential to positively or negatively affect all four of these measures.

Problematically, the effect of political micro-targeting on voter engagement is by no means easy to predict or measure. However, it may fairly be assumed that its efficacy depends on the characteristics of the political system in question, the forms, content and methods of personal political messaging employed, as well as the attributes and receptiveness of various voter cohorts. Recent research suggests that personalised messaging tends to have more effect on mobilising existing voters than on shaping political viewpoints.[39] Other studies also suggest that the segregating effect of online news consumption is likely to be relatively modest.[40] Although consumers prefer news media that coincide with their personal political preference, there are findings that the variety and accessibility of online media may also serve to expand the ideological spectrum of news that they encounter.[41] Notwithstanding the fact that practitioners of personalised political communication and the popular press may be prone to exaggerating its potential,[42] it remains true that the availability of modern personalisation tools has fundamentally changed political campaign strategies.[43] Even though proof of its utility remains scant and inconclusive, digital advertising is gaining an ever-increasing share of political campaign budgets.[44]

Despite recent changes, parties continue to have an important role in representative democracies. Aldrich and Griffin argue that parties make democracies more effective by providing a mechanism to reliably convert electoral preferences into competitive elections, as required for effective democratic governance.[45] Norris highlights their role in strengthening voter turnout as well as their other functions in

> simplifying and structuring electoral choices; organizing and mobilizing campaigns; articulating and aggregating disparate interests; channelling communication, consultation, and debate; training, recruiting, and selecting candidates; structuring parliamentary divisions; acting as policy think tanks; and organizing government.[46]

Yet, one of the challenges faced by modern political parties is how to 'reach politically uninterested voters and mobilise them to participate in politics'.[47] Communication is integral to their success in gaining support from voters and understanding citizens' priorities. Political parties and candidates have used a variety of communication methods to engage with voters, and these have developed over time in line with advances in technology. Modern data-driven communications make targeted messaging a much more feasible option and should increase the efficiency of political advertising. Provided that social media engagement is equally accessible to all players and comes at lower overall cost than traditional mass media advertising, this type of campaigning can have the positive effect of 'lower[ing] the entry barriers to the political communication market for smaller parties and enable parties with limited resources or with a more specific messages to reach out to constituents'.[48] However, parties or candidates with large campaign budgets can benefit disproportionately from these new forms of voter engagement because they can utilise online platforms more intensively and across wider sections of the population. These concerns about a level playing field between political competitors of different financial capacity can to some extent be addressed by introducing or recalibrating the spending limits for digital campaigns.[49]

An optimistic assessment would suggest that, provided that the fairness of political competition can be sufficiently protected, political micro-targeting has the potential to create a more diverse political marketplace that is more responsive to emerging voter concerns, provides voters more readily with the information they are seeking, and therefore allows them to make better informed and more conscious choices. However, a pessimistic account would emphasise the dangers of political micro-targeting, in particular the spectre of a fragmented polity with little knowledge of, or control over, its information sources.

13.3 POLITICAL MICRO-TARGETING AND INFORMATION PRIVACY

As micro-targeted political messages have the potential both to strengthen and to undermine political processes in the lead up to elections and in public discourse more generally, there is no clear path to developing the necessary regulation. Most jurisdictions are yet to respond to these emerging concerns and rely, for the time being, on regulatory toolkits that were conceived when political campaigning was largely analogue and that, unsurprisingly, reflect the peculiar political, cultural and legal traditions of each country. The centrality of personal data in developing and employing data-driven communication tools makes data protection laws an obvious starting point to deciding on the relative freedom of (micro-targeted) political communications.[50]

One end of the spectrum is occupied by the USA with its robust and overarching commitment to free speech – political or otherwise – under the First Amendment, its relaxed campaign financing laws and an absence of general data protection laws. These characteristics result in a highly permissive regime on political micro-targeting that also appears firmly entrenched.[51] Yet, considering that most of the large platforms through which micro-targeted political communications occur have their home in the USA, this permissive regime becomes a quasi-default for political communications on these platforms, unless local regulators are sufficiently empowered and determined to enforce stricter domestic standards.

Although not so explicitly framed in terms of a principled supremacy of free speech, a similar position is – in effect – also in place in Canada, where political parties are caught neither by the public sector Privacy Act 1985[52] nor by the private sector Personal Information Protection and Electronic Documents Act 2000 (PIPEDA).[53] It has been suggested that, in Canada, political parties simply '"fell through the cracks" of a privacy regime that regulates either public bodies, or organisations involved in commercial activity'.[54] To close this lacuna, there is now widespread support for amending PIPEDA 'to subject political parties to it, taking into account their democratic outreach duties'.[55] In contrast, the broad exemptions for politicians and political activities[56] under the Australian Privacy Act 1988 (Cth) were not the result of a fragmented privacy regime, but explicitly enacted. These statutory exemptions were justified on the basis that they were required by the implied doctrine of freedom of political communication in the Australian Constitution,[57] particularly considering the vital role played by parties and candidates in the functioning of democratic systems of government.

In contrast, the EU's General Data Protection Regulation (GDPR) – as complemented by the ePrivacy Directive[58] – does not exempt political communications from its regime.[59] Indeed as part of the requirement for lawfully collecting and using data, it stipulates 'explicit consent' as a precondition for collecting and using any personal data that reveal a political opinion.[60] One question this raises is whether micro data points that are mundane and non-sensitive by themselves, but insightful about political leanings when set against big data sets, belong to that special category [see Chapter 10]. In the absence of explicit consent by the data subject, processing of sensitive data is permissible only to the extent that it can be justified on specific grounds,[61] which are narrower than in the case of non-sensitive data. In any event, the restrictions in the GDPR concerning sensitive data do not apply to communications by a political party with its members, or with others who have regular contact with it.[62] As a consequence, those activities are subject to the lesser restrictions applicable to personal data more generally.[63] These lesser restrictions permit processing on the basis of consent, *or* where processing is necessary for the performance of a task carried out in the public interest, *or* where it is necessary for the purposes of the 'legitimate interests' of the controller or a third party except where those interests are 'overridden by the interests or fundamental rights and freedoms of the data subject which require protection of personal data'.[64] This results in a complex regime in which the lawfulness of data processing generally, consent aside, requires a balancing of the competing rights and interests involved.

It is also important to note that the GDPR allows for some derogations by Member States, of which the UK has availed itself. The Data Protection Act 2018 (UK) gives politicians and political parties important additional leeway because it provides that data processing that is necessary for 'an activity that supports or promotes democratic engagement'[65] *is to be regarded as* processing of personal data 'that is necessary for the performance of a task carried out in the public interest'.[66]

Data processing for democratic engagement, which includes communicating with electors and interested parties, opinion gathering, campaigning activities, activities to increase voter turnout and fundraising,[67] *is thereby lawful under the GDPR, provided it is necessary*[68] *and the task is laid down in domestic law, such as in electoral laws.*[69] This has the effect that the processing does not have to be justified on alternative grounds with more stringent limitations, such as the 'legitimate interests' of the data processor or the consent of the data subject.[70] It can, of course, be questioned whether data processing for political micro-targeting is *necessary* for communications by parties or their candidates with the electorate, given the concerns identified above. In its guidance, the Information Commissioner's Office has pointed out that the processing must 'be a targeted and proportionate way of achieving' the specific purpose and that it will not be *necessary* if there are less privacy-intrusive means to achieve that purpose.[71] However, available research suggests widespread reliance on this justification by MPs in the UK as a basis for collecting and using personal data.[72]

The GDPR appears implicitly to recognise the structural weakness of consent as a legitimising device for data processing, by setting up an overarching framework of 'background' duties on data controllers which are independent of user consent. These include the principles of 'privacy by default' and 'privacy by design'.[73] They also include the obligation to carry out a data privacy impact assessment for highly invasive activities, measured either by the scale of processing activity of 'sensitive data' or their effect on individuals,[74] with the view to identifying and minimising risks. Whilst these duties apply to political parties that employ micro-targeting in their campaigns,[75] they neither hinder such messaging nor necessarily prevent its manipulative variations. However, they do impose a more rigorous process of establishing practices that pay sufficient regard to the fairness and transparency of the data processing and its anticipated purposes.

Because of their regulatory focus on privacy, data protection laws also do not appear to be well equipped to be dealing with the dilemma of echo chambers and filter bubbles. A traditional response to the dangers of polarised and polarising media have been 'public service' broadcasters, whose news reporting is subject to the legal requirements of 'accuracy, impartiality, and fairness'[76] and thereby under an obligation to present a diversity of political viewpoints. As discussed above, the rise of digital networked media has been accompanied by a reduced penetration of traditional media, in particular the public service broadcasters, and a general fragmentation of the media. Although this fragmentation allows individuals theoretically to receive news from a more diverse range of media, this increased choice is practically undermined by the emerging trend that access to news on social media is mediated by a handful of dominant platforms (e.g. Facebook). Furthermore, poorly managed (or perniciously exploited), algorithmic personalisation results in fragmented narratives for *everyone*, thus combining the worst of both worlds: a media landscape that jeopardises civic unity without actually increasing diversity of sources.

In light of growing segmentation and 'emotionalisation'[77] of news, public broadcasters therefore continue to have an important role by supporting public interest journalism that generates broad benefits to society[78] and provides a shared platform for political communications and debate that is fundamental to democratic discourse.

13.4 CONCLUSION

The explanation for the lack of consensus on how micro-targeted political campaigns should be treated within data protection law lies partly in varying legal and political traditions and the relative novelty of the phenomenon. The exceptions for political campaigns from general data protection frameworks rely on the argument that their vital role in our system of democratic governance would be affected adversely by any (or too stringent) restrictions on the processing of personal information by political campaigners.

This chapter has argued that the unprecedented use of micro-targeted messaging in political communications in their manifold variations – ranging from the clearly deceptive or manipulative message to the confirmatory or engaging – requires a re-evaluation of the role of information privacy in political campaigns. In the light of the emergence of data-driven personalisation as a central force in political communication and the ability of parties to leverage information about voters to advance their political agendas, we submit that the widespread concerns about personalised political communications need to be taken seriously. It can no longer be assumed that the imposition of any privacy-based restrictions would be inherently detrimental to democracy and incompatible with the freedom of political communication.

In our view, there is no longer a good case for the retention in data protection laws of political exemptions, or overly broad provisions permitting data processing in political contexts. The example of the GDPR suggests that subjecting political parties to the general requirements of fair, transparent and lawful processing would go some way towards 'moderating' political micro-targeting in terms of creating a more rigorous and transparent process with regulatory oversight. This would help rebalance the legitimate functions and interests of political actors and digital intermediaries against the interests and fundamental rights of voters, thereby engendering more trust in political communications. Ultimately such protection could increase the transparency of profiling and targeted messaging, and provide some regulatory oversight at the input and process side of these practices, but would not deal with message content, including concerns about manipulation and dissemination of fake news. Even the GDPR – as the most stringent data protection regime currently in force – envisages and facilitates the micro-targeting of voters, and thus provides no answer to the issue of filter bubbles that micro-targeting tends to create and political elites can tap into and use for their purposes.

Subjecting political campaigning to data handling requirements applicable to other organisations can provide only part of the required solution to the information-based threats to personal and group autonomy identified above. Data protection laws commonly have limitations that affect their scope and effectiveness. Most notably, as indicated, they are not concerned with the content of political communications messaging that is its potentially manipulative or deceptive output. A number of countries have chosen to regulate fake news via legal prohibition,[79] but this is controversial because of the prospect of political censorship, which would be antithetical to democracy and constitutional guarantees of free speech.[80] Softer forms of regulation, including the establishment of fact-checking mechanisms, are designed to assist individuals in assessing whether purported 'news items' are in fact true. A more promising possibility is to strengthen political advertising laws, so that they provide additional limitations and more transparency in relation to political messaging. Enhanced transparency requirements are less likely to be in conflict with constitutional/human rights protections of free speech than any restrictions on the content or form of communications. The increasing fragmentation of public discourse also reinforces the need for maintaining public broadcasters to provide a shared platform of accurate, fair and impartial news reporting and political debate.

Data-driven personalisation of political campaigning requires regulation because it affects the privacy rights of voters and can interfere with personal autonomy essential for democratic legitimacy. It is open to doubt that blanket exemptions for political actors or very wide exceptions from data protection laws are warranted on democratic grounds. Political micro-targeting has the potential to enhance political engagement and to make it easier and more effective for political parties and movements to communicate with potential voters. However, to the extent that it is misused to misinform or manipulate voters, it undermines democracy. An unfettered segmentation of political communications also has the potential to undercut the civic disposition and common ground between voters which are fundamental to democratic discourse.

Data protection laws have an important role to play in limiting the processing of personal data and requiring practices to be designed in a manner that balances the protection of privacy and competing rights. We therefore argue that removing special exemptions for political parties and political messaging would serve to enhance the privacy of voters without inappropriately undermining the important values inherent in the doctrine of freedom of political communication.

NOTES

1 C Kang and S Frenkel, 'Facebook Says Cambridge Analytica harvested data of up to 87 million users' *The New York Times* (New York, 4 April 2018) www.nytimes.com/2018/04/04/technology/mark-zuckerberg-testify-congress.html.
2 S Illing, 'Cambridge Analytica, the shady data firm that might be a key Trump–Russia link, explained' (*Vox*, 4 April 2018) www.vox.com/policy-and-politics/2017/10/16/15657512/cambridge-analytica-facebook-alexander-nix-christopher-wylie.

3 See, for example, J Doward and A Gibbs, 'Did Cambridge Analytica influence the Brexit vote and the US election?' *The Guardian* (London, 4 March 2017)www.theguardian.com/politics/2017/mar/04/nigel-oakes-cambridge-analytica-what-role-brexit-trump.

4 See, for example, European Commission, Directorate-General for Communication Networks, Content and Technology, A multi-dimensional approach to disinformation: Report of the independent High Level Group on fake news and online disinformation (Publications Office of the European Union 2018).

5 House of Commons (UK), Digital, Culture, Media and Sport Committee, Disinformation and "fake news": Final Report (HC 2017–19, 1791). See also House of Commons (UK), Digital, Culture, Media and Sport Committee, Disinformation and "fake news": Interim Report (HC 2017–19, 363).

6 Information Commissioner's Office (UK), Guidance for use of personal data in political campaigning (9 March 2021) https://ico.org.uk/for-organisations/guidance-for-the-use-of-personal-data-in-political-campaigning/; for the earlier reports, see Information Commissioner's Office (UK), *Democracy disrupted? Personal information and political influence* (11 July 2018) https://ico.org.uk/media/2259369/democracy-disrupted-110718.pdf; Information Commissioner's Office (UK), Investigation into the use of data analytics in political campaigns: A report to Parliament (6 November 2018) 5-6 https://ico.org.uk/media/action-weve-taken/2260271/investigation-into-the-use-of-data-analytics-in-political-campaigns-final-20181105.pdf.

7 Electoral Commission (UK), Digital campaigning: Increasing transparency for voters (June 2018); GfK, Political Finance Regulation and Digital Campaigning: A Public Perspective (Electoral Commission, 24 April 2018) www.electoralcommission.org.uk/__data/assets/pdf_file/0019/244540/Electoral-Commission-political-finance-regulation-and-digital-campaigning-a-public-perspective.pdf.

8 European Commission, 'Code of Practice on Disinformation' (26 September 2018) https://ec.europa.eu/digital-single-market/en/news/code-practice-disinformation; see also European Commission, Tackling online disinformation: a European Approach (Com 2018/236, 26 April 2018).

9 HC Digital, Culture, Media and Sport Committee, Disinformation and 'fake news': Final Report (n 5); ICO, Investigation into the use of data analytics in political campaigns: A report to Parliament (n 6).

10 S Flaxman, S Goel and J M Rao, 'Filter bubbles, echo chambers, and online news consumption (2016) 80(S1) *Public Opinion Quarterly* 298.

11 D J Solove, '"I've got nothing to hide" and other misunderstandings of privacy' (2007) 44 *San Diego Law Review* 745. See generally, L Taylor, L Floridi and B van der Sloot (eds.), *Group Privacy: New Challenges of Data Technologies* (Springer 2016).

12 J Dunn (ed.), *Democracy: The Unfinished Journey – 508 BC to AD 1993* (Oxford Unversity Press 1992) vi.

13 J Kupfer, 'Privacy, autonomy, and self-concept' (1987) 24 *American Philosophical Quarterly* 81, 84; see also B van der Sloot, 'Privacy as human flourishing: Could a shift towards virtue ethics strengthen privacy protection in the Age of Big Data?' (2014) 5 *Journal on Intellectual Property, Information Technology and Electronic Commerce Law* 230, para 3.

14 *McIntyre v Ohio Elections Commission* 514 US 334 (1995), discussed in E Barendt, *Anonymous Speech: Literature, Law and Politics* (Hart Publishing 2016) 57ff; see also Y Akdeniz, 'Anonymity, democracy, and cyberspace' (2002) 69 *Social Research* 223.

15 This has in fact been a marker of their success, unlike polities still struggling to develop democracy, political discourse does not rely heavily on technically illicit communication.

16 See, for example, GDPR Art 9(2)(d). Regulation (EU) 2016/679 of the European Parliament and of the Council of 27 April 2016 on the protection of natural persons with regard to the processing of personal data and on the free movement of such data, and repealing Directive 95/46/EC (General Data Protection Regulation) [2016] OJ L119/1 (hereafter GDPR).

17 B Shiner, 'Political campaign methods and the need for fundamental reform' [2019] *Public Law* 362, 365.

18 See, for example, ICO, Democracy disrupted? (n 6); ICO, Investigation into the use of data analytics in political campaigns: A report to Parliament (n 6).

19 D Susser, B Roessler and H F Nissenbaum, 'Technology, autonomy, and manipulation' (2019) 8(2) *Internet Policy Review* https://doi.org/10.14763/2019.2.1410.

20 See, for example, B R Berelson, P F Lazarsfeld and W N McPhee, *Voting: A Study of Opinion Formation in a Presidential Campaign* (University of Chicago Press 1954) 308.

21 F J Zuiderveen Borgesius and others, 'Online political microtargeting: promises and threats for democracy' (2018) 14(1) *Utrecht Law Review* 82, 87.

22 See further L M Neudert and N Marchal, *Polarisation and the Use of Technology in Political Campaigns and Communication* (European Parliamentary Research Service, March 2019) 39 https://www.europarl.europa.eu/RegData/etudes/STUD/2019/634414/EPRS_STU(2019)634414_EN.pdf.

23 S A Munson and P Resnick, 'Presenting diverse political opinions: how and how much' (CHI '10: Proceedings of the SIGCHI Conference on Human Factors in Computing Systems, April 2010) 1457 https://doi.org/10.1145/1753326.1753543.

24 B Martens and others, *The digital transformation of news media and the rise of disinformation and fake news*, JRC Digital Economy Working Paper 2018-02 (Seville: European Commission, 2018) 29–30.

25 J Burkell and P M Regan, 'Voting Public: Leveraging personal information to construct voter preference' in N Witzleb, M Paterson and J Richardson (eds.), *Big Data, Political Campaigning and the Law: Democracy and Privacy in the Age of Micro-Targeting* (Routledge 2020) 47, 63.

26 I S Rubinstein, 'Voter privacy in the age of Big Data' [2014] *Wisconsin Law Review* 861, 909, citing E Pariser, *The Filter Bubble: What The Internet is Hiding From You* (Viking 2011) 155–56.

27 D Sunshine Hillygus and T G Shields, *The Persuadable Voter: Wedge Issues in Presidential Campaigns* (Princeton University Press 2008) 189.

28 D Helbing and others, 'Will Democracy Survive Big Data and Artificial Intelligence?' (*Scientific American*, 25 February 2017) www.scientificamerican.com/article/will-democracy-survive-big-data-and-artificial-intelligence/.

29 M Andrejevic and Z Volcic, 'From mass to automated media' in Witzleb, Paterson and Richardson (n 25) 17, 33.

30 M Haim, A Graefe and H B Brosius, 'Burst of the filter bubble? effects of personalization on the diversity of Google News' (2018) 6 *Digital Journalism* 330.

31 R Fletcher and R Kleis Nielsen, 'Are news audiences increasingly fragmented? A cross-national comparative analysis of cross-platform news: audience fragmentation and duplication' (2017) 67 *Journal of Communication* 476.

32 D Wilding and others, *The Impact of Digital Platforms on News and Journalistic Content* (Centre for Media Transition, University of Technology Sydney 2018) 57–61.

33 Ibid. 61–63.

34 R Gibson, 'Party change, social media and the rise of "citizen-initiated" campaigning' (2015) 21 *Party Politics* 183.

35 H Margetts, 'Rethinking democracy with social media' (2019) 90 *The Political Quarterly* 107, 108.

36 V Bashyakarla and others, *Personal Data: Political Persuasion – Inside the Influence Industry. How It Works* (2nd ed., Tactical Tech 2019) 7 https://cdn.ttc.io/s/tacticaltech .org/methods_guidebook_A4_spread_web_Ed2.pdf.

37 Campaign for Accountability, 'Partisan pogramming: how Facebook and Google's campaign embeds benefit their bottom lines' (August 2018) https://campaignforaccountability .org/work/partisan-programming-how-facebook-and-googles-campaign-embeds-benefit-their-bottom-lines/.

38 S Tormey, 'The contemporary crisis of representative democracy' (Papers on Parliament no 66, Australian Parliament 2016) www.aph.gov.au/About_Parliament/Senate/Powers_ practice_n_procedures/pops/Papers_on_Parliament_66/The_Contemporary_Crisis_of_ Representative_Democracy.

39 J Baldwin-Philippi, 'Data campaigning: between empirics and assumptions' (2019) 8(4) *Internet Policy Review* https://doi.org/10.14763/2019.4.1437.

40 Flaxman, Goel and Rao (n 10).

41 Ibid.

42 C J Bennett and S Oduro-Marfo, *Privacy, Voter Surveillance and Democratic Engagement: Challenges for Data Protection Authorities* V Bashyakarla and others, Personal Data: Political Persuasion (ICO and University of Victoria 2019) 16 https://privacyconference2019.info/wp-content/uploads/2019/11/Privacy-and-International-Democratic-Engagement_finalv2.pdf.

43 For a detailed overview of the broad array of methods in use and in development, see Bashyakarla (n 36).

44 A Macintyre, G Wright and S Hankey, *Data and Democracy in the UK: A Report by Tactical Tech's Data and Politics Team (Tactical Tech,* 8 August 2018) 11–15 https://cdn.ttc .io/s/ourdataourselves.tacticaltech.org/ttc-influence-industry-uk.pdf.

45 J H Aldrich and J D Griffin, *Why Parties Matter: Political Competition and Democracy in the American South* (University of Chicago Press 2018) 13.

46 P Norris, *Democratic Deficit: Critical Citizens Revisited* (Cambridge University Press 2011) 35.

47 Zuiderveen Borgesius and others (n 21).

48 B Bodó, N Helberger and C H de Vreese, Political micro-targeting: a Manchurian candidate or just a dark horse?' (2017) 6(4) *Internet Policy Review,* https://doi.org/10 .14763/2017.4.776.

49 S Hankey, J Kerr Morrison and R Naik, *Data and Democracy in the Digital Age* (The Constitution Society, 10 July 2018) recommendation 4.

50 Bennett and Oduro-Marfo (n 42) 17 identify five general patterns, which they describe as 'permissive, exempted, regulated, prohibited and emerging'.

51 See R J Krotoszynski, 'Big Data and the electoral process in the United States: constitutional constraint and limited data privacy regulations' in Witzleb, Paterson and Richardson (n 25) 186.

52 See the definition of 'government institution' in Privacy Act 2005, s3.

53 See PIPEDA, s 4(1) (application). For a more detailed discussion on Canada, see C J Bennett and M McDonald, 'From the doorstep to the database: political parties, campaigns, and personal privacy protection in Canada' in Witzleb, Paterson and Richardson (n 25) 141; on Australia, see M Paterson and N Witzleb, 'Voter privacy in an era of big data: time to abolish the political exemption in the Australian Privacy Act' in Witzleb, Paterson and Richardson (n 25) 164.

54 Bennett and Oduro-Marfo (n 42) 22. The exception is British Columbia, where political parties are subject to the Personal Information Protection Act (PIPA).

55 House of Commons (Canada), Standing Committee on Access to Information, Privacy and Ethics, *Democracy under Threat: Risks and Solutions in the Era of Disinformation and Data Monopoly*, December 2018, Rec 1.

56 See Privacy Act 1988 (Cth), s 6(1) and 6C (definition of 'organisation) and 7C (political acts and practices).

57 See further Paterson and Witzleb (n 53).

58 Directive 2002/58/EC of the European Parliament and of the Council of 12 July 2002 concerning the processing of personal data and the protection of privacy in the electronic communications sector (Directive on privacy and electronic communications) [2002] OJ L 201/37.

59 The other end of the spectrum is occupied by countries that completely prohibit data capture by political parties, such as Japan: see, e.g., Bennett and Oduro-Marfo (n 42) 37–39.

60 These are specified in GDPR (n 16) art 9(1).

61 GDPR (n 16) art 6.

62 GDPR (n 16) art 9(2)(d).

63 GDPR (n 16) art 6(1).

64 GDPR (n 16) art 6(1)(f).

65 GDPR (n 16) art 6(1)(e) and (f).

66 Data Protection Act 2018 (UK), s8(e), taking advantage of the derogation provision in the GDPR (n 16) art 6(2).

67 Data Protection Act 2018 (UK), Explanatory Notes, para 86.

68 The 'very wide' democratic engagement provision has been criticised by the ICO in the legislative process: Information Commissioner's Office (UK), 'Data Protection Bill, House of Commons Public Bill Committee: Information Commissioner's further written evidence' (19 March 2018) https://ico.org.uk/media/about-the-ico/documents/2258462/data-protection-bill-public-bill-committee-ico-further-evidence.pdf.

69 See GDPR (n 16) art 6(3) and Information Commissioner's Office, *Guidance on political campaigning*: (n 6) 30.

70 GDPR (n 16) art 6(1)(f).

71 Guidance on political campaigning (n 6) 30.

72 Gareth, 'British lawmakers are collecting their users' data to "promote democratic engagement"' (*Indivigital*, 21 June 2018) https://indivigital.com/news/british-lawmakers-are-collecting-their-users-data-to-promote-democratic-engagement/.

73 Ibid.

74 GDPR (n 16) art 33–36. European Commission, *Commission guidance on the application of Union data protection law in the electoral context* (Com 2018/638, September 2018) 8 https://eur-lex.europa.eu/legal-content/en/TXT/?uri=CELEX%3A52018DC0638.

75 Information Commissioner's Office (UK), Investigation into the use of data analytics in political campaigns (n 6).

76 Communications Act 2003 (UK), s 320; Royal Charter for the continuance of the British Broadcasting Corporation (December 2016), Cm 9365, Sch 3, s 3.

77 V Bakir and A McStay, 'Fake news and the economy of emotions: problems, causes, solutions' (2018) 6 *Digital Journalism* 154.

78 In its major inquiry on the digital platforms, and their effect on media and journalism, the Australian Competition and Consumer Commission recommended that the Australian public broadcasters be provided with stable and adequate funding in recognition of that role: Australian Competition and Consumer Commission, *Digital Platforms Inquiry, Final Report* (Commonwealth of Australia, 2019) rec 9.

79 G Haciyakupoglu and others, *Countering Fake News: A Survey of Recent Global Initiatives* (S Rajaratnam School of International Studies, 2018) http://hdl.handle.net/11540/8063

80 See A Schetzer, 'Governments are making fake news a crime – but it could stifle free speech' (*The Conversation*, 7 July 2019) https://theconversation.com/governments-are-making-fake-news-a-crime-but-it-could-stifle-free-speech-117654.

PART IV

The Future of Personalisation: Algorithmic Foretelling and Its Limits

14

Regulating Algorithmic Assemblages: Looking beyond Corporatist AI Ethics

Andrew Charlesworth

14.1 INTRODUCTION

The perceived potential of artificial intelligence (AI) systems, broadly characterised, has seen a massive surge of investment in research and development, and their penetration into many decision-making processes of commercial, political and public organisations.[1] The driver behind this surge and the improvements in AI technologies in recent years, especially in the field of machine learning, has been the development of vast digital data sets.[2] These data sets can be harnessed as training data to improve the AI system's ability to identify potentially significant correlations, which in turn can provide highly insightful intelligence on animate activity (e.g. human behaviour) or inanimate processes (e.g. weather patterns). Of course, large data sets (and actuarial assessments) existed long before the advent of digitisation, notably central and local government data sets (e.g. taxes, welfare), policing data sets (e.g. criminal records, fingerprints, photos), medical data sets (e.g. patient records, clinical trial data, surveys) and corporate credit data sets. Yet, what is new is their deep penetration into most spheres of private and public life. From shopping, entertainment, policing and fraud detection, to political campaigning, credit scoring, insurance quotes, social networking and news consumption, AI systems ubiquitously work behind the scenes to infuse decision-making processes with intelligence extracted from big data. In many of these contexts, this intelligence is used to develop highly personalised predictions or targeted services.

These automated decision-making processes have attracted public and regulatory attention, partly because of their sheer pervasiveness, and partly because the steady exposure to machine-generated outcomes has also made abundantly clear that the processes are no more neutral or objective than human judgements, but have values embedded within them. This in turn suggests that they ought to be subjected – in the name of transparency and accountability – to some regulatory oversight,[3] much like their analogue counterparts. Those employing AI ought not to be able to hide behind the machine and avoid being answerable for unlawful biases, damaging errors of assessment, or 'redlining' and discrimination against individuals and communities. Although such negative effects are usually the result of a failure in AI system design or flawed training data sets, some observers have suggested that certain AI-supported processes in government decision-making may have been quite deliberately designed to have exclusionary effects.[4]

At the same time, it has also become apparent that, even accepting that the personalisation phenomenon can provide notable efficiencies and economic gains in delivering services (e.g. precision medicine), or in allocating scarce state resources (e.g. predictive policing), it may often be accompanied by unintended negative effects[5] that should attract public debate. Take, for example, highly personalised insurance or credit score systems which apply a heightened user-pay logic to the provision of their services and are beneficial to privileged customers, but also liable to amplify existing social disadvantages, and implicitly undermine notions of distributive justice and communal solidarity. Equally, personalised news and entertainment consumption and the attendant 'filter bubble' effect cannot but undermine social cohesion.[6] Whilst media and academic accounts have focussed on the potential negative impacts on individuals or categories of individuals, there has been much less consideration of broader consequences or ripple effects of incorporating AI into existing social systems.[7] For example, although systems such as automated facial recognition technology or predictive policing promise more accurate and efficient policing (this is far from empirically proven), they also have unintended negative side effects. They divert limited public resources away from existing operational methods, such as community policing, that are demonstrably effective at achieving policing objectives, but which are human-resource intensive, and difficult to subject to audit and metric oversight. While greater recourse to such systems may generate revenue and data for the private sector, and produce auditable metrics for government, this will inevitably further isolate police officers and staff from direct engagement with the broader communities they serve, and whose co-operation they need.

This chapter explores these consequences and ripple effects through an 'AI ethics' perspective, which has become the dominant overarching discourse concerned with 'regulating' AI for the good of society. Yet, as the phrase suggests, 'AI ethics' is far removed from 'AI law' and broadly refers to self-policing by private corporate actors in their use of AI systems, as sanctioned by government. The discussion here critiques that self-policing, first, by locating AI ethics within long-standing traditions of corporate social responsibility and institutional ethical frameworks with all their in-built shortcomings, that frequently translate into a systemic inability to be truly Other-regarding. Second, this chapter shows, with reference to the recent EU AI ethics initiative, that even well-intentioned initiatives may shoot past their target by simply assuming the desirability of AI applications, regardless of their wider impacts. Such an approach restricts itself to tinkering with system details, the consequences of which are relatively minor in comparison to the much broader impacts of AI application within social systems, as captured by the idea of 'algorithmic assemblage'. Only a holistic analysis that goes beyond a focus on individual and group rights would be able to even engage with these broader impacts, but this is hardly likely to occur if AI ethics is constructed – as is currently the case – as an essentially corporate concern. For corporations, these wider effects of AI on society are frequently the direct *and* intended result of pursuing the bottom line.

14.2 A NEW ETHICAL DAWN OR THE ART OF 'ETHICS-WASHING'

14.2.1 *A Burgeoning Ethic Industry*

This public disquiet has not gone unnoticed by government, commercial entities and researchers seeking to develop or implement AI-supported personalisation. The European Commission explicitly included in its strategy for AI development 'ensuring an appropriate ethical and legal framework based on the Union's values and in line with the Charter of Fundamental Rights of the EU'.[8] Likewise, the UK Government's Office for Artificial Intelligence states, in its policy paper, *The AI Sector Deal* (2018), as a policy objective of its AI strategy 'leading the world in the safe and ethical use of data through a new Centre for Data Ethics and Innovation';[9] Google created, and then disbanded, an AI ethics council,[10] Microsoft has launched an AI ethics framework, and a range of companies including Facebook, Amazon, IBM and Salesforce are hiring ethicists to work on their AI strategies or funding AI initiatives.[11]

However, the developing interest in AI ethics in government and business, while on its face a positive reaction to public criticisms and fears, brings problems and concerns of its own. The establishment of ethics boards, ethics oversight committees and codes of practice for AI by corporate entities follows a familiar regulatory pattern, well established in the technology sphere, whereby industries seek to head off formal governmental regulatory intervention by providing putatively self-regulatory mechanisms to address the problematic impacts of their services or corporate activities. These are usually premised on subsidiarity arguments, and there is some evidence that they can be an effective means of achieving positive regulatory outcomes in specific circumstances.[12] However, self-regulatory regimes are often criticised in regulatory literature for failing to adequately protect public interests when these conflict with commercial imperatives, for lack of transparency and meaningful accountability, and for failing to engage in effective dialogue with civil society (a lack of tripartism).[13]

Of course, corporate embrace of ethical frameworks for AI is not necessarily a cynical attempt to avoid regulation by means of 'ethics-washing'. It may reflect genuine attempts to transfer values that contemporary public discourse (e.g. in the media) suggests are held or are likely to be considered desirable by primary stakeholders into a frame which corporations can more easily internalise: for example, transformation of those values into mechanisms for legitimising particular technology practices or business opportunities and thereby stabilising them. Personalised marketing would appear to be a prime example. This may open up a range of opportunities, from reconsideration of outdated corporate routine, to development of formal internal or industry codes of conduct, establishment of industry networks and wider stakeholder engagement. That said, those outcomes will not necessarily result in positive or effective approaches to resolution of social problems caused by AI. Much depends upon whether this approach to public values is truly institutionally assimilative or just deflective.[14]

14.2.2 *CSR Reinvented?*

Analysis of corporate moves to establish internal or industry-wide external AI ethics frameworks thus inevitably suggests parallels from the wider debate over the development and effectiveness of Corporate Social Responsibility (CSR). While CSR, in the broad sense of 'clearly articulated and communicated policies and practices of corporations that reflect business responsibility for some of the wider societal good',[15] has become a globally recognised concept, its roots lie firmly in the USA. Commentators have noted distinct differences between US and European approaches to CSR, suggesting that US CSR reflects a clearer explicit role for corporations in taking independent responsibility for societal interests, whilst European CSR implicitly envisages a 'partnership of representative social and economic actors led by government'.[16]

Given that corporate AI powerhouses are primarily of US origin, it is unsurprising that the initial response to concerns about the ethical implications of AI was premised on corporations developing solutions either through internal debate and procedures, or via trusted 'outsiders'. This meant that the AI ethics debate was 'Americanised' at an early stage, and a US corporate responsibility approach to AI ethics strongly underpins national and supranational policy developments. Thus, when the EU High-Level Expert Group on Artificial Intelligence was established by the European Commission in 2018, to make recommendations on ethical, legal and societal issues related to AI, the ethical discourse that it would engage in had already largely been framed. That framing embedded a corporate-centric perspective of potential ethical risks and the means to ameliorate them as the central focus of the dialogue.

Criticisms of the effectiveness of CSR in achieving long-term societal goods are long standing.[17] A key concern is that even where CSR practices are, or purport to be, beneficial for primary stakeholders, they fail to address issues of wider social importance – in other words that, in practice, most CSR initiatives are in fact 'direct influence tactics'.[18] An example of this in the AI domain can be seen in Google's recent attempts to address its employees' concerns about the direction of its AI R&D,

and in particular its relationship with the US military.[19] Google made a point of publicly distancing itself from controversial contracts, creating a set of AI Principles and establishing an AI ethics committee, which was disbanded after further employee protests about its proposed membership. These actions clearly sought to address the ethical concerns of a primary stakeholder group (its employees) relating to its corporate practices. However, Google continues to provide financial, techno-logical and engineering support to a range of start-ups that provide AI technology to military and law enforcement through a venture capital arm.[20] Thus the impact of the apparently 'responsible' actions is diminished, and the ethical considerations avoided rather than addressed. Indeed, placing ethically problematic R&D at one or more removes from Google, in a range of smaller, ostensibly independent, start-up companies is likely to make it harder to ensure that commercial practices that might breach, or come into conflict with, socially desirable ethical principles, can be identified, subjected to critical scrutiny and appropriately regulated.

14.2.3 *Structural Weaknesses of Corporate Self-regulation*

The problematics inherent in establishing when it is appropriate for government to permit corporate self-regulation combined with the criticisms of US CSR approaches (not least the difficulties in establishing the extent to which those approaches can plausibly be expected to identify, select and prioritise solutions that address wider social problems over those affecting primary stakeholders) also raises questions about the consultation process upon which guidance for national and supranational policymakers rests.

A critical assessment of the governmental/corporate approach to developing ethical AI should thus consider the extent to which bodies writing AI ethics guidelines on behalf of government, or ethics boards established by corporations to advise on policy, are truly independent and transparent.[21] For example, in the case of the EU High-Level Expert Group on Artificial Intelligence, what percentage of its fifty-two members were employed by corporate entities or interest groups, or funded by them? The Expert Group's report *Ethics Guidelines for Trustworthy AI* (2019) (*Ethics Guidelines*)[22] is silent on potential conflicts of interest amongst its members – an obvious ethical oversight. Similar problems can be found with corporate AI ethics boards: companies may refuse to divulge membership, identify who participates in meetings and discussions, reveal how rules and policies have been determined, and what action has been taken, if any, as a result of ethics board suggestions.[23]

This also implicates issues of accountability. If companies get to self-determine the parameters of the ethical landscape via their own ethical boards and through undeclared influence on the outcome of 'independent' governmental evaluations, key questions may simply never be adequately debated. Discussion can be framed in ways that fail to raise, or which marginalise, issues that are not readily amenable to the solutions that are acceptable to corporations, that is, solutions that place minimal regulatory constraints on their activities, or are of particular importance to their primary stakeholders. Reducing ethical investigation to checklists, or limiting consideration of the social impact of AI-supported personalisation to questions about whether individual rights, or the rights of particular groups, are disproportionately impacted, ignores issues that may not be readily addressed by checklists and that are of wider societal concern, and may range beyond the activities of an individual company or industry.

The self-regulatory approach that the use of ethics boards offers is one of weak accountability even for those issues that are addressed. Simply establishing an ethics board provides no guarantee of ethical behaviour without a clearly defined and transparent framework that sets out how the ethics board will operate, who its members are, how its recommendations should be acted upon by the company, and who is accountable, and how, if they are not. Similarly, a code of practice is of limited value without any publicly accessible evidence of what consequences of breaches there will be. Without these types of accountability mechanisms, ethics boards are likely to be simply a regulatory 'Potemkin Village' designed to deflect public concern and state regulation, but with little meaningful impact on corporate practices.

There is also an issue of the degree to which small groups of ethicists and experts drawn from a narrow range of disciplines or interest groups can adequately represent the broad concerns of wider civil society. Where the same individuals are also members of more than one ethics board or expert group – there is also an increased risk of 'groupthink'[24] that may lead to failure to access and exchange context-specific information, unwillingness to explore viewpoints or courses of action suggested by others outside the group, and as a result, the adoption of inadequate, incomplete or inflexible outputs.[25] A notable feature of much of the corporate-sponsored and governmental ethical debate about AI-supported personalisation has been its distance from both the general public and civil society groups. The High-Level Expert Group on Artificial Intelligence notes that 'Over the past months, the 52 of us met, discussed and interacted. . .'; yet a survey of its members listed suggests a very narrow range of discussants, dominated by corporate representatives and AI researchers from a select number of academic disciplines, notably computer science, law, philosophy and ethics.[26] A review of the literature cited in the *Ethics Guidelines* includes theoretical ethical material developed by members of the Group, and links to EU projects using or seeking to develop AI-based solutions to a range of social issues, but contains no citations to empirical work on the social impacts of AI, or to wider civil society critiques of impacts of new technologies. The document identifies that a key nontechnical method to secure and maintain Trustworthy AI is 'open discussion and the involvement of social partners and stakeholders, including the general public' and notes that '[m]any organisations already rely on stakeholder panels to discuss the use of AI systems and data analytics. . . includ[ing] various members, such as legal experts, technical experts, ethicists, consumer representatives and workers.'[27] Yet the

Group's pilot Assessment List appears to have been compiled without significant direct or indirect public input.[28]

The above concerns should not be taken as a criticism of specific individuals but should cause us to reflect upon the conscious or unconscious biases, preferences or concurrence seeking that drafting ethical guidelines under those conditions may encourage. A perceived problem of personalisation on the Internet is the filter bubble, that is 'an environment … in which people are exposed only to opinions and information that conform to their existing beliefs.'[29] In practice, filter bubbles of one sort or another have always existed, indeed, there are clear similarities with the concept of 'groupthink' mentioned above. Expert groups are no less prone to this problem than internet users. Indeed, as anyone who has been involved in drafting ethical frameworks, codes of practice or standards can attest, it is often relatively unproblematic to devise these in committee, particularly when the members of the committee share a common objective and similar backgrounds, but quite another to persuade others to apply them in practice in circumstances where there are divergent social, cultural or business attitudes.[30] Rules that look good to the committee on paper may not be assimilated without resistance into practices or applied to end-use cases. As the following section suggests, even with some degree of regulatory compulsion they may not lead to effective transparency, oversight, audit and accountability.

14.2.4 *Ethics Institutionalised*

As chair of an academic Research Ethics Review Committee, one obtains an interesting perspective into the way in which researchers in UK Higher Education interact with both the ethical guidelines pertaining to their discipline, and the procedural requirements created to give effect to those guidelines. There is often a perceptible disjoint between the 'understood' ethical principles and guidelines, and the actual willingness of researchers to act, or refrain from acting, in ways that ensure that those principles and guidelines are respected, and seen to be respected, in practice.

Researchers chafe at the 'red-tape', the 'administrative burden', the 'restriction on academic freedom' and the 'methodological constraints' of ethical oversight.[31] They cut and paste past responses to ethics review questions without considering the particular variables and risks of their proposed research, provide minimalist responses to questions about risks to research subjects and their data, and leave ethics review applications until the last moment before grant applications are to be submitted, or time-sensitive fieldwork begun. Their information for research subjects is written in impenetrable technical jargon, their consent forms are vague and confusing, and their risk assessments cursory. Then, when the research begins, how many of those gestures to ethical practice promised in ethics applications fall by the wayside when time is short? What ethical corners are cut when a 'research opportunity' is too good to miss? What are the perceived and actual consequences for individual or institution, if any, of breaches of ethical guidelines?

Equally, academic ethical review processes often leave something to be desired. Criticisms of ethical review encompass box-ticking exercises, institutional back-covering, excessive formality, lack of reflexivity and imposition of inappropriate discipline-specific requirements.[32] Often a primary institutional motivation for incorporating processes of ethical review of research across all academic disciplines is not a concern for the fair treatment of research subjects, as individuals or a group; for the welfare of researchers; or for the avoidance of possible negative impacts on wider society. Rather it is concerned with ensuring continued access to grants and avoiding embarrassing legal action or poor publicity,[33] or put another way, the need to pay attention to primary stakeholders. From that perspective, there are greater similarities between the objectives of such institutional research ethics policies and CSR policies in the wider commercial sector than might be anticipated. This 'institutional protection' may also perhaps be reflected in the nature of ethical oversight in academia – there is usually significant front-end oversight by commit-tees responsible for ethical review (although the nature and scope of that review may vary significantly between disciplines) at various levels of the institution.For some types of research, notably biomedical research, there may be formal oversight by external bodies,[34] but outside specific discipline domains, formal audit is unlikely, except in cases of egregious breaches of guidelines. There are numerous, often interlinked, reasons for this – lack of resources, lack of authority, lack of access and lack of will. Reliance is often placed on self-reporting of ethical breaches, reporting by those managing the researcher, or reporting by third parties, including research subjects, to ensure ongoing oversight.

It is suggested that the production of academic ethical standards and processes have, in conjunction with general legal requirements such as data protection law, resulted in a research environment where academics who deal with human research subjects are broadly cognizant of the general ethical principles applied to their research, even if they are sometimes rather hazy on the detail. However, in practice, those principles are often, consciously or sub-consciously, viewed as 'ethics for others', as researchers perceive that their own practices are somehow innately ethical, that any deviation by them from those principles is likely to be minor and excusable in the circumstances, and that it is other researchers that are more likely to significantly deviate from those principles and are thus more deserving of scrutiny than them. It is this perception that underlies at least some of the 'chafing' about the imposition of formal oversight.

A key question is then whether ethics guidelines and ethical review processes have resulted in better ethical practices in academic research, or simply led to the development of a carefully cultivated façade of ethical practice that suggests the existence of an effective and reflexive process of consideration and mitigation of individual, group and social risks that it cannot meaningfully deliver? Consideration of the outcome of that microcosmic assessment might provide a starting point from which to begin to understand the nature of the difficulties likely to arise when seeking to apply a general ethical framework to a phenomenon as potentially ubiquitous as the use of artificial intelligence in decision-making processes. If it is difficult to inculcate and embed effective ethical practice in a community of researchers which has produced numerous codes of ethical practice for research,[35] which supports several journals dedicated specifically to research ethics;[36] and which is subject to formal institutional, funder and increasingly, publisher, ethical review requirements; then one would have to seriously question the likely effectiveness of ethical guidelines alone in contexts with significant countervailing forces, such as governance and commerce.

14.3 AI ETHICS GUIDELINES DECONSTRUCTED

14.3.1 *Limited Tool Box: Those Who Cannot Remember the Past are Condemned to Repeat It*

It has often been said of army commanders that they tend to spend peace time studying how to fight the last war rather than strategising for the next one. Yet reacting to new problems by resorting to methods one used to address previous problems, even if the outcomes of those methods are less than optimal, is hardly confined to the realm of the military. One of the critical concerns relating to AI-supported personalisation is that of privacy, whether related to governmental surveillance and predictive profiling, or corporate profiling and manipulation of individuals and groups. Privacy and data protection have been key issues in the relationships between citizen vis-à-vis the State, and consumer vis-à-vis the private sector, for over 60 years. It seems fair to suggest that, to date, existing regulatory strategies to protect privacy and personal data have struggled to prevent their erosion by technology, even in those States which have constitutionally protected privacy rights and comprehensive data privacy laws. Equally, suggestions that technology (e.g., privacy-enhancing technologies) might be harnessed to either support or replace non-technological methods have not gained widespread traction in the private sector – to adapt a popular saying, it appears that the best way to make a small fortune investing in privacy-enhancing technologies is to start off with a large fortune.

With this in mind, it is instructive to look at the *Ethics Guidelines*. The technical measures it promotes are:[37] setting up processes for embedding ethical rules within AI system architecture (ethics by design), and secondary systems to monitor how compliant the primary systems apply those rules (Trustworthy AI); establishing methods that explain system behaviour to assess their reliability and to inform 'users' (explicability of output); testing and validating an AI system across its life cycle (oversight); and developing quality of service indicators to ensure a baseline that an

AI system has been tested and developed with security and safety considerations in mind. These are laudable objectives and have been suggested in some form or another, from a privacy-enhancing perspective, for many of the same AI systems. Indeed, the ethics-by-design suggestion is directly drawn from the GDPR and the data privacy research and practice upon which it rests. However, the real-world implementation of such technical measures in the privacy arena suggests at best a weak level of adoption and, even where adopted, the practical results often appear significantly attenuated from those suggested by regulators and theorists.

These technical measures are then followed by recommendations of non-technical measures including: *regulation* with references made to product safety legislation and liability frameworks; *soft law and co-regulatory approaches* with organisations signing up to the guidelines, codes of conduct, 'accreditation systems, professional codes of ethics or standards for fundamental rights compliant design' or certification regimes run by trusted intermediaries; *internal governance frameworks*, for example, by setting up ethics boards;[38] fostering *education* and awareness in all stakeholders including the general public, for example, by using stakeholder panels and engaging in social dialogue; as well as ensuring *diversity and inclusivity* amongst AI makers and users, that is amongst those who 'design, develop, test and maintain, deploy and procure these systems'.[39]

The idea that ethical AI can be promoted with the backing of product safety legislation and liability frameworks is interesting from a UK perspective, if only because of the limited application of both those regimes to computer software, and the degree of effort the software industry has, over the years, put into ensuring that this remains so.[40] Beyond this, most of these measures have also been mooted or utilised as part of the data privacy regulatory toolkit. With the arguable exception of data privacy legislation, most of these measures, while laudable in principle, have been of limited effectiveness in the data privacy sphere, and it is unclear why the *Guidelines* assume that they will be any more effective in creating 'Trustworthy AI' rather than simply producing (as we see with contemporary data privacy) a secondary industry ecosystem of consultants, certification bodies, e-training specialists and administrators, of varying quality, reliability and longevity.

Diversity and inclusivity from design to procurement and deployment is also, in principle, desirable, particularly considering that the technology industry has traditionally scored poorly on both counts, whether in terms of technology workers or organisational leadership. Yet, even if diversity and inclusivity can be increased, it is worth noting that the design side of the technology is often at a significant remove from the procurement and deployment of systems. A key element missing from the list is the 'selling' – what are the features upon which AI marketing rests, do purchasers understand the ethical implications of its use in particular contexts, and do the vendors themselves understand, and seek to communicate to the purchasers, the ethical issues that might arise from the use of their products? One can have an inclusive and diverse design, developer, testing and maintenance team which produces an ethical AI system, but still have it marketed, implemented and directed in ways that are problematic. The 'diversity and inclusivity' concerns are well illustrated by various manifestations of data-driven personalisation which, as shown in this collection, tend to reinforce existing socio-economic inequalities and vulnerabilities, few of which AI makers or their governmental or corporate users share or are particularly preoccupied with. Indeed, their personal or institutional interests often directly benefit from ethically questionable personalised applications, that come in the form of cheaper prices or credit (price or credit discrimination), greater public safety (predictive policing or sentencing) or smaller public health budgets (precision medicine) – regardless of their crippling consequences for the already disadvantaged, as discussed in a number of chapters of this book.

14.3.2 *Limited Perspectives on Affected Interests: An Atomistic Approach*

Much of the language of the *Ethics Guidelines* is couched in terms of fundamental rights and freedoms that are directed towards the individual or to particular groups of individuals who are perceived to be at risk because of particular characteristics or vulnerabilities. AI-facilitated personalisation will undoubtedly impact individual and group rights, and the *Ethics Guidelines* provide a lengthy, if sometimes mechanistic, *Assessment List* to aid consideration of the issues. Yet it pays little attention to the structural/societal impact of AI-facilitated personalisation. While the report makes gestures towards wider social issues,[41] only one of the 131 questions in the *Assessment List* is addressed to 'Society and Democracy' by alerting to the possibility of affected stakeholder interests over and beyond the end user.[42] This largely atomistic approach ignores the potential impacts of AI and personalisation on the wider community, preferring instead to concentrate on a series of discrete individual or group rights that can be neatly categorised, risk assessed and check boxed.

Several problems with this line of approach are identified by Hoffman.[43] The emphasis on avoiding breaches of legally protected individual or group rights tends to direct attention to the perceived need to avoid 'bad actors', that is, seeking to ensure that individuals or organisations do not deliberately or inadvertently embed discriminatory or damaging biases into AI. Alternatively, given the 'black box' nature of many AI systems, there is a growing tendency to shift the blame for unexpected or unpredictable outcomes from 'bad actors' to 'bad algorithms', that is, their model or training data. Solutions to these issues might typically be sought in enhancing diversity and inclusivity in human teams across the AI lifecycle, or by 'technical patches'. However, such fixes for individual or system behaviour inevitably displace more systematic attempts to explore and address the wider social and cultural processes and practices underlying the particular forms of discrimination that made them necessary in the first place.[44]

There tends also to be a focus on overcoming specific disadvantages faced by (legally) pre-categorised and often artificially homogenised groups without a clear understanding of how institutional or social contexts may affect the impact of a particular instance of AI decision-making on sub-groupings within and across those groups. Viewing AI decision-making solely from the perspective of avoiding building in specific types of disadvantage may result in a 'fair AI' in terms of avoiding obvious disparity between treatment of different groups by the AI. However, this approach is unlikely to call into question the discriminatory effect of any systemic advantages enjoyed by particular groups, whether these advantages are internal or external to the AI system.For example, an AI decision may have real-world consequences, the outcomes of which are entirely contingent upon external factors, such as wealth or social capital.[45] As Eubanks puts it:

> We all inhabit this new regime of digital data, but we don't all experience it in the same way. What made my family's experience [dealing with a negative AI decision] endurable was the access to information, discretionary time and self-determination that professional middle-class people take for granted.[46]

Neglecting to take a holistic view of potential structural inequalities, such as these, means that the unfairness of the AI outcomes tends to go unchallenged and unaddressed.

The legal and political debates around fair treatment and anti-discrimination also tend to home in on the distribution of rights, opportunities and resources. Hoffman argues that this is problematic on two grounds.[47] First, distribution of rights, opportunities and resources is in itself demonstrably insufficient to afford human dignity if such distribution is not simultaneously supported by changes in social structures and attitudes which prevent harms that do not lend themselves to effective remedy by distributive means. Second, making the central issue one of distribution of rights, opportunities and resources is to suggest that AI can be isolated from the wider social systems within which they are incorporated, when in fact they are intrinsic to the ongoing production of social and cultural meaning within those systems (see below).

The 'atomistic' approach thus reveals a core difficulty for the authors of the *Ethics Guidelines*. On the one hand they are tasked with considering the ethical issues arising from AI; on the other they aim to provide the *Assessment List* to aid organisations to incorporate ethical thinking into their processes and procedures. The former objective might reasonably be assumed to include a holistic assessment of the types of broad social issues and risks arising from AI beyond individual and groups rights. It might raise questions about whether use of AI-facilitated personalisation might drive undesirable social developments. For example, the potential for the concentration of power in the hands of those designing or controlling the design of the technology (we can already see how control of the use of personalisation has begun to affect the distribution of wealth [see Chapter 4]; the dismantling of systems based on communal solidarity or distributive justice, such as insurance; the further obstruction of social mobility, already in decline; or the erosion of social cohesion, driven by the expansion of 'filter bubbles' across all forms of technology-mediated communication. In contrast, the second objective demands an approach that eschews macro-policy considerations in favour of micro-risk assessment focusing narrowly on rights of individuals or groups of individuals. The risk with the latter approach is that it suggests that the broader social questions are out with the responsibility, concern or capacity of individual organisations or industries.

If that is the case, then it is even more problematic if governments, encouraged by the prime corporate movers, leave the legal and ethical regulation of AI to self-regulatory processes. In those circumstances the debate is likely to become one of how to implement business friendly, individual rights-focused, risk assessment-based regulation, and not one that actually engages with civil society representatives to develop an understanding of the limits of the social, economic and political trade-offs citizens might be willing to accept in return for the potential advantages that AI and personalisation might bring.[48] Major societal trade-offs obscured in a narrow debate premised on the desirability of personalised consumption from access to credit to medical services [see Chapter 9] are the values of communal solidarity or a recognition of structural disadvantages that makes this intensified 'user-pay' approach fundamentally problematic and at odds with concerns of redistributive justice. Equally, if one starts from an acceptance of personalised news consumption, the societal values of democratic debates across classes, cultures, generations are inevitably marginalised. Finally, in law, starting from an assumption of the legitimacy of predictive sentencing on the basis of its public safety benefits, obscures how those benefits can only come on the back of compromised fundamental values such as the presumption of innocence or just desert [see Chapter 8].

14.3.3 *Limited Problematisation of 'Algorithmic Assemblages'*

Finally, a striking omission from the *Ethics Guidelines* is any sustained attempt at reconsidering or challenging the predominant framing of the potential ethical risks and the strategies to address them. Recent literature in the Science and Technology Studies field argues that the majority of the discussion in this area to date has focused on relatively narrow and technical understandings of the effects and impacts of algorithms, and that it will be necessary to attempt a more holistic approach to framing if meaningful intervention to achieve broad social objectives such as fairness, justice and due process is to be achieved.[49]

Key to this argument is understanding that AI algorithms are not inherently free of values but have sociological and normative features which in their interactions with humans 'make some associations, similarities, and actions more likely than others'.[50] They become useful or reliable only by virtue of their interaction with data, end users or other systems, and in interacting are engaging in both technological and social functions 'structuring how information is produced, surfaced, made sense of, seen as legitimate, and ascribed public significance.'[51] The difficulty in creating guidelines for the ethical use of algorithms thus lies partly in the fact that such guidelines are not applying ethical values to a blank slate, but attempting to change values already embedded within particular algorithmic instances, and partly in the fact that ethical guidelines directed at affecting the behaviour of an organisation, or even an industry, are unlikely to be helpful when the need is to address the effect of 'algorithmic assemblages' that may span broad socio-technical networks:

> The efficacy of an algorithmic assemblage consists not only in its ability to process and identify patterns in vast amounts of data but also in its ability to manipulate adjacent computational routines, material infrastructures, and human beings. Depending on its domain of application, assembling a functioning algorithm requires the integration not only of hardware and digital flows but also of the organizational structures, analog infrastructure, and socioeconomic processes from which it draws its problems and on which it operates.[52]

The dominant framing of the AI ethics debate to date has adopted a US corporate-centric perspective of the potential ethical risks and the means to be taken to ameliorate them. This reflects a limited CSR-style approach to developing ethical guidelines, which focuses on the concerns of primary stakeholders, and takes an instrumental approach heavily premised on existing legally defined and narrow commitments to the protection of individual and group rights. This narrow framing of the ethics debate is unlikely to provide an effective basis for future ethical approaches to AI generally, and 'algorithmic assemblages' in particular. What is required is a clear understanding of how AI become incorporated into social processes, and the effect they have, and could have, on broader social developments. It is difficult to see how a pathway to such an understanding can be created if one begins from a starting point premised upon the social, political and economic presumptions and preconceptions baked into the CSR approach.

A fundamental rethink of the way that policymakers approach the problematic of AI and 'algorithmic assemblages' is needed. Recourse to ethical frameworks and regulatory models that do not attempt from the start to engage with the actual and potential structural inequalities that AI and 'algorithmic assemblages' retain, reinforce and reify is inevitably going to be a case of tackling symptoms and not causes. Consider, for example, how Amazon's market dominance, based on its first mover position on a personalised recommender system, is now deeply embedded within and enhanced by an intricate assemblage of algorithms extending far beyond analysing shopping habits to the analysing and optimising of workers, suppliers and competitors:

> The logistical algorithms at the core of an Amazon shipping center not only make predictions based on the analysis of past transactions, shipping events, and worker performance but also use those predictions to actively manage product inventories, control the position and performance of human workers, govern the flow of

packages through the physical space of the warehouse, and interact with external organizations such as FedEx or the postal service.[53]

This assemblage would already stretch the effective applicability of the *Ethics Guidelines'* Assessment List, and it is only a fragment of a far wider Amazon-centred social and economic 'ecosystem.' That ecosystem extends far beyond the boundaries of what Amazon.com, Inc. owns, or can exercise some degree of control over, even should it wish to, and is continually evolving. Developing an ethical framework that is capable of 'explicitly dismantling [those] structural inequalities' which Eubanks[54] fears may be inherent in such vast assemblages, is thus unlikely to come from a corporate ethics committee, even one which attempts to include all its key stakeholders, nor from an expert committee which focuses on producing outputs such as checklists and questionnaires for private and public sector organisations.

14.4 TOWARDS A MORE HOLISTIC AI ETHICS FRAMING

The contemporary corporate and governmental focus on developing ethics frameworks for AI is primarily concerned with the shaping of the future direction of the regulation of AI usage, including personalisation. The development of ethics frameworks, whether by the EU, nation states or corporate actors, alongside the creation of expert groups and institutional ethics boards, is a key element in making a case for self-regulation as capable of addressing the diverse range of risks and problems that may arise. As a corollary, it can be argued governmental regulation – whether through legislation, creation of regulatory agencies or other regulatory means – will thereby be rendered unnecessary.

This approach appears flawed in several critical respects. First, it is predisposed to assess the problematics of AI and 'algorithmic assemblages' via a limited CSR-influenced framing of the ethical risks and resort to a restricted range of 'established' regulatory techniques with which organisations are already familiar and can readily incorporate into established business practices. While this may have the advantage that it is easier to persuade organisations to adopt these techniques, it leaves open the question of whether those techniques are actually suited to the AI context and the particular issues it raises, and makes it more difficult to examine and, if appropriate, promote alternative techniques, whether technical or non-technical. This reliance on pre-existing regulatory theory and practices also fails to take advantage of a burgeoning contemporary science-and-technology-studies literature. That literature emphasises the importance of paying attention to the risks and biases inherent in the sociological and normative features of socio-technical networks created, or given new impetus, by AI, and counsels the wisdom of adopting as holistic an approach as possible to any framing of the discussion. It also opens up hitherto underexplored regulatory questions. For example, what is the extent to which a narrow concentration on avoiding specific categories of discrimination or disadvantage obscures the need to tackle less obvious, but potentially equally problematic, social and cultural issues, such as those derived from the unacknowledged leveraging of social and cultural advantages [see Chapter 7 Noelia]?

Second, those advocating ethical frameworks and oversight to prevent harms from AI systems underestimate the difficulty of making them work effectively against organisational constraints. Thus, for example, in contrast to the principles and objectives outlined in frameworks, such as the *Ethics Guidelines*, the real-world practice of ethical review and oversight within organisations designing, developing and deploying AI to date suggests a lack of transparency and limited understanding and practice of accountability.

Third, where national governments, or supranational actors, such as the EU, do not take a leading role in evaluating the ethical risks of AI, this inevitably cedes the regulatory initiative to the very entities who are the likely target of regulation – by leaving key issues, such as the choice of experts, advisors and stakeholders consulted, and the scope of the questions that are deemed necessary to address, in their hands. Those potential regulatory subjects are likely to give (indeed, in the case of corporations and their shareholders, may be effectively mandated to give) prominence to the opinions and positions of their key stakeholders, which may not capture critical issues of wider social importance. Even where policy guidance is sought from expert groups, if those groups are dominated by representatives of corporations producing or utilising AI, and individuals or organisations that have significant existing interactions or financial relationships with such corporations, this may call into question both a group's independence, and its ability or willingness to explore issues or courses of action that do not marry up to conventional CSR discourses. In the EU, the High-Level Expert Group on AI's *Ethics Guidelines* suggests that currently ethical policy guidance is being provided to the EU Commission and the Member States by a relatively small group of experts, by reference to a relatively narrow theoretical and disciplinary base, and on the basis of limited empirical evidence. There is little direct or indirect input from the public or civil society groups that might ground more nuanced understandings of existing and potential structural inequalities, and unexpected social and cultural impacts. Thus, by focusing upon business friendly, individual rights-focused, risk assessment-based regulation, the current ethics discussion cannot take a holistic view of the social impacts of AI and personalisation.

It is encouraging that, as was the case with Corporate Social Responsibility, there has been a growing critical response to the various iterations and aspects of 'ethical AI', from analysis of the 'abstraction traps' of *fair* machine learning methodologies,[55] to dissection of the failings of anti-discrimination law and practices when faced with complex socio-technical systems that require an intersectional-aware response.[56] The social sciences and humanities are already generating a wealth of evidence and analysis that are capable of grounding and supporting more sophisticated political and legal interventions into 'algorithmic assemblages' than have been envisaged to date. If that is the case, it is likely that the *Ethics Guidelines* will simply provide an early marker in the development of an evolving and reflexive field of regulatory practice.

NOTES

1 See, for example, J Council, 'Bosch launches AI training program for developers and managers' *WSJ Pro: Artificial Intelligence* (New York, 25 February 2020) www.wsj.com/articles/bosch-launches-ai-training-program-for-developers-and-managers-11582626602; A Loten, 'Trump wants to double spending on AI, quantum computing', *Wall Street Journal* (New York, 10 February 2020) www.wsj.com/articles/trump-wants-to-double-spending-on-ai-quantum-computing-11581378069.

2 T Scantamburlo, A Charlesworth and N Cristianini, 'Machine decisions and human consequences' in K Yeung and M Lodge (eds.), *Algorithmic Regulation* (Oxford University Press 2019) 49.

3 M Murgia, S Shrikanth, 'How Big Tech is struggling with the ethics of AI' *Financial Times* (London, 29 April 2019) https://www.ft.com/content/a3328ce4-60ef-11e9-b285-3acd5d43599e.

4 V Eubanks, *Automating Inequality* (St Martin's Press 2018).

5 J Angwin and others, 'Machine bias' *ProPublica* (propublica.com, 23 May 2016) https://www.propublica.org/article/machine-bias-risk-assessments-in-criminal-sentencing.

6 C O'Neil, *Weapons of Math Destruction* (Crown 2016).

7 AD Selbst and others, 'Fairness and Abstraction in Sociotechnical Systems' (2019) *FAT* '19: Proceedings of the Conference on Fairness, Accountability, and Transparency, January 2019, ACM* 59.

8 EU Commission, *Communication; AI for Europe* COM(2018) 237 final, Brussels (25 April 2018) 3; EU Commission, *Communication: Building Trust in Human-Centric AI* COM (2019) 168 final, Brussels (8 April 2019).

9 UK Department for Business, Energy & Industrial Strategy, *Industrial Strategy: Artificial Intelligence Sector Deal* (26 April 2018) www.gov.uk/government/publications/artificial-intelligence-sector-deal.

10 J Vincent, 'The problem with AI ethics' *The Verge* (3 April 2019) www.theverge.com/2019/4/3/18293410/ai-artificial-intelligence-ethics-boards-charters-problem-big-tech.

11 J Murawski, 'Need for AI ethicists becomes clearer as companies admit tech's flaws' *WSJ Pro: Artificial Intelligence* (New York, 1 March 2019) www.wsj.com/articles/need-for-ai-ethicists-becomes-clearer-as-companies-admit-techs-flaws-11551436200. In the wider research environment, UK Research and Innovation have, as part of their £100 million investment towards the development of AI research, funded the Centre for Doctoral Training in Interactive Artificial Intelligence at the University of Bristol to 'train the next generation of innovators in human-in-the-loop AI systems, enabling them to responsibly solve societally important problems'. University of Bristol, 'Press Release: University awarded an additional Centre for Doctoral Training in Artificial Intelligence'(21 February 2019).

12 A Ogus, 'Re-thinking self-regulation' (1995) 15(1) *Oxford Journal of Legal Studies* 97; NA Gunningham and J Rees, 'Industry self-regulation: an institutional perspective' (1997) 19(4) *Law & Policy* 363; C Parker, *The Open Corporation: Self Regulation and Democracy* (Cambridge University Press 2002).

13 I Ayres and J Braithwaite, 'Tripartism: gegulatory capture and empowerment' (1991) 16(3) *Law & Social Inquiry* 435; M Priest, 'The privatization of regulation: rive models of self regulation' (1998) 29 *Ottawa Law Review* 233.

14 C Besio and A Pronzini, 'Morality, ethics, and values outside and inside organizations: an example of the discourse on climate change' (2014) 119 *Journal of Business Ethics* 287.

15 D Matten and J Moon, '"Implicit" and "Explicit" CSR: a conceptual framework for a comparative understanding of corporate social responsibility' (2008) 33(2) *Academy of Management Review* 404, 405.

16 Ibid. 410.

17 See, for example, M Hopkins, 'Criticism of the Corporate Social Responsibility Movement' in R Mullerat (ed.), *Corporate Social Responsibility: The Corporate Governance of the Twenty-first Century* (Kluwer 2005); R Mullerat, *International Corporate Social Responsibility* (Kluwer 2009); P Fleming and MT Jones, *The End of Corporate Social Responsibility: Crisis and Critique* (Sage 2012).

18 ML Barnett, 'The business case for corporate social responsibility: a critique and an indirect path forward' (2019) 58(1) *Business & Society* 167.

19 S Shane and D Wakabayashi, '"The business of war": Google employees protest work for the Pentagon' *New York Times* (New York, 4 April 2018).

20 Lee Fang, 'Google continues investments in military and police AI technology through venture capital arm' *The Intercept* (23 July 2019) https://theintercept.com/2019/07/23/google-ai-gradient-ventures/.

21 O Williams, 'How Big Tech funds the debate on AI ethics' *New Statesman* (6 June 2019) www.newstatesman.com/science-tech/technology/2019/06/how-big-tech-funds-debate-ai-ethics.

22 High-Level Expert Group on AI, *Ethics Guidelines for AI, European Commission* (8 April 2019) https://ec.europa.eu/futurium/en/ai-alliance-consultation/guidelines.

23 A Hern, 'Whatever happened to the DeepMind AI ethics board Google promised?' *The Guardian* (London, 26 January 2017) www.theguardian.com/technology/2017/jan/26/google-deepmind-ai-ethics-board. Even where conflicts of interest are identified, it is clear that if a company decides the composition and membership of its ethics board, it will be in a position to indirectly influence the nature of discussions that take place, particularly if members have been, or could be, beneficiaries of research funding or consultancies; or might simply benefit from the association of their name (or that of their research institution) with an internationally recognised company. In essence, as one commentator has put it, in those circumstances, companies effectively get to 'choose their own critics.' (Poulsen quoted in Vincent (n 10)).

24 IL Janis, 'Groupthink' in R P Vecchio (ed.), *Leadership: Understanding the Dynamics of Power and Influence in Organizations* (2nd ed., University of Notre Dame Press 2007) 157.

25 CJ Nemeth and JA Goncalo, 'Influence and persuasion in small groups' in TC Brock and MC Green (eds.), *Persuasion: Psychological Insights and Perspectives* (Sage 2005) 171; E Pariser, *The Filter Bubble* (Penguin Press 2011).

26 *Ethics Guidelines* (n 22) 4 and 39. Representatives outside these categories are few and far between.

27 Ibid. 23.

28 Ibid. 26–31. The stakeholder participation element of the Assessment List itself (30) is brief and skewed towards workers and their representatives, possibly because one of the few participants who was not a corporate representative, AI researcher or academic, was a Trade Unions representative.

29 Pariser (n 25).

30 S Helin and J Sandström, 'Resisting a corporate code of ethics and the reinforcement of management control' (2010) 31(5) *Organization Studies* 583.

31 For example, KD Haggerty, 'Ethics creep: governing social science research in the name of ethics' (2004) 27(4) *Qualitative Sociology* 391; M Hammersley, 'Creeping ethical regulation and the strangling of research' (2010) 15(4) *Sociological Research Online* 16; J Taylor and M Patterson, 'Autonomy and compliance: how qualitative sociologists respond to institutional ethical oversight' (2010) 33(2) *Qualitative Sociology* 161.

32 L Stark, 'Victims in our own minds? IRBs in myth and practice' (2007) 41(4) *Law and Society Review* 777; R Eynon, R Schroeder and J Fry,'New techniques in online research: challenges for research ethics' (2009) 4(2) *Twenty-First Century Society* 187; S Clegg, 'The possibilities of sustaining critical intellectual work under regimes of evidence, audit, and ethical-governance' (2010) 26(3) *Journal of Curriculum Theorizing* 21; D Erdos, 'Systematically handicapped? Social research in the data protection framework' (2011) 20 (2) *Information and Communications Technology Law* 83.

33 A Charlesworth, 'Data protection, freedom of information and ethical review committees: policies, practicalities and dilemmas' (2012) 15(1) *Information, Communication & Society* 85.

34 For example, NHS Ethics Review Committees. Much of this oversight requires researchers to complete ethics review documentation for scrutiny, and often a dialogue between ethic review committees and researchers to ensure that institutional and discipline requirements have been duly observed and documented. If ethical clearance is granted, this documentation should, in theory, in combination with researcher's records of ongoing compliance with ethical requirements post-clearance, provide the basis for audit of ethical practice by the researcher at any point during or after their research.

35 For example, *AoIR Ethical Decision-Making and Internet Research: Recommendations from the AoIR Ethics Working Committee* (Version 2.0) (2012) http://aoir.org/reports/ethics2 .pdf; *SLSA Statement of Principles of Ethical Research Practice* (2009) www.slsa.ac.uk/ index.php/ethics-statement.

36 See, for example, *Research Ethics* (Sage); *Journal of Empirical Research on Human Research Ethics* (Sage); *IRB: Ethics & Human Research* (Hastings); *Accountability in Research* (Taylor & Francis).

37 *Ethics Guidelines* (n 22) 21f.

38 To provide 'oversight and advice' and developing interaction with industry and civil society groups.

39 *Ethics Guidelines* (n 22) 22f.

40 D Rowland, U Kohl and A Charlesworth, *Information Technology Law* (4th ed., Routledge 2011) Ch 12 on defective software.

41 *Ethics Guidelines* (n 22) 19.

42 Ibid. 31: Did you assess the broader societal impact of the AI system's use beyond the individual (end-)user, such as potentially indirectly affected stakeholders?

43 AL Hoffmann, 'Where fairness fails: data, algorithms, and the limits of antidiscrimination discourse' (2019) 22(7) *Information, Communication & Society* 900.

44 Ibid. 903f.

45 Ibid. 905ff.

46 Eubanks (n 4) 5.

47 Hoffman (n 43) 907ff.

48 In the data privacy context, this regulatory approach finds public sector medical data provided to the private sector without public consultation (C Stokel-Walker, 'Why Google consuming DeepMind Health is scaring privacy experts' *Wired* (14 November 2018) www .wired.co.uk/article/google-deepmind-nhs-health-data; A Hern, 'Google 'betrays patient trust' with DeepMind Health move' *The Guardian* (London, 14 November 2018) www .theguardian.com/technology/2017/jan/26/google-deepmind-ai-ethics-board); six million CCTV cameras on the UK's streets (S Carlo, 'Britain has more surveillance cameras per person than any country except China. That's a massive risk to our free society' *Time* (London, 17 May 2019) https://time.com/5590343/uk-facial-recognition-cameras-china/); and bulk interception of communications 'that intrudes upon every UK citizen's life in a way that would even a decade ago have been inconceivable' (P Bernal, 'How the UK passed the most invasive surveillance law in democratic history' *The Conversation* (the-conversation.com, 23Nov 2016) https://theconversation.com/how-the-uk-passed-the-most-invasive-surveillance-law-in-democratic-history-69247).

49 Selbst (n 7); Hoffman (n 43); H Rosenbaum, P Fichman 'Algorithmic accountability and digital justice: A critical assessment of technical and sociotechnical approaches' (2019) 56 (1) *ASIS&T* 237.

50 M Ananny, 'Toward an ethics of algorithms: convening, observation, probability, and timeliness' (2016) 41(1) *Science, Technology, & Human Values* 93, 97.

51 Ibid. 98.

52 I Lowrie, 'Algorithms and automation: an introduction' (2018) 33(3) *Cultural Anthropology* 349, 351.

53 Ibid.

54 Eubanks (n 4) 5.

55 Selbst (n 7).

56 Hoffman (n 43).

15

Scepticism about Big Data's Predictive Power about Human Behaviour: Making a Case for Theory and Simplicity

Konstantinos V. Katsikopoulos

15.1 INTRODUCTION

Concerns about an all-too-powerful computer elite are not new, as C. P. Snow wrote five decades ago:

> We have had two groups of persons in secret government: the circle of scientists who are knowledgeable about what is happening and which decisions must be made, and the larger circle of administrators and politicians to whom the scientists' findings have to be translated. My worry is that the introduction of the computer is going to lead to a smaller circle still ... We shall have a tiny circle of computer boys, a larger circle of scientists who are not familiar with the decision rules and are not versed in the new computer art, and then, again, the large circle of politicians and administrators...I suspect that the chap standing next to the machine, who really knows how it makes decisions, and who has the machine under his command, is going to be in an excessively influential position.[1]

Like Snow, I too am concerned about the hidden agendas that might be advanced by opaque algorithms, their appalling uses such as predatory lending and intrusive advertising for activities such as gambling, the concentration of power in the hands of a few computer experts, and so on. My chapter does not explore these issues directly but critically investigates a basic assumption that underlies them. This assumption is that *big-data* algorithms *do* in fact have the power to predict individual and group human behaviour, which then forms the basis for all sorts of agendas related to personalisation. The claim of big-data-algorithm enthusiasts – producers, champions, consumers – upon which such algorithms are being advocated, accepted, and implemented is that big-data algorithms are able to deliver insightful and accurate predictions about human behaviour. This paper challenges this claim.

My investigation of this claim has two parts: first, I perform a conceptual analysis and argue that big-data analytics is by design a-theoretical and does not provide process-based explanations of human behaviour, making it unfit to support deliberation, which is transparent to both legal experts and non-experts. Second, I review empirical evidence from dozens of data sets, which suggests that the predictive *accuracy* of mathematically sophisticated algorithms is not consistently higher than that of simple rules (rules that tap on available domain knowledge or observed human decision-making); rather, big-data algorithms are less accurate across a range of problems, including predicting election results and criminal profiling.

It should be emphasized that the arguments refer to understanding and predicting human behaviour and the use of predictive analytics in legal and regulatory contexts. Other applications of big-data analytics, such as predicting weather or biological processes, are not considered here. Finally, I synthesize the above points in order to conclude that *simple, process-based, domain-grounded* theories of human behaviour should be put forth as benchmarks, which big-data algorithms, if they are to be considered as tools for personalization, should *match* in terms of transparency and accuracy.

15.2 BIG-DATA ANALYTICS: LACK OF THEORY, EXPLANATIONS, AND TRANSPARENCY

15.2.1 *Theory and Explanations*

One of the foundational pieces of big-data analytics is Chris Anderson's short piece in *Wired* magazine in 2008, entitled 'The end of theory: the data deluge makes the scientific method obsolete'.[2] This title is striking. One might say that it is merely making a provocative point in order to attract attention, and is not to be taken literally. That could be. But let us look closer at what Anderson actually says:

> Petabytes allow us to say: 'Correlation is enough'...We can analyze the data without hypotheses about what it might show. We can throw the numbers into the biggest computing clusters the world has ever seen and let statistical algorithms find patterns where science cannot.

and

> This is a world where massive amounts of data and applied mathematics replace every other tool that might be brought to bear. Out with every theory of human behaviour, from linguistics to sociology. Forget taxonomy, ontology, and psychology. Who knows why people do what they do? The point is they do it, and we can track and measure it with unprecedented fidelity. With enough data, the numbers speak for themselves.[3]

So, the theory of big data is that human behaviour in any domain can be studied *without* a theory of this domain. Content and context supposedly do not matter. Rather, measurement and statistics suffice to reveal correlations, which in turn suffice to make accurate predictions. What about practice? Do big-data practitioners really try to predict what people will do without a behavioural theory?

It seems so. Consider, for example, Nate Silver's celebrated FiveThirtyEight website, and specifically how the result of the 2016 US presidential election was predicted:[4] the probability of winning was 71.4% for Hillary Clinton and 28.6% for Donald Trump. This prediction was broken down by state, the probabilities of interesting scenarios, such as a landslide for each candidate, were given, and so on. Silver's website explains 'How this forecast works': the method producing the predictions used the results of polls in 2016, taking into account the accuracy of election polls all the way back to 1972, and also demographic and economic data. Numbers were adjusted, weighted, and averaged in many different statistical ways, including by using linear regressions.

Based on Silver's documentation, there appears to be no political, economic, sociological, or psychological theory driving these calculations. By 'theory' I mean a construction that goes beyond unsurprising features such as including voter income as an independent variable in a regression. It is often argued that a statistical model, such as a linear regression, is equivalent to theorizing about the ways in which a voter's politics, economics, and psychology effect and interact in deciding whom to vote for. Of course, at some formal level, statistics can be seen as descriptions of behaviour. But describing a human behaviour formally is not the same as providing an explanation for how it came about, what goal it is achieving, and under which conditions it might change. This point has been made in the behavioural model-ling literature,[5] and has also been made in legal research. In the words of Vincent Chiao:

Machine-learning techniques, neural networks in particular, raise a distinct set of concerns. Machine learning is 'a-theoretical', in that a machine-learning algorithm 'learns' on its own to draw correlations between outcomes and inputs, including inputs that would not make much sense to a human. In the case of aero-planes, bridges and pharmaceuticals, even if lay persons do not understand how they work, still experts do. . .In contrast, in the case of a machine-learning algorithm, it may be the case that no one really understands the basis upon which it is drawing its correlations. Those correlations might be quite reliable, but it might be that no one is in a position to articulate quite why they are reliable and this surely does raise distinctive concerns about intelligibility.[6]

Chiao connects the lack of theory in big-data analytics to its lack of intelligibility. Big-data analytics cannot help us understand why a person behaved a certain way. It cannot provide explanations of the *process* by which a human behaviour comes about. Since the so-called cognitive revolution,[7] the description of the cognitive processes underlying observed behaviours is the pronounced goal of behavioural research. A cognitive process specifies the temporal order in which information-processing events occur in the mind, and how these events combine to lead to a decision.

For example, a voter might first consider the point that Trump is a populist. (Other voters might disagree with this judgment.) This might lead the voter to move closer to voting for Clinton, to the point that only one more point against Trump suffices to do so. The voter might then search his memory for further information on the two candidates. If he recalls that Trump has made racist remarks (again, others might disagree with this), then he would decide to vote for Clinton. No such process-based explanations are provided by Silver's algorithms for the voting of a person or a group. In fact, it is hard to see how there could be such explanations, given that there is no underlying theory about the politics, sociology, or psychology of voting. We will see such a theory and the explanation it provides below.

In sum, the workings of big-data algorithms are not transparent. Because of this, and other reasons discussed below, these algorithms are unfit to support deliberation.

15.2.2 *Support for Transparent Deliberation*

In the 2016 case of *State of Wisconsin v. Loomis*,[8] Loomis denied involvement in a drive-by shooting but pleaded guilty to a couple of lesser charges. Having accepted the plea, the Wisconsin court ordered a report to which a risk assessment based on the COMPAS algorithm was attached. Because the algorithm is proprietary and thus protected by trade secret law, as most algorithms are, the defendant was not given the chance to inspect its logic and challenge it in court. The COMPAS algorithm suggested that the defendant had a high risk of recidivism and the court used this, along with other considerations, to deny probation. The defendant appealed on due-process grounds based on his inability to challenge the accuracy and validity of the COMPAS's risk assessment, and on the fact that COMPAS takes gender and race into account in making the assessment. Yet, the Wisconsin Supreme Court rejected these grounds. Leaving aside the legal technicalities of the case,[9] I argue here that the big-data algorithm did not support transparent moral deliberation for experts or non-experts.

The Wisconsin Supreme Court expressed its anxiety about the use of algorithmic tools by requiring a 'written advisement' to accompany Presentencing Investigation Reports, which would alert judges to the inherent limits of these assessments.[10] Justice Bradley, writing for the court and uneasy about the use of COMPAS, cited a report by non-profit organization *ProPublica* about COMPAS that concluded that black defendants in Broward County, Florida, were far more likely than white defendants to be incorrectly judged as more likely to reoffend. Yet, she also noted that Northpointe, which had marketed COMPAS, had disputed ProPublica's analysis.[11] In the end, the Wisconsin Supreme Court held that the report added valuable information, and that in any case Loomis' sentence was based on other factors such as his criminal history and his attempting to flee the police.

This interaction of the legal experts with the COMPAS algorithm was far from useful. To start with, the argumentation and counter-argumentation seem strange. If Loomis would have received the same sentence without the COMPAS report, then the information added by the report is beginning to appear to be less valuable than claimed or at least less impactful. If so, why was it included? Perhaps there is some unique insight that was provided by the algorithm? Doubtful. Nobody in the trial, neither the court nor the defendant, had the opportunity to benefit from knowing the logic of the algorithm since nobody – except Northpointe, the marketer – had the chance to interact with the algorithm or having it explained to them. It is difficult enough to interact with complex algorithms, but in this case, where the algorithm was also secret, such interaction was made entirely impossible. In sum, it is difficult to see how algorithms such as COMPAS can support expert deliberation.

Consider now how non-experts interact with algorithms. Lipton focuses on the transparency of algorithms to decision makers and other stakeholders, including journalists and politicians, as well as the public.[12] Essentially he starts by identifying transparency with understanding. Then he puts forth simulatability as a main form of understanding. According to Lipton, simulatability means that a user can contemplate and interpret the whole algorithm at once. Lipton explicitly writes that 'an interpretable model *is* a simple model'[13] and suggests measuring simplicity by the number of an algorithm's parameters or its mathematical flexibility. An overly mathematically flexible algorithm, where multiple parameters interact, is too complex for people to interrogate it, understand it, and deliberate based on it. Today's neural networks, such as deep learning algorithms, are extremely flexible mathematically. This is how they manage to be successful in a wide range of engineering problems such as processing images, video, speech, and audio, which could in fact support personalization.[14] Yet, this success comes at the cost of loss of simplicity, lack of transparency, and ultimately the absence of support for deliberation.

15.3 BIG-DATA ALGORITHMS AND SIMPLE RULES: ACCURACY AND TRANSPARENCY

Asking how accurate a single algorithm is does not always make sense. Ninety % accuracy seems high, but not if many other algorithms have achieved 99% Likewise, 60% accuracy might seem low, but not if no other algorithm has exceeded 55%. Accuracy is relative, and so commonly in machine learning the accuracy of algorithms is judged by way of comparing a number of algorithms. Here, I compare mathematically sophisticated algorithms used in big-data analytics to another family of algorithms, called *simple rules*. Simple rules represent a diametrically opposing philosophy to big data for understanding and predicting human behaviour.

Simple rules have been discussed across disciplines such as economics,[15] psychology,[16] business strategy,[17] and also management science – which forms a core of analytics.[18] In law, Epstein has advocated simple rules,[19] and the concept of the 'reasonable man' has a long-established tradition in common law methodology as a leveller and driver towards simplicity.[20]

Simple rules can be defined as algorithms that process a *few pieces* of information and do so in *computationally simple* ways.[21] This is not a mathematical definition. How many pieces are 'few' and which computations are 'simple'? Case studies below from politics and law will help to contextualize these terms. The key point is that, in simple rules, the information used is available through knowledge that people – laypeople or experts – often possess or can access on the Internet; and the computations performed are within human reach, such as simply adding numbers or comparing them. For instance, recall the Clinton voter who decided based on just two binary pieces of information, Trump's alleged populism and racism.

The comparison between simple and more complex algorithms can be judged in two ways. Accuracy on predicting future outcomes is measurable quantitatively (in certain circumstances) and thus we will know which algorithm predicts better. Comparing the transparency of the algorithms is a more subjective exercise. Given the above discussion on the need for transparency of big-data-algorithms, it seems clear that simple rules are by design inherently more transparent. While I will not focus on transparency, I will comment on its benefits, such as providing theory and explanations of human behaviour, and thus also support for deliberating on it. I will outline[22] three cases: one predicting the 2016 US presidential election, and two on aspects of criminal profiling.

15.3.1 *Predicting US Elections*

As we saw, Nate Silver's big-data algorithms predicted a 71.4% chance of Clinton winning the 2016 election. Other polls and prediction markets made the same prediction about who had the clearly better chance of winning.

Historian Allan Lichtman, on the other hand, predicted that Trump would win. Lichtman relied on a simple rule he developed based on his domain knowledge, blending theories of politics, economics, sociology, and psychology.[23] Lichtman's rule, consisting of thirteen keys to the White House, does not deliver precise probabilities of winning, but simply a prediction of who will win. It is based on a historical analysis of the public's behaviour in every US presidential election from 1860 to 1980. The keys were fixed, once and for all, before the 1984 election. Each key is an issue that matters to US voters, that is a 'piece of information' in the cognitive-psychology jargon used above, or a 'feature' in machine-learning terminology. Lichtman's thirteen keys, each stated so that it is either true or false, are:

> *Key 1: Incumbent-party mandate.* Incumbent party holds more seats in the House of Representatives after this midterm election than the previous one.
> *Key 2: Nomination contest.* No serious contest for incumbent-party nomination.
> *Key 3: Incumbency.* Incumbent-party candidate is the sitting president.

Key 4: *Third party.* No significant third-party or independent campaign.

Key 5: *Short-term economy.* Economy not in recession during campaign.

Key 6: *Long-term economy.* Real annual per capita economic growth during the term equals or exceeds mean growth during two previous terms.

Key 7: *Policy change.* Incumbent administration effects major changes in national policy.

Key 8: *Social unrest.* No sustained social unrest during the term.

Key 9: *Scandal.* Incumbent administration untainted by major scandal.

Key 10: *Foreign or military failure.* Incumbent administration suffers no major failure in foreign or military affairs.

Key 11: *Foreign or military success.* Incumbent administration achieves a major success in foreign or military affairs.

Key 12: *Incumbent charisma.* Incumbent-party candidate is charismatic or national hero.

Key 13: *Challenger charisma.* The challenging-party candidate is not charismatic or national hero.

Lichtman's keys are combined in the following simple rule: *If six or more keys are false, the challenger will win.*

As an example, consider the 2012 election, where Mitt Romney challenged Barack Obama. Lichtman counted all keys as true except 1, 6, and 12, and correctly predicted that Obama would win. Some of the keys, such as whether the candidate is the sitting president, require no judgment, while others, such as charisma, do. Lichtman deals with this problem by defining standards and criteria. For instance, in Lichtman's definition, charismatic leaders include Franklin D. Roosevelt, Dwight Eisenhower, John F. Kennedy, and Barack Obama in 2008.

In late September of 2016, Lichtman considered the keys to be settled and counted. Keys 1, 3, 4, 7, 11, and 12 turned against Clinton, the incumbent-party candidate. Thus, the prediction was that Trump would win. There is one important caveat. According to Lichtman, the keys predict the majority vote, which Trump did not get. Thus, the thirteen-key rule got the president right, but not the majority vote. No prediction rule is perfect; still Lichtman's rule was closer to the outcome than polls and big-data algorithms; and its predictions have been accurate for all elections since 1984 when it was created.

Now, one might protest that a single case does not prove that big-data algorithms are less accurate than simple rules. Of course, it does not and proving anything like that is not the point anyway. The point is to raise the possibility that simple rules, based on domain theory, can compete with big-data algorithms, which are based on content- and context-free, formal approaches from statistics and computer science. Scholars such as Cartwright and Munro have argued that domain theory is key for better prediction,[24] and could help anticipate whether findings of randomized controlled trials may be generalized to novel situations.

It is important to discuss the possibility of using simple, *small-data* rules for making predictions because most of the public and expert discourse tacitly assumes that the most accurate data-driven algorithms must be big-data algorithms. But accepting this assumption without evidence is tantamount to committing the so-called 'big-data-hubris',[25] where 'small' or 'theory-based' data is considered inherently inferior to statistically processed big data. In contrast, Lazer and his colleagues have shown empirically that using a few variables publicly available on the website of the US *Center for Disease Control* in simple linear models led to more accurate predictions of flu-related doctor-visits than the famous *Google-flu-trends* algorithm.[26] Furthermore, I have shown that using a single variable by itself predicted even better.[27] One might note that the data on this website is also big. But there is no big-data algorithm there: essentially only counting is used to process it, as opposed to sophisticated statistics or machine-learning algorithms.

Before moving on to the next two cases, and to a review of the evidence, let me discuss the transparency of Lichtman's thirteen-key rule. It can be understood and learned by laypeople, and taught to laypeople. The rule also reveals an intriguing political logic that contradicts current campaign wisdom: the keys all refer to the party holding the White House and their candidate, not to the challenger (with the exception of the challenger charisma key; since 1984, this key has been negative only once, when Obama was the challenger in 2008). The keys deal with the economy, foreign policy successes, social unrest, scandals, and policy innovation. If people fared well during the previous term, the incumbent candidate will win, otherwise lose. The thirteen-key rule delivers a simple theory, explanations for its predictions, and creates a platform for discussion.

The two cases outlined next touch on two aspects of criminal profiling. The first refers to identifying the residential location of a serial offender and the second refers to deciding whether to grant bail to a suspected criminal before their trial. The former case focuses on which algorithm is more accurate, and is thus a prescriptive study of decision-making. The latter case focuses on how courts of judges actually make their decisions, and so it is a descriptive study. The law needs insight and accuracy in both prescribing and describing human behaviour. Which algorithms can do so?

15.3.2 *Criminal Profiling*

The claim that crime-related predictions are more accurate when made by a computer algorithm than the human mind is not unique to the big-data era. 'Actuarial techniques' have been used for decades,[28] and were eventually made available as software packages similar to COMPAS. Consider *geographical profiling*, where the geographical locations of a number of crimes (assuming that those were performed by the same offender) may be used to help identify the offender's residence. Such profiling has, for some time now, been entrusted to algorithms of which *CrimeStat*, a package provided by Levine and Associates (2000), is an example. It outputs the relative probabilities of any location in a pre-specified 2D-grid being the residence of the serial offender. The algorithm has been improved and calibrated with real-world data, even if such an amount of data might not qualify as big data by today's standards. Still, the description of CrimeStat by Snook, Taylor, and Bennell shows a fairly complex model, that they put to the test to see if it would outperform the judgment of people.[29]

Unlike the US election study, they probed the performance of laypeople. They recruited 215 prospective undergraduate university students and their guardians, and introduced them to a simple-rules approach to geographical profiling. For example, some participants were provided with the *circle heuristic*, which states:

The majority of offenders' homes can be located within a circle with its diameter defined by the distance between the offender's two furthermost crimes.

Unlike the thirteen-key rule, the circle heuristic does not lead to a unique answer, but is more of a guide to choosing the offender's residence.

The participants in the study had to solve ten geographical profiling problems (from real serial murder cases), represented on 2D maps produced by CrimeStat, based on the location of three murders. One group of participants had to work on their own unaided, another group was provided with the circle heuristic, and a third group was provided with another heuristic. Whereas the unaided group performed worse than the other two groups and CrimeStat, there was no statistically significant difference between the two groups supported with simple rules and CrimeStat's actuarial technique. In fact, the laypeople provided with the circle heuristic performed slightly better than the actuarial technique, as measured by the mean map distance between the predicted offender's residence and his or her actual residence.

Let us now assume that a suspected serial offender has been identified. While awaiting trial in jail, s/he may apply to be granted bail (unconditional release). In the UK, such decisions are made by volunteers called magistrates. How should they decide whether to grant bail or oppose it? The Bail Act 1976 and its subsequent revisions say that magistrates should pay regard to the nature and seriousness of the offence, to the character, community ties, and bail record of the defendant, as well as to the strength of the prosecution case, the likely sentence if convicted, and any other factor that appears to be relevant. The legal ideal of due process is based on a thorough analysis of the information available for each case. However, the law is mute on how exactly magistrates should combine the various pieces of information. What do magistrates then do?

Even though its status is weakening,[30] the ideal of a 'fully rational' standard economic actor is still a dominant description of human behaviour.[31] Whilst it has not been claimed that the human brain implements the most sophisticated of big-data algorithms (e.g., support vector machines or random forests), other such algorithms, such as linear regression – a statistical model that uses addition and multiplication in order to make predictions – are routinely proposed. Mandheep

Dhami tested empirically whether magistrate bail-or-jail decision-making is better described by a linear model or a simple rule.[32]

Dhami observed several hundred hearings in two London courts. The pieces of information available to the magistrates included the defendants' age, race, gender, strength of community ties, seriousness of offence, kind of offence, number of offences, relation to the victim, plea (guilty, not guilty, no plea), previous convictions, bail record, the strength of the prosecution case, maximum penalty if convicted, circumstances of adjournment, length of adjournment, number of previous adjournments, prosecution request, defence request, previous court bail decisions, and police bail decision. The magistrates also saw whether the defendant was present at the bail hearing, whether or not legally represented, and by whom.

Dhami evaluated algorithm accuracy, first, by calibrating each algorithm on a training set, which was half of the whole data set, and then by testing it in the other half. (This process was repeated multiple times to average out random variation.) Across the two courts, the family of algorithms which weighted and added 25 features achieved 79% predictive accuracy, whereas the family of simple rules that only used 3 features predicted 89% of the unseen data points. An example of a particular simple rule is the following:

Always opposcoure bail unless (1) prosecution granted bailed and (2) neither police nor previous courts imposed conditions on bail.

In other words, there is a huge gap between descriptions of how magistrates are deciding and the prescribed process that magistrates ought to follow.[33] To understand this gap, one needs to think about the magistrates' situation. Their task is to do justice to each defendant and the public, by balancing the likelihood of the two possible errors: a *miss* occurs when a suspect is released on bail and subsequently commits another crime, threatens a witness, or does not come to court. A *false alarm* occurs when a suspect is imprisoned who would not have committed any of these offences. Yet, magistrates do not have the information to balance the two errors. They do not know the frequency of these errors, nor does the law give them any instructions. English legal institutions do not collect statistics about the error rates in magistrates' decisions. Even if statistics were kept about how often misses occur, it would be impossible to do the same for false alarms; no method can determine whether jailed individuals would have committed a crime, had they been bailed. We cannot know whether following the prescribed process is more accurate than the actual decision process of magistrates.

In this situation, magistrates apparently focus on a task they are more capable of solving: to protect themselves. This is called *defensive decision making*.[34] Magistrates can be proven wrong only if a suspect who was released fails to appear in court or commits an offence or crime while on bail. To protect themselves against potential accusations by the media or the victims, they follow the defensive logic embodied in the simple rule above.

15.3.3 *Meta Studies of Performance of Complex Models and Simple Rules*

Were the above cases cherry picked? This final part compares the accuracy of mathematically sophisticated algorithms and simple rules across multiple data sets. Here I discuss four studies that used multiple data sets,[35] and even though the data sets are not 'big' in the usual sense, some of the algorithms tested are routinely used in big-data analytics.

First, in 1999 Czerlinski, Gigerenzer, and Goldstein used computer simulation to compare the performance of ordinary linear regression and simple rules, similar to those of Lichtman and Dhami, on twenty data sets from the fields of biology, economics, environmental science, demography, health, psychology, and transportation.[36] The authors considered choices between two options. Each choice had an objectively accurate answer; for example, in which one of two universities did professors have a higher average salary. On each data set, the algorithms were calibrated (i.e., their parameters were estimated) based on the information in half of the data set. On the average, the accuracy of regression and the best (most accurate) simple rule was equal, 76%. This finding was replicated in an experiment in 2010 that also found that the simple rules outperformed complex models such as linear regression and naïve Bayes by 5% or more, when there was little available data.[37]

Second, Martignon compared the predictive accuracy of two kinds of simple rules, similar to Dhami's rule, with two more complex models, logistic regression and Breiman's trees,[38] which are widely used in statistics and machine learning. The authors used thirty data sets from the UC Irvine Machine Learning Repository, where the objective was to assign objects, such as a medical patient, to categories, such as emergency care or a regular nursing bed.[39] The best complex model outperformed the best simple rule by 82% versus 78% when a lot of data was available to calibrate, that is improve, the models, but the difference shrunk to 76% vs. 75% when little data was available.

Third, Şimşek employed Czerlinski's twenty datasets[40] and added thirty-one more.[41] She used a state-of-the-art variant of regression (elastic net regularization). This regularized regression outperformed the best simple rule by 79% to 78%.

Fourth, in 2017 Lichtenberg and Şimşek used a similar database to Şimşek's earlier review, with sixty data sets, and focused on the performance of simple rules similar to that of Lichtman, comparing them with more complex models, such as regularized regressions and random forests.[42] The best complex model had an average error of 0.71, whereas the best simple rule scored 0.79. The results varied considerably across data sets and the authors concluded that while no single simple rule performed well across all data sets, in each data set there was a simple rule that performed well.

15.4 SIMPLE RULES AS BENCHMARK ALGORITHMS
FOR PERSONALISATION

This collection explores how algorithms change our society by leveraging big data to 'know' the individual. I myself hope that personalization will involve increasingly more evidence-based decision-making, also in the form of data-driven algorithms. Law and policy makers could then employ the accuracy and insight algorithms provide on human behaviour in order to improve the function of law, markets, and politics. Yet, together with many others, I worry about the way in which such developments are pursued today. These worries go beyond ethical concerns which have led some to ask data scientists to take an Hippocratic oath;[43] they refer to the actual capacity of big data to deliver insightful and accurate results.

I attempted to show that what is marketed as obviously superior big-data analytics and algorithms suffers from glaring drawbacks: it is a-theoretical, which limits (*i*) its support for processes we should hold dear, such as providing explanations of behaviour that we can understand and deliberate on, and (*ii*) its accuracy when trying to predict the behaviour of human individuals and groups. Data is necessary for algorithms but it has been shown again and again that more of it, and more complex ways of processing it, is not *necessarily* better (of course, sometimes it is, and we need a theory of when it is and when it is not).[44] Lazer's critique of big-data hubris in the case of Google-flu-trends,[45] as well as the accuracy of Lichtman's simple political theory of US elections,[46] should make us pause and ask: is there sufficient evidence that our accumulated, understandable, and reasonably accurate theories of human behaviour have now been matched by 'smart' machine-learning algorithms?! There might well be evidence for this in some cases, and there could soon be even more. What we should not do is to rush to a judgment without looking at the existing evidence. *That* would not be smart of us.

NOTES

1 CP Snow, 'Management and the computer of the future' in M Greenberger (ed.), *Computers and the World of the Future* (MIT Press 1962) 10–11.
2 Chris Anderson, 'The end of theory: the data deluge makes the scientific method obsolete' (*Wired*, 23 June 2008) www.wired.com/2008/06/pb-theory/.
3 Ibid.
4 FiveThirtyEight, '2016 Election Forecast' (*FiveThirtyEight*, last update 8 November 2016) https://projects.fivethirtyeight.com/2016-election-forecast/.
5 Konstantinos V Katsikopoulos, 'How to model it? Review of cognitive modeling (J. R. Busemeyer and A. Diederich)' (2011) 55(2) *Journal of Mathematical Psychology* 198.
6 Vincent Chiao, 'Fairness, accountability and transparency: notes on algorithmic decision-making in criminal justice' (2019) 15(2) *International Journal of Law in Context* 126, 136.
7 Ulric Neisser, *Cognitive Psychology* (Meredith Publishing Company 1967).

8 *Loomis v Wisconsin* 881 NW 2d 749 (Wis 2016).

9 For a discussion of the legal points, see Roger Brownsword and Alon Harel, 'Law, liberty and technology: criminal justice in the context of smart machines' (2019) 15(2) *International Journal of Law in Context* 107.

10 Editor, 'Wisconsin Supreme Court requires warning before use of algorithmic risk assessment in sentencing – *State v. Loomis*, 881 N.W.2d 749 (Wis 2016)' (2017) 130 *Harvard Law Review* 1530.

11 On this argument, see Alexander Holsinger and others, 'A rejoinder to Dressel and Farid: new study finds computer algorithm is more accurate than humans at predicting arrest and as good as a group of 20 lay experts' (2018) 82(2) *Federal Probation* 50.

12 Zachary C Lipton, 'The mythos of model interpretability' (ICML Workshop on Human Interpretability in Machine Learning, New York, June 2016).

13 Ibid. 4, emphasis added.

14 Yan LeCun, Yoshua Bengio and Geoffrey Hinton, 'Deep learning' (2015) 521(7553) *Nature* 436.

15 Ariel S Rubinstein, *Modeling Bounded Rationality* (MIT Press 1998).

16 Gerd Gigerenzer, Peter M Todd and the ABC research group (eds.), *Simple Heuristics that Make Us Smart* (Oxford University Press 1999).

17 Donald N Sull and Kathleen M Eisenhardt, *Simple Rules: How to Thrive in a Complex World* (Houghton Mifflin Harcourt 2015).

18 Robin M Hogarth and Natalia Karelaia, 'Simple Models for Multiattribute Choice with Many Alternatives: When It Does and Does Not Pay to Face Tradeoffs with Binary Attributes' (2005) 51(12) *Management Science* 1733; Konstantinos V Katsikopoulos, Ian N Durbach and Theodor J Stewart, 'When should we use simple decision models? a synthesis of various research strands' (2018) 81 *Omega The International Journal of Management Science* 17.

19 Richard A Epstein, *Simple Rules for a Complex World* (Harvard University Press 2009).

20 John Gardner, 'The many faces of the reasonable person' (2015) 131 *Law Quarterly Review* 563.

21 Özgür Şimşek, 'Linear decision rule as aspiration for simple decision heuristics' (2014) Twenty-six *Advances in Neural Information Processing Systems* 2904.

22 For more details, see Konstantinos V Katsikopoulos and others, "Classification in the Wild: The Science and Art of Transparent Decision Making" and date of publication to 2020.

23 Allan J Lichtman, *Predicting the Next President: The Keys to the White House 2016* (Rowman and Littlefield 2016).

24 Nancy Cartwright and Eileen Munro, 'The limitations of randomized controlled trials in predicting effectiveness' (2010) 16(2) *Journal of Evaluation in Clinical Practice* 260.

25 David Lazer and others, 'The parable of Google Flu: traps in Big Data analysis' (2014) 343 (6176) *Science* 1203, 1203.

26 Ibid.

27 Katsikopoulos and others (n 22).

28 Robyn M Dawes, David Faust and Paul E Meehl, 'Clinical versus actuarial judgment' (1989) 243 *Science* 1668.

29 Brent Snook, Paul J Taylor and Craig Bennell, 'Geographic profiling: the fast, frugal, and accurate way' (2004) 18(1) *Applied Cognitive Psychology* 105.

30 Daniel Kahneman, Paul Slovic and Amos Tversky (eds.), *Judgment Under Uncertainty: Heuristics and Biases* (Cambridge University Press 1982); Gigerenzer, Todd and the ABC Research Group (n 16).

31 See Konstantinos V Katsikopoulos, 'Bounded rationality: the two cultures' (2014) 21(4) *Journal of Economic Methodology* 361, and references therein.

32 Mandheep K Dhami, 'Psychological models of professional decision making' (2003) 14(2) *Psychological Science* 175.

33 Ibid.

34 Gerd Gigerenzer, *Gut Feelings: The Intelligence of the Unconscious* (Penguin 2007).

35 For a more comprehensive review, see Konstantinos V Katsikopoulos, Ian N Durbach and Theodor J Stewart, 'When should we use simple decision models? A synthesis of various research strands' (2018) 81 *Omega The International Journal of Management Science* 17.

36 Jean Czerlinski, Gerd Gigerenzer and Daniel Goldstein, 'How good are simple heuristics?' in Gigerenzer, Todd and the ABC Research Group (n 16).

37 Konstantinos V Katsikopoulos, Lael J Schooler and Ralph Hertwig, 'The robust beauty of ordinary information' (2010) 117(4) *Psychological Review* 1259.

38 Leo Breiman and others, *Classification and Regression Trees* (Routledge 1984).

39 Laura Martignon, Konstantinos V Katsikopoulos and Jan K Woike, 'Categorization with limited resources: a family of simple heuristics' (2008) 52(6) *Journal of Mathematical Psychology* 352.

40 Czerlinski, Gigerenzer and Goldstein (n 37).

41 Şimşek (n 21).

42 Lichtenberg, J., and Şimşek, Ö. (2017). Simple regression models. *Proceedings of the NIPS 2016 Workshop on Imperfect Decision Makers*. PMLR, 58, 13–25.

43 See for example Virginia Eubanks, 'A hippocratic oath for data science' (*virginia-eubanks. com*, 21 February 2018) https://virginia-eubanks.com/2018/02/21/a-hippocratic-oath-for-data-science/.

44 For more on this, see Katsikopoulos and others (n 22).

45 Lazer and others (n 25).

46 Lichtman (n 23).

16

Building Personalisation: Language and the Law

Alun Gibbs

16.1 INTRODUCTION

During a podcast on the *Joe Rogan Experience*, the maverick tech entrepreneur Elon Musk declared that it is possible that language could be obsolete in five to ten years, but could still be used for sentimental reasons.[1] This startling claim came about as he was discussing his tech business venture called Neuralink – which looks to develop a 'symbiosis' between human brains and artificial intelligence. The prediction about language, as well as the research itself, seems to merge reality with science fiction, but what has been clear is that innovations and the large tech companies that have advanced and developed new forms of computer-based technologies have transformed our experience of the world and ourselves. It would be a mistake to simply write these kinds of ideas off as some kind of folly of a tech-billionaire. Musk is no philosopher of language, but his work challenges something essential about how we have understood ourselves, particularly in relation to language. Without language what are we and how will we build our social and political institutions?

In the preface to his celebrated book about an interpretive theory of law, the American legal theorist Ronald Dworkin wrote that:

> . . .for we take an interest in law not only because we use it, for our own purposes, selfish or noble, but because law is our most structured and revealing social institution. If we understand the nature of our legal argument better, we know better the kind of people we are.[2]

This quotation neatly conveys part of the central features of constitutionalism and law that I intend to explore in this chapter. Firstly, law reveals something of our collective existence, our personhood, 'the kind of people we are'. Individual rules of law, legal institutions and so forth, taken as a whole, indicate something about the way we live as a collective and the social meanings that form how we make sense of the law. The second feature is the extent to which the law reveals or discloses this sense of the identity of our common political life, the solidarities that are shaped through our arguments about the nature of law.

This chapter sets out that personalisation technologies are fundamentally inimical to the way we have built our legal and political traditions: the building blocks, or the raw materials if you will, that make up the sources of the 'self' for technological personalisation are inimical to what has gone before. The advances in the use of personalisation technologies and the implications for how we understand our political and social lives through law (constitutionalism) hinge on the importance of language. There are risks posed by personalisation technologies to the building of *personality* and forms of *social solidarities*. The unprecedented confluence of the vast quantity of stored personal data and the ability to employ complex algorithms (and AI) to use this data results in the capacity to make accurate and detailed predictions about a whole range of behaviours and target these towards individuals. An expansion of personalisation, or the ability to make a set of predictive tailored choices for the individual in fields as diverse as criminal justice, healthcare, contract and insurance provision raises questions about regulation, ethical limits, and the kind of power that this technology entails. The challenge is not just that our behaviours may be shaped at the micro-level but that our personhood or 'self' can be 'built' by the options placed in front of us. This in turn has profound effects on the way that our social and political relationships form through the law and how we are able to make sense of them.

What we build with personalisation technologies is not part of our shared resource of language but is instead determined by data-sets which are capable of being interpreted by AI algorithms. Instead of shared and participatory forms of political meanings, there are measures or calculated personalised interventions which shape or structure decisions that are made. This may sound like an argument *against* the use of AI-driven personalisation technologies. This is not quite so. The ethical call here is to reflect on our collective intellectual resources and traditions to *think* about the technologies of personalisation and what may be appropriate uses for them, and what in the end they cannot substitute or make obsolete.

16.2 PERSONALISATION TECHNOLOGIES AND AN INITIAL CONSTITUTIONAL RESPONSE

Personalisation becomes possible due to the ability to harvest and store vast amounts of data (personal and other) alongside the capacity to process and direct this data towards tailored individual decisions or choices, increasingly through the use of AI algorithms. Often, we experience this in our daily life in the way that commercial decisions are facilitated through data providing evidence about our past choices or online preferences. So habituated have we become that we may not think twice about the relative sophistication involved in the ability of Amazon to offer interesting purchasing choices based on past searches. In other cases, personalisation serves a more subtle attempt to categorise behaviour as when, for instance, public health measures aim to tackle and reset harmful behaviour through targeted interventions.[3] Risky (from a health point of view) social behaviour such as drinking, smoking or lack of exercise can be measured against average data and then targeted with interventions to manage these risks. Heightened variations of this will see earlier interventions based on the risk of harm given the data about the subject. Tracing and tracking can open the door to governmental mass surveillance of decisions, choices and locations depending on the perceived overall risk. This is precisely the challenge that most countries have faced in respect of the public health emergency caused by the COVID-19 virus.[4] Governments turning to technological solutions can personalise the risk of the spread of a virus by gathering data through a tracing app about the location of those infected and those who as a result may have become infected. The impacts on personal privacy are obvious, and where the contact tracing app has been used most effectively, in countries such as South Korea, there have also emerged problems surrounding the potential for the disclosure of confidential information about individuals to the state and others.[5]

On both the individual and governmental/societal plane there is scope to conceive that personalisation technologies involve a *creativity* which can entail a sense of the liberation of the new. This kind of creativity can see the building of a new 'self' or the re-imagining of new societal structures. A relatively banal example of this could be the fitness apps enabling the use of biometric data to measure and work to encourage (or 'nudge') us towards effective exercise routines and personalised training plans which enable us to achieve fitness goals,[6] building the 'fit-self' and nurturing a desire towards physical transformation in the process. Also, at a societal level, it is possible to turn towards emerging modes of technological governance as the bringing about of the wholly new, a *tabula rasa* of possibilities. For example, this redesigning element has been brought out in David Gurnham's account, in chapter 8, of the use of data-driven technologies in predictive policing and criminal justice whereby traditional approaches to sentencing can be rebuilt based on complex data about the propensity for an individual to reoffend.[7] This kind of automated decision-making not only raises due process questions but would entitle us to ask what kind of data a public authority has about us and is prepared to use for policy ends. In this vein of rebuilding society in the 'post-Covid' world, the governor of the city of New York, Andrew Cuomo, was joined by leading figures from the tech industry to advance a vision of New York's post-Covid reality which would see the comprehensive integration of technology into every aspect of civic life. Naomi Klein draws an ironic comparison to the reconstruction of the New Deal in the aftermath of the great recession of the early 1930s – calling this tech inspired version the 'screen new deal'.[8] As Klein underscores, in the age of post-Covid, where fellow humans are viewed as potential bio-hazards, we may be more easily persuaded to assuage concerns about the widespread adoption of technological platforms simply in order to continue to undertake some semblance of economic, social and political life.

Building new personas or (re)imagining societal possibilities for technologies that are central to personalisation innovations can be creative but also Janus-like, since there is also the *deconstruction* of established practices. The well-documented controversy over the deployment of personal data harvested from Facebook by Cambridge Analytica for the US Presidential election in 2016 in order to mount targeted personalised political advertisements has led to a wider soul searching about the conduct of elections.[9] Misuse of personal data and the effective accountability of powerful tech firms is one aspect of the charge sheet, but equally the sophisticated way that social media platforms are able to use mass quantities of data in order to personalise and target political messages has arguably challenged the way common political dialogue is conducted. In a conventional understanding of election campaigning we tend to rely on an ideal (or myth) about a free marketplace of ideas and opinions. Of course, the reality is often imperfect and less than ideal but the debates, interviews, public adverts are *publicly* visible ways of communicating and exchanging the ideas, policies and opinions that will form the basis of a collective political choice. The kind of political campaigning in the age of personalised and targeted messaging, driven by the ability to use algorithmic analysis of data, can create a new form of politics. Equally, it may be pointed out that these new forms of political communication can only be achieved by distorting and deconstructing the established practice of public political dialogue.

In order to present a snap-shot of the underlying tectonics of change in personhood at an individual and societal level, it is critical to underscore the building blocks of this transformation: the ability to analyse enormous data-sets. Creative and deconstructive projects emerge, offering new possibilities as well as changing old certainties – transforming how we constitute our shared social and political lives. These pose constitutional questions and issues – but of what kind?

With any orthodox reading of constitutional theory, we find the understanding that law acts as a rational control or restraint over politics and power. Stemming from the rational enlightenment ideas of 'checks' and 'balances' within a designed constitutional framework, this tradition of constitutionalism is also rooted in the normative principles governing this regulatory framework of the constitution: rule of law, separation of powers, democratic accountability, individual and minority rights. If we strip back the specific technological complexities, are we facing a perennial issue of regulatory constitutionalism: how to hold to account and constrain power?

Clearly there are deeper complexities at play in this; firstly, what we are often confronted with in the form of new technologies and the impact on democracy stems from the monopoly of private power as well as the state – at least in the so-called 'west'.[10] It is the famous Silicon Valley tech companies that not only possess and can process vast amounts of personal data but these companies that also determine how our political dialogue is structured and what we see or how we see it. The 2016 US Presidential Election and the Brexit referendum exposed how the structures and procedures of the tech companies often fail to keep personal data secure.

Secondly, the challenge of addressing the structural power and wealth of technology is not something that can straightforwardly be resolved by any one state – any action to regulate would require a co-ordinated multinational response to be fully effective.

A paradigmatic effort towards legal regulation both in respect of personal data (privacy) and respect for due process concerns about the use of algorithmic AI in the analysis of data is the European Union's General Data Protection Regulation (GDPR),[11] which builds upon the rights-based approach taken by the EU to regulate the development of data processing. Under the GDPR regime, an individual is provided with rights to know and consent to personal data storage being undertaken by the 'data controller'. This includes, under Article 21, the right to object and also to know the process (usually algorithmic) by which the government or company is making automated decisions based on the personal data – a right of 'explanation'.[12] There is the clear advantage of protecting personal data and rights of privacy within the regulatory and multi-national regime created by the GPDR measure, but there is an equally significant incidental impact generated when individuals are able to challenge the way in which data is processed, revealing the inherent biases in many algorithmic processes for decision-making.[13] In conjunction with so called 'hard' legal regulation, a further strategy to enhance the rights of the data subject and further accountability over the process by which data-sets are used is to develop 'soft-law' industry-agreed standards. Codes of conduct and self-regulation may be ways of ensuring that key actors have an incentive to agree and adhere to common standards. Time-saving and effective at resolving the difficulties of transborder law enforcement, soft law measures can be attractive both to data subjects and to the industry leaders who may wish to avoid more heavy-handed forms of legal intervention.[14]

The regulatory response of the law (whether in its soft or hard law guise) is undoubtedly important to a rights-based approach to personal data and accountability for automated decision-making, but it is part of the argument in this chapter that if the constitutional response is confined to the regulatory paradigm then it is likely that the opportunity to explore wider questions is missed. Constitutionalism must also be able to respond to the way that the advance of personalised data technology creates and deconstructs personhood – both for the individual and society. What are these deeper kinds of constitutional issues? The answer involves the broader tradition of legal and constitutional thinking – the raw ingredients of constitutionalism, if you like, and in reflecting upon them we encounter the importance of language.

16.3 BUILDING CONSTITUTIONALISM: PERSONHOOD, AGENCY AND LANGUAGE

Moving the constitutional response to the challenges posed by personalisation technologies beyond the regulatory paradigm entails understanding the broader traditions underpinning the formation of constitutionalism as part of the broader political way of life. The focus here becomes the interlocking way that language makes possible the personhood and agency that is bound up with social meanings and solidarities. These are the building blocks of the wider understanding of constitutionalism as a political way of life.

Understanding what the law *is* has been interconnected with the question of personhood – or human nature. Tracing its origins back to ancient Greece (what is the essential difference between human things and natural and divine things?) and augmented by the work of the Church, the search for a substantive moral theory of law based on an enquiry into human nature, or natural law, has proven a durable aspect about identifying law.

Following World War II there was renewed interest in these natural law theories as a way of grounding the moral foundations of a universal human rights regime.[15] One such influential example is the idea of agency in the work of James Griffin, which directly draws on notions of personhood and choice as a grounding for a moral theory of human rights. Griffin writes about the notion of agency in the following way:

> What seems to me the best account of human rights is this. It is centred on the notion of agency. We human beings have the capacity to form pictures of what a good life would be and to try to realize these pictures. We value our status as agents especially highly, often more highly than our happiness. Human rights can then be seen as protections of our agency – *what one might call our personhood*.[16]

In a practical sense agency becomes the human capacity to choose a conception of a worthwhile life, and the substantive moral component of human rights enables us to do this.

The link between agency, moral choice and personhood also figures prominently in another influential political theorist, Charles Taylor. For Taylor, agency and personhood are connected to assessments or evaluations we make about our lives and collective social practices – and an irreducible component for agency is language.[17] The focus of Taylor's approach concerns how language enables us to recognise background social meanings and thereby form views about the possibilities of certain modes of living. It is because of language that it is also possible to appreciate that, meaning that events have a two-dimensional quality; they are particular events, but only in relation to a background meaning.[18] For Taylor this is the basis for the distinction that Saussure draws between *langue* and *parole*.[19] *Langue* depends upon the individual acts of speech (*parole*), and so there is an interdependency between the acts of *parole* and the overall language code (*langue*). Acts of *parole* recreate the background of *langue*, for instance, where misspeak and deviant usage catches on and becomes accepted as part of the wider language. Taylor, however, does not want to collapse *langue* completely into *parole* – because *langue* remains 'not an individual matter but the normative practice of a community'.[20] Taylor's principal contention is that there is an *irreducible social element to agency and personhood* (as brought out in language) that simply cannot be decomposed into individual acts.

Taylor develops an extensive argument about the importance of choices for agency.[21] Once again, the connection between the individual and social or collective component of personhood is brought out by language. What is distinctive to human agency is the ability to make assessments and evaluate those desires in order to determine a course of action.[22] Taylor develops this by adding that the ability to make assessments and choices is achieved because language possesses a vocabulary of qualitative contrast, for example 'noble or base', 'integrating or fragmenting', 'courageous or cowardly'.[23] The contrastive language about how we determine our choices also can be said to constitute our experience – such that 'certain modes of experiencing the world are not possible without certain self-descriptions'.[24] Meaning derives from the rich array of qualitative language to share or develop things in common between ourselves, thereby experiencing our agency in the world. Sustaining the richness of language is a social and political endeavour without which we imperil agency and personhood.

To centre our understanding of constitutions away from the regulatory model towards the notion of the form of life of living together – the manner of living of a society – known classically as *politeia* – is equally a task for understanding how language builds shared meanings.[25] Generating authentic meanings of social solidarities is more often a work of public argument, deliberation and exchange – through which claims are contextualised, adjusted and repositioned. Seyla Benhabib has described these as 'democratic iterations' encompassing the notion that the balancing and contestation of political meanings and solidarities take place through time in the political community.[26]

Bonds of solidarity that result from collective engagement with making and remaking (democratic iterations) of the political meanings that sustain the overarching collective project of democratic constitutional self-government can become strong points of 'identification' in acquiring a sense of collective personhood. Such identification can be attributed to the need for *active participatory agency* to reshape collective meanings through discussion, interpretation, deliberating – this in turn suggests the importance of language as the medium for social solidarities and identification. The interconnections between forms of political solidarity, language and identification are the hallmark of Robert Cover's pioneering contribution in the 1980s, finding that the capacity of law to sustain the normative dimensions of collective or common lives (what he terms *nomos*) depends upon the power of narratives. Cover put it famously in the following way:

> No set of legal institutions or prescriptions exists apart from the narratives that locate it and give it meaning. For every constitution there is an epic, for each decalogue a scripture. Once understood in the context of the narratives that give it meaning, law becomes not merely a system of rules to be observed, but a world in which we live.[27]

Language provides an orientation point around which collective meanings can be fashioned in the pursuit of the goals, and points of solidarity which shape how we live and how a sense of personhood and agency is exercised through political participation. There is also something else in the efforts of this diverse range of thinkers that have understood the need to think about constitutions as much broader than the institutional and governance matrix of rules and practices, and that is that this kind of understanding of the constitution as *politeia* is the opposite of *predictive rationality*. The *nomos* described by Robert Cover or the discursive 'iterative' practices of democracy for Seyla Benhabib are above all works of imagination, in the sense that for the interpretation of our political meanings to hold we must understand that these can be remade – that what holds and binds us to the political way of life is its *open-ended* nature. There are no predictive or determinative outcomes for a democratic political way of life – it should hold out the possibility that the *politeia* is remade – and in doing so reminds us of our own political agency.

The key to this section of the chapter is the appreciation that if it is possible to lose an understanding that political community indeed lacks fixed or predictive ends, then this will in turn threaten the capacity for using language and imagination to rethink the possibilities and presuppositions surrounding our collective political life. The point is most vividly conveyed by the Vienna-School philosopher Otto Neurath famously evoking the metaphor for a theory of knowledge and comparing it to a boat being built at sea: 'we are like sailors who on the open sea must reconstruct their ship but are never able to start afresh from the bottom...'.[28] Constitutionalism can be likened to this boat expressing the continuous, open-ended task of negotiation, compromise and disagreement that accompanies the constitution of political life.[29] The risk posed by personalisation technologies is that the raw materials that go into the constitutional project, namely language and agency, are stripped back and deconstructed in such a way that the collective effort to rebuild is made increasingly difficult.

16.4 CONSTITUTIONALISM AS RECOGNISING CATEGORY ERRORS IN OUR UNDERSTANDING OF PERSONALISED TECHNOLOGIES

How can the kind of excavation about constitutional thinking and its 'building blocks' help us to address what might be the wider (in the sense of going beyond the regulatory paradigm) response of constitutionalism? Thinking about what makes the building of personalised technologies possible alongside a comparison with the elements of our constitutional lives creates some room for comparison and enables the contours to be sketched about what might be the wider constitutional issues that are at stake in any response. In doing so it is possible to better understand the kind of tensions that may emerge as we use and expand how to employ personalisation technologies – particularly on societal scale projects such as those we are already seeing being advanced in public health and criminal justice.

In the argument presented here there is an unbridgeable distinction between the building of the 'self' in personalised technologies and how we have traditionally understood personhood and a political way of life, and it hinges around the problem of language. For the project of personalised technology, language is not directly necessary: what is required are points of data and an intelligent means of processing or analysing data points on a sufficiently large scale. As the foregoing section attempts to underline, how we have traditionally understood agency, law and social solidarities have evolved around language and our ability to convey meaning and the nature of collective decisions.

It does not necessarily follow from these observations that we are presented with a sort of radical Hobson's choice between the advantages stemming from the ability to personalise technology and the 'decline' of the building blocks of constitutionalism. After all, it seems futile to assume that the skills, knowledge and advancement pursued by using personalisation technology can be abandoned or disowned. The ethical dimension or choice might be better expressed, therefore, as a heightened awareness about the dangers or risks posed by personalisation technology and the precise ways in which they can be destructive of moral/political agency and social solidarities.

Being aware, in this sense, requires resources disclosed to us through the tradition of thinking about agency and constitutionalism; it is about recognising what we might call the 'category error' in our thinking. This might be about the misapplication of the technologies of personalisation or, in a related sense, the failure to grapple with the underlying presuppositions involved in relating new technologies to our practices of politics and law. For example, personalisation technologies tend to undermine or at least deny *connections* of solidarity in the way I attempted to account for in the preceding section – for these technologies, the connections that are made between individuals are generated by the mode of data analysis in the algorithm. Hence, whatever value might be disclosed through understanding the data connections between people, this cannot be made a substitute for the genuine sources of solidarity that result from the pursuit of political meaning.

To think about this problem in a more direct sense, we can return to perhaps one of the key democratic challenges that have emerged from personalisation technologies, namely, the mass surveillance necessary over personal data. What would be dangerous would be circumstances in which we assumed that mass surveillance of data was a politically meaningful activity and capable of sustaining a political way of life. This would be a category error in our thinking about personalisation technology, but it would also be the seeds of the inability to understand how technologies can corrode constitutional life. A further illustration of this point is to consider the individual through the lens of personalisation technologies – tailored choices or decisions which are personalised are in fact paradoxically the consequence of treating individuals as the *same* – that it is possible to be understood individually by reference to the data set analysed from millions of others. The building blocks of individual choices are the data-points of millions. This kind of 'code'-based understanding of agency is nevertheless of a different category to the creative interplay of choice and background culture developed through language; data-based decisions miss out this kind of hinterland in the way political and moral agency is exercised. This implies that we must recognise the risk posed by the 'category error' of assuming that personalisation technology actually can build moral or political agency or personhood; it does not provide us with *authentic* decisions. Ultimately, it might be remarked that the very notion of *personalisation* is a 'category' error in the description of what is happening to the extent that it implies that technologies can build personhood.

16.5 CONCLUSION

New technologies tend to encourage us to think about what we can gain – the creative possibilities, but it is equally significant to address what can be lost or at least reconstructed. This essay has been about what we cannot afford to lose from the way we conduct our political lives through commitments to constitutionalism. We make sense of our collective lives through exercising agency and building solidarities – this requires language. The risk is that a widespread commitment to building social action and individual personhood through the use of personalisation technologies will fundamentally undermine this. If constitutionalism presents a response beyond the regulatory model, it is to recognise what is critical about the building blocks of our constitutional way of life and how we might put this in jeopardy if these are substituted for something else.

NOTES

1 Tom Embury-Dennis, 'Elon Musk predicts human language will be obsolete in as little as five years: "We could still do it for sentimental reasons"' *The Independent* (London, 9 May 2020) www.independent.co.uk/life-style/gadgets-and-tech/news/elon-musk-joe-rogan-pod cast-language-neuralink-grimes-baby-a9506451.html.

2 Ronald Dworkin, *Law's Empire* (Fontana Press 1986) 11.

3 For a fuller discussion of these observations about the impact of personalisation technologies in the field of public health, see the chapter in this volume by Kieron O'Hara.

4 Evgeny Morozov, 'The tech "solutions" for coronavirus take the surveillance state to the next level' *The Guardian* (London, 15 April 2020) www.theguardian.com/commentisfree/2020/apr/15/tech-coronavirus-surveilance-state-digital-disrupt.

5 Nemo Kim, 'Anti-gay backlash feared in South Korea after coronavirus media reports' *The Guardian* (London, 8 May 2020) https://www.theguardian.com/world/2020/may/08/anti-gay-backlash-feared-in-south-korea-after-coronavirus-media-reports.

6 Chapter 8

7 Chapter 8

8 Naomi Klein, 'Screen New Deal: under cover of mass death, Andrew Cuomo calls in the billionaires to build a high-tech dystopia' (*The Intercept*, 8 May 2020) https://theintercept.com/2020/05/08/andrew-cuomo-eric-schmidt-coronavirus-tech-shock-doctrine/.

9 There is a vast wealth of commentary on the investigations into the impact of data misuse and the targeted personalised campaigns of disinformation and fake news. See the work of the investigative journalist Carole Cadwalladr who broke the story about the Facebook personal data misuse by Cambridge Analytica www.theguardian.com/profile/carolecadwalladr.

10 The situation in a country such as China is different – where there is considerable state control over technologies and their use.

11 EU Regulation 2016/678: https://eur-lex.europa.eu/legal-content/EN/TXT/?uri=CELEX%3A32016R0679

12 Andrew D Selbst and Julia Powles, 'Meaningful information and the right to explanation', 7(4) *International Data Privacy Law* 233 https://doi.org/10.1093/idpl/ipx022.

13 Karen Hao, 'This is how AI bias really happens and why it is so hard to fix' (*MIT Technology Review*, 4 February 2019) https://www.technologyreview.com/2019/02/04/137602/this-is-how-ai-bias-really-happensand-why-its-so-hard-to-fix/.

14 For a discussion of self-regulation in the tech-sector, see Sonya K Katyal, 'Private accountability in the age of artificial intelligence' (2019) 66 *UCLA Law Review* 54 www.uclalawreview.org/private-accountability-age-algorithm/.

15 Rowan Cruft, S Matthew Liao and Massimo Renzo (eds.), *Philosophical Foundations of Human Rights* (Oxford University Press 2015).

16 My emphasis in the final sentence. James Griffin, 'Discrepancies between the best philosophical account of human rights and the international law of human rights' (2001) 101(1) *Proceedings of the Aristotelian Society* 1.

17 Charles Taylor, 'Irreducibly social goods' in *Philosophical Arguments* (Cambridge University Press 1997) 131.

18 Ibid. 134.

19 Ibid. See also Ferdinand de Saussure, *Cours de linguistique générale* (Payot 1985) ch 4.

20 Taylor (n 17) 134.

21 Charles Taylor, *Human Agency and Language: Philosophical Papers Volume 1* (Cambridge University Press 1985); also Charles Taylor, *Sources of the Self: the Making of the Modern Identity* (Cambridge University Press 1989).

22 Ibid. 16.

23 Ibid. 19.

24 Ibid. 37.

25 Graham Maddox, 'A note on the meaning of 'constitution'' (1982) 76(4) *The American Political Science Review* 805.

26 Seyla Benhabib, *The Rights of Others: Aliens Citizens and Residents* (Cambridge University Press 2004).

27 Robert M Cover, 'The Supreme Court 1982 Term Foreword: Nomos and Narrative' (1983) 97 *Harvard Law Review* 4, 5.

28 Otto Neurath, *Anti-Spengler* (Callwey Verlag 1921) as quoted in Simon Blackburn, *Oxford Dictionary of Philosophy* (Oxford University Press 2018).

29 James Tully, *Strange Multiplicity: Constitutionalism in an Age of Diversity* (Cambridge University Press 1995).

17

Conclusion: Balancing Data-Driven Personalisation and Law as Social Systems

Jacob Eisler

17.1 INTRODUCTION

The contributions of this volume have examined the wide-ranging implications of data-driven personalisation. This conclusion will consolidate them through the use of systems theory. Systems theory identifies some entities as capable of sustaining themselves through adaptive reproduction of their own subcomponents and internal organisational schemas. These self-ordering systems are deemed *autopoietic* (Greek for 'self-producing'). While systems theory has its origins in the biological sciences, it has become a prominent means of understanding social systems as well. For social systems, 'the basic element...is communication'.[1] The defining feature of an autopoietic social system is that it autonomously reproduces itself through internal communication.

One way of imagining data-driven personalisation is as one of the subcomponents of society as a whole. Yet even more intriguing is the conceptualisation of data-driven personalisation as its own autopoietic system.[2] The idea is an elegant fit: data-driven personalisation consists of a recursive feedback loop between profiled persons who provide a continuously evolving mass data set, and an algorithm that, working only with such data, provides continuously updated recommendations to these persons. Data-driven personalisation system is thus iteratively self-replicating through communication between its two main subcomponents: profiled persons and a corresponding data set.

Imagining data-driven personalisation as a self-contained autopoietic system as well as part of the broader autopoietic system of society illuminates central themes in the volume and connects its diverse contributions. Firstly, such a conceptualisation unifies the inability of consent to adequately give persons control over data-driven personalisation. Because the substance of data-driven personalisation is continually redefined through interaction and adaptation, a static grant of permission is woefully inadequate to enable persons to control their information. Furthermore, insofar as data-driven personalisation redefines *persons themselves*, such involved persons are not appropriately positioned to monitor and control their role in personalisation. Secondly, recognising that data-driven personalisation is autopoietic explains why it is so difficult to purge the system of its power inequities. Systems theorists recognise that systems have moments of genesis and operate in environments that provide continuous external stimulation.[3] But once an autopoietic system has internalised the prejudices of its creation, these tendencies cannot be purged by deliberate intervention. By its very self-sustaining nature, the system cannot be 'reprogrammed' from the outside – a characteristic that explains many of the biases that plague data-driven personalisation.

This chapter concludes with a final thought as to how law can be leveraged to address these challenges of personalisation. Because any data-driven personalisation system is dynamic and self-contained, attempts to tame it through a single legal concept (equality, privacy, non-discrimination) will likely face problems that parallel consent: the system will simply internalise the efforts as environmental 'shocks' in its process of recursive self-perpetuation. However, system theorists have also explored another subcomponent of society, the legal system, as autopoietic. The status of law as autopoietic explains its potential as a counterweight to algorithmic data-driven personalisation. By adaptively balancing the invasive and hierarchical potential of personalisation, law may not be able to 'purify' personalisation of its pathologies, but it can soften its harmful impacts on society and individuals.

17.2 DATA-DRIVEN PERSONALISATION AS SOCIAL AUTOPOIESIS

Autopoietic systems are defined by the quality of autonomously replicating themselves and their constituent components over time.[4] Living organisms are the seminal example: an organism replicates itself (both through sustaining biological processes and through reproduction), but also replicates its constituent parts, such as cells and organs. From the perspective of the system, however, the 'elements...that constitute autopoietic systems have no <u>independent</u> existence.'[5] They are created and defined <u>by</u> the system. Animals again provide a vivid example. The constituent cells of an animal 'do not simply come together'[6] to create the animal, they are created by the animal as part of a grander totality, and for that animal only have meaning as part of that totality. A cell or organ in the body is its own autopoietic system as well as a subcomponent, though subcomponents such as cells and organs are not appropriately positioned to 'look upwards' and 'observe' the totality of the animal as a self-contained system.[7] It is worth noting, for context, that the parallel analogy is that society is an entire animal, and data-driven personalisation processes are like cells. Data-driven personalisation operates within society as a replicated subcomponent, but each data-driven personalisation system is also its own autopoietic system.

Social systems are autopoietic systems defined not by biological operations, but by communicative ones. It is communication that is the basic building block of social systems – not persons themselves.[8] While initially striking, this observation is inevitably true: a mere aggregation of living human bodies does not comprise a society, nor does a group of humans who emulate (from the perspective of an extra-systemic observer) a society, but do so in a deterministic exercise without the use of language to exchange ideas, preferences, and commands. Rather a society is defined by humans exchanging information – communicating – in order to form a stable and adaptive social order. Yet the communicative acts which create the social system are only real insofar as they exist within the system, and are defined wholly by their operation within it.[9]

That the fundamental unit of the system only has meaning within it explains one other feature of autopoietic systems: each is, *as a system*, closed. That is, an autopoietic system reproduces itself (its order and subcomponents) wholly as an internal process. Of course, systems depend on an environment for resources, and react to outside stimulus from their environments. But with regards to *reproduction*, an autopoietic system replicates itself and its constituent parts without outside instruction. A cell replicates on the basis of instruction contained with DNA; animals replicate on the basis of their internal biological configurations. These biological systems consume resources to reproduce, but these resources do not add information to the system. For a social system, there is neither communication entering the system, nor leaving it (if there were and the system were autopoietic, that communication would be part of the system).[10] Rather the society replicates by the terms of its own internally stable social dynamics – the system is 'sovereign'.[11]

Data-driven personalisation[12] can be understood as such a self-replicating system made up of at least two subcomponents: 'digital' persons (i.e., dynamic profiles of persons as 'perceived' by the personalisation system) who provide and receive information to inform a data set, and a correlated data set (mediated by an algorithm) that cyclically processes inputs from these digital persons and outputs information based on that recursively updated set. The totality is an autopoietic system of data-driven personalisation in a given domain. Once established,[13] the data-driven personalisation system can be described as follows:

> ... input-action by (digital) persons → data universe revised and correlations updated → recommendation to (digital) persons → input-action by (digital) persons → ...

This system perpetuates itself and its constituent subcomponents. The (digital) persons (from the perspective of the system, the personal profiles) and data set of group information are continually reproduced through system-internal communication, which updates the contours of the (digital) persons and the content of the data set. So long as the background environmental conditions (such as physical infrastructure and the presence of the encoded algorithm, which, notably, neither of the subcomponents perceive as such; rather these preconditions are 'environmental') persist, the personalisation process will self-perpetuate. The critical moments of communication are from the digital person to the data set, which, following updating and processing, returns recursive information back to the persons – a continuous cycle of adaptive communication.

This idea that persons, when they become participants in the system of data-driven personalisation, become 'digital' is inspired by two chapters of this volume. Kieron O'Hara's concept of digital modernity explores the destabilisation of both the bureaucratic system and the idea of the individual that is characteristic of the modern neoliberal order. 'Digital' persons – those who participate in data-driven personalisation – can be understood as a type of the 'inforg' described by O'Hara; and their new status as digital persons in an autopoietic system of algorithm-driven personalisation is an instance of the shift of data information from an epistemic to an ontological condition. By becoming a self-reproducing social system, data-driven personalisation becomes more than a static tool or intermediary employed by free actors, but a system with its own systemic ontology. The transformation of the person that is so effected by their involvement as a subcomponent in the personalisation system is elaborated by Marc Welsh's concept of the person as a 'datafied' subject. A 'digital' individual is subordinated to a personalisation system insofar as their reproduction as a person becomes dependent on that system, and only the information that they receive from *within* that system can compromise communication (as opposed to unintelligible 'noise' from the outside environment). The datafication of a person vis-à-vis a given system is thus illustrative of the type of Foucauldian power expression that Welsh describes.

17.3 ASSESSING DATA-DRIVEN PERSONALISATION FROM AN AUTOPOIETIC PERSPECTIVE

Systems of data-driven personalisation are (1) subcomponents of the grander autopoiesis of social organisation and (2) autopoietic within themselves. Each of these properties complicates the task (for individuals trying to position themselves within the system, or for critics such as scholars) of evaluating or controlling relationships to data-driven personalisation. In the case of (1), because the personalisation subcomponent shifts the identities of persons (another subcomponent of the social system), these persons are ill-equipped to take an objective perspective on the character of personalisation. In Welsh's terms, personalisation becomes an instrumentality of power to define persons located outside of persons themselves; in O'Hara's terms, personalisation creates 'avatars' who may struggle to turn back to look upon themselves. In the case of (2), the problem may be even more foundational, as within an autopoietic system, there is no intrinsic touchstone for making sense *of the system as a whole* by any subunit of the system.[14] Rather persons can only exchange information with the system, but the internal normative quality of the system is described wholly within the system.[15] Considering the closed system of personalisation alone, this makes the possibility of persons as participants in the systems performing a comprehensive evaluation even more daunting. These are both variations of a basic feature regarding any observation of an autopoietic system: they can only be performed by an outside observer. Data-driven personalisation entangles the identity of the person with the personalisation system itself, making standing outside impossible.[16]

Thus, both these problems can be understood as challenges for to evaluating systems of personalisation from a stable, 'objective' position – because the person performing the evaluation is dynamically integrated into such systems. Clarifying this instability requires further elaboration of the adaptive process of redefinition. Autopoietic systems do not exist in hermetic isolation, but rather within environments which may induce adaptive changes. At any moment autopoietic systems are in a state of fluctuation, with any current configuration ascribable to two types of factors: 'one from its previous state [a recursive term] and one from various interactions [an interactive term].'[17] This reflexive process of adaptation is constant. This perpetual process of adaptation means that such systems have no rigid baseline when examined at the relevant level of analysis (i.e., from the perspective of an entity *within* the system – a subcomponent cell looking at an animal or a digitalised person looking at a personalisation system, of which each is a part). An animal at any moment in time, for example, is the condition of both maintaining its bodily integrity through internal physiological processes, and adapting (including changing its nature) in response to external pressures – seeking sustenance, avoiding physical dangers, and so forth. The analogy for systems of personalisation considered as internally autopoietic would be changes in external personal preferences or changes in the outside system, which would, within the system, be environmental shocks. For example, a person might have their preferences change, with the result that their 'digital' self provides a different communication to the relevant personalisation system. This would by the system be treated as an interactive term, and be incorporated into the data set that guides algorithmic preferences. When this change – the environmental 'shock' of a changed preference – is communicated to the system of personalisation, the entire nature of the given personalisation system shifts.

A maudlin example illustrates how 'environmental' shocks exist outside personalisation as a system: following a romantic breakup a person selects an emotive song on YouTube, which uses a personalisation algorithm to suggest subsequent songs. This selection is unexpected given the profile of the person, who previously had shown no inclination for such music; the song selection results in an update to the person's profile (i.e., their 'digital personhood' within the system changes). The personalisation system may be more likely to recommend emotive songs in the future given that profile, and *also* updates its general data set. From the perspective of the personalisation system (both for the 'digital' person, i.e., the profile, and the data set), it does not 'know' anything about such changes in personal circumstances, nor can it know – such extra-systemic information is environmental 'noise'. Of course, as the data set grows more elaborate and the recommendations more complex, it may be able to predict what type of music selections are associated with such events, resulting in an uncanny ability to emulate knowledge of them. This in turn creates further changes in the behaviour of the person, continuing the process of recursive system reconstruction. But from the perspective of the music recommendation algorithm, these 'outside' personal events (such as a breakup) are part of the environment, not part of the system (unless, of course, the personalisation algorithm has the possibility of the person explicitly indicating a preference for music that is desirable following breakups).

It is possible to perform an assessment of an autopoietic system by standing outside of it.[18] Instead of acting as a participant in a system, one can act as an observer. However, because data-driven personalisation as a subcomponent of society operates upon individual human identity (a defining property of their position in the broader system of social organisation), it is difficult to step outside the system to assess it. A person trying to evaluate the technology has already been transformed by it. This is a demonstration of the sovereignty of autopoietic systems over their own subcomponents.

Trying to take an objective view of personalisation by considering the higher-level system of society is of limited use if one wishes to make the autonomous person the unit of analysis. Data-driven personalisation, as a new sub-component of society, is distinguished by impacting the condition of another system – that of the individual person. What is distinctive about the infiltration of data-driven personalisation is the way in which the internal autopoietic system of the person can no longer be understood without substantially incorporating the presence of personalisation. Since data-driven personalisation acts pervasively and fundamentally upon persons (as components of society as a system), it means that persons are incapable of making objective evaluations of the desirability of such a feature of the social system. The feature one wishes to evaluate has already been incorporated into personal identity, which is the fixed point which one wishes to use to evaluate it.

Under a liberal-Kantian worldview, then, the reflexive quality of data-driven personalisation complicates any ability to offer an independent evaluation of the *desirability* of the practice, because it acts upon the individual as the very unit of such evaluation. Personalisation operates by analysing a person's preferences in a given domain – commerce, politics, medicine, culture – and then heuristically changing the person's own experience, subsequently shifting the person's own preferences in the future. Personalisation thereby upsets the possibility of neutral moral observation of the practice, because ubiquitous data-driven personalisation changes the condition of the self-referential actor. In Niklas Luhmann's terms, personalisation perpetually 'decomposes' the person, at least vis-à-vis personalisation itself, such that the person cannot examine the process of personalisation from a fixed point within the social system.[19]

17.4 CHALLENGES OF AUTOPOIETIC PERSONALISATION SYSTEMS IN PRACTICE: THE INADEQUACY OF CONSENT

Social systems theory is notoriously abstract, but it provides an organising guide to common themes that shine forth from the chapters of this volume. Most notably, governments and legal systems have often turned to consent as a mechanism so individuals can moderate their own role in personalisation, but as many in this volume have observed, consent may not be up to the challenge. The idea of individuals acting freely as the determinant of rights guides legal reasoning across domains – from private law (particularly contract) to commercial law to criminal law (with its core in states of mind) to public law (ultimately vindicated by the free will of political participants).

The most salient practical illustration is Michèle Finck's incisive discussion of how the General Data Protection Act – the broadest catchall protection of user information in Europe – relies primarily on user consent to vindicate systematic use of data. Yet as Finck observes, 'freely' given consent seems almost impossible given the context and implications of personalisation. Many services are only available in a personalised form (such as, for example, credit as described by Noelia Collado-Rodriguez and Uta Kohl; or networked services such as Uber as described by Nick O'Donovan); and it is extraordinarily difficult to describe the full implications of personalisation. Even stickier, as Finck notes, is the problem of attempting to revoke a consent to use data – if the data has been used to train the algorithm, it is very difficult to undo a consent (at least if the person wishes to continue enjoying the benefits of accurate preference prediction that a personalised profile can confer). Finally, Finck notes that attempts to give certain types of data particularly protected status can be undone inadvertently (from the perspective of the algorithm's initial designer) by the algorithm identifying sensitive patterns simply by processing the data provided. Together these features illustrate the nature of personalisation as a system that incorporates persons into a self-replicating system, and which sustains itself in a closed manner, rather than requiring the guidance of some external intelligence. With varying degrees of cheer, Keith Syrett, Jan Poort and Frederik Zuiderveen Borgesius, and Moira Patterson and Normann Witzlieb observe similar features in the realms of medicine, personal finance, price discrimination, and political campaigns. In each domain, while consent may appear to offer the *philosophically* easiest way of reconciling technocratic power and personal decision-making, the reality of data-driven personalisation subverts this solution. This is not merely because the technocratic power is so great, but because the system is ultimately created by powerholders (even if, over time, it eventually becomes independent from them). Such systems obtain their own reality such that those whom the systems entangle cannot meaningfully take an outside perspective on them.

Relations of the difficulties noted by Finck are touched upon by other contributions to the volume. TT Arvind's analysis of the structural mismatch between

consent-driven contracts and privacy law, and the struggles that analogical jurisprudential reasoning has had with squaring the contract-and-privacy circle, points itself
to the distinctive nature of data-driven personalisation as a phenomenon. Because it
is self-perpetuating, standard legal paradigms that deal in entities with a level of
certainty struggle to manage data-driven personalisation. In effect, Arvind extends
some of Finck's observations from the doctrine to the nature of legal reasoning. The
structural parallel to this problem turns back to Welsh and O'Hara, and their
discussions of how persons are transformed by the digital world. The inability of
contract law to manage personalisation is a high-level instance of how the digital
integration of the person into a system of algorithmic personalisation generates legal
commitments that the neoliberal Kantian worldview cannot fully grasp. The autopoiesis of personalisation depends upon its capacity to redefine the person insofar as
they participate in the types of systems (commercial, political, social) that personalisation influences. Because individuals are, at least in some respects, *internal* to such
a system, they cannot obtain a complete view of it (at any single moment or
longitudinally) that makes any consent meaningful.

A schematic example illustrates both how personalisation can operate as an
autopoietic system, and the challenges that this poses to a consent-based approach.
Imagine a customer – who has no other online presence, and thus is, prior to such
an interaction, non-'digital' – decides to go online shopping for books. The person
has a set of characteristics and preferences, determined ex ante to becoming
involved in data-driven personalisation. However, the website the person chooses
to visit uses various personalisation technologies, and already has established a large
database of preferences of person with certain known characteristics and preferences.[20] When the customer provides data and proceeds to interact with the sales
website, they begin to participate in the recursive system of personalisation. This
might take any number of forms: the customer might provide information voluntarily and directly, as through a survey, or indirectly through browsing or purchase
habits. As such information is incorporated into the data set, it changes two
features: the 'digital personhood' (that is, the profile) of the customer; and the
actual content of the personalisation data set (which will influence recommendations made to any participant in the system). In autopoietic terms, the system of
personalisation uses this new communication to reconstruct itself by adding any
gleaned insights to its data set, and using this updated data set to define its future
state. As the system reconstructs itself, it changes how it communicates with the
customer. The customer transitions from being an outside interactive stimulus to
part of the system of personalisation, and evolves into a 'digital' person by developing a profile. Subsequently, the customer begins to undergo a different experience
of the personalisation system with each additional communicative iteration (i.e.,
each piece of information communicated by the customer to the system which it
can process, and each new piece of input the customer provided by the now
recursively-adapting personalisation algorithm). Given that persons (digital and

non-digital) are themselves autopoietic, one effect is that the customers' interface with the personalised recommendations changes them as well. From the perspective of the digital person who is conceived as existing within the personalised infrastructure, and whose identity is limited to the particular domain of interaction, this effect can be understood as recursive, that is, occurring with the autopoietic system of personalisation itself. From the perspective of the non-digital person (i.e., the whole person as a self-contained system), personalisation can be understood as an outside interactive stimulus.

In the initial engagement with personalisation, the customer may ostensibly choose to consent (and indeed, such consent is generally required under the GPDR by a data subject).[21] Yet unlike in a standard commercial transaction, the initial terms of this consent cannot capture the full ramifications of engagement with personalisation, as such participation recursively changes both the customer (particularly as a 'digital' person conceived as a self-contained system) and the system of personalisation. The system of personalisation will incorporate initial data about the person and, after synthesising this information into the data set, adjust the stimulus it provides to the person. This will in turn presumptively transform the experience and thus, as an external stimulus, the identity of the customer. Thus, a general consent to personalisation cannot be conceived of as permission to communicate or process a single piece of information, or even a series of pieces of information in the future. Rather it is an agreement to accede to the transformation of the system with which the customer interacts as both a provider and a recipient of information, and, presuming that the consent persists over time, to whatever communication the subsequent iterations of the system undertake. Thus the customer consents to interaction with a system whose future attributes cannot be anticipated at the moment of consent, because the system recursively adapts in response to future events. In short, the customer cannot know what they are consenting to. Yet even more strikingly, the meaning of such a consent is unpredictable because consenting to engagement with a system of personalisation *will change the customer as well*. The very wellspring of consent, the distinct identity of the person, is thereby destabilised by interaction with the system. A single consent – or even periodic consents – cannot capture the dynamic implications of such an agreement.[22] Adding a final but least predictable layer of complexity is that the significance of the consent is not determined simply by the relationships between the system of personalisation and the customer, but rather continuously fluctuates due to new information from *all* customers (a point made by Finck). A customer consents to receiving personalised recommendations, but these recommendations are determined by the totality of the data set gathered from all users. Thus, the meaning of the consent is continuously transformed through a series of communications which occur entirely beyond of the customer's permission (or awareness).

Thus, the closest analogy that can be drawn to participating in a system of data-driven personalisation is participation in a large-scale community or society. In such a society, most persons do not have face-to-face contact with the other constituent members, but the collective aggregation of their communication reproduces society. Moreover, this schematic (by presuming the person has no initial data footprint and that there is only one system) has vastly simplified the interactions of personalisation, ignoring the possibility that systems of personalisation can be cross-fertilising or aggregate multiple different sources of data. It seems unrealistic that a standard contractual consent could be adequate to capture this relationship (much as most individuals participate in society but have never explicitly consented to their membership).[23]

17.5 PRIVILEGED INFLUENCE AND MASS PARTICIPATION IN PERSONALISATION

Though instances of data-driven personalisation may become self-sustaining once the infrastructure and algorithms are established, their social position and their contextual relationships with other persons and society as a whole raise a different set of concerns. In particular, there is the spectre that the character of data-driven personalisation will be set by and serve the interests of those already in power. This does not mean, from a systems theory perspective, that such centralised elites *determine* personalisation. If their continual management of the process of person-alisation was required for its perpetuation, then data-driven personalisation could not be described as self-sustaining. Yet the very name of the process – *data-driven* – is what belies this necessity. Data-driven personalisation is distinctive from other types of recommendation or decision systems because it recursively gathers information by which it updates its own constitution, rather than requiring a set of specific instructions from an outside controller to so perpetuate itself. However, the condi-tions of initial formation, as well as the privileged opportunity to provide a high-level, system-wide stimulus to the system (as well as to destroy or reset the system), are established by those who design the initial algorithms and context of data-gathering, and who typically have an interest in deriving some benefit from the system.

A cogent example of this may be drawn from two chapters in this volume – the role of penology as described from different perspectives by Pam Ugwudike and by David Gurnham. As Ugwudike describes, data-driven predictions may replicate discriminatory pathologies in a society, often creating a feedback loop of disadvan-taged groups being further disadvantaged by personalised assessments; as Gurnham describes, pre-algorithmic technologies could also manifest these pathologies. For such systems, a foundational challenge is that processing of the data set will tend to reproduce existing social trends; if there are existing prejudices in policing or punishment, using algorithms that work off existing sets to make predictions will reproduce these. Thus, for example, if a certain disadvantaged subgroup is observed to be more likely to commit crimes or to have recidivist tendencies, the algorithm or programmatic assessment may reinforce that disadvantage.

The autopoietic nature of data-driven personalisation, however, exacerbates this risk, because it has the capacity, in response to new information, to recursively update itself, thus potentially introducing wholly new and subtle forms of reinforcement within the system. This is because unlike a static algorithm, data-driven personalisation will generate its own patterns that may not be transparent or built in by design. For example, a data-driven system given initial instructions to disregard race as a feature but otherwise set sentences to more harshly punish those with recidivist tendencies may come to show racial discrimination *via proxy* as it incorporates new information. Such tendencies may yield outputs that increase recidivist tendencies further. The communication by the system may then yield future inputs that reinforce the initial (exogenous) tendency. None of this, however, occurs through an explicitly prejudiced instruction within the personalisation system, conceived as self-contained. It merely moves from one state to another, incorporating new information and outputting communication that reflects the accumulated adaptive processing of that information. Given an initial state with a strong inclination, it may be impossible to simply eliminate a given prejudice without eliminating the system. A system given a certain initial function (such as minimising crime or setting sentences based on the likelihood of recidivism) will likely incorporate societal prejudices, regardless of its initial state (say, a data set that is race-neutral). Because the system replicates itself, any attempt to correct for later-introduced prejudices through an outside 'shock' designed to eliminate discriminatory tendencies cannot reset the system without destroying it. Rather such a shock can only become a new interactive term that the system will process on its own terms as it replicates itself.

The problem of privileged influence emerges from the fact that the initial condition of a data-driven personalisation algorithm will be set by those who have an initial set of interests, values, or an agenda. A penological algorithm designed to set sentences to minimise crime or more harshly sentence those predicted to commit crime again, for example, will have a particular initial state from which later states will, through recursion and adaptation, be derived. The tendencies of this initial state will persist throughout the system through recursion. In the absence of some stimulus, that fundamentally reorients the system, that initial tendency of the system will likely survive. Yet if the system loses that initial tendency, it likely means that it has failed in its initial purpose, and might well be scrapped by those with power over it.

Underlying this is a property of data-driven personalisation systems generally. While internally autopoietic, such systems are part of larger self-replicating systems of society. Many of these systems include privileged actors whose communications reproduce or accelerate certain features of the system that are to their own advantage. In the penology system, it may be that dominant groups within the larger society provide a consistent set of interactive terms (initial features of the algorithm or data points, initially or later) to the algorithm that leads it, in its perpetual redefinition, to adopt certain properties. It is critical to note that the privileged actors are not explicitly *instructing* the personalisation system to adopt certain features; were such instruction necessary, the system would not be autopoietic. Rather they are merely providing terms that effects the state of the system at any given time. Because the system of personalisation replicates itself, the nature of such influence is non-intentional. Indeed, this is what makes data-driven personalisation as an autopoietic system such a subtle and effective replicator of the interests and biases of those in a privileged position. Instead of taking the form of explicit instruction, command, or oppression, it adopts the form of stimulus that may look objectively neutral or unbiased, but which induces the personalisation system to adapt itself in a particular way.

Two authors in this collection offer insights particularly relevant to how data-driven personalisation, even when it operates under its own momentum, can reinforce the privileged positions of centralised actors. As O'Donovan observes, as a system of personalisation grows more accurate (i.e., replicates itself after incorporating additional information from communication with users), it can offer material benefits to the actor who originated them. As users receive more and more precise recommendations, they become increasingly attached to the *quality* of the network. This can be understood as a refinement of customers' status as 'digital' persons within the system of personalisation. O'Donovan focuses on the commercial context of personalisation, which creates more accurate recommendations for users, and greater market share (or market entrenchment) for the companies who are the centralised actors that originate the system of data-driven personalisation. But similar benefits are offered to *any* actor that benefits from a personalised system, *on the normative terms that serve to animate the system.* Thus, for commercial recommendation services, the nature of the second-order effect is to offer more accurate recommendations to customers, with the market share benefit for companies that are ancillary to the autopoietic nature of the personalisation system. Conversely, for, say, a credit company (the type of context discussed by Collado-Rodriguez and Kohl) the personalisation system communicates with both the credit applicant (who provides applicant information) and the creditor (who receives feedback from the system and ultimately feeds a different type of information back into the system). In this case both applicant and creditor are 'digitalised' by the personalisation system, but the benefits of the first order (more accurate default rate information) *and* the second order network effects (greater profits from selecting the 'right' lendee) both accrue *directly* to the mortgage company.

This language of 'accurate' and 'right' decisions flowing from effective data-driven personalisation exemplifies another quality of the system which Andrew Charlesworth's chapter addresses. Charlesworth observes that 'AI ethics' – often the gloss adopted to develop normatively acceptable personalisation algorithms – are often informed by corporatist interests, whether through the corporate influence over normative debate or through the assumption that corporate ends (efficiency and profit maximisation) are the morally weighty ones. Charlesworth's point can be generalised from 'ethics-washing' to the very purposes that personalisation systems seek to effect. A personalisation system interprets data – that is to say, gives it meaning – within the context of the replicating system.[24] Thus, a product recommendation system incorporates data and outputs data insofar as that data is relevant to providing products customers are likely to buy; a penological personalisation system does the same with regards to (say) preventing recidivism; a credit system with regards to the likelihood of determining defaults. What these terms mean changes once the personalisation process begins to replicate itself and incorporates new data. But three points are particularly relevant with regards to privileged actors. With regards to the genesis of the algorithm, privileged actors have the opportunity to set the initial state of the system,[25] thus privileging their interests, values, and so forth – initial direct control over what Charlesworth calls an 'algorithmic assemblage'. Secondly, insofar as they stand outside the system of personalisation, these privileged actors are typically positioned to continually provide stimulus to serve their own interests, thus inducing the personalisation system, as it processes these interactions, to continue to serve their interests.[26] Finally with regards to their own position in a broader self-replicating social system these privileged actors play an outsized role in recursively setting the terms of personalisation (as one subcomponent of society).[27]

The power of privileged actors over personalisation sharpens the problem of trying to use consent to manage personalisation systems. Not only do personalisation systems transform a given person such that consent to the system of personalisation can have stable meaning, the meaning of the system is under constant pressure from privileged actors whose interests are likely orthogonal to those who are subject to the personalisation system itself. Thus a consent is not only unstable because of future processing by the system and future changes to the person *in response* to the system, but it is likely that such future processing will occur under the gravitational pull of actors who lies outside the system (conceived as closed), who are not perceived from the perspective of the personalised communication itself, and yet who have specific and likely self-serving interests.

17.6 LOOKING FORWARD: PRESERVING THE INTEGRITY OF LAW AS AN INDEPENDENT SOCIAL SYSTEM

System theory provides a framework that synthesises many of the concerns about data-driven personalisation expressed by the scholars in this volume. Because data-driven personalisation is so fluid and pervasive, it threatens to run roughshod over the standard mechanisms that maintain the power balance between individuals and institutions. This can be attributed to the fact that data-driven personalisation is not merely a static object that can be accepted, declined, or negotiated over, but rather a dynamic system that not only changes itself but changes the identities of those whom it profiles.

Could a shift from consent to a dedicated conception of the right to (say) privacy or equality adequately prevent personalisation from becoming a mechanism by which elite actors cyclically transform the identities of citizens and consumers, and thereby achieve a better power balance? Such a shift in the substantive focus of rules has an initial gleam, but it faces a mismatch with the character of personalisation. Since personalisation is a reflexive process that redefines the very terms of analysis, striving to constrain the pathologies of personalisation through a fixed norm seems procedurally inadequate. Personalisation will adapt; a clearly defined substantive norm (such, for example, as the liberal ideal of consent) will not. Underlying this attribute is the status of any given autopoietic system – including those of data-driven personalisation – as 'closed'. They self-perpetuate on their own terms. Attempts to modify or shift them might operate as an interactive stimulus to which they adapt, but seeking to simply transform how they operate will fail, a challenge demonstrated by the difficulty of instructing systems not to 'uptake' or recognise racial bias in the data itself. But this will not purge the presence of underlying tendencies that, from a perspective of a moral observer outside the system, are undesirably discriminatory. For better or worse, the system of personalisation 'learns' the reality which composes it, and replicates it. Asserting that the system must recognise consent, or privacy, or equality, as an ideal, will not fix it.

One could, of course, attempt to exclude the domain of personalisation as a general matter – but such Ludditism tends to be submerged by the movement of history. Moreover, as this volume has also detailed, personalisation does offer significant benefits,[28] in domains ranging from medical treatments to accurate pricing to urban design. While efforts might be taken to use regulation to precisely dictate the domains in which personalised information could be deployed, such a 'static' regulatory approach invokes again the basic problem of power imbalance. It would be elite hierarchies that would be trusted to appropriately manage personalisation and its concomitant power over human identity.

The most promising solution is to leverage another sub-societal autopoietic system (that is, another system that is a subcomponent in greater society)[29] against the dynamism of personalisation. Both this volume (through critique) and systems theory point the way: that system is law. Like personalisation, law is a closed system, comprised of judicial reasoning and state action following from it.[30] Law thus has the capacity to self-replicate itself as a system that advances certain norms as values without being guided from the outside. But this does not mean that law does not recognise forces – such as personalisation – that lie outside of it. It takes notice of them, but treats them as environmental factors rather than those intrinsic to law. It is 'normatively closed and cognitively open'.[31]

As Gunther Teubner observes, this closure of law as a system of self-sustaining norms gives it great potential to act as a socially transformative force. 'The more the legal system gains in operational closure and autonomy, the more it gains in openness toward social facts, political demands, social science theories, and human needs.'[32] If law is 'sealed' against the influences of personalisation, it can advance norms of justice with a self-perpetuating fluidity that matches personalisation as a system. Indeed, the potential for this counterbalancing dynamic is established by their mutual existence within the greater autopoietic structure of society: while considered as distinct systems, they act on each other as stimulus, but while as sibling subcomponents of a contextualising system they communicate information in the process of broader social replication.

How can the interaction of personalisation and law be made to serve justice? The most important step may be to ensure that the legal system remains insulated from the influence of personalisation, in the autopoietic sense of perpetuating itself *without* incorporating, as a subcomponent, the characteristics of personalisation.[33] This is not because personalisation is itself pernicious, but because the independence of the legal system from the qualities of personalisation demands the legal system's closure. Indeed, rule of law requires neutrality of evaluation before the law and recognition of the person's intrinsic legal standing. It thus stands at odds with the tendency of data-driven personalisation to submerge the identity of the individual into aggregated profile information, and the capacity of privileged institutions to shape the substance of communication.

The chapter in this volume that bears on this most directly is Alun Gibbs's analysis of how the construction of legal institutions through language stands at odds with the patterns of personalisation. As Gibbs observes, '[l]anguage provides an orientation point around which collective meanings can be fashioned in the pursuit of the goals, points of solidarity which shape how we live and how a sense of personhood and agency is exercised through political participation.'[34] The self-perpetuation of data-driven personalisation, which integrates individuals into a predictive system and displaces the opportunity for deliberate, participatory governance with algorithmic-driven suggestions, is at odds with the communicative character of a free system of law. Gibbs's analysis can be understood as establishing the normative backdrop for Charlesworth's explanation of why elite determination of personalisation is problematic. Construction of the terms of self-rule by autonomous persons is fundamentally at odds with a centralised system controlled by elite actors which in fact dissolves, rather than protects, the terms of personal autonomy. Perhaps no doctrinal area illustrates this better than the concerns of the use of mass data analysis in criminal law; both Ugwudike and Gurnham point to the need to retain the individual as the locus of penological justice.

This register of concerns – from the background norms of legality, to a conceptually specific threat from the implementation of data-driven personalisation, to a specific domain of law in which this issue has bite – shows why the legal system must self-perpetuate its norms in a manner 'closed' to personalisation. This does not mean, of course, that the legal system cannot address disputes and challenges evoked by personalisation; that it can do so is precisely what gives it its power. But it must treat the problems of personalisation as external to the law's own values and operation. In the terms of autopoietic theory, questions of personalisation must be processed as environmental stimulus, rather than as normatively meaningful communications that are part of law's internal reproduction. This means that law will never 'conquer' data-driven personalisation, because the system of personalisation will always perpetuate itself outside of law. But it means that the value of law, and the conceptual integrity that underlies that value, will also endure.

This collection should be taken as a call to understand the potential of law to counter-balance the impact of personalisation on the social order as a whole. That it is a starting point, rather than an ending point, for the exploration of a social phenomenon is appropriate, for data-driven personalisation is still in its early days. By exploring the depth of conceptual issues, and the wide array of substantive concerns, evoked by personalisation, this volume has hopefully served as a guide to how moral integrity of the self can be reconciled with a world transformed by, and for, the individual self.

NOTES

1 Gunther Teubner, 'Introduction to autopoietic law', in *Autopoietic Law: A New Approach to Law and Society* (Gunther Teubner, ed.) (de Gruyter, 1988) 1 at 4.

2 While some leading scholars of social systems theory argue that only societies as a whole can be described as completely autopoietic, this has not prevented them from analysing other systems (such as legal systems) as autopoietic. Niklas Luhmann, 'The unity of the legal system', in *Autopoietic Law: A New Approach to Law and Society* 12 at 18.

3 Niklas Luhmann, *Theory of Society, Volume I* (Stanford University Press, 2012: Rhodes Barrett trans) at 32. However, insofar as autopoietic systems are internally complete, they are closed off from these environments. David Seidl, 'Luhmann's theory of autopoietic social systems' (Munich Business Research No. 2004-2) (2004). Retrieved from www.zfog .bwl.unimuenchen.de/files/mitarbeiter/paper2004_2.pdf.

4 Niklas Luhman, 'The autopoiesis of social systems' in *Sociocybernetic Paradoxes* (Felix Geyer and Johannesvan der Zouwen eds.: Sage, 1986) 172 at 174.

5 Luhman 2012 at 32 (emphasis added).

6 Id.

7 Niklas Luhmann, 'Closure and openness: on reality in the world of law', in *Autopoietic Law: A New Approach to Law and Society* (Gunther Teubner, ed.) (de Gruyter, 1988) 335, at 339.

8 Teubner 1988 at 3.

9 Luhman 1986 at 174–5.

10 As Luhman 2012 at 32 describes, any information from the environment (as opposed to communication internal to the system) is 'noise'. That external information is noise explains why the system is closed; it can only make sense of information internal to the system in its process of redefinition.

11 Luhmann 1986 at 174.

12 Personalisation that is not data-driven and thus does not self-replicate as an autopoietic system can also occur, but the essential shift is that it does not replicate itself or its subcomponents. It is static. For a description of such systems, see the chapter in this volume by Poort and Borgesius at [x] (describing how price discounts for e.g. students can comprise a form of price discrimination).

13 The preconditions of its establishment are discussed in Section III below, but that such a moment exists for autopoiesis systems is described by Luhmann 2012 at 32. Such systems need not be Augustinian first movers.

14 Luhman 'Closure' 1988 at 339.

15 Luhman 'Unity' 1988 at 21. A legal analogue to this is described by HLA Hart, *The Concept of Law* (Oxford University Press, 1994) at 89. For a scaling up of this internalism-and-meaning question to the international relations arena, see, for example, Maren Hofius, 'Towards a 'theory of the gap': addressing the relationship between practice and theory', 9 *Global Constitutionalism* 169 (2020).

16 Luhmann 2012 at 35.

17 Loet Leydesdorff, 'Luhmann, Habermas and the theory of communication' 17 *Systems Research and Behavioral Science* 273, at 276 (2000).

18 Such 'operation requires self-reference'. Luhmann 1986 at 175. Leydesdorff 2000 calls this 'hyper-reflexivity', or perhaps more simply, 'taking a perspective', at 276.

19 Luhmann 1986 at 175.

20 The customer may try elaborate measures to avoid providing any data that could be used to personalise an experience – blocking all cookies, refusing to answer questions about identity, purchasing with randomised, anonymised online accounts, and so forth. If the customer successfully takes all of these steps, they remain non-'digital' by never communicating with the online system, either as a provider or recipient of information.
    It is worth noting that in this commercial schematic, the aptly named customer has more discretion to engage or not engage with the system. In other personalised systems – such as mortgage applications or the criminal justice system – such opt-outs may be impossible, and the personalisation system will roll ahead regardless of their efforts. The online book shopping example is helpful merely because it is easier to conceptualise casual repeat interactions.

21 Michèle Finck (Chapter 5).

22 The generic form of this is Luhmann 2012's discussion of meaning at 18.

23 See Frank Lovett, 'Can justice be based on consent' 12 *J. Pol. Phil* 79, 87 (2004).

24 Luhmann 2012 at 18.

25 Luhmann 2012 might refer to this as the initial 'historical state[]' of the system', at 32.

26 Critically, from the perspective of the personalisation system, this stimulus is from the environment, and, in Luhmann's terms, 'random'. Luhmann 2012 at 32. Thus for example in the case of a personalisation system (conceived internally) that recommends products to customers, the internal autopoietic system consists of the communication between customers (who become 'digital' once they participate) and provides information regarding preferences of types of persons (which the personalisation system uses to redefine itself) and a data-driven algorithm that seeks to provide the 'best' possible products. Insofar as it only does this the system is closed. But the environment in which this operates (which

neither the customer nor the algorithm 'perceives' as such) the environment is the profit-seeking of the entity which originated the algorithm and seeks to sell to customers. But the personalisation output is not directly determined by this profit motive (if so, it would simply be hierarchical instruction by the seller, which is not data-driven); this profit motive lies outside the personalisation system and is rather part of the environment. See Luhmann, 'Closure' 1988 at 337. This idea of the impact of environmental shocks being perceived as 'random' by the system seems preferable to the idea that they are 'indirect', as described by Richard Lempert, 'The autonomy of law: two visions compared', in *Autopoietic Law: A New Approach to Law and Society* (Gunther Teubner, ed.) (de Gruyter, 1988) 152 at 153. The effect may be direct – but the system does not conceive of them as communication.

27 In this analogy, personalisation, its subjects, and the privileged actors are subcomponents of a larger system of society (much as animals are themselves autopoietic systems, but are part of larger autopoietic systems such as ecosystems). The privileged actors have, in the recursion of the state of the broader social system, an outsized capacity to determine the character of the personalisation subcomponent.

28 See in particular Chapters 4, 10, and 12 in this volume.

29 Luhmann, 'Unity', 1988 at 19.

30 Luhmann, 'Unity', 1988 at 21.

31 Lempert 1988 at 153.

32 Teubner 1988 at 2.

33 Indeed, France has a heavy-handed linear step towards such insulation with Article 33 of the Justice Reform Act (Law no. 2019-22, 23 March 2019, available at www.legifrance.gouv.fr/eli/loi/2019/3/23/2019-222/jo/article_33), which prohibits the use of personalised evaluation of judicial personnel.

34 Alun Gibbs (Chapter 16) at 284.

Index

For EU product safety concerns, contact us at Calle de José Abascal, 56–1°, 28003 Madrid, Spain or eugpsr@cambridge.org.

www.ingramcontent.com/pod-product-compliance
Ingram Content Group UK Ltd.
Pitfield, Milton Keynes, MK11 3LW, UK
UKHW020400140625
459647UK00020B/2564